American Psychiatric Press

Review of Clinical Psychiatry and the Law

Volume 2

American Psychiatric Press

Review of Clinical Psychiatry and the Law

Volume 2

Edited by

Robert I. Simon, M.D.

Clinical Professor of Psychiatry
Director, Program in Psychiatry and Law
Georgetown University School of Medicine
Washington, DC

American Psychiatric Press, Inc.

Washington, DC
London, England

Note: The authors have worked to ensure that all information in this book concerning drug dosages, schedules, and routes of administration is accurate as of the time of publication and consistent with standards set by the U.S. Food and Drug Administration and the general medical community. As medical research and practice advance, however, therapeutic standards may change. For this reason and because human and mechanical errors sometimes occur, we recommend that readers follow the advice of a physician who is directly involved in their care or the care of a member of their family.

Books published by the American Psychiatric Press, Inc., represent the views and opinions of the individual authors and do not necessarily represent the policies and opinions of the Press or the American Psychiatric Association.

The paper used in this publication meets the minimum requirements of the American National Standard for Information Sciences—Permanence of Paper for Printed Library Materials ANSI Z39.48-1984. ♾

Manufactured in the United States of America
First Edition
91 92 93 94 4 3 2 1

American Psychiatric Press, Inc.
1400 K Street, N.W., Washington, DC 20005

ISSN 1045-1609
ISBN 0-88048-376-8

Dedicated with love and admiration to
Ann:
I marvel at your goodness.

R.I.S.

Contents

Features

Contributors

Steven B. Bisbing, Psy.D., J.D.
Mental Health Law Consultant (private practice), Takoma Park, Maryland; and Clinical Assistant Professor of Psychiatry, Georgetown University School of Medicine, Washington, DC

Neil Blumberg, M.D.
Clinical Instructor in Psychiatry, University of Maryland School of Medicine, Institute of Psychiatry and Human Behavior, Baltimore, Maryland

Thomas G. Gutheil, M.D.
Associate Professor of Psychiatry, Harvard Medical School; Co-Director, Program in Psychiatry and Law, Boston; and President, Law and Psychiatry Resource Center, Brookline, Massachusetts

Edmund G. Howe, M.D., J.D.
Associate Professor of Psychiatry, Uniformed Services University of the Health Sciences, Bethesda, Maryland

Carol C. Kleinman, M.D., J.D.
Clinical Assistant Professor of Psychiatry, Uniformed Services University of the Health Sciences, Bethesda, Maryland

Ellen G. McDaniel, M.D.
Adjunct Associate Professor of Psychiatry, University of Maryland School of Medicine, Baltimore, Maryland

Robert D. Miller, M.D., Ph.D.
Training Director, Forensic Center, Mendota Mental Health Institute, Madison; Clinical Professor of Psychiatry and Lecturer in Law, University of Wisconsin—Madison; and Associate Clinical Professor of Psychiatry, Medical College of Wisconsin, Milwaukee, Wisconsin

Jeffrey D. Robertson, J.D.
Partner, Wilson, Elser, Moskowitz, Edelman and Dicker, New York, New York

Robert L. Sadoff, M.D.
Clinical Professor of Psychiatry, University of Pennsylvania School of Medicine, Philadelphia, Pennsylvania

Stephen W. Siebert, M.D.
Coordinator, Inpatient Managed Care Program, Sheppard and Enoch Pratt Hospital, Towson, Maryland

Stuart B. Silver, M.D.
Clinical Assistant Professor of Psychiatry, University of Maryland School of Medicine, Baltimore, Maryland

Robert I. Simon, M.D.
Clinical Professor of Psychiatry and Director, Program in Psychiatry and Law, Georgetown University School of Medicine, Washington, DC

Selwyn M. Smith, M.D.
Consultant in Psychiatry, Ottawa, Canada; formerly Professor of Psychiatry, School of Medicine, University of Ottawa; and Past President, American Academy of Psychiatry and the Law

Kenneth Tardiff, M.D., M.P.H.
Professor of Psychiatry and Professor of Public Health, Cornell Medical College, New York, New York

Consulting Editors

Foreword

The practice of psychiatry continues to evolve and has changed dramatically over the past quarter of a century. Much of what I learned as a resident in psychiatry has changed profoundly following the revolution of the 1960s and 1970s. Major changes in psychopharmacology and biological understanding of clinical entities have affected the manner in which psychiatrists treat patients. The law has been cognizant of these changes and has kept pace. The legal regulation of psychiatric practice has grown and intensified during the past several years, causing confusion among psychiatrists and frustration for those who have not kept abreast of the legal changes affecting psychiatric practice.

Textbooks have been written on forensic psychiatry, on psychiatry and the law, and on psychiatric malpractice, generally addressing the issues facing the psychiatric clinician. However, the changes sometimes occur so rapidly that textbooks become obsolete within a decade or less. The *American Psychiatric Press Review of Clinical Psychiatry and the Law* is an attempt to plug the gap in our information source to keep us up to date on recent changes that affect all psychiatrists.

Volume 1, also edited by Dr. Robert I. Simon, contained the essentials of most of the issues facing the practicing psychiatrist. It should be read and digested by all clinicians to keep abreast of the changes that affect us all. Volume 2 expands on these practical applications of legal principles to practicing psychiatrists.

Psychiatric practice has been regulated over the years, and regulations change with different legal cases. When psychiatrists read of their colleagues being sued for malpractice for reasons that are difficult to understand, they begin to have increasing anxiety about their own practice. For example, the concept of "dangerousness" is one that has affected us all. Commitment statutes require that a patient be both mentally ill and represent a clear and present danger of harm to self or others before that patient may be committed involuntarily to a psychiatric hospital. Who defines dangerousness? What are the clinical parameters of dangerous or violent behavior? Can a psychiatric patient be "dangerous" in some circumstances and not in others? What are the duties and responsibilities of the treating psychiatrist to ensure safety to the community and to avoid violent behavior by a dangerous patient? Finally, who should decide on the discharge of the dangerous patient to the community from a psychiatric hospital? Is this a psychiatric decision alone, as it always has been, or is it now more a community decision to be determined by a judge or others?

The clinician is at the front lines of treatment and must take the responsibility for clinical decisions that are made about patients. But the law has been looking over the clinician's shoulder to ascertain the validity and correctness of those clinical decisions.

One of the major changes that have affected psychiatric practice is the emergence of the autonomy of the patient. No longer is the patient to be considered incompetent to make decisions, and no longer may the psychiatrist act in a paternalistic way toward the patient, except in an emergency. Thus, the whole concept of informed consent has evolved into an important issue that has divided physicians and attorneys. How much information is given, and in what circumstances? How much autonomy should a competent patient have in determining the treatment he or she receives at the hands of the psychiatrist?

With the changes in psychiatry have come modifications in treatment through the mental health system. Psychiatrists often act as supervisors and consultants, whereas nonpsychiatrists conduct the therapy. What responsibility do psychiatrists have in such supervisory positions? What are the ethical implications involved in doctor-patient relationships and doctor- and psychiatrist-student relationships?

The major changes of recent years require all psychiatrists to keep abreast of clinical practice and legal regulations affecting the clinician. Dr. Simon has provided a service to us all by collecting and editing this series of updates and reviews in clinical psychiatry and the law. The presentations are clearly written and helpful for all practicing psychiatrists.

I join my colleague, Dr. Jonas R. Rappeport, who wrote the foreword to Volume 1 of the *Review*, in his praise of the contents and in anticipation of a continuing series of helpful, practical comments reflecting the changes in psychiatry and law that affect us all.

Robert L. Sadoff, M.D.

Preface

It is with great enthusiasm that I present to my psychiatric colleagues Volume 2 of the *American Psychiatric Press Review of Clinical Psychiatry and the Law*. This volume addresses four major areas of pressing clinical concern to psychiatrists. The first section covers the psychiatrist's legal duties and liabilities in the practice of psychotherapy. Although the field of psychotherapy itself defies clear definition, most therapists nevertheless hold basic ideas concerning what constitutes patient exploitation. Yet, it is precisely this issue of maintaining boundaries that causes therapists the greatest problems both clinically and legally.

In Section I, "Psychotherapy and Malpractice," I define treatment boundaries according to Freud's principle of abstinence. No therapeutic alliance can develop with the patient if the therapist does not abstain from using the patient for his or her own personal gratification. A duty to neutrality also is recognized in case law. Furthermore, the therapist-patient relationship is considered by law to be fiduciary, where the therapist in whom the patient reposes trust acts strictly in the best interest of the patient. The maintenance of treatment boundaries is the cornerstone of good clinical care and legal-liability prevention.

In Section II, Robert D. Miller, M.D., Ph.D., presents a comprehensive analysis of involuntary civil commitment. This section is essential reading for psychiatrists who have responsibility for the care of patients, either directly or indirectly. Dr. Miller also graces the reader with a unique, international perspective on involuntary civil commitment.

Unfortunately for many psychiatrists, civil commitment appears so encumbered with legal issues that its value as a clinical management tool frequently becomes obscured. Contrary to much of the libertarian commentary by lawyers on the subject of involuntary civil commitment, a significant number of patients have expressed gratitude for their involuntary hospitalization and treatment. Nor should the psychiatrist unduly fear being sued for medically certifying the mentally ill patient who meets the substantive standards for involuntary hospitalization. Following legal requirements, conducting an adequate examination, and abstaining from malice in seeking involuntary hospitalization will successfully counter most allegations of improper commitment. Dr. Miller helps the psychiatrist maintain an essential clinical position in the utilization of involuntary civil commitment procedures.

In Section III, Kenneth Tardiff, M.D., M.P.H., presents the psychiatrist with an extremely valuable literature review and clinically based discussion of the assessment and management of the violent patient. The only way a psychiatrist can avoid violent patients is to avoid seeing patients. It is the character-disordered patients, the "bread and butter" patients for many psychiatrists, who not infrequently present the vexing problem of prediction and management of violence. Although professional standards do exist for the assessment of violence, the actual prediction of violence remains a judgment call. In the *Tarasoff* case, the court determined that the assessment of violence would be judged according to a professional standard, whereas the prediction of violence would be judged by an ordinary negligence standard (lay standard). Without any clinical basis for the long-term prediction of violence, frequent short-term assessments of the patient for the potential for violence is a sensible alternative. Dr. Tardiff presents the reader with specific methods for the assessment of the risk of violence. The thoroughness and clinical practicality for the total management of the violent patient provided by Dr. Tardiff is without peer.

Section IV, edited by Carol C. Kleinman, M.D., J.D., tackles an area that is now and will be in the future of ever-increasing concern and complexity for psychiatrists. In the past, most psychiatrists had minimal contact with nonmedical professionals. Rarely did they come into close contact with the public, as occurs now through radio and television appearances. For many psychiatrists, their professional fare consisted mainly of individual therapy within a solo practice.

The professional isolation of psychiatrists from the community is now history. Psychiatrists who do not meet with nonmedical professionals and interact with the public quickly find that they are isolated from important referral sources. However, with new relationships come new problems. For example, psychiatrists who work with health care provider organizations must be aware that the contractual agreement with the provider may ration professional resources to patients and sometimes will create obstacles to good clinical care. Good business and good psychiatric care are not always identical.

Psychiatrists also must be sensitive to the myriad double-agentry roles that arise when they attempt to serve the patient and nonmedical third parties simultaneously. Dr. Kleinman's section brings together the stimulating views of a number of authors on the psychiatrist's relationship with nonmedical professionals and the public.

The Features section brings back the forensic psychiatric experts of Volume 1. "Recent Legal Developments and Psychiatry" by

Steven B. Bisbing, Psy.D., J.D., keeps psychiatrists abreast of important recent legal developments and their clinical significance. In "Expert Opinion," Thomas G. Gutheil, M.D., and Robert L. Sadoff, M.D., present an analysis of a complicated case of tardive dyskinesia from both the plaintiff and defense experts' positions. Jeffrey D. Robertson, J.D., and I, in "The Psychiatrist in the Courtroom," discuss psychiatric testimony in suicide cases. With Volume 2, we begin a new feature titled "The Canadian Connection: A Canadian Perspective on Clinical Psychiatry and the Law." It is an honor to have Selwyn M. Smith, M.D., as Section Editor. Dr. Smith brings to this task a very high level of professional knowledge and competence in the area of psychiatry and the law. These chapters illustrate the interactions between psychiatry and the law.

It is virtually impossible to practice competently yet remain ignorant of the legal requirements governing psychiatry. The legal regulation of psychiatric practice will only increase in the years ahead. It is the legally informed psychiatrist who will be in the best position to provide good clinical care to patients. Knowledge and management of legal requirements governing clinical psychiatric practice can be expected to become an increasingly integral part of the professional standard of care.

Robert I. Simon, M.D.

Acknowledgments

Over the past 5 years, I have had the very good fortune to work closely with the American Psychiatric Press. No author could ask for a more gratifying relationship with a publisher. I want to express my gratitude to Carol Nadelson, M.D., Ron McMillen, Tim Clancy, Karen Loper, Richard Farkas, Pam Harley, and Julie Glass, all of the American Psychiatric Press, for their unfailing support.

I also want to express my deep appreciation to the section and feature editors as well as to the consulting editors of Volume 2 for the excellence of their contributions. They continue to demonstrate their expertise as top forensic professionals.

My many thanks go to my secretary, Susan Breglio, whose patience and steadfastness are invaluable.

To my wife, to whom I dedicate this volume, I promise to no longer promise that I will not write or edit any more books.

Section I

Psychotherapy and Malpractice

Robert I. Simon, M.D., Section Editor

Chapter 1

The Practice of Psychotherapy: Legal Liabilities of an "Impossible" Profession

Robert I. Simon, M.D.

Countless patients have been helped by the various psychotherapies. Yet, the task of conducting psychotherapy remains impossible given the enormity of human problems and psychological dysfunctions addressed regularly by psychotherapists. The limitations of therapists, patients, and scientific knowledge set real limits on the effectiveness of psychotherapy in achieving specified goals. Moreover, the very factors that limit psychotherapy often are the ones that create legal liabilities for the psychotherapist.

Psychiatric malpractice is medical malpractice. It consists of acts or omissions by the psychiatrist in his or her professional capacity that cause or aggravate an injury to a patient. The injury is the result of a failure to exercise the degree of care, knowledge, and skill ordinarily possessed and exercised in similar situations by a member of the profession in the same field (1). The legal elements of malpractice (the "four Ds") are duty, dereliction of duty, damage, and direct causation. A plaintiff (person bringing a suit) must establish these four elements by a preponderance of the evidence to prevail in a malpractice action. That is, the plaintiff must show that a psychiatrist-patient relationship was created that established a *duty* of care for the patient, that the psychiatrist breached this duty by an act or omission that was a *dereliction* of professional stan-

Portions of this article are excerpted and modified with permission from Simon RI: Clinical Psychiatry and the Law. Washington, DC, American Psychiatric Press, 1987.

dards, that the patient was *damaged,* and that the harm to the patient was *directly* caused by the psychiatrist's breach of duty.

Practitioners need basic knowledge about medical negligence law so that they themselves do not fall prey to unrealistic fears and fantasies about psychiatric malpractice. If they are not to practice too defensively, mental health professionals must know the legal realities governing their professional lives. Denial is no less maladaptive for therapists than it is for patients. For example, if a psychiatrist provides substandard treatment and the patient is not damaged, there is no malpractice. Even if the patient alleges damage from the provision of substandard care, no malpractice can occur unless damage is directly (proximally) caused by the deviation in care. Furthermore, there can be no malpractice unless a doctor-patient relationship establishing a duty is formed.

The therapist is not a warrantor of correct diagnosis and treatment. Therapists may make mistakes without necessarily incurring liability, provided that they have used due care in diagnosis and treatment. Thus, to avert liability, therapists would be prudent in recording risk-benefit analysis regarding treatment intervention. Clinical judgments that later prove to be wrong cannot be shown to be negligent when the therapist has used reasonable care and the reasoning is documented. The law is not interested in punishing errors in judgment as such (2).

An allegation of psychiatric malpractice often is not so much a result of bad practice as it is a failure in the development or maintenance of the therapeutic alliance. As Gutheil points out, malpractice is a consequence of bad results and bad feelings (3).

Psychiatrists are specifically trained in managing feelings inimical to the development of a therapeutic alliance. Nevertheless, the vicissitudes of the therapeutic alliance may be the fundamental consequence of the patient's psychiatric disorder and may not indicate that the psychiatrist lacks skill. Alliance-resistant patients not only remain at high risk for psychiatric complications but also may become sources of future litigation against the psychiatrist. With such patients, specific recommendations that psychiatrists adopt or avoid certain practices to diminish their vulnerability to malpractice may be of little avail.

CREATION OF THE PSYCHIATRIST-PATIENT RELATIONSHIP

No professional duty of care is owed a patient unless a psychiatrist-patient relationship exists. Once that relationship exists, the duty of care required of the psychiatrist is imposed by society through tort law, independent of any agreement between the psychiatrist and the patient (4).

King states that the courts tend to seize on almost any act by physicians to find an undertaking that would support a duty to the patient (4). In *O'Neill v. Montefiore Hospital* (5), the court dealt with the question of whether a telephone conversation was sufficient to create a doctor-patient relationship. The appellate ruling in *O'Neill* held "that the jury could have concluded that the physician undertook to diagnose the ailments of the deceased and could have decided whether he abandoned the patient, inadequately or improperly advised him, or conversely, made a proper diagnosis fully appropriate under the circumstances, or offered an examination which was rejected." The appeals court ordered the reversal of the lower court's dismissal of the case, and a new trial was ordered.

Occasionally a new patient who calls for an appointment will want to engage the therapist in a lengthy discussion. Therapists should tactfully discourage such discussions. Clearly, the telephone should be avoided in making diagnoses or initiating treatment. In general, the telephone should be used primarily for making or breaking appointments with patients.

In *Giallanza v. Sands* (6), a physician allowed his name to be used as a favor so that a patient could be admitted to a hospital for emergency treatment by the staff. Although the physician never saw the patient, the court held that a triable issue of fact existed about whether a doctor-patient relationship was created. In *Rainer v. Grossman* (7), the plaintiff suggested that the opinion of a medical school professor expressed during a teaching conference that surgery was indicated for the plaintiff made the professor liable for malpractice. The court declined to find liability, stating that "[p]resumably every professor or instructor in a professional school hopes, expects or foresees that his students will absorb and apply in their own careers at least some of the information he imparts. Does he thereby assume a duty of care and potential liability to those persons who may ultimately become clients or patients of those students? We think not."

In *Hammer v. Polsky* (8), the plaintiff alleged that the psychiatrist willfully and negligently diagnosed his condition as "schizophrenia, paranoid in type" when the psychiatrist saw the plaintiff with the plaintiff's wife, who was the "basic patient." The court held that the complaint failed to allege that the relationship of the plaintiff to the defendant psychiatrist was that of a patient and therapist. The defendant moved to dismiss the case. The motion was granted with leave to the plaintiff to serve an amended complaint.

Although in *Hammer* the traditional view was adopted that limits the therapist's duty of care only to persons with whom a therapist-patient relationship has been established, judicial decisions holding therapists liable to nonpatient third parties have increased in recent years. Thus, family members involved in the therapy of a "basic patient" may assert a relationship with the therapist or claim an expanded duty to nonpatient third parties. This issue is quite separate from the therapist-patient relationship established with all members in formal family or group therapy. Should any doubt exist, the therapist must make clear to family members who are seen in conjunction with the patient's treatment that no therapist-patient relationship exists with them. Family members who require individual psychiatric attention should be referred to another therapist. These legal considerations should not dissuade the psychiatrist from involving a family in a patient's care when this course is clinically indicated, however.

Many times, friends, neighbors, or colleagues may ask therapists for advice about problems. Therapists should make clear that in listening or giving advice, they are doing so only as friends. Note that providing psychoactive drugs to such individuals creates a doctor-patient relationship with responsibility for liability if the new patient suffers an adverse reaction. Some state statutes require doctors to keep a medical record when they prescribe controlled substances (9). Psychiatrists who wish to treat in informal situations must understand they have created a duty of care to their friend, neighbor, or colleague.

Radio and television shows, newspaper and magazine columns, and lectures to large groups with special interests often invite therapists' views and opinions. Unless they want to risk creating a duty of care, therapists who engage in informational, educational activities directed toward the general public must make clear that they are speaking about general principles only and are not specifically advising individuals in the audience. The American Psychiatric Association offers guidelines for psychiatrists who make radio and television appearances (10).

Third-party requests for treatment may create a duty of care. When parents request that a therapist treat their child, the therapist who accepts owes a duty to the child. When a therapist employed by a company treats an employee and is negligent, the right to sue the company-employed therapist may be denied based on the old common-law principle that the employer is not responsible for the injuries one employee causes another (9). Worker's compensation laws may be the only remedy. Psychiatrists may be sued for the negligent evaluation of disability claimants. Psychiatrists may owe duties to third parties even if a therapist-patient relationship does not exist when, during the course of an evaluation, the therapist discovers a danger to others such as child abuse, contagious disease, or threat of violence.

When performing evaluations rather than treating patients, therapists do not usually create a therapist-patient relationship. Generally, where the benefit of the examination or evaluation inures to the employer, no doctor-patient relationship is found by the courts. If some benefit is deemed to accrue to the examinee through even a hint of advice or treatment, then a doctor-patient relationship is created. Ordinarily, physicians who perform preemployment or insurance examinations do not incur a sufficient duty to the patient to be liable for malpractice (11). Therapists who examine litigants at the request of the court are immune from liability even if negligent.

Psychiatrists appointed by the court in civil commitment cases generally are protected from liability. But when psychiatrists commit their own patients, to whom they owe a duty of care, they may be liable to claims of negligence or intentional torts. When a psychiatrist-patient relationship exists, courts are less inclined to grant immunity on the grounds that psychiatrists owe a greater responsibility to their own patient than they do to individuals whom they examine exclusively for the purpose of commitment (12).

As hard as therapists may try to maintain an evaluatory stance toward a patient initially, this stance may not hold up in actual clinical practice. Therapists usually do not know how sick a new patient is after seeing the patient for the first time. On the other hand, some patients are floridly psychotic or may present clinical situations in which danger to self or others threatens. Here, the therapist may decide to intervene and forgo the evaluation period. But what if the therapist does not want to accept the patient for treatment? Therapists often feel trapped when confronted with a patient in a crisis that requires immediate attention. Therapists who do not want to accept the patient for treatment should attempt to find immediate competent treatment for the patient. In some instances, this may require accompanying the patient to a hospital emergency room. Therapists who remain indifferent to a patient's immediate crisis could be sued for negligent evaluation. In any case, professional concern for patients in crisis dictates that therapists direct them to immediate help.

Defensive psychiatrists may find concerns about litigation an additional incentive to see prospective patients for a clearly defined and mutually understood period of evaluation. Psychiatrists have become increasingly vulnerable to suits by patients they have seen for a short time—often as short as 30 days (13). A previously unknown patient seen in the absence of a therapeutic alliance, who perhaps has unrealistic expectations, who harbors discontents, and who may be litigious, may create a high potential for a liability suit. It is also known that 8 out of every 10 persons who commit suicide pay a visit to a physician within 6 months of their decision (14).

The Legal Basis of the Psychiatrist-Patient Relationship

The legal basis of the psychiatrist-patient relationship is founded on contract and "undertaking" theory (4). When a psychiatrist agrees to accept a fee in exchange for the treatment of an individual, a contract is created with corresponding duties and rights. When a specific agreement about the terms of treatment is reached between the patient and the psychiatrist, an express contract exists. Courts will infer that an implied contract exists from surrounding circumstances, such as when a patient consents to treatment, and a psychiatrist has the expectation of payment for services. The most common type of legal relationship between psychiatrist and patient is through contract, either expressed or implied.

Circumstances arise in professional practice that do not always fit into the traditional contract model. Unconscious patients may be treated without their knowledge or consent. Patients also may be treated free of charge. Although these situations do not fit into traditional contract theory, they are covered by "undertaking" theory, which holds that a psychiatrist who undertakes to treat a patient creates a professional relationship with a duty of care to the patient. Thus, a cardiologist who reads an ECG of a patient whom the doctor does not see and whom he or she treats gratuitously still owes a duty of care to that patient. Similarly, when psychiatrists treat patients without charge, the psychiatrist remains liable for any negligence in the course of diagnosis and treatment.

Although the psychiatrist-patient relationship usually is based on contract theory, the contract is not a guarantee of specific results but rather a promise to provide an acceptable standard of care. Furthermore, psychiatrists should distinguish between legal contracts and therapeutic contracts. The latter ordinarily do not have legal force but rather memorialize a treatment prescription. For example, a treatment contract with a suicidal patient acknowledges the patient's willingness to contact the psychiatrist in a suicidal emergency.

The No-Duty Rule

The "no-duty" rule states that a psychiatrist who is self-employed and not required by the policies of others to accept patients owes no duty to enter into a professional relationship with a patient. King (4) feels, aside from common-law precedent holding that no duty is owed by one individual to come to the aid of another, that medical practice is essentially a private enterprise, consistent with individualism and independence, as part of our nation's history and jurisprudence. The courts have refused to abrogate the right of an individual to say no in a free society.

Evaluation and treatment often blur into each other during an initial session. However, as suggested above, therapists may wish to undertake a brief, clearly defined and mutually understood period of evaluation before accepting a patient. For such evaluations, psychiatrists must notify the patient and make it expressly clear that no treatment will be rendered. On completion of the evaluation, both the therapist and the patient may decide whether to begin treatment. Therapists who are conducting an initial evaluation only must scrupulously avoid advice, interpretation, or any other intervention that might be interpreted as treatment, because courts seem to have little difficulty in finding a "sufficient undertaking" to establish a professional relationship with the patient. Obviously, in addition, psychiatrists should not undertake the treatment of patients whose problems are beyond their ability and training.

Psychiatrists have no legal obligation to provide emergency medical care. Nevertheless, as the American Medical Association's *Current Opinions of the Judicial Council,* Section 8.10 (15), advises, "The physician should . . . respond to the best of his ability in cases of emergency where first aid treatment is essential." Only the Massachusetts Board of Registration in Medicine requires licensees to render emergency medical treatment (16).

When a psychiatrist undertakes to render assistance to a person "at the wayside," the psychiatrist is protected by Good Samaritan statutes, enacted by all states, against suit for damages arising out of any professional act or omission performed in "good faith" and not amounting to gross negligence (17). Good Samaritan laws cover the physician who is not licensed in the state where emergency care takes place as well (17).

Once psychiatrists have decided to render emergency "wayside" aid, they have a duty not to abandon the rescue and to use whatever reasonable means are available to continue the rescue effort, without jeopardizing themselves. Psychiatrists must either wait until competent medical assistance arrives or must accompany the victim to the hospital and into the hands of competent medical care. Good Samaritans, acting in good faith, do not send trauma victims a bill for services.

Halleck (9) feels that an ethical psychiatrist should come to the rescue of an accident victim. But psychiatrists who are accustomed to practicing their profession in the quiet of their offices may no longer possess even rudimentary medical or first aid skills. Thus they may decide to refrain from providing help to trauma victims unless immediate lifesaving actions are necessary. This lack of action is not so much out of a fear of legal liability but rather to avoid further harm to the victim. The old saw that "a psychiatrist is a physician who is afraid of blood" may contain a certain truth here. For whatever reason, some psychiatrists may be unable to function satisfactorily in an accident-trauma situation. Psychiatrists themselves present a wide spectrum of attitudes on this subject.

Supervision of Other Psychotherapists

Under the doctrine of *respondeat superior,* or vicarious liability, a supervisor may become responsible for the acts and omissions of a training psychotherapist who is treating a patient. The doctrine of vicarious liability originated from the master-servant relationship (18), and, in fact, *respondeat superior* means "let the master answer." The doctrine states that the one with the right of control must pay money damages to the successful plaintiff. The law's assumption is that the master has the deeper pocket than does the servant. Under the doctrine of respondeat superior, vicarious liability may be imposed on an individual therapist or institution for negligent acts of employees under the clinician's supervision (19). But liability for a subordinate's negligence exists only if the professional has the right or ability to control the subordinate at work. Yet even in the absence of an employer-employee relationship, a therapist exercising extensive control over the employee of another employer may be liable for negligence of the subordinate under the "borrowed servant" doctrine. Still, when a subordinate deviates too far from assigned work and becomes engaged in "frolic and detour," liability of the employer will no longer exist.

The American Psychiatric Association's "Guidelines for Psychiatrists in Consultative, Supervisory, or Collaborative Relationships With Nonmedical Therapists" (20) states that the psychiatrist is responsible for the patient's diagnosis and treatment plan and for the supervision of the nonmedical therapist to ensure that the treatment plan is properly administered with suitable adjustments to the patient's condition. The guidelines do not specify the frequency of supervision. Thus, psychiatrists, when supervising nonmedical therapists, are responsible for the supervisees' patients as if the patients were their own (20). The guidelines explicitly state: "The psychiatrist remains ethically and medically responsible for the patient's care as long as the treatment continues under his or her supervision."

For psychiatrists supervising other psychiatrists, psychiatric residents, or interns, the situation is somewhat different. If an intern or resident is treating a psychiatrist's patient, the intern may be considered a "borrowed servant," whereupon the psychiatrist will be vicariously responsible for any negligence that leads to harm. Likewise, interns and residents treating their own patients but supervised by a psychiatrist may themselves incur direct liability, whereas the psychiatrist may be vicariously liable when he or she has exercised supervisory control.

The determination of vicarious liability may depend on the disparity in training and experience between supervisor and supervisee. The lesser the training gap, the less likely is the imposition of vicarious liability if the supervisees are treating their own patients. Psychiatrists supervising other graduate psychiatrists may be viewed as "independent contractors" and may not bear liability for acts of negligence by supervised psychiatrists. Because of the considerable independence and freedom of action that physicians possess in the practice of medicine, it is unlikely that one psychiatrist will be viewed as the "servant" of another. Although not strictly consultative, the supervisory relationship between psychiatrists appears closer to the consultative model, even though it occurs on a continuing basis.

The psychiatric team concept has gained considerable popularity in treating patients. The team may contain a psychiatrist, psychologist, social worker, and other mental health professionals, with a concomitant increase in the liability of individual members (17). Therapists may be held liable for the negligent acts of partners, even though the therapists themselves have never seen the patient. Vicarious liability also may be imposed for the negligent acts of employees committed within the scope of their employment.

Establishing a Standard of Care and Dereliction From It

The plaintiff is required to establish a standard of care, and the psychiatrist's dereliction from that standard generally is established through an expert witness (1). Treatises and articles from professional journals may be used in lieu of expert testimony in states that permit the use of the learned treatise as an exception to the hearsay rule in establishing the professional standard of practice. The plaintiff is relieved of his or her "burden of production" if the facts allow for laypersons to conclude whether there was a failure to conform to the applicable standard of care or under the rule of *res ipsa loquitur* (the thing speaks for itself; e.g., a sponge left in the patient's abdomen). No expert is necessary. The plaintiff presents evidence of the injury and the circumstances of the occurrence of the injury. In the past, courts have applied standards from the defendant's locality, but most courts now judge the psychiatrist by national standards (21).

Psychiatric diagnosis and treatment are still an imprecise science despite the *Diagnostic and Statistical Manual of Mental Disorders, 3rd Edition, Revised* (DSM-III-R) (22). Some psychiatrists feel that diagnosis and treatment is more of an art than a science. Hence, one therapist's "deviation" in care may be another's "cornerstone" in managing patients. Therapists disagree concerning the indications and effectiveness of the myriad psychotherapeutic modalities. Differences of opinion are evident even within the same school of psychotherapy. For example, one behaviorist might treat phobias through systematic desensitization, whereas another might treat the same ailment through implosion techniques. Psychiatrists also differ on basic treatment approaches. Some prefer insight psychotherapy for phobias, whereas others are adamant about using tricyclic antidepressants or specific benzodiazepines. Others advocate a combined approach. Psychiatry has a tradition of being hospitable toward diverse and competing schools of thought. At last count, there were more that 450 separate schools of psychotherapy (23).

Lazare (24) describes four distinct conceptual models used in treating patients in contemporary psychiatry: biological, behavioral, psychodynamic, and social. The biological and behavioral models are currently ascendant, whereas the psychodynamic and social models are declining in use (25). The eclectic psychiatrist is under pressure from subspecialization in these areas. Biological psychiatry has ready credibility with the medical community. Behavioral principles appeal to pragmatic physicians because they allow for relatively direct, uncomplicated approaches to treatment. In these areas, standards of care are clearer and are better defined. Still, courts may be reluctant to find psychiatrists negligent if they follow methods approved by at least a respectable minority of the profession (1). On the other hand, experts are less reluctant now to testify against colleagues. Hence, attorneys can no longer claim a "conspiracy of silence" within the medical profession.

The court usually derives the standards of the profession from expert testimony of psychiatrists and by evaluating how the ordinary and prudent practitioner of the profession would have acted under the same or similar circumstances (26). The law takes the position that it does not prefer one form of treatment over another. It will measure a therapist's care by the standard of the therapist's school of treatment if that school is supported by a respectable minority of fellow professionals. In some instances, the applicable standard may be defined by statute or by a court that imposes judicial standards, as in *Tarasoff v. Regents of the University of California* (27). For example, as a result of the ruling in *Helling v. Carey* (28), tonometry examinations in the state of Washington are required by law on all patients, regardless of the infrequency of glaucoma in patients under age 40. The intentional infliction of emotional distress is another example of a judicially imposed standard (29).

Standards of care also may be derived from drug manufacturers' instructions and by medical treatises under the federal Rules of Evidence in many states (30). Governmental and nongovernmental regulatory agencies may specify standards of care. Informed consent statutes and other legislative mandates setting standards for peer review and record keeping are increasingly more common (30). Third-party payers—including private, state, and federal insurance programs—are establishing standards for treatment. Long-term psychotherapy is being drastically limited as an "appropriate" treatment modality for a number of psychiatric diagnostic categories. Treatment manuals recently developed for the various types of psychotherapy provide standards for this very ambiguous area (31,32). The American Psychiatric Association Task Force on Treatments of Psychiatric Disorders (33) has published a complete, multivolume text on the treatments of psychiatric disorders. Inevitably, the standard of care will be influenced and shaped by third-party decision makers.

Psychiatrists have an ethical and professional duty to stay abreast of new developments. *The Principles of Medical Ethics With Annotations Especially Applicable to Psychiatry* (34) states: "Psychiatrists are responsible for their own continuing education and should be mindful of the fact that theirs must be a lifetime of learning" (Section 5, Annotation 1). The law has imposed a duty on all physicians to stay abreast of changing concepts and new developments (35). In fact, the duty to keep up with medical and psychiatric advances is much clearer for specialists than for general practitioners (36). Psychiatrists are held to the standards and advances in diagnosis and treatment commonly used throughout the country (36). Knowledge concerning treatment efficacy and adverse effects of drug therapy is burgeoning. Psychiatrists who prescribe drug therapy must apprise themselves of current developments in psychopharmacology.

Nonmedical therapists who present themselves as specialists in the treatment of emotional and mental illness also will be held to the higher standard of the specialist. If nonmedical therapists undertake diagnosis and treatment of medical disorders, then they will be held to medical standards (4). Finally, specialists are held to higher standards of care than nonspecialists, even in cases involving the same problem. Thus, psychiatrists who do psychotherapy should not represent their work as psychoanalysis nor themselves as analysts if they are not so trained. The couch traditionally used in psychoanalysis should not be used in psychotherapy or by therapists not prepared to handle the transference complications that may develop. The couch is not just a convention.

Psychoanalysts and other psychodynamic therapists heretofore have been almost totally immune from malpractice suits because of virtually insurmountable technical and legal reasons. Yet patients dissatisfied with the lack of improvement after prolonged psychodynamic treatment may have found a way around these legal obstacles —a way provided by biological psychiatry. That is, they may sue for malpractice because biological treatments were not administered. In *Osheroff v. Chestnut Lodge et al.* (37), the plaintiff asserted that he was inappropriately treated by psychotherapy for depression, needlessly extending his hospital stay and causing him other emotional and financial harms. This case was eventually settled, but it has generated considerable controversy and discussion among mental health professionals and attorneys (38).

Some therapists may be proficient in psychoanalytic psychotherapy only. Others may be expert primarily in psychopharmacology. Combined treatment approaches often are necessary. Yet some therapists who are proficient in only one or two forms of therapy insist on applying their treatments in Procrustean fashion— to all patients who enter their office. Thus the specter exists of an analyst futilely but intrepidly treating a bipolar patient with five-times-per-week psychoanalysis, or of a biological psychiatrist unleashing a pharmacopoeia of antidepressant drugs on a neurotically depressed patient. According to Klerman (39), the use of one type of psychotherapy or pharmacologic intervention in treating all affective disorders is not supported by the literature. Affective illnesses are highly heterogeneous in origin. Treatment decisions thus depend on careful evaluation of the patient according to rapidly developing research data.

Establishing Damage

No matter how clear the deviation from a reasonable standard of care, malpractice cannot be assessed where there is no harm to the patient. The courts rely on the testimony of expert witnesses to determine the presence or absence of harm to the plaintiff. Until the 1960s and 1970s, the courts denied liability in negligence actions causing emotional distress in the absence of physical injury or impact (30).

Although the courts during the past 10–20 years are finding compensable psychic impairment without physical injury or impact, judges and juries remain skeptical of the claim of emotional injury without physical damage. Proofs of psychic injury or its causes are considered highly speculative.

In allegations of psychiatric malpractice, the presence of "emotional injury" may be very difficult to determine, because emotional difficulties are inherently preexistent. Furthermore, plaintiffs must establish and courts must determine that the emotional injury claimed is caused by the psychiatrist's negligent actions and is not a result of the natural progression of the emotional or mental illness being treated. When emotional distress is accompanied by physical injury, courts are more likely to find allegations of emotional harm more compelling. For example, severe emotional distress following a suicide attempt with physical injuries such as fractures and neurologic damage may lead to substantial monetary damages for pain and suffering if negligence is found. For emotional harm to be compensable, it does not necessarily have to meet DSM-III-R criteria for a mental disorder. Simple pain and suffering may suffice. In tardive dyskinesia (TD) cases, the physical injury is clear and compelling. Courts have awarded six- and seven-figure monetary judgments where the TD was causally linked with a deviation in the standard of neuroleptic treatment.

Showing Direct Causation or Proximate Cause

When a psychiatrist deviates from a standard of care in the diagnosis and treatment of a patient who alleges harm, no malpractice can be assigned unless the damage is the direct result of the deviation from the standard of care.

The law divides causation into *cause-in-fact* and *legal* or *proximate cause* (40). Cause-in-fact is expressed in the "but for" rule, which attempts to show that the psychiatrist's conduct was a necessary antecedent to the patient's injury. If the injury would have occurred without the psychiatrist's conduct, no causation exists. Further, where there is more than one cause of injury, the "but for" test also may deny recovery.

Yet when several causes act together to bring about an injury of which any one cause alone would have been sufficient to cause the injury, it is sufficient if the conduct of the defendant was a "substantial factor" in causing the injury (41). For example, two fires meet at a building and burn it down. Either fire alone would have destroyed the building. Under the "but for" test, neither fire was the cause, because the building would have been burned by the other. The courts avoid this conundrum by considering as causes all the factors that were sufficient or substantial factors in causing damage or injury.

When two or more individuals have been negligent, but it is unclear which individual or individuals caused the plaintiff's injury, the "alternative cause" approach may be used. Here, the plaintiff must prove that harm has been caused by one of the individuals, even if the plaintiff does not establish which one. The burden of proof then shifts to the defendants, and each much show that his or her negligence is not the actual cause. For example, two shotguns are negligently fired in the direction of the plaintiff, who is hit by a pellet. The plaintiff cannot determine which shotgun fired the shot. Under the alternative cause approach, the defendants who fired the guns will have to prove that the pellet did *not* come from their gun. If neither defendant is able to do so, both may be liable.

In addition to the cause-in-fact, the defendant's act or omission must be the *proximate cause* of the injury. Proximate or legal cause exists where an uninterrupted chain of events occurs from the time of the defendant's negligent conduct to the time of the plaintiff's injury. Intervening causes may occur after the time of a negligent act but may combine with the negligent act to cause injury to the plaintiff. Here, the defendant is liable for harm caused by foreseeable intervening forces. For example, a physician who is initially negligent by harming a patient is usually liable for aggravation of the patient's condition caused by the negligent conduct of a subsequent treating physician.

A *superseding intervening force* breaks the causal connection between the initial wrongful conduct and the ultimate injury and becomes a direct, immediate cause of such injury. An intervening force is superseding when it is not foreseeable and relieves the first person from liability. For example, a borderline patient becomes impulsively involved in a sexual relationship between once-per-week psychotherapy sessions. Despite a clear understanding between the therapist and the patient to call the therapist if the latter encounters a crisis, the patient does not call the therapist after experiencing a severe rejection in the new relationship. Instead, the patient becomes enraged, abuses alcohol, and takes an overdose of antidepressants that the patient has stored up over time. The patient survives but is brain damaged. Here, despite the existence of an explicit understanding to call the therapist should a crisis occur, the patient's uncommunicative and impulsive behavior may be considered an independent superseding variable that produced the damage, and the psychiatrist is not negligent.

The concept of proximate cause is extremely elusive and has little resemblance to Aristotelian logic as applied to scientific injury. Slovenko (42) points out that proximate cause is used as a convenience for public policy considerations and a rough sense of justice. The law arbitrarily stops tracing the causes of a series of events beyond a certain point. Thus, proximate cause often refers to the last factor in a series of events—the "straw that breaks the camel's back"—rather than to the first or primary cause.

Causation of emotional and mental illness is imperfectly understood. It is sometimes very difficult to distinguish emotional harm allegedly caused by the psychiatrist's negligent act or omission from the natural course of the disorder or from other causes in the patient's life. But note that medical causation in clinical practice is quite different from the legal concept of proximate cause.

Standards of Proof

When a malpractice case goes to trial, the jury is instructed on the standard of proof required. Malpractice cases are civil suits requiring plaintiffs to prove their allegations by a preponderance of the evidence. *Preponderance* refers to the weight of evidence that must be more probable than not (e.g., 51% versus 49% for the plaintiff to prevail). Criminal proceedings, in contrast, require that a defendant's guilt be proven beyond a reasonable doubt (90–95% range of certainty). In *Addington v. Texas* (43), the U.S. Supreme Court determined that the level of evidence for involuntary civil commitment proceedings must be at least clear and convincing (75% certainty). Percentages are used merely to illustrate the legal concepts. The law does not attempt to assign percentages to these standards of proof.

Because malpractice cases are determined by a preponderance of the evidence, the outcome of these suits is somewhat difficult to predict. Thus, defendants who perceive themselves vulnerable for heavy damages often may choose to settle for a given amount.

MALPRACTICE STATISTICS

Slawson and Guggenheim (44) examined 217 malpractice actions against psychiatrists from 1974 to 1978 using the detailed analysis of the National Association of Insurance Commissioners' nationwide study of 71,788 malpractice claims filed against American physicians. Ten psychiatric procedures account for approximately 50% of all psychiatric claims: tranquilizers, 17 claims; psychotherapy, 16; mental health evaluations, 16; electroconvulsive therapy (ECT), 13; general psychiatric examination, 13; general medical examination, 9; unspecified drug, 8; antidepressant drug, 6; neglect, 6; and other psychoactive drug, 4. The most common complaint about psychiatric procedures was that they were improperly done or not indicated.

The average indemnity paid to patients harmed by these procedures was $26,000. The average indemnity for tranquilizers was $5,000; for ECT it was $3,500. The largest average paid indemnity of $109,000 was paid for the general examination category. On average, both the patients and psychiatrists involved in the malpractice litigation were middle-aged. More often than not , the psychiatrists were board certified, and the majority were in private practice.

The most frequent causes of injuries in psychiatric claims, accounting for 95 (44%) of the total claims, were diagnostic errors, 36 claims; suicide or self-injury, 26; death, 7; medical complications, 7; inadequate physical examination, 6; surgical complications, 5; tranquilizers, 4; and antidepressants, 4. The average indemnity paid for the 10 most frequent categories was $21,500.

The 10 most frequently listed psychiatric diagnoses accounted for 112 claims (52%): depressive neurosis, 32 claims; other neuroses, 20; psychosis (type not specified), 13; paranoid psychosis, 13; schizophrenia, 14; anxiety neurosis, 5; major affective disorders, 4; general psychiatric examination, 4; schizoaffective disorder, 4; depressive disorder not elsewhere classified, 3. The neuroses were the largest diagnostic group and were associated with 16 fatalities and 6 permanent injuries with an average indemnity of $44,000. The largest indemnity paid was $250,000 for injury leading to blindness from a homicidal assault. A majority of the psychiatrists were board certified.

Although underreporting of suits against psychiatrists by some insurance companies may have skewed the figures, the claims against psychiatrists represented only 0.3% of the 71,788 claims against all physicians. These statistics led Slawson and Guggenheim (44) to conclude that psychiatrists should be reassured by the proportionately low figures for psychiatry. They suggest that the data indirectly support the inference that the psychiatrist's facility with interpersonal relationships is a significant factor in maintaining low malpractice rates.

Slovenko (21) states that psychiatry ranks eighth among medical specialties in relative frequency of malpractice suits. In almost every suit in which liability was imposed, tangible physical injury was demonstrated. Suits usually arise in all medical specialties when an unexpected bad result occurs, a large bill is owed, and the relationship between physician and patient has been poor (45). Slovenko suggests that the number of suits against psychiatrists may be small because patients are reluctant to expose a psychiatric history, because it is difficult to prove that the treatment was the cause of injury, and because psychiatrists are skilled in managing patients' negative feelings. Suits against psychiatrists have been primarily for negligent diagnosis and evaluation, improper certification for commitment, suicide injuries and harmful effects from ECT and psychotropic drugs, breach of confidentiality, and undue familiarity with patients. However, judging by the steep rise in current premiums for professional liability insurance for psychiatrists, psychiatry's reputation as a backwater of litigation is changing rapidly.

Boundary Violations: The Royal Road to Malpractice Litigation

Breach of a Psychiatrist's Fiduciary Relationship With a Patient

In a strictly legal sense, the term *fiduciary* refers to a relationship in which a person manages money or property for another who has the legal right to place great trust and confidence in the manager. More broadly, it refers to any relationship in which one person is under a duty to act for the benefit of another. Fiduciary relationships may be formal, as with a banker and an investor or a guardian with a ward. Or they may be informal, as with an adult and a child, an adult and an aged parent, or a husband and a wife. Fiduciary relationships are usually established when the confidence placed in one person is accepted by the other. Merely respecting another's judgment or trusting an individual's character is not usually enough to create a fiduciary relationship.

Fiduciary relationships may be personal, domestic, moral, or social. In every case in which confidence is placed by one person and accepted by another with resulting dependence of one party on the influence of another, a fiduciary relationship is created. The psychiatrist's relationship with the patient is a fiduciary relationship.

Persons acting as fiduciaries are not permitted to use the relationship for their personal benefit except with the full knowledge and consent of the other person. The person giving such consent must be mentally competent for the courts to consider the consent valid. Courts carefully scrutinize transactions between individuals in fiduciary relationships, especially if the dominant individual profits at the expense of the individual over whom influence is exerted (46).

Case law has affirmed that a physician in whom a special trust or confidence is placed is required to act in good faith and in the interest of the person reposing the trust (47). Because of the special training and knowledge of the physician and "the ignorance and helplessness of the patient regarding his own physical condition," the physician-patient relationship is a fiduciary relationship (48). For example, one of the fundamental principles underlying the doctrine of informed consent is that the physician, as a fiduciary, discloses to the patient all pertinent facts about the patient's condition and the treatment recommended (49). In *Hammonds v. Aetna Insurance Company* (50), the court defined the fiduciary relationship between psychiatrist and patient as the "aura of trust and the expectation of confidentiality, . . . an undivided loyalty." In this case, an attorney induced a psychiatrist to divulge confidential information about his patient on the pretext that his patient intended to bring a suit for malpractice. The psychiatrist was found blameless, because he was deceived by the attorney.

Neutrality in Psychotherapy

A general consensus exists concerning the appropriate treatment boundaries among most of the more than 450 current schools of psychotherapy. Many years ago, Freud enunciated the principle of abstinence—that psychiatrists must refrain from gratifying themselves at the expense of patients.

Good psychotherapeutic techniques help to preserve the therapist's neutrality and to avoid misalliances with the patient. The therapist's position of neutrality ensures that treatment intervention is made on behalf of the patient. Therapeutic neutrality also dictates that the patient's agenda is given prime consideration. The personal needs and undue influences of therapists should not be allowed to contaminate the treatment situation. In addition, case law implicitly recognizes a duty to neutrality by therapists toward patients.

A corollary of the principle of abstinence is that the psychiatrist's main source of personal gratification should arise from conducting the psychotherapeutic process and from helping the patient. The only direct material reward received from the patient is payment for the therapist's services. Treatment boundaries are violated when the primary source of the psychiatrist's gratification is achieved *from* the patient directly rather than by engagement in the therapeutic process *with* the patient.

The duty to neutrality is soundly based in the legal concept of the fiduciary relationship, requiring all mental health professionals to act in the best interests of their patients through a position of personal neutrality. This should not be confused with "impersonal" attitudes or the psychoanalytic therapist's technical position of neutrality, in which the analyst attempts to remain equidistant between reality and the patient's superego, ego, and id. Although such a position does militate against self-serving intervention in psychoanalysis, it also serves other important treatment purposes in psychoanalytic therapy. Not infrequently, however, psychiatrists need to support a patient's defenses and conscience, or even help a patient to define reality. These are all legitimate treatment interventions for the needs of specific patients. The duty to neutrality refers not to these technical issues but rather to the obligation of therapists to curb any tendencies to manipulate or exploit patients for the therapists' personal gain.

Double Agentry

Double agentry is the royal road to malpractice litigation. Double agentry occurs when mental health professionals have conflicts of interest that interfere with their fiduciary responsibility to act solely in the best interest of the patient or the person being evaluated. Obviously, conflicts of interest with patients undermine the therapeutic alliance. Without a healthy, functioning alliance with the patient, treatment will likely founder. Double-agent roles distract the therapist from fully concentrating on the welfare of the patient and the conduct of treatment. Patients inevitably react to this situation with feelings of rejection (hurt and anger). As Gutheil (51) points out, bad feelings combined with bad results lead to malpractice suits.

The occasions for double-agent roles in clinical practice are more numerous than mental health practitioners generally realize. In fact, the practice of psychotherapy practically bristles with moral dilemmas.

Double-agent roles may be societally imposed, as, for example, when a therapist seeks involuntary civil commitment primarily on the basis of dangerousness rather than the need for treatment. The conflict of interest may be stated or unstated. Where the conflict of interest is stated, the patient or evaluee presumably has been put on proper notice. But instances arise in which—even though the patient or evaluee is aware of the mental health professional's conflict of interest—coercion is present that nullifies this knowledge of conflict. Consider an example given in the *Opinions of the Ethics Committee on the Principles of Medical Ethics With Annotations Especially Applicable to Psychiatry* (52), published by the American Psychiatric Association. This work examines the potential ethical conflicts of a student health psychiatrist who sees some patients for treatment and others for administrative reasons. The American Psychiatric Association opinion on this case states that a classic example of double agentry exists if an administrative opinion is rendered about a patient with whom the psychiatrist has a therapeutic contract. Even if a student gives consent for the administrative report after a period of psychotherapy, the conflict of interest may not be resolved if the consent is not given freely but is coerced. The opinion further states that the psychiatrist should define his or her role clearly and in advance with the student.

In this chapter, the concept of double agentry has been broadened to include actions of mental health professionals in which the therapist's interests are inserted before those of the patient. Direct conflicts between the therapist's selfish interests and the treatment needs of the patient are not discussed as often in the professional literature as are the more traditional conflicts of loyalty to external agencies. Yet it must be conceded that psychotherapists are no better or worse than any other human beings. One hopes they possess a special skill that allows them to work intimately with individuals suffering from emotional and mental disorders. Nevertheless, the best training available does not protect against the character deficiencies in therapists that lead to exploitation of their patients.

Despite their efforts to remain therapeutically neutral, psychotherapists have their own powerful value systems. Should psychiatrists make their values explicitly known to patients—as a kind of *Miranda* warning? Patients then would know exactly where the therapist stands, and they would not be subject to the therapist's hidden agendas or values.

Slovenko (53) describes other occasions of double agentry. For example, double agentry may occur when a mental health professional writes an article about a patient, about a research subject, or about the subject of a forensic examination rendered on behalf of an attorney or the court. Here, the conflicting interests are of confidentiality versus dissemination of scientific information.

In *Roe v. Doe* (54), a university social work professor initiated a legal action to prevent publication of a book by her therapist that contained intimate details of her life. The patient contended that her right of privacy and the confidential nature of the doctor-patient relationship had been violated. The psychiatrist claimed that the patient gave a verbal agreement. The patient argued that the consent given during the course of treatment was invalid because passive and dependent attitudes were induced toward the therapist through transference. Although the U.S. Supreme Court ultimately dismissed the suit as "improvidently granted," a New York appellate court enjoined distribution of the book. Slovenko (55) questions whether an informed consent could be obtained if the patient had not seen the manuscript. Furthermore, when writing about patients, does the therapist prolong treatment to obtain material? Are interpretations skewed by the need to develop certain material of interest to potential readers? Was note taking done for the purpose of writing the book, possibly inhibiting the treatment process? Finally, does disclosure of negative information about a patient violate the therapist's ethical and legal obligation not to harm the patient?

Therapists may attempt to disguise the identity of a patient, but this is often difficult. Moreover, too much disguise may undermine the scientific veracity of a case, making the patient into a fictional creation of the therapist. Sometimes, no disguise is attempted except to withhold the patient's name. A number of recent books contain verbatim therapy sessions. These books are purported to be of educational value, but the patient's consent in many cases was not obtained (55).

Publishing research or clinical studies that support new discoveries is a professional obligation, of course. At the same time, conflicts between service and research obligations may disrupt the therapist's fiduciary relationship with the patient. Thus, no matter how well disguised case material appears to the therapist, the therapist should discuss the issues with the patient and obtain permission in writing for publication.

Therapists who exploit their patients sexually egregiously violate their fiduciary trust relationship with the patient. In *Roy v. Hartogs* (56), a leading sexual misconduct case, the court held that the psychotherapist-patient relationship was a fiduciary relationship analogous to a guardian-ward relationship. The court further stated that "there is a public policy to protect a patient from the deliberate and malicious abuse of power and breach of trust by a psychiatrist when the patient entrusts to him her body and mind." Stone (57) feels that emphasis on the fiduciary relationship removes the patient consent issue in sexual misconduct cases. A patient's capacity to consent is irrelevant, in Stone's view.

Another form of double agentry may occur when patients who have been sexually abused by a therapist are referred to another therapist for much-needed treatment. Subsequent therapists with forensic interests or unstated moral vendettas have converted the treatment relationship into a forensic case, encouraging a suit and initiating ethical and licensure proceedings against the former therapist. The patient who seeks treatment should be offered the choice of treatment or forensic advocacy, but the latter should not be misrepresented to the patient as treatment. It must be remembered that sexually abused patients have already experienced a devastating deception through a conflict of interest by the previous therapist.

Mental health professionals may themselves feel isolated and lonely, and may seek the friendship and companionship of current and past patients. Although overtly nonsexual, such intrusions into the patient's treatment or residual transferences left over from the terminated therapy may be confusing, upsetting, gratifying, or reassuring to the patient, but they are blatant examples of double agentry. "Once a patient, always a patient" is a principle that allows patients to go about their lives free of the shadow of their therapists. In *Landau v. Werner* (58), an English case, a psychiatrist encouraged a patient to become emotionally involved with him, continuing social visits with her after she had "fallen in love" with him. There were no allegations of any sexual advances. The court stated that medical testimony condemned the insertion of social visits into the treatment of an emotionally attached patient and held that the psychiatrist would be liable for any serious decline in the patient's condition if deterioration was proximately caused by the therapist's negligence.

One of the real deprivations of psychiatric practice, in contrast to most other medical specialties, is the prohibition against socializing with patients, both current and former. Note, however, that a useful distinction can be made between maintaining a friendly interest in former patients and striking up social relationships with them. From time to time, therapists receive letters from former patients about their current lives. These contacts provide important follow-up data. Although these communications may contain manifest or latent psychological overtones in relation to the therapist, the human response is to answer these letters unless doing so is clearly contraindicated. "Once a patient, always a patient" should not become an inhuman dictum.

Some psychiatrists involve their patients in business deals. Unfortunately, such exploitations are not that rare. The reverse situation tends to be more common—a therapist is induced to enter a business deal offered by a patient. Some therapists have asked patients to include them in business deals that patients have discussed during the course of therapy. Others have accepted large bequests from patients. In still another instance, a psychiatrist used a stock tip obtained from a patient during the course of therapy to turn a large profit (59). After the Securities and Exchange Commission learned from the patient of this transmission of "insider" information about a merger, it charged the psychiatrist with profiting illegally. The psychiatrist neither admitted nor denied the charges but surrendered profits of $26,933.74 and paid a fine of the same amount.

Using information obtained during therapy is not only unethical, but it also invites litigation. Therapists who become involved in business dealings with patients may later be accused of undue influence if they have purchased valuable goods or property from the patient at below market value, or if the patient leaves the therapist a large amount of money in a will (9). Litigation usually is aimed at voiding the business contract or will. Damages against the therapist usually are not sought. The burden of proof usually will be on the patient or litigant to show that undue influence was brought to bear.

Double-agentry breaches of fiduciary trust cut through all schools of psychiatric treatment and occur at all levels of training. Honesty and integrity in the practice of one's profession appear to reflect innate character. It is something that can be learned only to a limited degree.

Fees

Self-serving interventions may occur concerning billing and fees (2). Most therapists explain their fees at the initiation of treatment so that patients can either agree, disagree, or enter into negotiations for a mutually agreed-on fee. However, double-agent roles can arise over billing for times reserved or through discounting and inflating bills.

Therapists are free to bill at rates they have established for services. Billing for missed appointments is appropriate if the patient is advised from the beginning of this practice (1). *The Principles of Medical Ethics With Annotations Especially Applicable to Psychiatry* (60) provides ethical guidelines permitting billing for missed appointments, but "always with the utmost consideration for the patient and his/her circumstances" (Section 2, Annotation 6). If the therapist charges for phone conversations or for preparing reports or lengthy insurance forms, the patient should be notified in advance. The American Medical Association's *Current Opinions of the Judicial Council* (15) states that "the attending physician should complete without charge the appropriate 'simplified' insurance claim forms as part of his service to the patient to enable the patient to receive his benefits. A charge for more complex forms may be made in conformity with local customs" (Section 104, 6.06).

Legal commentators state that charges for missed sessions should not be represented as treatment sessions to third-party payers (1). Doing so could be interpreted as misrepresentation. Some therapists feel that they do not want to place themselves in the position of the patient's conscience; hence, they inform the patient that conflicts with the insurance carrier over payments for missed appointments will need to be handled by the patient. But therapists should make clear on the bill that all appointment times are reserved. Some therapists stipulate conditions on the bill, such as "sessions reserved, 50 minutes each" (2). Other therapists indicate directly on the billing statement all missed appointments even if patients object. Then patients' feelings are addressed as treatment issues. In any case, not to clarify billing procedures with third-party payers may raise the question of collusion with a patient against a carrier.

When a patient has insurance but is unable to pay his or her own portion of the bill, "discounting" of the bill occurs if the therapist accepts no payment or a smaller amount from the patient (61). The effect of this practice is to nullify the insurance company's position that services are unlikely to be overly or inappropriately used when patients pay their part for the therapy. In most instances, insurance companies are responsible for a percentage of the psychiatrist's usual and customary fee. When the psychiatrist accepts the insurance reimbursement as payment in full, but collection of the copayment from the patient is permissible, the insurer actually is paying 100% of the bill. Insurance carriers look on this practice as fraudulent, because the physician is pocketing their "overpayments."

"Inflating" bills refers to charging the insurance carrier a higher fee than the therapist is actually charging the patient. When this happens, the therapist pockets the difference or applies it to the patient's portion. Also, therapists must distinguish between three separate billing situations: illegal balance billing, charging one's insurance company profile fee to the insurer, and charging the patient a normal discounted fee—which is perfectly reasonable and is universally done (62). For example, it is illegal under most Blue Cross agreements in most states to bill a patient $100, accept the $60 Blue Cross payment and bill the patient for the balance of $40. It is a perfectly acceptable approach for the psychiatrist to bill Blue Cross for his or her profile fee of $60 but charge a patient who is paying out of pocket only $40. The profile fee, in this instance, is being discounted but not within the agreement with Blue Cross.

Although therapists are not agents of the insurance company, neither should therapists be agents of the patient against the carrier. A position of neutrality on insurance matters maintains the therapist's integrity (2). Aside from ethical concerns, double-agent roles are certain to be exposed in court, and the credibility of the therapist will be severely undermined should the therapist become entangled with the patient in litigation.

In *Metropolitan Life Insurance Company v. Ditmore* (63), the First Circuit Court of Appeals reinstated an insurance company's lawsuit against a psychiatrist for damages for overpayments allegedly resulting from fraudulent claims. The insurance company charged the psychiatrist with making three types of statements amounting to misrepresentations: listing himself as the "attending physician" when the therapy was actually conducted by nonmedical therapists; indicating services rendered as "psychotherapeutic sessions" without specifying whether the sessions were individual or group; and charging $100 per session regardless of the kind or duration of the sessions. Summary judgment was granted in favor of the psychiatrist by the district court. The psychiatrist admitted to the allegations but pointed out that the state statute permitted delegation of medical services and that insurance claim forms were general and did not call for specific information. However, the court stated that "partial disclosures and half truths are under some circumstances tantamount to misrepresentations of the fact." The court sent the case back for full trial after concluding that a genuine issue of material fact existed as to whether the psychiatrist's statements amounted to misrepresentations.

The *American Psychiatric Association Legal Consultation Plan*

Newsletter, in discussing this case, states, "What is certain is that both the insurance companies and courts are now likely to review a psychiatrist's billing practices with great care" (64).

Patients in treatment may become financially impecunious but continue to need treatment. They may attempt to barter cars, jewels, property, or other valuable items for continued treatment. In one instance, a patient tried to barter a car for another year's treatment. The only medium of exchange when psychiatrists accept payment from patients should be the coin of the realm—literally, money. Patients who desperately feel they need treatment or are under the influence of transference feelings often are unable to render an arms-length assessment of the monetary value of their possessions.

Slovenko (42) discusses the problems of therapists who accept paintings, poetry, sculpture, and other valuable items. The only therapeutic reason for the therapist to receive such property is to view it as part of the patient's personal productions to be analyzed and understood for the purposes of the therapy. When the treatment relationship is concluded, these items should be returned. Similarly, therapists should tactfully refuse large gifts from patients, and, if possible, they should investigate the meaning of the gift for the benefit of the patient's treatment. This is not always easily accomplished, because some patients will feel devastated by having their gifts questioned. Small gifts given by patients at the termination of therapy should be accepted graciously and best left unanalyzed. As suggested earlier, a good rule to follow is that the payment for work with patients is through the fee received and from the professional gratification derived from conducting competent therapy.

Physicians have long struggled with what has appeared to be an inherent conflict of interest between the patient's interest and the pecuniary interest of the physician. Physicians determine treatment intervention while deriving income from serving the patient. What distinguishes professionals from nonprofessionals is that professionals are "first and foremost dedicated to serving the patient's interest" (65). Thus, economic benefits accruing to a physician are not necessarily in conflict with acting in a patient's best interest. To a conscientious, dedicated professional, the patient's interest is intrinsic; money is part of the transaction but extrinsic to a central concern for the patient's welfare.

The Hastings report makes three fundamental recommendations in dealing with the problems of double agentry (66). First, separate functions should be assigned to mental health professionals who manage different roles. Second, following a *Miranda* model, patients need to be informed of the priorities and purposes of mental health professionals in advance, including which sets of obligations, rules, and agendas are being followed. Third, mental health professionals must assume active responsibility to "clean their own houses."

INFORMED CONSENT FOR PSYCHOTHERAPY

Very few therapists warn patients of risks of a proposed method of psychotherapy, although they may extol the potential benefits. Yet it is well known that untoward transference reactions, regressive dependency states, and worsening clinical conditions occur with some regularity in psychotherapy (67). Prolonged nontherapeutic stalemates also are not unusual. Yet, as Halleck (9) notes, the informed consent doctrine has not yet been judicially tested as applied to individual, group, or family therapy.

Reisner (19) gives two reasons why informed consent has been limited to the biomedical field. The first reason relates to the law of damages, where physical harm is required. Thus, in psychotherapy, where no physical damage can be demonstrated, the patient is unlikely to qualify for more than nominal damages when deprived of a right to give informed consent. However, because courts in recent years have demonstrated a marked tendency to compensate for nonphysical injuries, therapists may have an increased risk for liability under the informed consent doctrine.

The second reason informed consent actions have not occurred against psychiatrists and psychologists for psychotherapy is the difficulty of proving that an injury was proximately caused by the psychotherapy. Nevertheless, Reisner predicts that despite these difficulties, the concept of informed consent will be applied increasingly to "nonmedical" treatment situations. Clearly, as the scientific study of the treatment efficacy of psychotherapy moves forward, therapists will be expected to discuss with patients at the outset the qualitative and quantitative outcome data of alternative therapies.

Slovenko (68) points out that under classic tort theory, nonconsensual touching is battery. The administration of drugs or ECT, although therapeutic, is battery when given without the patient's consent. Any unauthorized touching outside of ordinary social interaction constitutes a battery. Punitive and actual damages may be imposed because unauthorized touching is an offense to the dignity of the patient and is an invasion of the right of self-determination. No touching occurs in purely talking therapies; therefore, no cause of action for battery is present (68).

Foster (69) indicates that both the law and medical ethics impose a duty of loyalty to the patient based on the physician as a fiduciary owing the highest duty of care to the patient. One of the pillars of the informed consent doctrine rests on the fiduciary relationships between doctor and patient, requiring that the patient be adequately informed of any proposed treatments or procedures.

With the ascendancy of the "reasonable man" standard of informing patients, therapists are required to provide sufficient information for the reasonable patient to make a knowledgeable decision. Providing insufficient consent may be actionable under negligence law. In contrast with a battery claim, an action brought under negligence will have a longer statute of limitations as well as the availability of malpractice coverage that determines the nature and extent of claims.

The application of strict liability (i.e., where proof of negligence is not required) to the field of psychotherapy is recommended by Furrow (70). He outlines three standards of informing patients: the *professional custom standard* (what other therapists do), the *objective lay standard* (what a reasonable patient would want to know), and the *subjective lay standard* (what a particular patient would want to know). He recommends the last for psychotherapy because professional opinions about risks and benefits are so uncertain and diverse. In principle, most psychotherapists would agree that prospective patients should be permitted adequate time to ask questions about their specific concerns. This may be observed more in the breach than in actual practice, however.

Although therapists often balk at obtaining informed consent for psychotherapy, consent at least has two immediate salubrious effects. First, the psychiatrist is encouraged to think of alternative therapies. Second, unrealistic expectations of the patient concerning treatment may be curbed.

Psychotherapy, no matter what type, can only take place in the presence of a working alliance. The legal requirement that informed consent must be obtained from the patient usually can be turned to clinical account as an alliance builder. Promoting the patient's autonomy is a common goal of both psychiatry and the law.

For the surgical patient, consent is obtained to render the patient unconscious and a "nonparticipant" for a specific surgical procedure. In psychotherapy, informed consent has the effect of awakening the patient to choice, autonomy, and freedom. The success of any psychotherapy is largely the result of the patient's own efforts and active participation in the treatment process.

Providing Information

Slovenko (68) quotes Freud as advising against "lengthy preliminary discussions before the beginning of treatment." Freud felt it important, however, that the patient know of the difficulties and sacrifices of analytic treatment so that the patient would not be deprived "of any right to say later on that he had been inveigled into a treatment whose extent and implication he did not realize." Nevertheless, many psychodynamic therapists still tend to express concern that sharing detailed psychological information or discussing a diagnosis may scuttle the newly launched psychotherapeutic process. This potential distorting or subversive effect of the doctrine of informed consent on the therapeutic process is discussed by Epstein (71) and Robitscher (72).

An initial period of evaluation allows the patient time to assess the therapist, the therapist's technique, and the interactional process between therapist and patient. This time also allows the therapist to make a reasonable diagnostic assessment. The nature of the patient's difficulties should be described in plain language using descriptive terms that underlie psychiatric nosology.

Benefits

Anticipated benefits may be discussed in terms of altering maladaptive defenses and resolution of underlying conflict, symptomatic relief, or crisis intervention, as best suits the patient's situation. Obviously, no promises of cure can be made. For therapists who are prone to promising too much to patients, Freud's comment that the object of psychoanalysis is to substitute for neurotic misery ordinary human unhappiness may temper therapeutic overzealousness. Bibring's (73) classification of psychotherapies according to the singular or combined use of catharsis, suggestion, manipulation, clarification, and insight can be a useful conceptualization for the therapist who is seeking to explain to the patient the methods used in any given psychotherapy. As treatment outcome studies become available, this information also can be shared with patients.

Risks

The risks of psychotherapy are more difficult to state. Where the evaluation reveals past regressive episodes during a personal crisis, it is reasonable to consider with the patient whether such a recurrence might happen in the course of long-term insight psychotherapy. A history of previous serious psychosomatic illnesses, marked dysfunctional periods, or intense transference reactions toward others should alert the therapist to a possible similar recurrence in the psychotherapeutic situation, providing an indication of potential risks to the patient. Although major life changes can occur as the result of long-term, intensive psychotherapy, specific events such as divorce or occupational or financial reverses that may seriously stress other family members often are not foreseeable risks.

Prognosis

Prognostic statements should be made with great caution. In discussing prognosis, Freud used the example of the king who, to determine which of two subjects was bewitched, required each to be boiled. Presumably, the bewitched subject did not boil. Similarly, only after the patient has been "boiled," or treated over a period of time, can the therapist be reasonably certain of the outcome. Another analogy may be useful to the clinician. Long-term, intensive psychotherapy is like a journey taken with a guide over an uncharted territory to reach a distant land. No maps exist, and paths are often uncertain and sometimes treacherous. Travelers occasionally may encounter difficult, hostile inhabitants. Not infrequently, the journey fails or never gets started beyond some initial forays. Those who complete the journey successfully often experience a great sense of achievement, confidence, and a new personal perspective. Prospective travelers need to have the guide explain the anticipated risks and benefits of the proposed journey. Obviously, for some patients, only a shorter journey over familiar terrain can be attempted. Sometimes the wisest course for patients is just to stay at home or at least be helped to appreciate the pleasures of their own backyards.

The expected outcome of a particular mental disorder without treatment is extremely difficult—if not impossible—to determine. Many unforeseen life factors and the inherent course of any given mental disorder influence outcome considerations. Spontaneous remissions are not uncommon. Nevertheless, certain mental conditions such as phobic disorders or the schizophrenias have recurrent or chronic courses.

Which Therapy?

Therapists need to discuss alternative therapeutic modalities with their patients. No longer can the psychiatrist recommend only one form of treatment. More than 450 schools of psychotherapy abound

(2). Although therapists may not be competent in more than a few basic treatment approaches, they should be up-to-date in their knowledge of the standard treatments used by competent, ethical therapists. Therapists at least should be able to explain intelligently the various treatments available to the patient. The phobic patient can be treated by behavior therapy, psychodynamic therapy, medications, or group therapy, or by a combination of therapeutic modalities that best serve the patient's treatment needs. The therapist who primarily uses dynamic, insight psychotherapy should be reasonably knowledgeable about the methods, indications, and contraindications of biological therapy, behavior therapy, cognitive therapy, and crisis intervention, to name just a few alternatives. Patients have a right to know about the various therapies that may be reasonably expected to help their condition. This is not to recommend a "supermarket" approach, in which the patient picks from a vast array of therapies. Therapists should give an opinion concerning the most desirable treatments.

Confidentiality

The therapeutic alliance can be enhanced by initial discussions with the patient about the length of sessions, cost, frequency of visits, vacation schedules, missed-appointment policies, and confidentiality issues. Patients should give their informed consent to any waiver of confidentiality involving third-party payers. Patients need to understand that information about history, diagnosis, treatment, and prognosis may be requested by governmental agencies, insurance companies, or peer review committees. Psychiatrists should know that a number of state laws enacted in the 1970s provide a certain degree of protection for patients' records from legal discovery by peer review. But protection may not exist at all in federal antitrust or civil rights litigation. Malpractice actions or denial of staff privileges, in some instances, may lead to discovery of peer review records.

The patient should be informed that absolute confidential handling of personal data cannot be guaranteed once it leaves the therapist's office. In jurisdictions requiring *Tarasoff* warnings that may breach confidentiality, the question arises whether the patient should receive a *Miranda*-type warning concerning disclosure of dangerous intentions. This issue is discussed in detail elsewhere (74). Suffice it to say here that although informed consent is a means of protecting patients from harmful disclosures, as Roth and Meisel (75) point out, it also can be an important way for therapists to share with patients their dilemma over the duty to protect third parties from threatened harm. Thus, one hopes, a mutually constructive action can be formulated without breaching confidentiality.

Supervision

Another area of concern regarding informed consent involves supervision of therapists. If a therapist will be supervised while treating a patient, consideration should be given to informing the patient. Informed consent problems involving supervised cases and the attendant limitations on confidentiality may arise when patients are not informed of the actual status before beginning treatment (2). Although many therapists feel that informing patients of the supervised status of the therapy or of the confidentiality issues this raises is not necessary, this issue cannot be shrugged off so lightly as in the past. For example, patients may be seeking a graduate psychoanalyst or psychiatrist and may not know, unless informed, that their therapist is in training or is a nonmedical therapist. Sometimes even medical students are passed off as "doctors" or as fully trained therapists. A strong case can be made that patients, as informed consumers, should not be kept ignorant of the training status of the therapist. Furthermore, important ethical and clinical issues are raised: Is the therapist deceiving the patient while expecting honesty from the patient? Is not also the quest of truth one of the highest values shared between therapist and patient engaged in the psychotherapeutic process? What are the possible countertransference issues raised by "keeping a secret" from the patient?

A common apprehension of training personnel is that therapists-in-training will have their authority undermined or perhaps be perceived as needing help—which, of course, they do. The paradox of encouraging patients to seek help while denying a similar need in the therapist-in-training is indeed curious. Although patients do need to have confidence in their therapists, it hardly seems necessary to create the illusion that the therapist is omnipotent to achieve this goal. Such an illusion also precludes the reassuring idea that patients may benefit from the experience and judgment of two therapists.

Another concern expressed by psychoanalysts is that informing patients of the presence of a supervisor will permit an external intrusion into the analysis that may skew the transference and offer a rallying point for intractable resistance (2). Robitscher (72) states that giving patients detailed information will alter but not necessarily harm the therapeutic relationship. In speaking of psychoanalysis, he feels that a less omnipotent relationship between patient and analyst has many advantages. It "would lead to a different kind of psychoanalysis," he admits, "but it would not necessarily be a worse kind of psychoanalysis."

Innovative Therapies

Innovative or experimental therapies require a full explanation of all foreseeable risks (76). Written disclosures should be made and the patient's written consent obtained. Informed consent and experimental therapies are discussed elsewhere (74).

Questions and Answers

Patients should be given an opportunity to ask and receive answers to questions about psychotherapy even when aspects of their questions are overdetermined by emotional factors that are clearly treatment issues. Informed consent is not a solitary event that occurs just at the initiation of treatment. Rather, it is a continuous process throughout the therapy. Issues such as increasing the frequency of visits or altering the goal of therapy require risk-benefit analysis with the patient.

The professional background and credentials of the psychiatrist should be divulged if requested by the patient. Informed consumers of psychotherapy may rely on the information about the therapist's training to come to a reasonable treatment decision. Has the therapist been analyzed? Has the therapist been trained primarily in only one school of psychiatric thought? Is the therapist proficient in using more than one treatment modality, or will he or she recommend the same treatment for anyone who comes through the office door? Of course, an unvarying policy of revealing one's bona fides may not be appropriate for all patients, and a policy of not displaying diplomas or certificates has some theoretical justification for analytical therapists. In general, however, a lack of frankness about a therapists' qualifications can be prejudicial to a patient's decision-making process (2).

CONFIDENTIALITY

Confidentiality refers to the ethical duty of the psychiatrist, arising out of the physician-patient relationship, not to disclose information obtained in the course of evaluating or treating the patient to any other individual or party without the express permission of the patient. The duty of confidentiality is also legally protected from unauthorized disclosure of information. If statutory regulation or public policy is violated, a legal action may result. Moreover, if information is negligently disclosed that directly damages the patient, a lawsuit for professional negligence may be brought.

Ethical and Legal Obligations to Maintain Confidentiality

Since the time of Hippocrates, physicians have had an ethical duty to maintain the confidentiality of their patients. The Hippocratic oath states: "Whatsoever things I shall see or hear concerning the life of men, in my attendance on the sick or even apart therefrom, which ought not to be raised abroad, I will keep silence thereon, counting such things to be as holy secrets." *The Principles of Medical Ethics With Annotations Especially Applicable to Psychiatry* (34) states: "Confidentiality is essential to psychiatric treatment. This is based in part on the special nature of psychiatric therapy as well as on the traditional ethical relationship between physician and patient" (Section 4, Annotation 1).

The American Psychiatric Association in 1978 in its *Position Statement on Confidentiality* (77) set forth some examples where common sense and good judgment, after careful evaluation of the patient and the issues, could lead to a decision to break patient confidentiality. The situations presented were, first, a patient will probably commit murder, and the act can be stopped only by the psychiatrist's intervention; second, a patient will probably commit suicide, and the act can be stopped only by the psychiatrist's intervention; and third, a patient who is charged with serious responsibilities, such as an airline pilot or bus driver, shows marked impairment of judgment.

Aside from statutory disclosure requirements and judicial compulsion, no legal obligation exists to provide information, even to law enforcement officials (78). In a 1985 case, *State v. Miller* (79), the Oregon Supreme Court held that the ethical obligation of a psychotherapist rarely justifies disclosures of a patient's confidence to police and "never justifies" a full disclosure in open court. Jerry Lee Miller, in a telephone conversation with a receptionist at Dammasch State Hospital, said that his problem was "murder." The receptionist promptly called the local sheriffs' department and summoned the hospital's psychiatrist on duty, who spoke with Miller for about 15 minutes. Meanwhile, the police traced the call and arrested Miller. The supreme court disallowed introduction into evidence of the preliminary incriminating statements made by Miller to the receptionist and the psychiatrist.

The psychiatrist has an ethical obligation to maintain confidentiality. Confidentiality is an ethical issue until it is breached. A breach of this ethical obligation may result in a legal action based on implied contract of confidentiality, breach of the duty of confidentiality, invasion of privacy, and violation of the statutory protection of confidentiality.

Obtaining Valid Authorization

A valid, informed authorization for the release of information protects a psychiatrist ethically and legally (80). State law and mental health confidentiality statutes generally specify the requirements for a valid authorization. Statutes also may forbid release of certain information even when the patient consents, as with information supplied to third-party payers.

Consent should be obtained in written form as a permanent record of the fact and the scope of consent. Patients need to be able to make a considered judgment about the impact of their decision. Written forms do possess this advantage. Psychiatrists have been sued for breach of confidentiality when they have relied only on oral authorization to release information—patients can and do forget or deny giving oral permission.

Therapists should avoid blanket consent forms. Rather, consent should be given for a specific release of information. The purpose and any limitation should be specified. The form should have a place to indicate whether a one-time or continuing consent is being given. Patients should also be informed on the form that they have the right to revoke consent at any time, as well as a right to inspect and copy any information authorized for release.

The Principles of Medical Ethics With Annotations Especially Applicable to Psychiatry (34) states: "The continuing duty of the psychiatrist to protect the patient includes fully apprising him/her of the connotations of waiving the privilege of privacy" (Section 4, Annotation 2). Psychiatrists should satisfy themselves that the patient understands the kind of information requested and the type of information in the record. Whenever possible, therapists should allow patients to see all information to be released to others and should permit the patient to be the final decision maker about any release. The information can be provided to the patient in an addressed envelope without a stamp—the intent not being to save the therapist postage but to emphasize to patients their responsibility and consent in releasing such information. A walk to a mailbox has produced a change of heart in some patients in regard to releasing information. If the patient does not wish to know the content of the disclosure, the psychiatrist should assess whether this is a competent request and should record the fact of the patient's wish in the medical record.

The American Psychiatric Association Task Force on Confidentiality (81) states that psychiatrists are most concerned about statutory requirements of disclosure and judicial compulsion. Apart from these requirements, however, there is no other legal requirement to provide information. By far, the most frequent occasions for release of information are by patients themselves when they authorize disclosure by the psychiatrist for insurance, employment benefits, welfare benefits, driver's licenses, or even charge accounts (82). It is surprising, however, that psychiatrists often needlessly reveal the identity of patients in correspondence involving the peer review process, even though peer review is set up to maintain patient anonymity.

The situation is entirely different when an evaluation is being performed for a third party, as in court evaluations, preemployment interviews, or disability evaluations. Unless a treatment relationship has been established between the therapist and the patient, a duty of confidentiality does not arise. That is, no duty exists when, from the very beginning of the examination, the person being examined is told that the examination is at the request of a third party (20). Apart from legal constraints, the individual should be told at the outset that information obtained is not confidential and that the individual will not be given a report by the psychiatrist. The report will be sent directly to the interested third party, whether it may be for security clearances or suitability for a job, or to determine legal competence. Consent is implied when the individual proceeds with the evaluation. *The Principles of Medical Ethics* (34) clearly states the proper procedure: "The psychiatrist must fully describe the nature and purpose and lack of confidentiality of the examination to the examinee at the beginning of the examination" (Section 4, Annotation 6).

The psychiatrist's duty of confidentiality remains even when blanket consent forms are signed. *The Principles of Medical Ethics* (34) states that "ethically, the psychiatrist may disclose only the information which is relevant to a given situation. He/she should avoid offering speculation as fact. Sensitive information such as an individual's sexual orientation or fantasy material is usually unnecessary (Section 4, Annotation 5).

Confidentiality of Minors

The "law of adolescence" is evolving. Until recently, the legal status of all minors from ages 7 to 17 was considered the same. Currently, the rights of 15- to 17-year-olds are not the same as those of a 6-year-old. These changes are reflected in the U.S. Supreme Court holding that state statutes providing for parental permission in abortion decisions of pregnant teenagers are unconstitutional. In addition, all states by statute allow young people to consent independently to treatment for venereal disease. Most states permit young people to secure birth control devices without parent notification. States are beginning to lower the age of medical consent from 18 to 14 or 15 (83).

During the past 30 years, no lawsuits for civil damages or criminal charges have been brought against physicians who have beneficially treated a minor over 15 for any condition on the consent of the minor. Because of alarming rises in rates of venereal disease, alcohol and drug abuse, and teenage pregnancy, states have passed "enabling laws" that allow minors access to medical care without parental approval.

A general rule is that confidentiality accompanies the legal ability to consent to treatment. Mental health confidentiality statutes usually provide a definition of who is a "young minor." The American Psychiatric Association suggests that therapists may consider it prudent and safe to rely on parental consent for children under age 12 (84). With young minors, the parents or guardians are the legal decision makers. Thus, parents have a right to know about the course of treatment as well as the diagnosis and prognosis. Obviously, revealing confidential information must be done cautiously so that damage is not done to the treatment or to the child's relationships with caretakers. States require the reporting of child abuse, some even of *suspicion* of child abuse. The psychiatrist is fully protected by the reporting statute from suit for breach of confidentiality in these cases. Moreover, every statute has criminal penalties for not reporting.

For therapists to release medical records or testify about treatment of young minors, the consent of one parent is generally sufficient. But if divorce or custody litigation is taking place, parents may disagree about waiver of confidentiality. The therapist should wait before releasing confidential information until the court has ruled on the validity of the waiver or, in the absence of a court ruling, should consult state law requirements (1). In some jurisdictions, the state may require an attorney to represent the interest of the child regarding waiver of confidentiality. If a minor is too young to personally exercise the privilege, courts may appoint a guardian to act in the best interests of the child. Under such circumstances, the parents may not agree or may refuse to waive the privilege on the child's behalf (85).

Just as some minors are able to consent to treatment independently and legally, they are able to control disclosure of medical information. Usually from ages 14 to 15, young people may be considered "emancipated minors" when they do not customarily live at home or when they are self-supporting. Or they may be considered "mature minors" when they are judged by physicians to possess sufficient maturity to understand and consent. Consent of a parent is never required in a genuine emergency. For the protection of the community, minors, emancipated or not, can be treated in all states for venereal disease without consent or knowledge of parents.

Relying on parental consent alone for young people in transitional states of maturity is clearly insufficient. When disclosures are made to interested third parties, consent of both the patient and parents may be advisable. For each of the four categories of legally cognizant youth—those not dwelling at home, those who are self-supporting, those who are decreed "mature," and those who may be unemancipated but in need of emergency or special treatment—the risk of treatment is an important consideration in intervention provided without parental consent and knowledge. In psychiatry, the use of psychoactive drugs, for example, increases the risk of treatment, not only because of adverse drug side effects but also because the psychoactivity of the drugs may affect important activities such as educational or athletic performance or newly learned driving skills. Thus the risk of the treatment and the maturity of the minor are crucial questions for a therapist to weigh in proceeding with or without parental consent.

Whether the minor patient has consent rights or not, therapists should make every effort to preserve confidentiality for the sake of the treatment. Still, the conflicting interests of the minor's independent right to confidentiality with the parents' need to have information for making reasonable treatment and confidentiality decisions are always present. *The Principles of Medical Ethics* (34) are sensitive to these conflicting interests: "Careful judgment must be exercised by the psychiatrist in order to include, when appropriate, the parents or guardian in the treatment of a minor. At the same time the psychiatrist must assure the minor proper confidentiality" (Section 4, Annotation 7).

In psychiatric practice, the parents of minors undergoing treatment often will need to be involved at some level. The problems of minors often are inextricably interwoven with those of their parents. Ground rules for confidentiality must be set from the beginning of treatment. For the most part, therapists may choose to avoid disclosure as much as possible, perhaps encouraging the child and parents to improve communications with each other. The parents must live with the child from day to day, and it is often the parents who feel the psychic pain of their child's emotional disturbance. Their intimate knowledge of the child and of the family's emotional dynamics is a source of essential information to the therapist.

Economic reality rather than legal theory may determine the right to confidential information. Therapists or hospitals often will be unwilling to treat a minor patient without the signature of a financially responsible person. When a parent receives an itemized bill or statement from a therapist or an insurance provider, privacy is no longer an issue. When parents do not consent to nonemergency treatment of a minor, they are not responsible for payment of care. Some state statutes, as in California, spell this out clearly (83).

Confidentiality After a Patient's Death

Unless there is a specific court decision or statute providing for the release of patient records after death, the legal duty to maintain confidentiality that existed in life follows the patient in death. If legal duty is sometimes ambiguous, an ethical duty to preserve confidentiality certainly persists after death. The American Psychiatric Association's *Opinions of the Ethics Committee on the Principles of Medical Ethics With Annotations Especially Applicable to Psychiatry* (86) presents the following question and answer asked by a psychiatrist on this very point:

> *Question:* Can I give confidential information about a recently deceased mother to her grieving daughter?
>
> *Answer:* No. Ethically, her confidences survive her death. Legally this is an unclear issue varying from one jurisdiction to another. Further, there is a risk of the information being used to seek an advantage in the contesting of a will or in competition with other surviving family members.

Many patients feel they have horrible secrets that must be hidden at all costs. If the confidentiality of their therapy ceased to exist after their death, many patients would be deterred from treatment. This is particularly true if death seems imminent, as for the patient considering suicide or for patients with terminal illnesses.

Often therapists are asked for information after a patient's death, and, for a variety of reasons, therapists sometimes disclose such confidential information in the face of ethical and legal strictures. Circumstances that commonly raise such temptations are criminal investigations, will contests, and meetings with families seeking information about the patient as part of their grieving. When a patient commits suicide, for example, family members may request a meeting with the treating psychiatrist. It is a stressful time for the family and for the psychiatrist. The family almost invariably feels guilty, angry, and blaming. The therapist often feels defeated, guilty, and defensive. In such circumstances, psychiatrists may reveal too much information in an effort to exculpate themselves. Therapists must avoid inflicting additional painful details of a patient's life that are not relevant to the family's inquiry. The therapist's task is to console the family and to assist in their grief work. Psychiatrists should not refuse to see a family unless the family has instituted litigation against them.

If a psychiatrist feels compelled to reveal confidential information after a patient's death, the therapist can minimize legal risks by providing just enough information for the task at hand. Details of the patient's therapy are rarely, if ever, required. Relevancy is the guiding rule. Second, revealing information about third parties learned from the patient may be legally dangerous. Slovenko (53) points out that the dead or their survivors cannot sue for defamation or the invasion of privacy, because these are personal rights that die with an individual. Even if a person is defamed while alive, under common law the cause of action dies with the person. A cause of action may exist, however, when words contained in a medical record independently reflect on and defame those living. Slovenko states: "One who divulges an allegation by another may find himself liable although he did not indicate his own belief in the truth of the statement." Thus, unless privilege exists to make disclosures, mental health professionals are responsible for statements made, even though the views are purported to be those of the patient.

The Clinical Record

Keeping a record during the course of the patient's treatment serves a number of important clinical purposes. Review of the record between sessions as well as the exercise of summarizing treatment sessions permits a better understanding of the patient and the treatment process. If a patient interrupts or terminates treatment but later decides to return, the therapist will find records helpful in refreshing his or her own memory. Accurate record keeping will also help in disputes over billing. Moreover, pressure for record keeping is increasing because of the need to maintain quality assurance, for accreditation, for financial reimbursement, and for legal purposes (87).

Technically, the law considers things not recorded as things not done. The record should document major management and treatment decisions. Medication records should accurately reflect the amount of medication prescribed, instructions given the patient about taking the medication, and warnings issued to the patient about risks. The record also should contain the risk-benefit assessments surrounding important treatment interventions. Informed consent obtained from the patient and any waivers of confidentiality should be noted. Noncompliance with psychiatric treatment, including failure to take psychoactive drugs, is important to note. Significant telephone conversations with patients should be made part of the medical record. The treatment record that accurately portrays the reasoning behind treatment intervention or nonintervention, particularly when careful risk-benefit analyses are conducted, may be the psychiatrist's best friend should litigation arise. Errors in psychiatric diagnosis and treatment are not actionable as such. Good records can go a long way in showing that although a psychiatrist may have erred, he or she used reasonable skill and diligence in arriving at treatment decisions.

Gutheil and Appelbaum (88) distinguish between *process notes* and *progress notes.* The former contain "anything that comes to mind and are not for therapeutic or investigative use." The latter contain "operational, descriptive information for treatment and administrative purposes." Usually, no useful purpose is served by noting the patient's fantasies, derogatory opinions of others, or any other information not directly relevant to documenting treatment decisions. Where a record of intimate details is necessary for supervision of student psychotherapists or analysts, these records should not be kept after their educational function has been served. Therapists should consider developing a consistent policy for destroying process records. Medical records can be disposed of by burning or shredding. Confidentiality must be maintained during this process. The destruction can be certified and the certificate kept permanently. A certificate of destruction is not a legal requirement, however.

State law actually may forbid destruction of records where the intent is to prevent disclosure at a judicial proceeding. But if the psychiatrist discloses at judicial hearings that he or she routinely and consistently destroys records, such testimony will tend to negate questions about credibility. Writing self-serving statements into a record in the hope of exonerating oneself should a lawsuit arise is foolhardy and useless. Both the record and the psychiatrist will be subjected to searching cross-examination, and any discrepancy between testimony developed in court and self-serving information recorded in a psychiatric record may deal a severe blow to a psychiatrist's credibility.

Psychiatrists must also realize that the psychiatric record can become an iatrogenic factor in exacerbating a patient's condition, particularly if it contains damaging or frightening information. Many states allow patients access to their records. But who owns the medical records? The actual record maintained by the psychiatrist is the physical property of the psychiatrist. But information contained in that record belongs to the patient, and therapists should be prepared to provide a copy of the record to their patients. Therapists should never relinquish an original record to a patient.

The rules governing patients' access to their own records are complicated and vary considerably in each jurisdiction. The rules also vary according to the type of record. When a lawsuit is filed against a psychiatrist, every state permits the patient to subpoena the records. Again, the therapist should provide only a copy of the record.

A number of states have enacted patient access statutes permitting patients to have access to medical records in the absence of litigation, after paying administrative costs. Some jurisdictions draw a distinction between mental health records and other medical records. Access to records may also depend on who is making the request (i.e., patient, next of kin, or legal representative) and the reason for the request. At least 18 jurisdictions permit direct access by the patient's attorney, physician, or near relative but not by the patient. Many states provide an exception for the release of mental health treatment records on the grounds that the psychological welfare of the patient might be impaired by knowledge of the contents of the record.

A few states have passed statutes expressly prohibiting the release of mental health records to anyone except under court order (89). Under the Federal Privacy Act of 1974, all patients receiving medical care under the federally administered Medicare program, all patients in Veterans Administration hospitals, and recipients of Social Security or supplemental security income benefits have access to their records (90). In some states, the statute protects institutional records independently of the therapist's obligation to maintain confidentiality. This is frequently the case in state hospitals for the mentally ill and retarded. However, some states treat state hospital records as nonprivileged public documents or privileged under government privilege statutes that are subject to waiver by the government without the patient's consent (19).

The therapist should be present to answer questions whenever patients wish to inspect their records. Patients can become very distressed over what they discover or misinterpret in their records, and they may need the assistance of the therapist. The therapist also should be present to prevent any alteration of an original record.

Therapists sometimes keep two separate sets of records: one set for diagnosis, prognosis, and treatment decisions; the other for speculations of the therapist and the fantasies and intimate details of the patient's life. Although the American Psychiatric Association's *Model Law on Confidentiality of Health and Social Service Records* (91) recognizes this distinction, only two jurisdictions permit dual records (92,93). The Illinois statute segregates personal notes, which are defined as follows: information disclosed to the therapist in confidence by other persons on condition that such information would never be disclosed to the recipient or other persons; information disclosed to the therapist by the recipient that would be injurious to the recipient's relationships to other persons; and the therapist's speculations, impressions, hunches, and reminders. No court has allowed such a distinction, and the work-product privilege that protests attorneys' records has not been applied to medical practice. Slovenko (42) warns against keeping two sets of records. Because concealing records is a violation of the law, Slovenko advises the psychiatrist not to keep dual records but instead to exercise "extreme caution" when writing in a patient's record.

Laws and administrative codes in a number of states require psychiatrists to keep a record for each patient. Records should be kept until the relevant statute of limitations has lapsed (1). Each state has its own statutory period, usually 2 or 3 years from the time of the last treatment or from the time of discovery of the injury caused by the treatment. But note that the statute of limitations for breach of contract is usually 6 years, and state statutes may be *tolled* (stopped from running) while the patient is a minor or is incompetent. Thus, even therapists who retire should keep their records at least until the statute of limitations runs out. For minors or incompetent patients, it may be prudent to hold records for a considerably longer period. After a patient's death, a clinical record should be kept for at least 10 years.

Medical records may be kept in written form, on microfilm, on audiotape, or on a computer disk. Although no specific recognition of computerized records exists, there is no specific prohibition of their use. Confidentiality and access to these records must be carefully protected. In addition, therapists may need to modify computerized systems to meet state statutes. For example, most statutes require the record to be signed. Some states require that the record be written in ink. A therapist will not usually be held liable for entrusting confidential reports to a secretary for typing (42). However, by extension, the secretary is under the same obligation of confidentiality as the therapist.

The practice of keeping no records of patient care places the psychiatrist in an extremely disadvantageous position should a legal action arise. Properly kept medical records can be the psychiatrist's best ally in malpractice litigation. The absence of records may raise questions about the psychiatrist's competence and credibility in general. Moreover, failure to keep a medical record may violate state statutes or licensing provisions. Of course, failing to keep medical records may arise not from incompetence or perversity but from a psychiatrist's concern to protect the patient's treatment information. Total confidentiality is an admirable ideal, but in real life the psychiatrist may be subpoenaed and compelled under certain circumstances to testify directly about confidential treatment matters. It is better to have a contemporary and adequate record to support such testimony.

Confidentiality and the Patient's Bills

No ethical principles forbid therapists from using collection agencies or the courts to collect bills. The physician-patient privilege is not held as a bar from suing to collect rightful fees. Ethical and legal obligations to protect the patient's confidentiality continue, however, even though the patient breaches the treatment contract by not paying the bill. Of course, patients may not want to reveal their status as patients, and they may sue for breach of confidentiality when disclosure of such information is made to a collection agency or in a court proceeding. Suits brought solely on such grounds are untenable, however, because privilege does not apply in litigation between doctor and patient. This is true whether the litigation involves bill collection or malpractice.

Although therapists have some legal protection in using third parties for recovering fees, they first should try to use means other than collection agencies or the courts. Then, if the patient is unresponsive, the therapist may decide to bring suit or employ a collection agency. Before therapists use such means, they should inform the patient of the action they intend to take if the bill is not paid within a specified period of time. Moreover, therapists who use a collection agency or who sue are ethically and legally obligated to reveal *only* essential information that is specific for the purpose of fee collection. "Essential information" means the patient's name and the amount owed. Itemized bills should be general, indicating "office visits" rather than the type of therapy.

Some states have enacted laws that outline specific steps that must be followed when a therapist refers an account to a collection agency. These laws include the information that may be revealed. The District of Columbia Mental Health Information Act (94) requires that a psychiatrist not turn over a patient's account to a collection agency or lawyer until the patient receives "written notification that the fee is due and has failed to arrange for payment . . . within a reasonable time after such notification." If recourse to a collection agency or lawyer is taken, the act states that disclosure should include only "administrative information," defined as the patient's name, age, sex, address, identifying number, dates and character of the sessions (individual or group), and fee (94).

The therapist should select a reputable collection agency that does not harass patients or use abusive tactics. Therapists themselves may not harass patients with threats of criminal prosecution or with threats of disclosure of false information to ruin a credit reputation. Therapists may not pursue bills by contacting the debtor's employer before they have obtained a judgment, and they may not make unjustified disclosure of information about the debt, use abusive language, or engage in other harassing tactics (1). Although clearly against the law in various jurisdictions, such tactics may also lead to a lawsuit based on the intentional infliction of emotional distress, or they may be the basis of an ethics complaint. therapists also must not withhold services they are legally and ethically required to provide to put pressure on patients for payment. Even though the American Medical Association sanctions the charging of interest on overdue accounts if patients are properly informed of such charges, in the psychotherapeutic context this practice appears to be an unseemly commercialization of the doctor-patient relationship. In fact, whether interest is paid or not, overdue accounts place the therapist in the position of a moneylender, with all the attendant transference and countertransference problems occasioned by patients who continue to come for treatment without paying.

The Impecunious Patient

The ethical issues involved in continuing to treat a nonpaying patient are complex, particularly in the mental health field. In general, therapists have no legal duty to treat patients who do not pay. However, therapists must be careful not to abandon their patients (2). The American Medical Association Judicial Council places a physician's duty to provide care above monetary considerations but defends the doctor's right to choose patients and the terms of treatment (95). When treating a nonpaying patient over a long period, a therapist is at high risk for negative countertransference. Private therapists usually do not have a large volume of patients and rely on the treatment of relatively few patients for their income. Thus, treating a nonpaying patient may represent a significant loss of income to the therapist and the situation may produce resentment both in the therapist and the patient, disrupting the therapy (96).

Because therapists in private practice may freely choose their patients, the countertransference and transference issues that inevitably will arise with the nonpaying patient must be considered openly. Therapists who see patients infrequently or only for medication management may be able to handle the nonpayment issue more easily. The patient who runs out of money during the course of therapy, however, presents more difficult problems. Terminating the therapy may be very destructive to the unique relationship that develops between the therapist and the patient. In fact, because the entire therapeutic modality may be founded on the unique rapport that exists between therapist and patient, it might not be readily possible to find a workable substitute for the therapist.

The therapist may treat the patient for a token fee until the patient's financial situation improves, at which time a new fee can be negotiated. This option is particularly pertinent to psychiatrists practicing in rural areas who may have no place to refer nonpaying patients who require continued treatment. Obviously, free therapy may arouse insurmountable negative transference and countertransference reactions. Still, Freud (96) found exceptions in which free treatment was very successful and in fact advocated free treatment for the poor (97).

Asking the patient to pay the money owed at a later date places the therapist in the position of the patient's creditor. This may interfere with the therapist's efforts to maintain a position of neutrality. Similarly, entering into a barter arrangement with a nonpaying patient should be avoided. The therapist-patient relationship does not place both parties on an equal footing, and the patient may not be in the position to evaluate properly the value of what is exchanged. Where others assume financial responsibility for the patient, the therapist may wish to formalize the arrangement with a written agreement.

Some psychiatric patients have the means to pay but do not do so for various important psychological reasons. Thus, a depressed patient may feel unreasonably impoverished, a narcissistic patient may feel entitled to free treatment, and a hostile and controlling patient may want to withhold money from the therapist. Money issues are always an integral part of therapy. The only "real thing" that the patient must give the therapist is money. Whenever possible, the treatment issues surrounding nonpayment should be thoroughly explored with the patient before collection efforts are initiated.

Billing and Bad Results

Therapists must weigh the risks and benefits of attempting to collect a fee from a patient who has suffered a bad result and is unhappy. The circumstances of the particular case are determinative in charting the appropriate response by the therapist. The patient's pain and suffering, complications, additional therapy required, the extent of dissatisfaction and unhappiness, and the risk of potential damages if one loses a suit must be considered. One must also consider the expenditure of time and effort as well as the loss of income that results from defending a suit. Such considerations may lead a therapist simply to close the account and absorb the loss. Moreover, therapists should be aware that in some jurisdictions, suing for nonpayment of a bill may extend or revive the statute of limitations on malpractice.

Alton (98) suggests that if they feel they must pursue payment, therapists should wait until the statute of limitations for filing a malpractice claim expires. Usually statutes of limitations on malpractice are many years less than statutes for breach of contract. Alton also suggests that whether or not therapists pursue payment to the legal limits, they must send bills for services rendered. Patients may feign dissatisfaction with services as an excuse for nonpayment. Moreover, even if a threat of a patient suit exists or it is not likely that the patient will pay, the therapist must send bills. Generally the receipt of bills will not trigger lawsuits by patients. Alton states that in most instances, nonpayment will satisfy the patient's desire to punish the therapist. In addition, if legal action does ensue, failure to send a bill may be considered an admission of fault. Alton feels that therapists might as well proceed on the assumption that if patients sue after receiving a bill, they probably were planning a suit anyway. By similar logic, the therapist should make the bill for a reasonable amount rather than an unusually low amount. Patients should not be told that no bill will be submitted or that the bill will be reduced because of complications or poor results. Be aware that failure to follow up on a bill that was sent will not necessarily be considered an admission of fault. As long as normal billing procedures are carried out, no negative inferences can be drawn.

The relentless pursuit of an unpaid bill reflects an unfortunate attitude that places greater importance on money than on patient care. Of course, the two fundamental gratifications afforded therapists in the treatment of patients are a genuine, personal enjoyment of the treatment process itself and reasonable remuneration for services rendered. But emphasis on the latter, without the former, perverts the therapist's professional duty of devotion to the best interests of the patient.

ABANDONMENT

A therapist in private practice generally has no duty to accept any patient. Once the therapist agrees to treat the patient, however, a therapist-patient relationship is formed with the duty to provide treatment as long as is necessary. Where the therapist-patient relationship is unilaterally and prematurely terminated by the therapist without reasonable notice, the therapist may be liable for abandonment if his or her services are still needed by the patient (4). The patient must prove that the cause of the injury was the abandonment. Once abandonment is proven, the burden of proving causation may be less rigorous than in other malpractice cases.

Abandonment may be either quite obvious or implied by a failure to attend, monitor, or observe the patient. Intentional abandonment has become confused with the negligent failure to follow the patient diligently (4).

If the therapist uses poor judgment in terminating therapy or does not diligently attend the patient, the therapist may be liable for negligence. On the other hand, if the therapist consciously terminates with the patient knowing that the latter needs continuing care, the therapist may be liable for intentional abandonment. In negligence cases, expert testimony will be required about the standard of care. When the abandonment is egregious, no expert may be necessary. Many courts have widened the concept of abandonment where delay and inattention in providing care caused injury, terming it *constructive* (as if) *abandonment* (99).

Often, the therapist's legal and ethical duties in terminating therapy with the patient depend on the circumstances (1). In *Brandt v. Grubin* (100), the court noted that where a physician is employed for a specific occasion or service, no liability for abandonment exists if treatment ceases after the performance of the specific purpose. Thus, if a patient attends a phobia clinic for the sole purpose of being treated for specific phobias over a specified number of sessions, abandonment should not exist when treatment ceases after the prescribed time. However, this may not apply where the patient has reason to believe the physician has assumed a continuing treatment role as a "personal physician" and will be available to the patient as needed.

When no emergency or crisis exists, a therapist may terminate the therapy if the therapist gives reasonable notice, if the therapist offers the patient assistance in finding another therapist, and if the therapist makes the patient's records available to the new therapist on request. In addition to notifying the patient verbally, the therapist also should give the patient written notice. Proper notice really is essential for the patient to find a substitute therapist. If the patient is in an emergency situation, however, the therapist should see the patient through the period of stress. Certainly, this is an extremely difficult task with patients who seem to be in perpetual crisis. Yet therapists who terminate therapy with patients who have suicidal tendencies and who are under great stress may only exacerbate the situation by fleeing in fear of a suit if the patient commits suicide. The additional stress of terminating therapy could cause the patient to suffer further regression or even to commit suicide. Courts are less likely to find that a therapist adequately discharged his or her responsibility when the therapist ceases to attend the patient during a crisis or emergency. Therapists should defer terminating therapy with patients who are in crisis unless an appropriate referral can be made.

Therapists must realize that certain actions by the patient do not automatically terminate the therapist-patient relationship. Mere nonpayment of a bill, failure to be compliant, unilateral consultation with another mental health professional, or failure to keep an appointment are not causes for termination when the patient continues to need treatment (101). Furthermore, these issues should be taken up initially as treatment matters. Suppose the patient stops coming to regularly scheduled appointments. Does the therapist have a duty to contact the patient? The answer to this question depends on the extent to which the patient's absence is a direct function of mental illness. The more severe the illness, the more the therapist should assume the responsibility for contacting the patient. The specific steps required in terminating therapy with patients are discussed elsewhere (102).

Abandonment in Psychotherapy

The patient has the right to leave treatment at any time and without notice. In some instances, the patient may terminate therapy by simply not showing up for appointments. But a patient who is mentally ill and a danger to self or others may make an incompetent termination of therapy. In such cases, the therapist's duty to care for the patient continues and requires that the therapist intervene. Although not absolutely required to do so, therapists should send a letter to competent patients to confirm that the patient has willingly terminated the therapy and to ensure that no misunderstanding exists about the termination.

Therapists who mismanage countertransference feelings may unwittingly abandon a patient when such feelings explode into the therapeutic situation. Angry outbursts or corrosive ill will can destroy years of therapeutic work. In *Hess v. Frank* (103), the court dismissed a suit for negligence brought against the psychiatrist who, during a regularly scheduled session, allegedly used abusive language toward the patient in an argument that developed over fees and the appointment schedule. The psychiatrist had been treating the patient for more than 8 years. The case was dismissed because the court inexplicably viewed the argument as being outside of the treatment relationship. Although in this case the patient did not allege abandonment, a vitriolic argument between a therapist and a patient may destroy the treatment relationship, leaving the patient devastated and essentially bereft of the therapist's help. Under such circumstances, a patient could be considered "abandoned."

Borderline patients who careen from crisis to crisis may sorely tax a therapist's energy and patience, leading to a countertransference-based, abrupt, and ill-advised termination that can bring allegations of abandonment. Malignant narcissistic personalities and certain severe borderline patients may continually act out destructively to manipulate the therapist. Because therapists cannot practice with a psychological gun to their heads, they may need to terminate therapy with such patients appropriately.

All therapists' difficulties with patients are not necessarily countertransference. Some patients are genuinely difficult and demanding in their own right, often presenting unique problems that some therapists can handle better than others. Therapists must realize their limitations and abandon grandiose notions that they can treat anyone. But therapists may not terminate therapy with patients for capricious reasons and must give them time to work through the termination (9).

During the month of August, an exodus occurs among psychiatrists. Patients may find that when they call a designated covering psychiatrist, they are referred through a series of psychiatrists who have signed out to each other. On one such occasion, a psychoanalytic candidate was asked by a recently graduated psychoanalyst to cover his practice during the month of August. The candidate discovered later that the other analysts, including his own, had signed out to the recent graduate. Thus, to his not unpleasant amazement, the candidate found himself covering for his analyst, his fellow analysands, and himself. It is important that disturbed patients not be subjected to such runarounds. Feelings of discouragement and rejection may inhibit patients' efforts to obtain help and could lead to an allegation of abandonment (4).

When obtaining coverage, therapists should seek out other therapists of similar experience and training. Clinical information about patients who may call should be provided to the covering therapist. Selection of a covering therapist should be done carefully. If difficulties arise between the patient and the covering therapist, the patient may allege that the therapist was negligent by engaging an unqualified practitioner. If it can be shown, however, that the covering therapist was fully qualified and the patient was fully informed of the therapist's period of absence, imposition of liability is unlikely.

A therapist who uses a substitute is not liable for the substitute's negligence unless the substitute therapist was acting as an agent in the performance of treatment or the original therapist did not exercise due care in selecting the substitute therapist (104). If a fixed stipend is paid to the covering therapist from fees collected, an agent (employee) relationship is established. If the patient is billed, and the proceeds are shared with the covering therapist after expenses, then a partnership is created. To avoid the possible legal entanglements of such relationships, the covering therapist should bill independently for services rendered.

Another form of abandonment may occur when therapists do not list a home telephone number in the directory or with directory assistance. Instead, an answering machine collects overnight calls for the next day. Even for the psychiatrist with a quiet practice, this procedure is replete with untoward clinical and legal consequences, because emergencies can arise at any time, with any patient. It is a clinical fact that hiding from patients measurably increases their anxiety and causes some patients to go to extraordinary lengths to find the therapist. Ready availability, in contrast, appears to diminish patients' anxiety, resulting in fewer telephone calls to the therapist and possibly lessening claims of abandonment, if an emergency does arise.

A creeping form of abandonment occurs through two great enemies of the practicing psychotherapist—boredom and fatigue. Inattention, ennui, and impatience, followed by cutting back of patients' visits and dissatisfaction with psychotherapeutic practice, are all symptoms of therapist boredom and fatigue. When a crisis arises in a patient's life, the bored and tired therapist may consciously or unconsciously downplay its significance, providing either negligent treatment or abandoning the patient outright.

Failure to instruct the patient concerning side effects of medication, failure to stay abreast of the patient's condition, failure to admit the patient to a hospital when warranted, failure to follow the patient during hospitalization, premature discharge of the patient from the hospital, and improper referral of the patient may all constitute abandonment of the patient (101). When it is clinically appropriate, therapists who are unable to treat their own patients who are hospitalized should stay in contact with their patients through the admitting psychiatrist or by shifting temporarily into a consultative role.

Finally, patients may be improperly abandoned when their insurance benefits run out. Psychiatric hospitals and other health care providers including health maintenance organizations, preferred provider organizations, and other prepaid plans providing psychiatric care must be careful not to terminate patients summarily based strictly on financial considerations rather than on the treatment needs of the patient. Mental health professionals working for such groups must be careful to resist erosion of their professional duty to patients by financial and administrative pressures.

In *Wickline v. State* (105), a patient sued Medi-Cal (State of California Medical Assistance Program) following amputation of a leg allegedly resulting from premature discharge from the hospital. The court of appeals held, among other things, that the physician who complies, without protest, with limitations imposed by a third-party payer cannot avoid ultimate responsibility for patient care. In this case, the physician, not Medi-Cal, was held liable for the discharge decision. The lesson from this case is clear: When confronted by "orders" from third-party payers that are inimical to good patient care, physicians must not abrogate their duty of care to the patient.

Defenses Against Claims of Abandonment

Particular circumstances dictate which legal defenses may be asserted against a claim of abandonment. If a competent patient unilaterally severs the relationship, the therapist's duty is terminated. This occurs most commonly when the patient fails to return. Proper notice to find a substitute is another defense against the claim of abandonment.

If a suitable substitute is provided, a therapist's intervening illness will not ordinarily be considered an abandonment of the patient. Section 6-C of the American Psychiatric Association's *Opinions of the Ethics Committee on the Principles of Medical Ethics With Annotations Especially Applicable to Psychiatry* (86) considers this issue:

> *Question:* Because of ill-health, it has become necessary for me to retire. I have sent a written announcement to that effect to all my patients 90 days in advance. Full-fee patients have been accepted by other psychiatrists but I am having great difficulty placing my Medicaid patients. The local public clinics have long waiting lists. Will I be abandoning my patients?
>
> *Answer:* No. Ninety days written announcement is quite adequate. It is unfortunate you are having such difficulty placing your Medicaid patients but you have done all you can be expected to do. Your colleagues might wish to consider their roles as ethical practitioners in assisting you and your patients in your time of need (April 22, 1978). See Opinion 8.10 of *Current Opinions of the Judicial Council of the AMA,* 1981: "Once having undertaken a case, the physician should not neglect the patient, nor withdraw from the case without giving notice to the patient, relatives, or responsible friends sufficiently long in advance of withdrawal to permit another medical attendant to be secured."

Under circumstances of a therapist's acute illness, the therapist may need to refer patients to emergency facilities if colleagues cannot provide coverage. Note, however, that patients have sued for abandonment when the substitute is many miles away or when access to the therapist is difficult or unduly burdensome (106).

A malpractice action by the patient against the therapist may allow the therapist to serve notice of termination (101). Although this course of action by the therapist is not absolutely protected, and legal opinion should be sought on specific cases, termination of the therapy appears appropriate to protect the interests of the therapist. Clinically, it seems inconceivable that a therapist should continue to treat a patient who is suing him or her, both because of the adversarial legal circumstances and because the negative transference and countertransference problems would almost certainly break the therapeutic alliance.

In *Hammonds v. Aetna Insurance Company* (50), the insurance company, fearing a lawsuit, induced the psychiatrist to abandon his patient. The court held that a physician, when threatened by a suit for malpractice, can terminate the physician-patient relationship, but only after "the claimant knows or suspects that he is the victim of medical malpractice and has expressed an intent to pursue his legal rights." The psychiatrist and insurance company complained that this stringent requirement would allow the "plaintiff an unfair advantage to fully prepare his case while the doctor is proscribed against the first defensive measure." The court disagreed, believing that the plaintiff rarely enjoys an advantage in any lawsuit.

PRESCRIBING DRUGS

A leading cause of malpractice suits against psychiatrists involves injuries to patients from prescribed medications. Tardive dyskinesia, in particular, has resulted in six- and seven-figure judgments against psychiatrists (107). Some dynamically trained psychotherapists have eschewed acquiring knowledge or skill in administering drug therapy. They, as well as nonmedical therapists, frequently ask a medical colleague to prescribe medications for their patients. This practice introduces an artificial split into the intimate connection between psychopharmacotherapy and psychotherapy. To be effective, the therapeutic process should not be fragmented. Ostow (108) also disagrees with fragmented treatment practices because the data obtained from psychotherapy are necessary for proper administration of drug therapy. In addition, to understand the patient, drug effects must be distinguished from psychopathological processes.

Slovenko (30) points out that in fragmented treatment the transference may be split and that division of treatment is doubly expensive. Psychiatrists have an ethical duty to keep abreast of scientific developments in their specialty. Particularly in the burgeoning area of psychopharmacology, psychiatrists who prescribe medications need to keep apace of new developments. Psychiatrists can no longer afford to be therapeutically one-dimensional, knowledgeable in only one method of treatment. Obviously, however, psychiatrists who are unfamiliar with a specific treatment modality should avoid its use.

Lesse (109), speaking about the treatment of depression, states that "those who treat severe depressions should have the broadest possible knowledge of the limitations of various psychotherapeutic techniques. Similarly, they should have an intimate knowledge of the benefits and limitations of the antidepressant drugs." In *Osheroff v. Chestnut Lodge et al.* (37), the plaintiff alleged that his major depression was inappropriately treated by intensive psychotherapy, unnecessarily prolonging his hospitalization and suffering. After transfer to another hospital and the initiation of antidepressant medication, the plaintiff improved rapidly. The case was eventually settled. This case is discussed extensively in the literature (38). Somatic therapies and the law are discussed in detail in Volume 1 of the *American Psychiatric Press Review of Clinical Psychiatry and the Law* (110).

The Borderline Patient

Patients with borderline personality disorder have a spectrum of clinical features that are not only difficult to manage therapeutically but also are laden with potential liability consequences for the therapist. In addition, countertransference problems arise frequently in therapists who treat borderline patients.

The classic features of borderline personality disorder are good-bad splitting devaluation, intense rage, narcissistic entitlement, rapidly developing psychotic transferences, impulsivity, and projective identification (111). Not infrequently, borderline patients make a good initial clinical impression, particularly if they possess high intelligence or other attractive qualities and personal accomplishments. Therefore, the therapist should allow for a period of evaluation that will permit an accurate diagnosis, differential diagnosis, and treatment plan. Patients who have manifestations of severe psychopathology or regression in the past may likely develop these difficulties again in the course of therapy. With accurate diagnosis, a reasonably predictable clinical course can be expected.

Gutheil (51) points out that the various clinical aspects of this disorder pose special problems for therapists, particularly in creating vulnerabilities to legal action. Intense feelings engendered by borderline patients may interfere with sound clinical judgment. Patients who demand special entitlements may create angry, withholding reactions in their therapists, leading to destructive power struggles that may be acted out between patient and therapist (51). It is critically important to maintain, as much as possible, a position of therapeutic neutrality with the borderline patient. In psychoanalytic terms, the therapist as participant observer is poised equidistant between reality and the patient's ego, superego, and id. Borderline patients frequently attempt to dislodge the therapist from his or her treatment role in an attempt to live out or "actualize" their conflicts. Without reacting directly to the provocative patient, therapists should ask themselves, "What does it mean that the patient puts me in this position?"

Therapists also may become frightened by the rapid regression of a borderline patient. Psychotic transferences can develop very rapidly, leading to overreactions by the therapist. Breaches of confidentiality, ill-advised intervention, or abandonment through inappropriate referral or discharge may result. Therapists cannot treat patients who hold them hostage at the point of a psychological gun because of destructive acting out. Acting out that cannot be controlled through usual treatment intervention may require the structured setting of a hospital, particularly if the acting out is destructive to the patient's treatment. Mental health professionals who treat borderline patients must be prepared to hospitalize patients who are in a crisis or at least should be able to refer the patient for hospitalization.

Psychotherapists must distinguish suicidal behavior as an emergency state from suicidal behavior as a chronic maladaptational life-style (112,113). The acute suicidal state often presents in the context of depression with the associated vegetative features of sleep disturbances and weight changes. For patients in acute suicidal states, therapists make all efforts to assist the patient through the crisis until the self-destructive impulses have passed. Hospitalization is often necessary. In the chronically suicidal patient, therapeutic intervention is aimed at enabling the patient to face and master conflicts rather than to avoid or escape through suicide. Rage rather than depression appears to underline recurrent suicidal episodes. Paradoxically, the option of suicide is a solace to some patients who fear being overwhelmed by feelings and impulses. The idea of suicide may provide the patient with the feeling of control. However, chronically suicidal patients may have life-threatening exacerbations of self-destructive impulses.

VICISSITUDES OF PSYCHOTHERAPY

Countertransference problems are inevitable in the treatment of the borderline patient. The therapist's ability to use these reactions for the benefit of the patient's treatment is critical. All therapists, being human, have certain vulnerabilities and limitations. Therapists who treat borderline patients should have a good working knowledge of their own conflicts and defensive operations. Vulnerabilities that exist inevitably will be tested by the borderline patient. Therapists who remain ignorant of their own professional limitations may become rudely acquainted with them in a court of law.

In *Hess v. Frank* (103), the psychiatrist treated the patient from 1961 to September 1969. On 26 September 1969, the patient alleged that during a regularly scheduled session, without just cause, the psychiatrist became abusive to the patient, uttering various words and phrases. The plaintiff charged that the psychiatrist knew or should have known in his professional capacity that his behavior would cause grave mental anguish and be injurious to the health of the patient. The alleged abusive statements were uttered during the course of an argument over fees and the appointment schedule. The patient sought $100,000 in damages.

The court dismissed the patient's case against the psychiatrist by viewing the argument as outside of the professional treatment relationship. The court stated: "The conduct complained of, however, was not part of the course of treatment and there is no claim or indication that defendant failed to provide medical services in accordance with accepted standards or that he did not exercise requisite skills in the treatment of the plaintiff." Assuming that the plaintiff's allegations were correct for the purpose of discussion, the court did not consider mismanagement of the countertransference as a factor when the psychiatrist who, after treating the patient for 8 years, "without any just cause, became abusive to the patient."

A therapist's childhood and personal psychodynamics have no direct bearing in a civil case, and these issues cannot be raised as a defense in a malpractice suit. Nonetheless, therapists should have a reasonably thorough awareness of their personal strengths and weaknesses especially when treating and managing certain psychiatric patients. This facilitates good clinical practice and helps to avoid legal entanglements with patients.

Borderline patients cannot always be adequately treated even by experienced therapists. Therapists are not born with the knowledge of how to treat these difficult patients. All therapists must begin from a state of inexperience. Still, therapists should consider supervision by and consultation with clinicians who have more training and experience when the original therapist is having difficulties understanding or managing the care and treatment of a patient. Rappeport's maxim about consultation is extremely important to remember: "When in doubt, shout" (114). As Slovenko (30) notes, therapists are liable for failure to refer when they should have known that a problem existed that they were not competent to manage.

The importance of making a psychiatric diagnosis of each patient cannot be overemphasized. Psychodynamic formulations are important, but they do not have the prognostic significance of an accurate diagnosis. Psychiatrists are less likely to be surprised by the patient's clinical course when formulating a working diagnosis. The DSM-III-R diagnosis of borderline personality disorder emphasizes chronically suicidal and self-mutilating tendencies as major characteristics of these patients. Diagnostic formulations should be made as a matter of course.

Slovenko (30) states: "Good sense, the law, and professional ethics would all maintain that one should not undertake services in a matter outside of one's competence. If services are undertaken by a therapist who discovers that he or she cannot properly care for the patient, an affirmative duty exists to seek qualified help." Qualified help also can mean treatment for the therapist, if indicated. Therapists should consider a period of self-analysis or "analytic toilet," as advocated by the English psychoanalyst Edward Glover, when they experience consistent difficulties in treating certain patients.

Because the treatment of borderline patients is replete with unexpected clinical twists and turns, careful documentation of the reasoning behind treatment interventions should be made. Sometimes the therapist is required to make a treatment intervention that appears contrary to a layperson's logic, such as a well-thought-out, clinically indicated hospital discharge that is complicated by regression at the time of discharge (51). This discharge appears to be inappropriately flying in the face of the patient's regression, even though clinical assessment has been careful and indicates that the patient can tolerate the temporary anxiety surrounding discharge from the hospital. The reasoning governing the clinical decision should be carefully documented. Therapists who treat seriously disturbed patients must be in a position to hospitalize these patients should a crisis arise that requires inpatient treatment. Ideally, therapists should be able to hospitalize their own patients to maintain continuity of care. If this is not possible, however, direct referral by the therapist should be made to a psychiatrist who is readily available to hospitalize and treat emergency patients.

Therapists who treat borderline and other disturbed patients must be able to tolerate some degree of being "on call" to these patients during times of crisis. Late-night calls are not unusual. Often, the therapist must be prepared to give the patient his or her home telephone number. Therapists who cannot tolerate this type of intensity and involvement probably should not treat these patients. Moreover, therapists must be able to withstand the uncertainty and calculated risks involved in the treatment of very disturbed patients. Therapists who find it difficult to tailor their treatment interventions to the needs of disturbed patients will inevitably provide ineffective or even harmful treatment, leading to possible allegations of negligent psychotherapy.

The psychotherapy of borderline patients increases the therapist's risk of liability because of their unique psychopathology. Certain of these patients pull a "gotcha" reaction, goading and provoking the therapist into a treatment mistake, then feeling, through the use of projective defenses, "Aha! My split-denied projective identification has worked! I can kill myself with a clear conscience, knowing all the hostility and guilt lies on the therapist's side" (115). Abusive, provocative behavior needs to be interpreted immediately. If interpretation proves insufficient, direct confrontation of the patient with the consequences of his or her behavior is required. The therapist cannot conduct therapy amidst continuing abuse and threatening behavior. In these instances, consultation should be considered. Hospitalization of the patient may be necessary. Acting-out behavior should be therapeutically engaged as soon as it emerges and before it can unleash feelings in the therapist that may become destructive to the patient's therapy. Strategies for structuring the outpatient treatment of borderline patients so as to limit acting out and to preserve the therapy are described by Kernberg (115).

Negligent Psychotherapy: A Rarity

With the exception of suits involving sexual misconduct, abandonment, and gross therapist acting out, malpractice suits alleging negligent psychotherapy are very rare (116). Negligent psychotherapy suits are difficult to win because establishing a standard of care and a departure from that standard is nearly impossible. Many therapists disagree concerning the indications and effectiveness of the manifold therapeutic modalities in use. Proximate cause is equally difficult to establish, because so many factors can influence the course of an illness. The impulsive, unpredictable, and destructive acts of certain malignant borderline patients may be beyond the realistic control and management of the psychotherapist. Until recently, courts did not allow for a determination of psychic damage apart from physical damage, and skepticism still abounds regarding psychic injury alone. What one therapist considers a symptom of psychic damage, another may welcome as a sign of progress. It is axiomatic among therapists that progress cannot occur in therapy without some psychic pain.

In professional negligence or malpractice actions, the standard of care is the degree of skill and learning that is ordinarily possessed and exercised by members in good standing of that profession (30). The plaintiff must find an expert to testify about the standard of care and the deviation from that standard. A psychiatrist is judged according to his or her school and mode of therapy, even if that school represents only a respected minority of professionals. Note, however, that single practitioners following their own idiosyncratic theoretical principles do not constitute a "respected minority." But with so many schools of psychotherapy in existence, therapists usually do not find it difficult to find a supportive expert.

Increasing efforts to standardize psychiatric treatment through the development of treatment manuals may establish a standard of care. In the late 1970s, researchers began to develop treatment-specific manuals to form a basis for comparing the various psychotherapies. Without endorsing any particular form of therapy, an American Psychiatric Association task force has published a report describing the state of the art for treating 26 different disorders (117). Blue Shield in California has specified rigid "standards of treatment" for psychotherapy and ECT but emphasizes chemotherapy as the treatment of choice. Psychotherapy may be indicated in some cases but requires justification (30). Insurance carriers can be expected to expand standard settings for psychiatric treatments that eventually may be referred to as a standard of care in psychiatric malpractice cases. Insurance carriers, which are understandably bound by profit-and-loss motives, cannot be relied on to set professional standards of psychiatric care.

Given the multiplicity of therapeutic schools and the courts' disinclination to judge the appropriateness or efficacy of competing reputable psychotherapies, determinations of standard of care become extremely problematic (118). Nonetheless, when therapists use outmoded treatments when more effective therapies are available, claims of negligent treatment may be raised (30).

The term *negligent psychotherapy* often is erroneously applied to gross misconduct situations involving intentional torts (e.g., assault and battery, fraud, misrepresentation, the intentional infliction of emotional distress, breach of contract, and false imprisonment). For example, the landmark psychiatric battery case was *Hammer v. Rosen* (119). Dr. John Rosen originated the innovative though controversial therapy of *direct analysis*. Schizophrenic patients were initially bombarded with id-type interpretations. Sometimes, the therapist assumed the position of an all-powerful parent, using physical methods to make contact with severely regressed patients. The court held that the beatings Alice Hammer received over the course of 7 years of treatment with Dr. Rosen constituted improper treatment and malpractice.

In another case, *Abraham v. Zaslow* (120), a 22-year-old graduate student agreed to undergo an experimental treatment called *rage reduction* or *Z-therapy*. This form of treatment was designed for autistic children. The patient is restrained, tickled, and poked when unsatisfactory answers are given to questions asked by the therapist. Ms. Abraham was continually poked and abused for 10–12 hours, suffering extensive bruising and acute renal failure. She was awarded $170,000 in damages.

Finally, in California, the Center for Feeling Therapy was sued by former patients for fraud, breach of contract, false imprisonment, battery, intentional infliction of emotional distress, lack of informed consent, and malpractice based on allegations of "mind control" and "undue familiarity." This case, *Rains v. Center Foundation et al.* (121), was ultimately settled. In *Going Sane: An Introduction to Feeling Therapy* (122), the center's unorthodox techniques are described: "You will be asked to do many things. . . . You may be asked to scream loudly, to use profanities, to shout at others presently in your life and from your past, to push, shove or make physical contact with fellow patients or therapists . . . to undress, to refrain from smoking, drinking or using narcotics."

Miles (123) discusses novel theories of litigation in psychotherapy that focus primarily on issues of "brainwashing" and "mind control."

The Stalemated Patient

The continued treatment of any patient in the face of deterioration or lack of improvement over many years may raise the issue of negligent psychotherapy. The therapist has a duty to terminate treatment that is ineffective or harmful (70). Therapists have the duty to act in good faith toward patients by informing them when necessary that a certain treatment is of no benefit (124). The duty to terminate also requires that patients who need continued treatment be referred to specialists who might provide other or better treatment, when the psychiatrist knows or should know that the present treatment is not proving effective in relieving or curing the patient's condition (2). If termination is not considered feasible, at the very least, a consultation should be obtained. Patients who remain in long-term psychotherapy without improvement but then improve rapidly with psychopharmacologic treatment may claim negligent treatment (25). Some patients express a preference for psychotherapy over drug treatment, even though the latter might bring quicker results and is clearly indicated. This preference may be honored if the patient is properly informed of alternative therapies that may be more effective, and if psychotherapy is not contraindicated.

Prolonged stalemates in psychotherapy are not unusual. Patients regularly produce infantile, dependent transferences that may remain intractable to psychotherapeutic intervention over many years. It is often difficult to distinguish between the patient who requires years or even a lifetime of supportive therapy to function at a job, to remain within a family, or to prevent frequent hospitalizations, from the patient stalemated in a relationship that has ceased to be therapeutic. The former situation is much like the diabetic patient who requires maintenance insulin therapy throughout life. For example, the treatment of patients with personality disorders may require many years of psychotherapeutic work. During this time, Axis I disorders may develop that temporarily worsen the patient's clinical course. A legitimate goal of long-term therapy of personality disorders can be to help the patient maintain stability in interpersonal and occupational functioning. If general improvement occurs, it would be considered a bonus.

The stalemated patient resists making any substantial internal or external changes but rather lives in and for the therapy. Many of these patients have endured difficult families and deprived circumstances. The best relationship that they have had with anyone is often the therapist, so that the temptation to replace life with therapy is very strong. Thus the treatment itself becomes a defensive avoidance. Stalemated patients and patients who manifest negative therapeutic reactions to gains in treatment should be considered for termination only after they prove intractable to concerted efforts at appropriate therapy. Consultation with another therapist is wise. Consideration also should be given to obtaining supervision from a knowledgeable and experienced therapist before termination is implemented.

How should the therapist attempt to terminate the permanently stalemated patient? Even after thorough consideration of the psychological implications of termination with the patient, the therapist may fear that the patient will undergo a severe emotional crisis or psychotic episode. Where indicated, termination and transfer to another therapist may have to occur within the hospital context.

The fear that a patient will regress should not, by itself, prevent the therapist from transferring or terminating a patient who is permanently stalemated.

Therapists and patients often have a distorted sense of time when it comes to length of therapy. It is altogether too easy to rationalize stalemates that go on for years until the therapist realizes, in a moment of agonizing truth, that no substantial progress has been made and that hundreds of hours and thousands of dollars have been spent fruitlessly. Moreover, the patient may have been diverted from a more effective treatment. Diverting a person from therapy that may have provided a "substantial possibility of recovery" may be considered malpractice (125). Of course, one may not know that a treatment is efficacious, except in hindsight. Nevertheless, a disillusioned patient may seek legal redress for an alleged provision of negligent psychotherapy and loss of chance (2).

The Suicidal Patient

The most common cause of a malpractice suit involving psychiatric care is the failure to reasonably protect patients from harming themselves. In essence, theories of negligence involving suicide can be grouped into three broad categories—failure to properly *diagnose* (assess the potential and/or severity of suicide), to *treat* (use reasonable treatment interventions and precautions), and to *implement* (treatment is negligently carried out). Each of these theories applies correspondingly to inpatient and outpatient settings and is based on the defendant's failure to act reasonably in exercising the appropriate duty of care to the patient. Patient suicides leading to wrongful death suits essentially are based on the legal concepts of foreseeability and causation. That is, they are based on claims that the suicide was not diagnosed and treated properly, causing the patient's death.

As a general rule, a psychiatrist who exercises reasonable care in compliance with accepted medical practice will not be held liable for any resulting injury. This would include situations in which a patient's suicide was not reasonably foreseeable or in which the suicide occurred as a result of intervening factors.

Foreseeable Suicide

As an accepted standard of care, an evaluation of suicide potential should be done with all patients, even those who do not present overtly with suicidal complaints. A review of case law shows that reasonable care requires that a patient who is either suspected or confirmed to be suicidal must be the subject of certain affirmative precautions. A failure either to reasonably assess a patient's suicidality or to implement an appropriate precautionary plan once the patient's suicide potential becomes foreseeable is likely to render a practitioner liable if the patient is harmed because of a suicide attempt. The law tends to assume that suicide is preventable if it is foreseeable.

Outpatients

Psychiatrists are expected to assess the severity and imminence of a foreseeable suicidal act that generally dictates the nature of the duty of care options. But most courts have reasoned that when an outpatient commits suicide, the therapist will not be held to have breached a duty to safeguard the patient from foreseeable self-harm because of the difficulty in controlling the patient (126). For example, intervening variables leading to patient suicide over which the clinician has no control constitute a valid legal defense. The borderline patient who suffers a significant rejection between therapy sessions and impulsively commits suicide without attempting to contact the therapist is an example of such an intervening variable.

Assessment

Providing a reasonable standard of care in *assessing* suicidal patients preempts the very problematic issue of *predicting* suicide, for which standards do not exist. When a risk-benefit analysis is noticeably absent, the court is less able to evaluate the appropriateness of the decision-making process in assessing the risk of suicide. All suicide assessments should be recorded in the patient's chart *at the time of evaluation.* For the suicidal patient, assessment should be made at each outpatient visit. The hospitalized patient also should have frequent assessments, particularly when a change in status is considered, such as room or ward change, pass, or discharge.

Risk-Benefit Analysis

Risk-benefit analysis provides a systematic assessment of the balance of clinical factors favoring or opposing the treatment intervention under consideration. A risk-benefit evaluation also allows the psychiatrist more therapeutic latitude with the suicidal patient where fears of malpractice inhibit appropriate therapeutic intervention. It is not unusual for psychiatrists to be so fearful of a malpractice action when treating a suicidal patient that they overly restrict the patient, to the latter's therapeutic detriment. Specific risks for any given psychiatric intervention should be recorded in a risk-benefit note in the patient's chart. The record should reflect what sources of information were consulted, what factors went into the clinical decision, and how the factors were balanced by the use of risk-benefit assessment.

Suicide usually is the result of a complex interplay of factors. Thus, it is a multidetermined act. Clinicians rely on many clinical variables in assessing the suicide potential of patients. Some of the variables are vague and difficult to interpret. Furthermore, it is extremely difficult for the clinician to determine the weight to be given to the various factors that might signal suicide risk. Risk variables identify too many false-positive patients to be useful in long-range suicide prediction. Still, their clinical usefulness is much greater for short-range assessment of suicide risk in the patient undergoing an acute suicidal crisis (127). I describe elsewhere a method of assessing suicide risk that permits judging low, medium, or high potential for suicide (128).

Because time attenuates predictive accuracy, the "weather forecast" model has a certain applicability to the prediction of violence. That is, short-term predictions—about the weather or about human behavior—are much more accurate than long-term predictions, because in the short term, the parameters that influence future occurrences can be specified with greater precision. For psychiatric predictions made at a greater distance in time, the clinician loses the ability to specify both psychological and environmental determinants of behavior, and thus to predict with precision the likelihood of particular outcomes. Accordingly, patients undergoing a suicidal crisis should be seen frequently, and their suicide risk should be assessed from session to session.

Suicide has a low base rate of occurrence. Even when an extremely high suicide rate of approximately 180 per 100,000 exists—as with affective disorders, schizophrenia, or alcohol or drug abuse—this still means that 99,820 will not commit suicide. Thus, in most instances, the therapist is much more likely to be correct in predicting that the patient will not commit suicide. Although standards for assessing suicide exist, predictions of suicide originating from such assessments become progressively less accurate beyond the immediate short term (i.e., 24–48 hours). Every suicide is a unique event that defies easy analysis, even in retrospect.

Probability determinations of suicide potential are *judgments* based on risk assessment. Once such judgments are made, however, appropriate clinical interventions must be initiated (e.g., hospitalization, more frequent patient visits, or medication adjustments). No one suicide risk variable can be counted on exclusively in assessing suicide potential. However, one of the most significant "predictors" is the lack of an ongoing therapeutic alliance. The therapeutic alliance is defined as the conscious and unconscious working relationship between therapist and patient in which each implicitly agrees to collaborate in the process of treatment. The presence of a therapeutic alliance is a bedrock indicator of the patient's willingness to seek help and sustenance through personal relationships during serious emotional crises, and it is the most important nonverbal statement of a desire to live. The presence or absence of the therapeutic alliance can be used by clinicians as a here-and-now indicator of the patient's suicidal vulnerability. Note, however, that for new patients or for patients seen in emergencies, sufficient time may not have elapsed to establish and evaluate a therapeutic alliance.

I have discussed suicide and legal liability more extensively elsewhere (129,130).

THE POTENTIALLY VIOLENT PATIENT

As a general rule, one person has no duty to control the conduct of a second person to prevent that person from physically harming a third person (131). As applied to psychiatric care, this rule traditionally meant that psychiatrists had only a limited duty to control hospitalized patients and to exercise due care in deciding on discharge. This rule changed, however, after the *Tarasoff* case (132). This case significantly expanded the therapist's legal duty and potential liability. In *Tarasoff*, the California Supreme Court first recognized that a duty to protect third parties was imposed only where a *special relationship* existed between the victim, the individual whose conduct created the danger, and the defendant. The court stated "that the single relationship of a doctor to his patient is sufficient to support the duty to exercise reasonable care to protect others" from the violent acts of patients.

In some jurisdictions, courts have held that the need to safeguard the public well-being overrides all other considerations, including confidentiality. Therefore, a psychotherapist has a duty to act affirmatively to protect an endangered third party from a patient's violent or dangerous acts. Although a few courts have declined to find a *Tarasoff* duty in a specific case, a majority of courts have recognized some variation of the original *Tarasoff* duty. No court has rejected this duty outright as an invalid principle.

Some courts and state legislatures have determined that a duty to exercise reasonable care to protect others arises when a psychotherapist determines, or should determine, according to the standards of the profession, that a patient poses an imminent threat of serious harm to a third party. This so-called duty to protect has been acknowledged by legal commentators as vague and wide open to interpretation. For example, determining the "standards of the profession" to be followed for evaluating an imminent threat (predicting dangerousness) and specifying how the duty should be carried out makes this area of mental health law one of the most controversial and vexing. Nevertheless, clinicians have found that the duty to protect also provides more latitude for treatment interventions than just the duty to warn. Except in states with specific legislation mandating a duty to protect (i.e., California, Colorado, Florida, Kentucky, Louisiana, Massachusetts, Minnesota, New Hampshire, and Washington), no hard-and-fast rules have been applied. In jurisdictions where no duty to warn or protect currently exists, precedents from other states may be applied in future cases alleging such a duty. Some states have specified statutory limitations for psychiatrists' liability when their patients harm others (133).

Discharging the Duty

A number of courts and at least nine state statutes have addressed the duty to protect doctrine. The statutes usually require that an identifiable victim be warned and the police notified. Courts typically focus on whether the violence was foreseeable and whether the element of control was sufficiently present. Generally, the psychiatrist who is appropriately exercising this duty of care must address three threshold factors:

1. The threat of dangerousness must be assessed.
2. The potential object of that threat must be identified.
3. Some affirmative, preventive act must be implemented.

Foreseeability is much more difficult when a class of persons or society is threatened. Courts have been divided on the issue of control of outpatients in imposing a duty to protect.

Assessing the Threat

Despite psychiatrists' inability to predict long-term dangerousness, the law requires that therapists exercise reasonable care in making such an assessment. This type of evaluation only requires compliance with ordinary assessment procedures used in the profession. Such steps as a thorough pretreatment history, asking about and exploring past or present violence, and consideration of factors reasonably thought to contribute to violent behavior likely will satisfy a reasonable standard of care.

Psychiatrists may experience interference with their ability to properly assess potentially violent patients. Many psychotherapists rarely see violent patients and may become highly uncomfortable in the presence of such patients (134). A hallmark of competent psychotherapists is their ability to listen without too much discomfort to unacceptable thoughts and feelings expressed by patients. The therapeutic alliance with a patient who is threatening violence can be strengthened by this process of listening and attempting to understand. With many patients, the pressure to commit violence may be considerably lessened if the therapist can maintain reasonable calm toward the expression of violent thoughts and feelings.

Victim Identification

If psychotherapists determine that the threat of violence exists, they are clinically and legally obligated to follow up that assessment with a determination of who might be the object of the threat. Earlier cases and a growing number of recent court decisions have held that the duty to protect applies only when there is a "specific threat to a specific victim" (135). Yet at least one court has broadened this finding by requiring a duty to protect whenever there is a "foreseeable risk of harm" to the public at large (136). Whether or not a specific victim can be identified, psychiatrists should act in some affirmative way to safeguard against a potential risk of harm.

Exercising an Affirmative Act

The liberal language used in the current duty to warn or protect case decisions affords the therapist certain latitude in determining "what(ever) steps are reasonably necessary" to discharge that duty. As always, the therapist should attempt to integrate the *Tarasoff* duty into the clinical work with the patient. Thus, states that have statutory provisions limiting the *Tarasoff* duty to warning when an identifiable victim is endangered may distract psychiatrists from providing the full spectrum of clinical interventions appropriate for these cases (137).

Beck (134) points out that once a clinical assessment that a patient is potentially violent is made, three options are open: to deal with the violence in the therapy; to discuss the problem with a third person such as the victim and/or the police; or to arrange for the voluntary or involuntary hospitalization of the patient. If the therapist is satisfied, after careful assessment, that the patient will not commit violence before the next scheduled appointment, then the therapist can continue to treat violence as a purely therapeutic issue. If the therapist believes the patient will become violent within 24–48 hours, hospitalization is generally the treatment of choice. When, as in most cases, an intermediate position exists where the therapist feels that violence is a distinct possibility but is not imminent, then the best course usually is discussion with some third person, such as the victim. Warning may also be the intervention of choice when it appears that a patient will become violent before the next session but is not committable. To keep the focus clinical and to defuse not just the liability but the actual dangerousness of the situation, the patient should be encouraged to do the warning when warning is indicated.

As with weather forecasts, short-term assessments of potential for violence are more accurate than long-term predictions. The greater the distance in time, the more the clinician loses the ability to specify both psychological and environmental determinants of behavior. Thus it becomes more difficult to predict with precision the likelihood of particular outcomes. Accordingly, potentially violent patients should be seen face to face *frequently*, and their risks for violence should be reassessed each time.

Note that assessment is not an academic exercise. Its sole purpose is to guide patient management. Appelbaum aptly states: "Clinicians have learned to live with *Tarasoff*, recognizing that good common sense, sound clinical practice, careful documentation, and a genuine concern for their patients are almost always sufficient to fulfill their legal obligations" (138). I have developed a method of assessing the violent patient (139).

Special Considerations

Time limitations. The courts have never specifically addressed the time limits of a therapist's duty to protect. Instead, it appears that the reasonableness of a therapist's evaluation of a patient's dangerousness plays a more important role in a court's finding of liability than the amount of time elapsing between the last therapy contact and the injury of a third party. In *Laird v. State* (140), a judgment against Dr. Naidu and others was made on the plaintiff's allegation of gross negligence in releasing a mental patient who, while in a psychotic state, subsequently killed the plaintiff's husband in an automobile accident. The accident occurred more than 5 months after discharge. On appeal by Dr. Naidu and others, the case was affirmed by the Delaware Supreme Court (141).

Confidentiality and liability. Even in jurisdictions affirmatively endorsing the duty to warn with the concomitant necessity for breaching confidentiality to safeguard society, the therapist still can be sued for breach of confidentiality. The disclosure must be made with discretion and in a manner that would preserve the patient's privacy to the fullest degree possible while preventing potential harm. Moreover, it must be based on a reasonable risk of danger. Courts not recognizing the duty to warn and thus adhering to the common-law recognition of doctor-patient confidentiality will likely favor a reasonable clinical alternative to breaching patient confidentiality, such as hospitalization.

Unforeseeable violence. Basically, liability will not be imposed if the evaluation that a patient is not dangerous is based on acceptable and reasonable clinical considerations and judgment. Therefore, in situations in which liability is found despite a clinical judgment of nondangerousness, the evidence generally shows that the therapist's evaluation and treatment procedures were substandard or that the therapist substantially departed from acceptable clinical practice.

Patient self-harm: duty to third party? The danger of physical harm must be to others, not to the patient. Therefore, a psychotherapist does not have a duty to inform another party (e.g., a parent) if a patient is going to harm himself or herself. However, sound clinical practice may require that the family be brought into treatment of the suicidal patient.

Warning endangered third parties. Just issuing a warning as a legal formalism is not an acceptable approach to managing the violent patient. The duty to warn has been hopelessly overvalued because of the original *Tarasoff* decision (142). This decision was superseded by the duty to protect in the court's second hearing, known as *Tarasoff II* (143). Furthermore, warning alone is almost never enough. There are very few situations in which warning is justified without also calling the police. Although at least nine states have defined the *Tarasoff* duty by statute and have narrowed the potential liability, the psychiatrist who does not exercise reasonable professional judgment in managing the violent patient still may be vulnerable to a suit. Therapists must be reasonably certain that the threat of harm to a specific, foreseeable victim is imminent. The danger must be substantial, involving serious bodily harm or death (144).

Moreover, reasonable efforts to control the patient must be made before issuing a warning to the intended victim. If a warning is issued, reasonable follow-up should be attempted. Whether the law mandates it or not, therapists have a moral, ethical, and professional duty to protect patients and their potential victims. The obligation is primarily professional. Legal imposition of this duty is incidental to the therapist's professional duty. When the duty to warn is implemented, every effort should be made to keep it a treatment issue. The violent patient and the *Tarasoff* duty are discussed comprehensively in Section III in this volume by Dr. Kenneth Tardiff and elsewhere in the psychiatric literature (145,146).

SEXUAL MISCONDUCT

Civil Liability

Psychiatrists who sexually exploit their patients are subject to civil and criminal actions as well as professional licensure revocation proceedings. Malpractice is the most common area of liability. As explained earlier, the patient-plaintiff must establish the four requisite elements of a tort claim: duty of care, breach of that duty, damages, and causation. In a sexual exploitation case, the plaintiff will have the difficult burden of proving, by a preponderance of the evidence (e.g., better than 50% chance), that the exploitation actually took place.

This burden is best met when the plaintiff can provide corroborating evidence to support the claim, such as testimony from other abused (former) patients, diaries, letters, and hotel or motel receipts. If the defendant practitioner admits to the exploitation, then the plaintiff is left with the responsibility of showing that he or she sustained injuries as a result of the sexual activity. Typically, patient injury occurs in the form of emotional injury (e.g., worsened psychiatric condition). Expert psychiatric testimony usually is required to establish the type and extent of psychological damages, as well as to establish that a breach of the standard of care occurred.

A few states have statutorily made sexual activity civilly and, in some cases, criminally actionable. For instance, Minnesota recently enacted legislation that states:

> A cause of action against a psychotherapist for sexual exploitation exists for a patient or former patient for injury caused by sexual contact with the psychotherapist if the sexual contact occurred: 1) during the period the patient was receiving psychotherapy . . . or 2) after the period the patient received psychotherapy . . . if a) the former patient was emotionally dependent on the psychotherapist; or b) the sexual contact occurred by means of therapeutic deception. (Minnesota Statute Annotated Chapter 372, Section 148A.02 [Supplement 1984])

Mental health professionals and state legislators in Minnesota have developed methods to improve reporting, management, and rehabilitation of therapists who sexually exploit patients (147). Only six states have civil statutes proscribing sexual misconduct (Ohio, Florida, Minnesota, New Hampshire, Wisconsin, and Michigan). But a number of states prosecute psychiatrists under their sexual assault statutes.

Other Civil Theories and Defenses

In a minority of states, spouses of injured patients also have legal standing to initiate their own lawsuits against an exploitative practitioner on the grounds of loss of consortium (interference with the marital relationship).

If a sexual exploitation case goes to trial, the accused therapist will almost invariably deny the charges because he or she cannot reasonably expect to justify them. In a few cases, accused therapists and their attorneys have raised a variety of defenses admitting sexual contact but seeking to diminish or protect against liability. For example, defendants have contended that the patient "consented" to the sexual contact; that the patient was aware that sex was not a part of treatment; that the sex occurred outside the treatment setting; or that treatment ended before the sexual relationship began. All these arguments have been explicitly rejected by the courts. Furthermore, no "respected minority" in the profession claims that sexual relations with patients are therapeutic. At one time, this position had a few adherents, but if it still has adherents, they no longer advocate the point of view publicly.

Criminal Sanctions

Sexual exploitation of a patient may be considered rape or some analogous sexual offense and therefore criminally actionable. Typically, the criminality of the exploitation is determined by one of three factors: the practitioner's means of inducement, the age of the victim, or the availability of a relevant state criminal code.

Sex with a current patient may be criminally actionable if the patient can prove beyond a reasonable doubt (e.g., 90–95% certainty) that he or she was coerced into engaging in the sexual act. Typically, this type of evidence is limited to the use of some form of substance (e.g., medication) to either induce compliance or reduce resistance. To date, claims of "psychological coercion" via the manipulation of transference has not been successful in meeting the criteria for coercion necessary for a criminal case. In cases involving a minor patient, the issue of consent or coercion is irrelevant, because by law minors and incompetent patients (including incompetent adults) are considered unable to provide valid consent. Therefore, sex with a child or an incompetent person is automatically considered a criminal act. A few states have statutorily made sexual relations between a therapist and a patient a criminal offense. For example, a Wisconsin statute holds that

> [a]ny person who is or who holds himself or herself out to be a therapist and who intentionally has sexual contact with a patient or client during any ongoing therapist-patient or therapist-client relationship regardless of whether it occurs during any treatment, consultation, interview or examination is guilty of a class ***D felony. Consent is not an issue in an action under this sub-section. (148)

Professional Disciplinary Action

Licensing boards that adjudicate allegations of professional misconduct typically are granted certain regulatory and disciplinary authority by state statutes. As a result, state licensing organizations, unlike professional associations, may more effectively and punitively discipline an offending professional by suspending or revoking his or her license. Because licensing boards are not as restrained as civil and criminal actions by rigorous rules of evidence in trial procedures, patients generally find it less difficult to seek redress through this means. A review of published reports of sexual misconduct adjudicated before licensing boards revealed that in a vast majority of cases where the evidence has been sufficient to reasonably substantiate a claim of exploitation, the professional's license was revoked or suspended for varying periods, including permanent suspension.

Ethics and Malpractice

The Principles of Medical Ethics With Annotations Especially Applicable to Psychiatry (34) of the American Psychiatric Association unequivocally prohibits sex with patients:

> The requirement that the physician conduct himself with propriety in his/her profession and in all the actions of his/her life is especially important in the case of the psychiatrist because the patient tends to model his/her behavior after that of his/her therapist by identification. Further, the necessary intensity of the therapeutic relationship may tend to activate sexual and other needs and fantasies on the part of both patient and therapist, while weakening the objectivity necessary for control. Sexual activity with a patient is unethical. (Sec. 2, Annot. 1, 1985)

This ethical position has a venerable history. One version of the Hippocratic oath that dates back at least 2,600 years sets the following standard: "In every house where I come, I will enter only for the good of my patients, keeping myself far from all intentional ill-doing and all seduction and especially from the pleasures of love of women and men."

Sex between the psychiatrist and the patient is malpractice per se. That is, the sexual activity is presumed to be a deviation from the standard of care. It is another question whether the patient is damaged or whether that fault caused the damage (149). As stated earlier, psychiatrists who indulge in sex with patients can become embroiled in civil, criminal, and licensure proceedings.

Evaluation, Consultation, and Group Therapy

In an evaluation or consultation situation, the usual doctor-patient relationship may not exist. Thus, whether the patient could bring a malpractice claim for sexual misconduct may be in question. However, the ethical issue remains unchanged. Often, the sickest patients are the ones who are seen more often for medication appointments than for psychotherapy. Nevertheless, because of the extent of regression, powerful transference phenomena frequently occur. The therapist is at a disadvantage in not having an ongoing therapy situation that permits assessment of transference developments. Not surprisingly, some therapists who see patients infrequently espouse theoretical orientations that do not place much emphasis on recognizing or managing the transference. Group therapy situations also are rife with intense transference that can become focused on the therapist but without the benefit of the close scrutiny that a one-to-one therapy might provide.

All psychiatrists, whether psychodynamically or biologically trained, must have an appreciation for the power of both conscious and especially unconscious transference and countertransference feelings. Psychiatrists cannot give medications to patients without developing some transference in the patient. Just the image of physician alone is powerfully evocative of such feelings. Furthermore, it is axiomatic that sexual involvement with patients does not occur in the absence of other deviations in care. Above all, psychiatrists should know more than anyone the destructive effects on patients of sexual exploitation.

Trainee-therapists must abide by the same ethical principles as do fully trained therapists. Supervisors should be aware of sexual issues as they develop from the trainee's supervision. Failure to do so may render them civilly and ethically liable. Professional principles as well as the management of sexual feelings in both the trainee and the patient need to be openly discussed and should be an integral part of every training program.

As with individual psychotherapy, the potential for exploitation of psychologically needy and often very regressed patients is ever present in all these clinical situations. Borderline, dependent, and histrionic personalities appear particularly vulnerable to sexual exploitation because of the common development of intense dependent and erotic transferences. Patients with borderline personality disorder tend to evoke boundary violations in psychotherapy, including sexual interactions with therapists (150).

Transference and Countertransference

Transference is the primarily unconscious tendency of an individual to assign to others in the present those feelings and attitudes originally connected with significant figures during the course of early development. In psychodynamic psychotherapy, the patient identifies the therapist with the parents or other significant early figures. The transference may be either positive (affectionate) or negative (hostile). Analysis of the transference feelings is a major therapeutic tool in individual and group therapy, enabling the patient to gain insight and understanding into the origins of personal difficulties and behavior (151).

Countertransference is the primarily unconscious emotional response of the therapist toward the patient. Greenson (152) states that countertransference is a transference reaction to the patient. Grossman (153) defines countertransference as the therapist's reaction to the patient's transference. However defined, it is shaped by the therapist's inner needs and based on the conflicts and defenses that reflect the developmental psychological history of the therapist. For example, countertransference to the patient as a prohibited sexual object may unconsciously represent a compelling, early incestuous object for the therapist. Unfortunately, countertransference feelings, particularly of the erotic variety, have become associated with mismanagement of the patient's treatment and are viewed with shame and embarrassment by some therapists. However, the work of Winnicott (154), Little (155), and Heimann (156) stimulated a significant literature underscoring that countertransference, when properly managed, can be used as a valuable therapeutic tool. Most of the psychiatric literature on this subject underscores that *ignorance* of the countertransference may harm the therapeutic process and even the patient.

Transference feelings, in contrast to transference neurosis, may be broadly described as primarily conscious feelings that the patient has toward the doctor. Transference phenomena are thought to be universal, but they may be particularly prominent in caretaking and service relationships, such as doctor-patient, attorney-client, teacher-student, and priest-penitent relationships. Depending upon whether an orthodox analytic view or a more generic definition is used, transference and countertransference may hold very different meanings. For example, countertransference may mean simply disliking the patient.

In *Zipkin v. Freeman* (157), the defendant was found to have manipulated the patient to his advantage by convincing the patient during the course of psychotherapeutic treatment to become his mistress and to leave her husband. The patient alleged that she had sex with the psychiatrist and attended "group therapy" that involved nude swimming. The patient complained that the psychiatrist mishandled the transference that a psychiatrist is expected to handle properly. The judge stated that

> [o]nce Dr. Freeman started to mishandle the transference phenomena, with which he was plainly charged in the petition and which is overwhelmingly shown in the evidence, it was inevitable that trouble was ahead. It is pretty clear from the medical evidence that the damage would have been done to Mrs. Zipkin even if the trips outside the state were carefully chaperoned, the swimming done with suits on, and if there had been ballroom dancing instead of sexual relations.

The jury awarded the plaintiff $17,000 in damages. The court reduced the award to $5,000. However, since the mid-1970s, six-figure judgments have not been uncommon. In *Walker v. Parzen* (158), a $2.5 million settlement was agreed on after a jury rendered an initial judgment of $4.6 million.

At one point, malpractice in sexual misconduct cases was

couched in terms of negligent handling of the transference that was considered a central part of the psychotherapy. To a large extent, this was an artifice designed by defendants to come under the negligence coverage provided by the professional liability insurance. Otherwise, sex with the patient would be construed as an intentional tort (battery) and would not be covered under the policy. However, sex with a patient is a clear deviation in patient care, whether mishandling of transference or other reasons are involved.

Managing "Love Transferences" in Therapy

Love transferences often are not what they appear to be. Transferences, like dreams, have a manifest and latent content. Thus, Freud emphasized that "transference love" must be understood as a specific treatment phenomenon not identical to the experience of "falling in love" as it occurs outside of therapy. He stated that the analyst

> must recognize that the patient's falling in love is induced by the analytic situation and is not to be ascribed to the charms of his person, that he has no reason whatsoever to be proud of such a "conquest," as it would be called outside analysis. (159)

The therapist who only considers the "love" or manifest aspect of the patient's feelings seriously misjudges the situation. Most patients have felt deprived of warmth and affection in their important relationships. Behind these powerful yearnings for love objects often lurk feelings of rage and revenge. Litigation is frequently initiated against psychotherapists when they attempt to extricate themselves from the relationship with the patient. Often, sexually abused patients are rudely rejected by their exploiters. These patients feel terribly rejected, enraged, and seek redress through the law. Some forensic commentators have wryly observed that a therapist who begins a sexual relationship with a patient must never go away on vacation or must marry the patient to avoid litigation.

It is unethical for any physician to engage in sex with patients (160). However, psychiatrists hold a special position. Unlike the general physician, who intrinsically works within the ambit of a positive transference that provides hope and succor to the patient, the psychiatrist often works directly with transference as a therapeutic tool. As part of their treatment strategy, therapists may encourage development of the transference, but they are expected to keep any countertransference feelings in check for the benefit of the patient. The very act of intently listening and caring is itself a seductive process for both the patient and the therapist.

A higher standard of care is required of the psychiatrist in appreciating and managing in a nonexploitative manner unconscious, powerful feelings arising in both patient and therapist. Furthermore, psychiatrists, more than other physicians, should know better—that is, that sex with a patient is exploitative and psychologically damaging.

A significant number of sexual misconduct cases are not just the result of a mishandling of transference or countertransference. Psychotherapists with malignant character disorders manifesting severe narcissistic, antisocial, or perverse character traits entice patients to have sexual relations for reasons quite apart from countertransference issues. Analogously, severely character-disordered patients may attempt to seduce or entrap the therapist into a sexual relationship. Nevertheless, therapists are expected to maintain a treatment position with these difficult patients.

Sexual Relationships With Former Patients

"Once a patient, always a patient" represents a sound clinical position (161). When patients terminate therapy, the positive state of their transference may help sustain psychological stability for a lifetime. A subsequent relationship with the patient—even social—may inflame troubling transference feelings that can destabilize the patient. Furthermore, patients may need subsequent treatment during the course of their lives. Therapists should maintain their availability to former patients as much as possible.

Currently, there is no official American Psychiatric Association policy that *unequivocally* states that a sexual relationship by a psychiatrist with a *former* patient is unethical. However, in 1988, the Assembly of District Branches and the Board of Trustees voted to accept the following addition to Section 2, Annotation 1, of the *Principles of Medical Ethics With Annotations Especially Applicable to Psychiatry:* "Sexual involvement with one's former patients generally exploits emotions deriving from treatment and therefore almost always is unethical" (162).

A case-by-case analysis of such relationships is conducted by district branch ethics committees. Close scrutiny is given to whether the relationship is exploitative. Particular emphasis is placed on transference exploitation. For example, a therapist who has a sexual relationship with someone the therapist had seen once in consultation 10 years previously probably would not be considered exploitative. But a therapist who terminates—or more accurately, interrupts—treatment with the patient on one day and initiates a sexual relationship on the next day most likely would be found to have committed an ethical violation based on exploitation. The length of time following termination is not, by itself, determinative, however. To date, psychiatrists who have faced ethics charges in these situations generally have been found in violation of ethical standards governing the exploitation of patients.

A small but growing number of states have enacted statutes that specify a period of time after therapy ends during which a psychotherapist will incur liability for engaging in a sexual relationship with a former patient (163).

Reporting Sexual Misconduct

Reporting the alleged sexual misconduct of other therapists is fraught with complex clinical, ethical, and professional issues (164). Requiring mandatory reporting may create serious double-agent roles that can critically undermine treatment interventions with the exploited patient (165). Clinical flexibility rather than rigidity is required in the treatment and management of these often difficult patients. Minnesota (166) requires the reporting of allegations of sexual contact between a patient and a prior therapist. California (167,168), by law, requires psychotherapists to provide and discuss with patients their rights and remedies. Stone (169) proposes a therapist-consultant split in managing the sexually exploited patient. The treating psychiatrist attempts to work in a protected psychotherapeutic relationship with the patient while the consultant works with the patient in managing, reporting, and litigation matters.

Malpractice Insurance

Malpractice insurance coverage is defined by specific language contained in the policy. Both what is and is *not stated* in the insurance policy will determine coverage. Many insurance carriers will not insure for sexual misconduct, excluding it as an intentional tort or criminal action. What is not practice is not considered malpractice. In some malpractice policies, the psychiatrist may be able to obtain coverage for the costs of litigation but not for damages. Other carriers will only insure the therapist if the charges are denied. The American Psychiatric Association position of discouraging sexual misconduct has led to dropping coverage for undue familiarity from its member malpractice insurance plan. After 1 May 1985, the plan no longer paid claims for undue familiarity, but it continues to provide legal defense up to $100,000. It is implicit that for legal expenses to be covered, the charge of sexual involvement must be denied. Otherwise, no basis for a defense would exist. The American Psychiatric Association plan does not permit the carrier to settle a claim without the psychiatrist's explicit permission. This is an important feature for the psychiatrist who is erroneously accused of sexual misconduct.

Prevention

Therapists who feel they are losing their grip on countertransference feelings should consider a number of options. First, therapists must *recognize* their own slippage from a therapeutic stance. Such slippage occurs when a therapist begins to think that the patient's sexual feelings are directed at him or her personally rather than created by the *role* of being the therapist. Therapists' involvement with patients usually does not happen all of a sudden. Except in cases in which a patient is forcibly raped by the therapist, treatment boundaries rarely are violated suddenly but tend to erode gradually over time (170). Thus, sufficient time is ordinarily present to obtain help.

In obtaining help when therapists find their own objectivity slipping, therapists might consult a colleague, who, like a "Dutch uncle," might restore some perspective. In more serious cases, particularly when therapists themselves are experiencing personal difficulties, they should consider psychotherapy or analysis for themselves.

Finally, therapists need to culture a sense of humility. Certain patients will present special difficulties for the therapist. Therapists should forthrightly acknowledge their own limitations of their skills with certain patients, and these patients should be referred. If therapists are "stricken" by the physical beauty or attractive personal qualities of a new patient, they should consider immediate referral. A therapist's "where have you been all my life?" reaction to a patient is a certain sign of future trouble. Psychotherapy is difficult enough without such burdensome feelings. It is not shameful to admit that one has limitations and to acknowledge that the mishandling of transference is an occupational hazard of the profession of psychotherapy.

The specialty of psychiatry tends to be a lonely, isolated endeavor. Enforced collegiality often is not available. However, a full personal life for the psychiatrist also may help buffer temptations to exploit patients. Love relationships, friends, hobbies, recreation, and physical activities may help certain therapists to resist a tendency to live in and for their practices. Freud made similar recommendations years ago.

Conclusion

The provision of good clinical care, the maintenance of a working therapeutic alliance with the patient, a knowledge of legal requirements governing clinical practice, documentation, and good malpractice insurance will go a long way in mitigating malpractice fears. Concern for the patient, not fear of being sued, is the appropriate attitude toward the patient. Unduly defensive practices should not be allowed to erode the psychiatrist's affirmative professional, ethical, moral, and legal duty to provide quality care to the patient.

The practice of psychotherapy is an "impossible" task because of unavoidable limitations of therapists, patients, and knowledge. It is incumbent on therapists and patients to recognize these limitations. Litigation may arise from unfettered expectations of cure by disillusioned patients.

The therapeutic alliance is the best insurance against a malpractice action because it creates an optimal clinical climate for improvement of the patient. The therapeutic alliance is a two-way street. The patient must do his or her part. The therapist must maintain treatment boundaries to avoid exploitation of the patient. Treatment boundaries are crossed whenever the therapist gains gratification directly from the patient rather than from the treatment process *with* the patient. Patients who feel exploited are a major source of litigation against psychotherapists.

Although the task of psychotherapy is impossible in any ultimate sense, it is often gratifying and life-enhancing both for patients and for therapists. Knowledge and insight into the causes of litigation can help psychotherapists preserve the tranquility and composure necessary to the therapeutic alliance and the practice of psychotherapy.

Notes

1. Klein JI, Macbeth JE, Onek JN: Legal Issues in the Private Practice of Psychiatry. Washington, DC, American Psychiatric Press, 1984
2. Simon RI: Psychiatric Interventions and Malpractice: A Primer for Liability Prevention. Springfield, IL, Charles C Thomas, 1982
3. Gutheil TG: Legal Issues in Psychiatry, in Comprehensive Textbook of

Psychiatry/V, 5th Edition. Baltimore, MD, Williams & Wilkins, 1989, p 2109
4. King JH: The Law of Medical Malpractice. St. Paul, MN, West, 1977
5. O'Neill v Montefiore Hospital, 11 AD 2d 132, 135–36, 202 NYS 2d 436, 439–40 (1960)
6. Giallanza v Sands, 316 So 2d 77 (Fla App 1975) (per curiam)
7. Rainer v Grossman, 31 Cal App 3d 539, 107 Cal Rptr 469 (1973)
8. Hammer v Polsky, 36 Misc 2d 482, 233 NYS 2d 110 (1962)
9. Halleck SL: Law in the Practice of Psychiatry. New York, Plenum, 1980
10. American Psychiatric Association: Official Actions: Guidelines for Psychiatrists Working With the Communication Media. Am J Psychiatry 134:609–611, 1977
11. Batistella v Society of the New York Hospital, 9 AD 2d 75, 191 NYS 2d 626 (1959)
12. Davis v Tirrell, 110 Misc 2d 889, 442 NYS 2d 136 (1981)
13. Rappeport JR (chairman): Malpractice: problems and solutions. Presented at the 15th annual meeting of the American Academy of Psychiatry and the Law, Nassau, Bahamas, Oct 24, 1984
14. Medicine devoting increasing attention to rising incidence of teenage suicides. AMA News, Aug 2, 1985, p 36
15. American Medical Association: Current Opinions of the Judicial Council. Chicago, IL, American Medical Association, 1984
16. Klein JI, Macbeth JE, Onek JN: Legal Issues in the Private Practice of Psychiatry. Washington, DC, American Psychiatric Press, 1984, p 11
17. Md Cts & Jud Prac Section 5-309 (1984)
18. Quimby CW: Law for the Medical Practitioner. Washington, DC, Aupha Press, 1979
19. Reisner R: Law and the Mental Health System. St. Paul, MN, West, 1985
20. American Psychiatric Association: Guidelines for psychiatrists in consultative, supervisory, or collaborative relationships with nonmedical therapists. Am J Psychiatry 137:1489–1491, 1980
21. Slovenko R: Forensic psychiatry, in Comprehensive Textbook of Psychiatry, 4th Edition. Edited by Kaplan HI, Sadock BJ. Baltimore, MD, Williams & Wilkins, 1985, pp 1960–1990
22. American Psychiatric Association: Diagnostic and Statistical Manual of Mental Disorders, 3rd Edition, Revised. Washington, DC, American Psychiatric Association, 1987
23. Simon RI, Smith JT, Robertson JD: Psychiatric Malpractice. Washington, DC, Federal Publications, 1984
24. Lazare A: Hidden conceptual models in clinical psychiatry. N Engl J Med 288:345–351, 1973
25. Stone A: The new paradox of psychiatric malpractice. N Engl J Med 311:1384–1387, 1984
26. Colten RJ: The professional liability of behavioral scientists: an overview. Behavioral Sciences and the Law 1:9–22, 1983

27. Tarasoff v Regents of the University of California, 118 Cal Rptr 129, 529 P2d 553 (1974), reargued, 17 Cal 3d 425, 55 P 2d 334 (1976)
28. Helling v Carey, 83 Wash 2d 514, 519 P2d 981 (1974)
29. Hirsh HL: Judicially imposed standard of care: prophecy in medicine. Medical Trial Technique Quarterly 28:1–8, 1980
30. Slovenko R: Malpractice in psychiatry and related fields. Journal of Psychiatry and Law 9:5–63, 1981
31. Klerman GL, Weissman MM, Rounsaville BJ, et al: Interpersonal Psychotherapy of Depression. New York, Basic Books, 1984
32. Beck AT, Rush AJ, Shaw BF, et al: Cognitive Theory of Depression. New York, Guilford Press, 1979
33. American Psychiatric Association: Treatments of Psychiatric Disorders, Vols 1, 2, 3. Washington, DC, American Psychiatric Association, 1989
34. American Psychiatric Association: The Principles of Medical Ethics With Annotations Especially Applicable to Psychiatry. Washington, DC, American Psychiatric Association, 1985
35. Holder AR: Failure to "keep up" as negligence. The Best of Law and Medicine 116:107, 1973
36. Weintraub A: Physician's duty to stay abreast of current medical developments. Medical Trial Technique Quarterly 31:329–341, 1985
37. Osheroff v Chestnut Lodge et al, #66024 Circuit Court, Montgomery County, MD
38. Malcolm JG: Treatment choices and informed consent in psychiatry: Implications of the *Osheroff* case for the profession. Journal of Psychiatry and the Law 14:9–107, 1986
39. Treatment with drugs, psychotherapies found most effective. Psychiatric News, May 3, 1985, p 18
40. Kionka EJ: Torts: Injuries to Persons and Properties. St. Paul, MN, West, 1977
41. Multistate Bar Review: Torts. New York, Harcourt Brace Jovanovich, 1982
42. Slovenko R: Psychiatry and Law. Boston, MA, Little, Brown, 1973
43. Addington v Texas, 441 US 418 (1979)
44. Slawson PF, Guggenheim FG: Psychiatric malpractice: a review of the national loss experience. Am J Psychiatry 141:979–981, 1984
45. Sommers PA: Malpractice risk and patient relations. Legal Aspects of Medical Practice 13:1–4, 8, 1985
46. Family Legal Guide. Pleasantville, NY, Reader's Digest Association, 1981
47. Miller LJ: Informed consent: I. JAMA 244:2100–2103, 1980
48. Miller v Kennedy, 11 Wash App 336, 522 P2d 852, 860 (1974), citing Hunfer v Brown, 4 Wash App 899, 484 P2d 1162 (1971), aff'd 81 Wash 2d 465, 502 P2d 1194 (1972)
49. Natanson v Kline, 186 Kan 393, 350 P2d 1093 (1960)
50. Hammonds v Aetna Insurance Company, 243 F Supp 793 (ND Ohio, 1965)

51. Gutheil TG: Medicolegal pitfalls in the treatment of borderline patients. Am J Psychiatry 142:9–14, 1985
52. American Psychiatric Association: Opinions of the Ethics Committee on the Principles of Medical Ethics With Annotations Especially Applicable to Psychiatry. Washington, DC, American Psychiatric Association, 1985
53. Slovenko R: The hazards of writing or disclosing information in psychiatry. Behavioral Sciences and the Law 1:109–127, 1983
54. Roe v Doe, 420 US 307 (1975)
55. Slovenko R, personal communication
56. Roy v Hartogs, 81 Misc 2d 350, 366 NYS 297 (1975)
57. Stone AA: Law, Psychiatry and Morality. Washington, DC, American Psychiatric Press, 1984
58. Landau v Werner, 105 Sol J 1008 (1961)
59. Northrup B: Psychotherapy faces a stubborn problem: abuses by therapists. Wall Street Journal, Oct 29, 1986, p 1
60. American Psychiatric Association: The Principles of Medical Ethics With Annotations Especially Applicable to Psychiatry. Washington, DC, American Psychiatric Association, 1985, Section 2, Annotation 6
61. Robitscher J: The Powers of Psychiatry. Boston, MA, Houghton Mifflin, 1980
62. Gutheil TG, personal communication
63. Metropolitan Life Insurance Company v Ditmore, 729 F2d (1st Cir 1984)
64. American Psychiatric Association Legal Consultation Plan Newsletter, Summer 1985, pp 6–7
65. Reports of the Judicial Council of the American Medical Association, Dec 1984. JAMA 253:2424–2425, 1985
66. In the Service of the State: The psychiatrist as double agent (Special Supplement). Hastings-on-Hudson, The Hastings Center, 1978
67. Hadley SW, Strupp HH: Contemporary views of negative effects in psychotherapy. Arch Gen Psychiatry 33:1291–1302, 1976
68. Slovenko R: Forensic psychiatry, in Comprehensive Textbook of Psychiatry, 4th Edition. Edited by Kaplan HI, Sadock BI. Baltimore, MD, Williams & Wilkins, 1985, p 1981
69. Foster HH: Informed consent of mental patients, in Law and the Mental Health Professions. Edited by Barton WE, Sanborn CJ. New York, International Universities Press, 1978, pp 71–96
70. Furrow BR: Malpractice in Psychotherapy. Lexington, MA, DC Heath, 1980
71. Epstein GN: Informed consent and the dyadic relationship. Journal of Psychiatry and the Law 6:359–362, 1978
72. Robitscher J: Informed consent and psychoanalysis. Journal of Psychiatry and the Law 6:363–370, 1978
73. Bibring E: Psychoanalysis and the dynamic psychotherapies. J Am Psychoanal Assoc 2:745–770, 1954
74. Simon RI: Clinical Psychiatry and the Law. Washington, DC, Ameri-

can Psychiatric Press, 1987, pp 319–322
75. Roth LH, Meisel A: Dangerousness, confidentiality, and the duty to warn. Am J Psychiatry 134:508–511, 1977
76. Stone AA: The right to refuse treatment. Arch Gen Psychiatry 38:358–362, 1981
77. American Psychiatric Association: Position Statement on Confidentiality. Washington, DC, American Psychiatric Association, 1978
78. Slovenko R: Forensic psychiatry, in Comprehensive Textbook of Psychiatry, 4th Edition. Edited by Kapaln HI, Sadock BJ. Baltimore, MD, Williams & Wilkins, 1985, p 1986
79. State v Miller, 709 P2d (Ore Sup Ct 1985)
80. Slovenko R: Accountability and abuse of confidentiality in the practice of psychiatry. Int J Law Psychiatry 2:431–454, 1979
81. American Psychiatric Association: Confidentiality: A Report of the Conference on Confidentiality of Health Records. Washington, DC, American Psychiatric Association, 1975
82. Slovenko R: Psychotherapy and Confidentiality: A Report of the Conference on Confidentiality of Health Records. Washington, DC, American Psychiatric Association, 1975
83. Law of adolescence gradually maturing. American Medical News, Sept 9, 1983, pp 7, 12
84. Sloan JB, Hall B: Confidentiality of psychotherapeutic records. J Leg Med (Chicago) 5:435–467, 1984
85. Nagel v Hooks, 460 A2d 49 (Md 1983)
86. American Psychiatric Association: Opinions of the Ethics Committee on the Principles of Medical Ethics With Annotations Especially Applicable to Psychiatry. Washington, DC, American Psychiatric Association, 1983
87. Slovenko R: On the need for record keeping in the practice of psychiatry. Journal of Psychiatry and the Law 7:399–440, 1979
88. Gutheil TG, Appelbaum PS: Clinical Handbook of Psychiatry and the Law. New York, McGraw-Hill, 1982, pp 22–23
89. Bromberg J, Hirsh HL: Medical records and hospital reports. Med Law 1:253–272, 1982
90. Slovenko R: Forensic psychiatry, in Comprehensive Textbook of Psychiatry, 4th Edition. Edited by Kaplan HI, Sadock BJ. Baltimore, MD, Williams & Wilkins, 1985, p 1982
91. American Psychiatric Association: APA Model Law on Confidentiality of Health and Social Service Records. Am J Psychiatry 136:138, 1979
92. Illinois Stat Ann 91-1/2, 802, § 2(4) (iii) (Smith-Hurd Supp 1985)
93. DC Code § 6-2003
94. District of Columbia Mental Health Information Act, DC Code Ann 6-2001, et seq (1981)
95. American Medical Association: Current Opinions of the Judicial Council, Section 6.03, Chicago, IL, 1984
96. Freud S: On beginning the treatment (1913), in The Standard Edition of

the Complete Psychological Works of Sigmund Freud, Vol 12. Translated and edited by Strachey J. London, Hogarth Press, 1958, pp 121–144

97. Freud S: Lines of advance in psychoanalytic therapy, in The Standard Edition of the Complete Psychological Works of Sigmund Freud, Vol 17. Translated and edited by Strachey J. London, Hogarth Press, 1958, pp 157–168
98. Alton WG: Malpractice: A Trial Lawyer's Advice for Physicians. Boston, MA, Little, Brown, 1977
99. Mains J: Medical abandonment. Medical Trial Technique Quarterly 31:306–328, 1985
100. Brandt v Grubin, 131 NJ Super 182, 329 A2d 82 (1974)
101. Hirsh HL: Abandonment: actual or constructive premature termination of the physician-patient relationship. Trans Stud Coll Physicians Phila 6:207–222, 1984
102. Simon RI: Clinical Psychiatry and the Law. Washington, DC, American Psychiatric Press, 1987, pp 371–372
103. Hess v Frank, 47 AD 2d 889, 367 NYS 2d 30 (Sup Ct App Div 1975)
104. Alsobrook HB, Conason RL: Medical Malpractice. Washington, DC, Federal Publications, 1982
105. Wickline v State, 228 Cal Rptr 661 (Cal App 2 Dist 1986)
106. Marco CH: A case of abandonment? Legal Aspects of Medical Practice 12:3, 1984
107. Simon RI: Clinical Psychiatry and the Law. Washington, DC, American Psychiatric Press, 1987, pp 72–74
108. Ostow M: Is it useful to combine drug therapy with psychotherapy? Psychosomatics 20:731, 1979
109. Lesse S: Editorial comment. Am J Psychother 19:105, 1965
110. Simon RI: Somatic therapies and the law, in American Psychiatric Press Review of Clinical Psychiatry and the Law, Vol 1. Edited by Simon RI. Washington, DC, American Psychiatric Press, 1989, pp 3–79
111. Kernberg O: Borderline Conditions and Pathological Narcissism. New York, Jason Aronson, 1975
112. Olin HS: Psychotherapy of the chronically suicidal patient. Am J Psychother 30:570–575, 1976
113. Schwartz DA, Flinn DE, Slawson PF: Treatment of the suicidal character. Am J Psychother 28:194–207, 1974
114. Rappeport J: Ethics and forensic psychiatry, in Psychiatric Ethics. Edited by Block S, Chodoff P. Oxford, Oxford University Press, 1981, pp 255–276
115. Kernberg OF: Psychotherapy with borderline patients, in Specialized Techniques in Individual Psychotherapy. Edited by Karasu BT, Bellak L. New York, Brunner/Mazel, 1980
116. Gutheil TG, personal communication
117. American Psychiatric Association: Treatments of Psychiatric Disorders. Washington, DC, American Psychiatric Association, 1989
118. United States v Klein, 325 F2d 283 (2d Cir 1983)

119. Hammer v Rosen, 7 NY 2d 376, 165 NE 2d 756, 198 NYS 2d 65 (1960), 395, 402, 421, 424
120. Abraham v Zaslow, No 245862 (Santa Clara County Sup Ct Oct 26, 1970) 424
121. Rains v Center Foundation et al, C 384 972 (Cal Super Ct, filed June 9, 1981)
122. Hart J, Corriere R, Binder J: Going Sane: An Introduction to Feeling Therapy. Los Angeles, CA, Center for Feeling Therapy, 1975
123. Miles DE: Psychotherapy Malpractice: Theories of Liability From Mind Control to Undue Familiarity. Washington, DC, Medicine and Law Committee, American Bar Association, 1989
124. Malpractice: Physicians' Failure to Advise Patient to Consult Specialist or One Qualified in a Method of Treatment Which the Physician Is Not Qualified to Give, 35 ALR 3d 349 (1971)
125. Hicks v United States, 368 F2d 626 (4th Cir 1966)
126. Speer v United States, 512 F Supp 670 (ND Tex 1981)
127. Fawcett JA: Acute versus long-term clinical predictors of suicide. Presented at the 140th annual meeting of the American Psychiatric Association, Chicago, IL, May 11, 1987
128. Simon RI: Concise Guide to Clincal Psychiatry and the Law. Washington, DC, American Psychiatric Press, 1988, pp 92–93
129. Simon RI: Clinical Psychiatry and the Law. Washington, DC, American Psychiatric Press, 1987, pp 248–275
130. Simon RI: Concise Guide to Clinical Psychiatry and the Law. Washington, DC, American Psychatric Press, 1988, pp 83–98
131. Restatement (Second) of Torts § 315(a) (1965)
132. e.g., Tarasoff v Regents of the University of California, 17 Cal 3d 425, 131 Cal Rptr 14, 551 P2d 334 (1976)
133. Appelbaum PS, Zonana H, Bonnie R, et al: Statutory approaches to limiting psychiatrists' liability for their patients' violent acts. Am J Psychiatry 146:821–828, 1989
134. Beck JC: Violent patients and the *Tarasoff* duty in private practice. Journal of Psychiatry and the Law 13:361–376, 1985
135. Thompson v County of Alameda, 27 Cal 3d 741, 167 Cal Rptr 70, 614 P2d 728 1980; Brady v Hopper, 751 F2d 329 (10th Cir 1984); White v United States, 780 F2d 97 (DC Cir 1986)
136. Lipari v Sears, Roebuck and Co., 497 F Supp 185 (D Neb 1980)
137. Simon RI: Clinical Psychiatry and the Law. Washington, DC, American Psychiatric Press, 1987
138. Appelbaum PS: Implications of Tarasoff for clinical practice, in The Potentially Violent Patient and the *Tarasoff* Decision in Psychiatric Practice. Edited by Beck JC. Washington, DC, American Psychiatric Press, 1985, pp 93–108
139. Simon RI: Concise Guide to Clinical Psychiatry and the Law. Washington, DC, American Psychiatric Press, 1988, pp 108–109
140. Laird v State, No 79C-JA-97 (Jan 12, 1982)
141. Naidu v Laird, 539 A2d 1064 (Del Supr 1988)

142. Tarasoff v Regents of the University of California, 118 Cal Rptr 129, 529 P2d 553 (1974)
143. Tarasoff v Regents of the University of California, 17 Cal 3d 425, 131 Cal Rptr 14, 551 P2d 334 (1976)
144. Simon RI: Concise Guide to Clinical Psychiatry and the Law. Washington, DC, American Psychiatric Press, 1988, p 107
145. Simon RI: Clinical Psychiatry and the Law. Washington, DC, American Psychiatric Press, 1987, pp 306–337
146. Simon RI: Concise Guide to Clinical Psychiatry and the Law. Washington, DC, American Psychiatric Press, 1988, pp 99–120
147. Gartrell N, Herman JL, Olartes S, et al: Management and rehabilitation of sexually exploitive therapists. Hosp Community Psychiatry 39:1070–1074, 1988
148. Wisc Stat Ann § 225(2) (Supp 1982)
149. Slovenko R, personal communication
150. Gutheil TG: Borderline personality disorder, boundry violations, and patient-therapist sex: medicolegal pitfalls. Am J Psychiatry 146:597–602, 1989
151. Kapland HI, Freedman AM: Comprehensive Textbook of Psychiatry, 3rd Edition. Baltimore, MD, Williams & Wilkins, 1980
152. Greenson RR: The Technique and Practice of Psychoanalysis, Vol 1. New York, International Universities Press, 1967
153. Grossman CM: Transference, countertransference, and being in love. Psychoanal Q 34:249–256, 1967
154. Winnicott D: Hate in the countertransference. Int J Psychoanal 30:69–75, 1949
155. Little M: Countertransference and the patient's response to it. Int J Psychoanal 32:32–40, 1951
156. Heimann P: On countertransference. Int J Psychoanal 31:81–84, 1950
157. Zipkin v Freeman, 436 SW 2d 753 (Mo 1968)
158. Walker v Parzen, Cal San Diego Super Ct July 7, 1982, digested in 24 Atla L Rep 295 (1981)
159. Freud S: Observations on transference-love (1915), in the Standard Edition of the Complete Psychological Works of Sigmund Freud, Vol 12. Translated and edited by Strachey J. London, Hogarth Press, 1958, pp 159–171
160. American Medical Association: Current Opinions: Council of Ethical and Judicial Affairs of the American Medical Association. Chicago, IL, American Medical Association, 1989, Section 8.14
161. Simon RI: Sexual misconduct of therapists. Trial 21:46–51, 1985
162. Psychiatric News 24:35, May 5, 1989
163. 148 A02 Minn Stat Ann 1986 § (2)
164. Pope KS, Bouhoutsos JL: Sexual Intimacy Between Therapists and Patients. New York, Praeger, 1986
165. Simon RI: Clinical Psychiatry and the Law. Washington, DC, American Psychiatric Press, 1987, pp 296–298
166. Minn Stat Ann §§ 147.111, .091 (1) (t) (Supp 1987)

167. California Business and Professions Code § 337
168. California Business and Professions Code § 728
169. Stone AA: Law, Psychiatry, and Morality. Washington, DC, American Psychiatric Press, 1984, pp 191–216
170. Simon RI: Sexual exploitation of patients: how it begins before it happens. Psychiatric Annals 19:104–112, 1989

Section II

Involuntary Civil Commitment

Robert D. Miller, M.D., Ph.D., Section Editor

Chapter 2

Involuntary Civil Commitment

Robert D. Miller, M.D., Ph.D.

Throughout history, societies have treated mentally ill people through coercion. What has changed has been the way in which this coercion has been implemented, and by whom. The increasing depth and sophistication of historical research on the treatment of the mentally ill has revealed that previous concepts have often been too simplistic, assuming that identical events were occurring across the country. A further cause of oversimplification of historical accounts can be found in the attempts of many authors to place their data within (unarticulated) ideological frameworks.

Many of the conceptual differences between clinical and legal professionals have been discussed in the literature (1). For the purpose of this analysis, the most significant differences include *1*) the law's focus on liberty interests (defined as freedom from external restraints), as contrasted to psychiatry's focus on treatment needs and the internal restraints imposed by the mental disorder itself; *2*) the law's emphasis on procedural rights, as contrasted to the clinical emphasis on outcome; and *3*) the criminal justice representation model, which requires concentration on the rights of individual clients without regard to the rights of others who might be affected by the individual's behavior, as contrasted to the interest of clinicians (particularly those who work in inpatient settings where patients have less opportunity to avoid each other or staff) in the rights of all patients and staff in a given facility.

Frequently and accurately, clinicians have been characterized—both by themselves and by their critics—as paternalistic in their approach to patients (2). Unfortunately, *paternalism* has come to have a pejorative connotation because of the history of abuses in psychiatric facilities that was justified in its name. Paternalism and the need-for-treatment rationale for involuntary hospitalization that was based on it have become suspect. That is, paternalism has been equated by critics with unjustified deprivation of liberty under an unsupervised, clinically dominated power structure. This *post hoc propter hoc* fallacy has led many clinicians, particularly those who work in inpatient facilities, to become defensive about their "paternalistic" motives and to denounce them publicly even while continuing to subscribe to them privately.

Kaplan and Miller (3) have put forth one reason for the paternalistic tradition in medicine that is directly relevant to this discussion. Drawing on Lévi-Strauss's historical analysis (4), Kaplan and Miller point out that the Greek philosophers conceived of moral worth in terms of rationality. For the Greeks, the highest moral duty was to assist others to achieve their potentials for rational thinking and action. They based their political system on the principle that the duty of the wise person was to lead others along the path of rationality, and the duty of the less-wise was to follow that lead. Similarly, they believed that physicians possessed wisdom concerning health and that patients had a moral duty to follow their advice. It is no coincidence that the ethical principles that still form the basis for medical practice were established at the time of the Hellenic Greeks.

Physicians, including psychiatrists, are still socialized (implicitly if no longer explicitly) under the belief that it is their duty not only to offer the best clinical advice possible but also to ensure that the patient follows it. This concept becomes particularly significant in psychiatry, in which the patient's rationality itself is often affected by illness. Thus, it is easy to understand how psychiatrists interpret the "right to treatment" as the right of the treater to impose needed treatment on the patient (5). It also explains why many psychiatrists reject the concept of a "right to refuse treatment," which prevents them from fulfilling their moral responsibility to treat patients whose rationality has been impaired through illness. Even worse, recognizing the right to refuse makes clinicians responsible for incarcerating patients without providing the treatment necessary for their release.

The process of civil commitment itself changed less during the 1980s than in the previous decade. Yet although the recent developments in commitment law per se have represented fine-tunings and corrections to changes made in the 1970s, they demonstrate that the process is still evolving. This chapter examines the trends that have arisen or continued during the 1980s, beginning with the two most recent and controversial areas in which legal changes have affected psychiatric practice—the duty to protect society and the right to refuse treatment.

The Duty to Protect Society

The first of these trends, which is still under evolution, is that of the establishment of psychotherapists' duty to protect potential victims of their patients. Since 1973, both the American Medical Association (6, Section 9) and the American Psychiatric Association (7, Section 4, Annotation 8) have established provisions for breaching the confidentiality of the physician-patient relationship if it is necessary to protect the welfare either of the patient or of the community. Similar provisions exist in the ethical codes of psychologists and social workers. Thus, the *Tarasoff* decisions of the mid-1970s in California (8) did not create a duty previously unrecognized by mental health professionals themselves. What *Tarasoff* did was to significantly lower the legal thresholds obliging professionals to take direct action when patients appear to pose a risk of dangerous behavior. Now, as a result of social trends toward protecting society at the expense of individual rights, current legal pressure is almost all on the side of involuntary hospitalization rather than of treatment in the community and toward reluctance to release patients who have been hospitalized (9) because they have been decreed dangerous.

Because of recent social trends, clinicians are faced with a heightened ethical dilemma. They are impelled on the one hand to exercise clinical judgment and to emphasize treatment in the least restrictive setting, and on the other hand they are charged with ensuring the short-term protection of society and themselves by increasing their use of involuntary hospitalization and by delaying releases of patients until the responsibility can be passed to judges at commitment review hearings.

The whole concept of the *Tarasoff* duty has been reviewed recently by Felthous (10), and it need not be discussed here in depth. Several scholars have discussed the relationship between the duty to protect and civil commitment. In an influential 1974 law review article, which was cited with approval by the *Tarasoff* court, Fleming and Maximov (11) argued in favor of a duty to *warn* rather than to *protect*, because they viewed breaking confidentiality as less harmful to patients than commitment. Stone (12) responded by arguing that commitment was more appropriate clinically, that it was a more effective response to potential patient violence, and that it was less destructive to the therapist-patient relationship. More recently,

Felthous (10) argued that hospitalization is usually brief, whereas warnings are not time-limited and may result in more lasting damage, such as loss of a job or divorce. Also, he noted, the propriety and justification for commitment are determined by courts, whereas warnings are not. He concluded that neither alternative is more damaging than the other, as such. Rather, he argued that the choice should depend on the circumstances of the case.

Appelbaum (13) has postulated that psychiatrists might resist the pressure to commit potentially dangerous patients for whom hospitalization would serve not as an appropriate treatment but rather as preventive detention and as protection for the therapist. Psychiatrists could do so by officially deciding that a *professional* standard of care did not countenance commitment purely for preventive detention. He points out, however, that some courts appear to hold clinicians to a lay—not a professional—standard of reasonableness. If so, the suggested approach might expose clinicians to an increased risk of liability because a lay standard might be likely to weigh public protection more strongly than the rights of prospective patients. Efforts to change the "professional" standard of liability also run into the problem of a lack of professional consensus about who should be hospitalized.

Schopp and Wexler (14) argue that Appelbaum's suggestion that organized psychiatry refuse to hospitalize patients solely to prevent violence would not be effective because too many clinicians would continue to hospitalize patients for this reason and thus would provide a basis for challenging the proposed standard. Schopp and Wexler suggest going to the other extreme; by initiating commitment proceedings whenever there appears to be *any* possibility of violence, clinicians would overwhelm the courts and hospitals, and perhaps force society to deal with the consequences of the *Tarasoff* concept rather than allowing society to dump the problem into psychiatry's lap.

Appelbaum et al. (15) review 12 state statutes that attempt to define and limit the duty to protect. Five of them explicitly mention involuntary hospitalization as an appropriate way in which to discharge the duty. Indiana, Massachusetts, and Utah ask only that the clinician "seek" commitment. Kentucky asks that the clinician take "reasonable steps" to secure hospitalization; but New Hampshire requires that if clinicians choose this option, they "obtain civil commitment." Pending legislation in Wisconsin specifies that the duty to protect exists if there is a specific threat to an identifiable victim or if the patient meets civil commitment requirements. Wisconsin thus would permit a reasonable effort at commitment as an option to discharge the duty. The one federal court that has explicitly examined arguments that clinicians have an affirmative duty to initiate commitment whenever they feel that their patients are potentially dangerous has rejected those arguments (16). No court or legislature to date has held that civil commitment is the *only* option available to clinicians who feel that their outpatients are potentially dangerous, although several courts have held that inpatient clinicians have a duty not to release patients who are still dangerous (17).

Felthous (10) has pointed out that one beneficial effect of the duty-to-protect cases is that they provide a stimulus to improve clinicians' abilities to predict future dangerousness. Whether such studies have been motivated by a heightened fear of liability or not, several have appeared recently. These studies use more appropriate methodology than their predecessors, which generally examined the dangerousness of long-term hospitalized patients when they were released into the community. By looking at dangerous behavior immediately after the predictions are made, these studies more closely approximate the kinds of decisions required in duty-to-protect cases.

Segal and colleagues (18) devised the *TRIAD* (Three Ratings of Involuntary Admissibility) scale, a reliable ($r = .89$) index of behavioral indicators of danger to self, danger to others, and grave disability. The TRIAD severity (dangerousness) score had an interrater reliability of .65, on levels 1–4, with higher numbers indicating increasing dangerousness. Use of this rating scale, and of the Clinician's Global Rating (CGR) scale, predicted dispositional decisions of 70 emergency room clinicians in 251 cases. Eighty-five percent of patients with TRIAD danger scores of 4 were retained for commitment; 57% were retained for levels 2 and 3; and 30% who were rated at level 1 were retained. Predictions based on retention only for level 4 scores were correct in 76% of cases. The authors concluded that clinicians are consistent in their evaluations of dangerousness. They believe that the TRIAD approach more accurately reflects the actual decision-making process used by clinicians than do the measures used in previous studies, which reported less consistency.

In a second study (19), Segal and colleagues compared the severity of mental disorder and ratings of dangerousness. They developed the Indicators of Mental Disorder Scale (IMDS) to measure severity and found that danger scores (on either TRIAD or CGR) were significantly positively correlated with major disorders (psychosis or affective disorders), not correlated with personality disorders, and significantly negatively correlated with other diagnostic categories. A very strong relationship existed between IMDS ratings of impulsivity and dangerousness, even with personality disorders. Danger to others was most correlated with severity of disorder, whereas danger to self was least correlated. Grave disability had both positive and negative correlations. The authors argued that impulsivity is so strongly correlated with all three types of dangerousness that policymakers should consider making it a specific criterion for commitment.

In a third study, Segal and colleagues (20) looked at the effects of dangerousness and mental disorder on decisions to retain or release in emergency rooms. Seventy percent of retained patients had diagnoses of a major disorder (equivalent to psychosis or major affective disorder), whereas 46% of released patients had a diagnosis other than major disorder or personality disorder. The TRIAD danger scores accurately predicted retention (gamma = .71 for new patients, gamma = .73 for readmissions). Ninety-three percent of patients who scored high on grave disability were retained; 88% of those who scored high on danger to self; and 83% of those with high danger to others scores. The authors argued that fears that danger criteria select for those dangerous to others and not treatable were not confirmed. Overall, 82% of dispositions were correctly predicted by a discriminate function, which included severity of illness and dangerousness. Impulsivity was the most important factor in the clinicians' decisions, even more so for new patients than for readmissions.

In a retrospective chart review of 253 patients in an acute psychiatric inpatient unit, McNiel and Binder (21) looked for evidence of threats and violence in the 2 weeks before and the 3 days after hospitalization. Fifty-eight percent of patients who had made threats in the community required seclusion, and 32% physically assaulted someone. The correlation between pre- and postadmission violence was especially strong among schizophrenic patients. Schizophrenic patients who had threatened were more likely to be both physically and verbally assaultive after admission, whereas manic patients who had threatened were more likely to be verbally assaultive. Twenty-four percent of the patient sample had made threats before admission (35% of schizophrenic patients, 28% of manic patients, and 14% of patients in other diagnostic groups). Those who had threatened were significantly more likely to physically assault, to verbally assault, or to be secluded in the hospital than those who had not threatened.

Beck and Bonnar (22) also studied the relation of violence in the community before involuntary hospitalization to behavior in the hospital during the first 72 hours for 100 consecutive emergency admissions. They used an operational definition of violence, recording threats and violence to self and to others. Of the patients Beck and Bonnar studied, 10 threatened or assaulted; 3 of 16 patients who had assaulted in the community did so in the hospital; and 2 of 84 who had not assaulted in the community did so in the hospital (a nonsignificant difference). A significant relationship was found between patients who had assaulted in the community and hospital violence (including threats), but not between community threats and hospital violence. Most violence occurred on the first day of hospitalization. They found that manic patients were the most likely to be violent, whereas schizophrenic patients were less than 25% as likely to be violent, and no other diagnostic category was significantly related to violence.

The Right to Refuse Treatment

The right to refuse treatment remains a subject of concern and litigation across the United States. The majority of jurisdictions still do not have court decisions or statutes explicitly governing the rights (if any) of involuntarily committed mental patients to make decisions concerning treatments such as psychosurgery, aversive conditioning, electroconvulsive therapy, or psychotropic medication (23). Those that have examined the issues invariably have determined that some qualified right exists, but in every jurisdiction there are exceptions that permit clinicians to treat patients involuntarily. The differences are in the procedures required to override refusal.

Because much of the controversy over somatic treatments other than medication has largely been resolved, both legally and clinically (24), I will concentrate here on medication. Two major trends are evident. First, the Supreme Court's decision in *Youngberg v. Romeo*, which held that professional judgments in clinical decisions such as the use of seclusion and restraint are presumptively valid and that judges were less capable of making such decisions than clinicians (25), has caused the federal judiciary to become increasingly deferential to clinical decision-making about seclusion and restraint (26–28).

Many state courts, however, have been willing to maintain the trend away from control by the treating psychiatrist (29) and have required external review of such decisions (30). The current case law has been surveyed by several authors, who have divided it into the types of review of patient treatment refusal required (24,31). There also have been empirical studies of the implementation of these procedures in Massachusetts (32,33), Minnesota (34), Ohio (35,36), California (37,38), and Oregon (39,40). More recently, state courts in New York (41) and Wisconsin (42) have overturned previous federal decisions that permitted in-house clinical review of patient refusals. In addition, a state decision invalidated the clinical review process established by administrative code in Minnesota (43). In New York, the *Rivers v. Katz* decision grafted a full judicial review process onto the state's existing administrative/clinical review, thus requiring *both* types of review sequentially, although abbreviating the clinical review.

Studies of five different hospitals in New York after the *Rivers* decision (one private university hospital, three state hospitals—one with university affiliations—and one county hospital) have revealed some unexpected results. Cournos et al. (44) studied Manhattan State Hospital for 1 year before and after the decision. Of 21 petitions for involuntary treatment before *Rivers*, 20 were approved and 1 was denied; after *Rivers*, 18 of 21 were approved. The time between petition and decision was 5.4 weeks before the *Rivers* case and 5.8 weeks after *Rivers*. Attorneys for the state-funded Mental Health Legal Services did not argue that any patient was competent to make treatment decisions. Rather, they argued about what treatment would be in the patient's best interests. Side effects were prominently mentioned by the attorneys in 19 of 21 cases, and they were the sole legal objection in 11. One judge ordered a specific medication, based on the patient's report of side effects to the physician's first choice of another antipsychotic. Judges approved involuntary treatment for varying periods ranging from 30 days to 6 months, with an average of 3.7 months. Review of the continued need for medication required a new petition, often before a different judge. Cournos et al. concluded that the lack of independent clinical review was the greatest deficiency of the process. They hypothesized that the process may be impossible in smaller private hospitals without access to legal services.

Rachlin (45) examined changes in results of treatment refusal in the Nassau County Health Care Center before and after *Rivers*. He reported that the refusal rate of newly admitted patients dropped from 2.8% to 1.9%, with no other significant changes in demographic characteristics or the dispositions of the review.

Zito et al. (46) reported on Rockland Psychiatric Center, a state hospital with university affiliations. During the year after *Rivers*, there were 2,538 admissions, 63% of which were involuntary. The authors studied 295 refusers and 296 controls matched on legal status and diagnosis. Petitions were filed on 20 committed patients (1.3% of involuntary admissions). The court approved treatment in 13 of 15 cases reviewed (87%). The incidence of criminal patients in the refuser group was higher (20%). Four patient objections to medication were judged meritorious. Illness-based refusal was judged responsible for the rest of the refusals. The mean delay before the court decision was 42 days (range, 5–109 days).

Ciccone et al. (47) studied a private university facility and a state hospital for a year before and a year after *Rivers*. The incidence of reported refusal dropped after *Rivers* from 2.95% to 1.2% at the university hospital and from 4.5% to 1.6% at the state hospital. Time to resolution increased from 10.5 days to 31.4 days at the university hospital and from 21.1 to 68.2 days at the state hospital. Delays caused transfers to public hospitals when insurance ran out.

Although no formal research data have appeared yet from Minnesota after its forced conversion from an in-house clinical review to a judicial review system, preliminary indications are that judicial review consumes significantly more time for staff, delays treatment significantly longer, and results in fewer refusals being upheld than under the previous clinical review (48).

Comprehensive data are not yet available from Wisconsin, but Miller et al. (49) have found that the imposition by the state supreme court in *Jones et al. v. Gerhardstein et al.* of judicial review had significant results in a forensic patient population. Because of the statutory provisions, which had been upheld in a previous federal court challenge (27), no formal data had been kept on treatment refusals. After the *Jones* decision, the highest incidence of refusal ever reported was found—29% of patients already on medication and 75% of newly admitted patients refused treatment initially. All refusals were overridden by the court. That outcome has continued throughout the nearly 2 years since the decision (50). The time to disposition ranged from 3 to 132 days.

Data from Wisconsin's other forensic facility, which does not provide maximum security, also indicate very high refusal rates, although not as high as in the maximum security hospital. The second facility had no refusals of forensic patients sustained by courts during the first year after the *Jones* decision, and it experienced similar prehearing delays (51). Anecdotal data from several civil inpatient and outpatient programs in the state have indicated much shorter delays but a significant incidence (approaching 50% in some programs) of patients who were permitted to refuse medication.

One reason for the higher rate of refusal reported by Miller's group was the fact that the clinicians filed petitions on every persistently refusing patient who was felt to be incompetent to make treatment decisions. Others have reported that because of the staff time and legal costs associated with judicial review—4.5 *months* in Massachusetts's maximum security forensic facility (33)—staff were reluctant to initiate petitions for review. Rachlin (45) hypothesized that such reluctance explained much of the apparent drop in refusal rates after *Rivers*, and Ciccone et al. (47) reported that before *Rivers*, the staff at both hospitals studied encouraged the use of clinical review procedures, perhaps in part because of their rapidity. After *Rivers*, the attorneys at both hospitals discouraged petitioning. Legal fees at the private hospital were a significant factor in the increased rate of transfer to public facilities. Similarly, reports from Wisconsin's non-maximum-security forensic facility indicate that its lower rate of documented refusals resulted, at least in part, from the reluctance of some of their psychiatrists to become involved in the process (G. Hupfer, personal communication, 1988).

Although there has been considerable concern about the type of review process (clinical versus judicial), about the percentage of refusals sustained, and about the delays involved, other aspects of the review process have received less attention.

Criteria for Overriding Patient Medication Refusal

Although all courts have agreed that medication may be administered involuntarily in emergency situations involving some type of dangerousness, there is less agreement about the criteria for overriding refusal in nonemergency situations. The majority of states require a determination that the person is incompetent to make treatment decisions (43,52–54).

Other states set other criteria in addition to incompetency to make treatment decisions. Washington (55) requires a showing that "the administration of the drugs is both necessary and effective for furthering the patient's interest in treatment," and the state also sets forth four criteria for overriding refusal: *1*) preservation of life, *2*) protection of third parties' interests, *3*) prevention of suicide, and *4*) maintenance of the ethical integrity of the medical profession. The judge is required to weigh the patient's prognosis with and without the proposed treatment and must consider alternative treatments.

In Wisconsin (42), refusal may be overridden only if the judge finds that the patient lacks the capacity to understand the advantages, disadvantages, and alternatives to the proposed treatment, and if the judge determines that the treatment would not interfere with the person's capacity to participate in future legal proceedings.

Colorado had a statutory requirement for judicial determination of incompetency to make treatment decisions and a balancing of the state interests (including the police power to protect society and to keep order within institutions and the parens patriae power to treat persons incapable of procuring treatment for themselves) and patient interests. The state appeals court (56) held that in addition the judge must observe the patient personally, must inquire into the patient's own views of the treatment, and must give those views great weight, even if the patient is incompetent. The judge also must consider the prognosis with and without treatment, alternatives to that treatment, potential risks and side effects, the patient's religious beliefs, the views of patient's family or guardian, and the interests of others in and out of the institution in deciding whether to authorize involuntary medication.

The Arizona statutes require allegation of incompetency to make treatment decisions, but do not require such *findings*. They provide for involuntary administration of medication as part of a written treatment plan and pursuant to regulations promulgated by the Department of Mental Health. In reviewing these statutes, the court (57) explicitly did not examine the right of a person judicially determined incompetent to refuse treatment. It accepted the statutory system of nonjudicial determination of the need for involuntary treatment.

In Massachusetts (58), judges may override patient refusal only if the patient is found incompetent to make treatment decisions *and* the judge determines that the patient would have accepted medication if competent. Appelbaum (30) reports anecdotal data that indicate that hearings tend to concentrate more on the appropriateness of treatment than on patient competence.

The New Hampshire statutes require, for involuntary medication in nonemergency situations between the probable cause and final commitment hearings, that a physician determine that *1*) the patient is unable because of mental disorder to understand his or her need for treatment; *2*) no one who is legally responsible for the patient can be contacted; and *3*) a reasonable person would consent to the treatment. The legislature sought to relax these requirements, that is, to require only that the patient is unable because of mental disorder to understand his or her need for treatment and that a reasonable person would consent to the treatment. It asked the state supreme court to rule on the constitutionality of the changes. The court (59) did not reject the proposed criteria, but it ruled that the changes were inadequate to provide necessary procedural protections for patients.

In New York (41), if a court determines that a patient is incapable of making treatment decisions, it must go further to determine whether the proposed treatment "is narrowly tailored to give substantive effect to the patient's liberty interest, taking into consideration all relevant circumstances, including the patient's best interests, the benefits to be gained from the treatment, the adverse side effects associated with the treatment and any less intrusive alternative treatments." Rachlin (45) cites actual cases in which judges make such treatment decisions, such as specifying the particular antipsychotic medication to be prescribed; limiting the clinicians to one drug at a time, with a new review required for each change; prescribing acceptable schedules for dose changes; and requiring antiparkinsonian medication at the first sign of any side effects.

Who Should Be the Substitute Decision Maker?

Another difference among current approaches to patient refusals concerns who has the authority to make decisions for patients judged to be incompetent to do so. Several states, such as Colorado (56), do not explicitly address the issue. Others, such as New York, Minnesota, Wisconsin, and New Hampshire, authorize (either explicitly or in practice) treating clinicians to make the decisions, although in New York the judge retains significant input into the type of treatment to be administered. Florida (60) and Oklahoma (54) require the appointment of an independent guardian to make treatment decisions. The Wisconsin Supreme Court rejected a recommendation for a similar system (42). In Massachusetts (58) and Washington (55), the judge acts as substitute decision maker.

Discussion

The data currently available reveal that few committed patients are ultimately permitted to continue to refuse clinically appropriate medication once their refusals are formally reviewed by whatever mechanism is required in a given jurisdiction (31). Commentators have pointed out advantages of a formal review mechanism. It encourages clinicians to work with their patients rather than simply to prescribe treatment without any attempt at collaboration (61,62). In addition, it contributes to ultimate monetary savings through reduction in the inappropriate use of medication (62). Although it is unfortunate that the threat of judicial interference has been necessary in some jurisdictions to accomplish this goal, the goal itself is sufficiently important to withstand the methods, even at the cost of unnecessary time spent on legal procedures by clinicians who were already working collaboratively with their patients.

Another advantage of external review (clinical or judicial) of treatment refusal that has not been prominently discussed is the protection against civil liability that review provides for treating clinicians. Clinicians do not need judicial input into a decision about whether to prescribe chlorpromazine or fluphenazine, but clinical training does not provide the expertise for evaluating the relative importance of the therapeutic effects versus the side effects of a given treatment. Ultimately, only patients, if they are competent, can decide whether the side effects of treatment outweigh the benefits. Particularly when patients appear to be at significant risk for conditions such as tardive dyskinesia, a formalized external review procedure for patients whose competency is questionable may provide more protection against future lawsuits than the more usual process of informal peer review.

Few would continue to argue that competent patients should be forced to take medication against their wills (although many feel that clinicians should not be forced to keep such patients hospitalized). Clinicians object strenuously (and in my opinion justifiably), however, when judges go beyond the legal determination of competency to become involved in decisions such as which antipsychotic medication to use, in what dosage range, and whether or not to prescribe antiparkinsonian medication (44,45). Decisions to permit such judicial oversight, which almost invariably emanate from appellate courts far removed from the necessity of actually *making* such decisions, reflect the continuing misunderstanding of the judiciary of the real risk-benefit ratio of the treatment under consideration. As Gutheil and Appelbaum have pointed out (63), the legal literature, on which judges base their decisions in this area, continues to reflect an almost monolithic bias against psychotropic medications, calling them "mind altering" and either ignoring their therapeutic effects or misrepresenting those effects as the results of overtranquilization (49).

Judicial reluctance to authorize the involuntary administration of psychotropic medication has also been based, in our experience in Wisconsin as well as in the experience of other jurisdictions, on arguments presented in briefs or in testimony in treatment hearings themselves, almost invariably by "experts" who will not have any responsibility for the treatment or management of the patients in question. Nonmedical witnesses in particular often state that psychotropic medication is not only unnecessary for the treatment of severe psychoses or depressions but that it is actually inferior to psychological approaches such as group, individual, or even "milieu" therapy. Lacking the expertise even to determine who the real "experts" are, judges often have a difficult time in making specific treatment decisions. Most judges prefer not to do so.

Another common misunderstanding by judges and attorneys, even of the governing legal decisions themselves, is that "dangerousness" is required in nonemergency situations to medicate a patient involuntarily (50). Such misunderstandings have been, in our experience, most common in cases of reviews by criminal courts, which have much less experience than do civil courts in dealing with issues of competency (other than to stand trial).

There appears to be a trend for state courts to find grounds to require judicial review of medication refusal. It therefore would behoove state psychiatric organizations in jurisdictions without either statutes or case law setting forth the procedures necessary for review of such refusals to be prepared to testify before courts, legislatures, or both. Such testimony would provide decision makers with the considerable amount of information that is available, and that reveals that independent clinical review is much more efficient than judicial review and that clinical review is more likely to permit patients to refuse medication. Such briefs also should address the inadvisability of requiring judges to serve directly as substitute decision makers or to make specific decisions about particular medications. As the recent experience in Wisconsin has demonstrated, briefs arguing for total control of the decision-making process by treating psychiatrists are unlikely to be effective and may reduce the chances of forging a more acceptable compromise.

DEVELOPMENTS IN COURT DECISIONS ON INVOLUNTARY HOSPITALIZATION

A major revolution in statutory criteria (both substantive and procedural) for civil commitment occurred in the 1970s, when all states except New York added dangerousness as a requirement for commitment (24). During this period, the federal courts took the lead in revising civil commitment laws. Landmark decisions in Wisconsin (64) and Hawaii (65) established basic parameters then considered constitutionally necessary to protect the rights of persons subject to involuntary confinement in mental hospitals. Juvenile law was another legal system that had been supposed to be exempt from due process protection because of its therapeutic purpose (66–68). Taking a lead from Supreme Court decisions in this area, federal and state courts struck down the distinction between criminal and civil proceedings that had preserved the psychiatric dominance of civil commitment.

The courts examined both the substantive criteria (setting forth the conditions that must be met before persons may be committed) and the constitutionally required procedural protections necessary to ensure that the substantive decisions are made fairly. Most federal courts through the 1970s found that the substantive criteria in existing commitment statutes were deficient for two main reasons. First, they were overly broad (64). Second, their clinical definitions of concepts such as "need for treatment" were circular and abdicated too much power to clinicians, who were not considered to be sufficiently objective to be the appropriate decision makers when loss of liberty was involved (65).

The significant conservative trend of the Supreme Court in recent years has led the Court toward a "hands off" policy with respect to the operation of state institutions. Concomitantly, the Court has decided that clinicians are in a better position to make most of the decisions associated with commitment than are judges (25). As lower-level judges are replaced with those of a similarly conservative legal philosophy, the federal courts have virtually ceased to be an effective forum in which to discover new constitutional rights. Thus, advocates seeking protections greater than those established by the more liberal federal judiciary of earlier years now have turned to state courts and legislatures (29). In fact, except for one decision from the circuit court for the District of Columbia, all of the other 25 recent decisions reviewed here come from state courts. For clinicians to present their viewpoints effectively to the courts and legislators, they must understand how the courts have conceptualized the commitment process (69).

Decisions through the 1970s favored commitment based on a *dangerousness* standard, because it was argued that people's need for *treatment*—no matter how beneficial the treatment—was not sufficient to deprive them of their liberty, and because the courts were already familiar with making decisions (bail, probation or parole, release) based on standards of dangerousness. Most observers believed that under a dangerousness standard, judges would be less likely to defer to clinical testimony.

In fact, following the 1970 court decisions requiring "dangerousness," legislatures in every state except New York revised their commitment statutes to require evidence of dangerousness for involuntary hospitalization (23). Such requirements have not proved to be the panaceas their advocates anticipated, however. Definitions of dangerousness and evidence necessary to establish its future likelihood have remained matters for complex litigation. Two different New York State trial courts ruled in 1988 that dangerousness was constitutionally required for involuntary hospitalization, even though not required by statute (70,71) and not required by the federal constitution.

Evidence required to establish statutorily mandated dangerousness was examined by the Wisconsin Court of Appeals in 1988 (72). The court held that dangerousness can be established by evidence of threatened bodily harm even if the person so threatened was not present or otherwise aware of the threat. The court held that persons other than the intended victim may be placed in fear by such threats and that thus the statutory requirements were met.

The Colorado Supreme Court upheld that state's commitment statutes, although "dangerousness" was not explicitly defined, because due process was satisfied as long as the state proved by clear and convincing evidence that there was a reasonable basis to believe the individual's mental illness resulted in a present danger to self or others (73).

The Washington State Supreme Court rejected the claim that a definition of dangerousness without the qualifier "imminent" was unconstitutional. It held that the statutory requirement for a "substantial risk of serious harm" was sufficient to satisfy constitutional requirements. It did find that the state statutes were unconstitutional, however, because the procedures under which clinicians have the authority to detain patients without review by an impartial judicial officer, and even without seeing the prospective patient, did not satisfy the due process requirements (74).

Virtually all commitment statutes require the combination of mental illness and dangerousness, with a necessary causal relation between the former and the latter. In practice, as predicted by the proponents of police power commitments, judges rarely examine the evidence for mental illness with the degree of scrutiny that they apply to the evidence of dangerousness. With the proliferation of liability suits for failure to protect third parties from dangerous patients, clinicians have become more concerned about dangerousness and are reluctant to release patients whose mental illnesses are in remission if they consider that these individuals continue to pose threats in the community.

Courts have ruled on such situations. In *Reome v. Levine* (75), the federal district court in Minnesota considered the case of a patient, diagnosed as suffering from antisocial personality, who was certified as mentally ill and dangerous and who was committed. Less than a year later, an appeal panel of the state supreme court heard the patient's petition for discharge. The hospital director testified that the patient was still considered dangerous, but that he did not consider antisocial personality to satisfy the statutory definition for mental illness. Reome was released, and the state appealed. After further review by the panel, the court ruled that although Reome was not mentally ill, he should be kept in the hospital because dangerousness was the essential factor justifying commitment. The federal district court reversed this ruling, holding that continued commitment required both mental illness *and* dangerousness. It held that to confine on dangerousness alone would constitute impermissible preventive confinement.

The reverse situation has also been examined. In the Minnesota case *Matter of Stewart* (76), Stewart was committed to a hospital for treatment and evaluation of whether he was mentally ill and dangerous after he was charged with assault. (The Minnesota statutes provide a specific category of commitment for such persons.) On rehearing, testimony indicated that Stewart was still mentally ill and might become dangerous again if he were released and stopped his medication, which he had done in the past. The trial court ordered recommitment. On appeal, the state court of appeals ruled that the statutes required specific findings that a person was dangerous before recommitment could be ordered.

In *B.A.A. v. Chief Medical Officer, University of Iowa Hospitals* (77), a patient was admitted voluntarily as catatonic and depressed. His parents refused both electroconvulsive therapy (ECT) and medications, and the hospital sought commitment, which was granted. After ECT, the patient improved, and petitioned for release. The trial court ordered him released, because he was no longer dangerous. The hospital appealed, arguing that dangerousness was not required for *continued*—as opposed to *initial*—commitment. The state supreme court affirmed the trial court's dismissal of the commitment.

Courts have continued to examine other issues involving the substantive criteria for involuntary hospitalization. After determining that the minor patient before it did not meet the statutory criteria for mental illness, a North Carolina state trial court went on to find that the state's statutes governing the voluntary admission of minors (i.e., "voluntary" on the part of the parents or guardian, not necessarily of the minor) were unconstitutional because terms such as "age appropriate" and "age adequate" were impermissibly vague. It also held that minors should have to meet the adult criteria for dangerousness before they can be involuntarily hospitalized. The appeals court affirmed the decision, but the state supreme court held that once the trial court had determined that the minor did not meet the specified criteria for mental illness and released him, it lost jurisdiction to rule on the constitutionality of the statutes themselves. The supreme court thus reversed the findings of constitutional violations (78).

Several courts have examined the issue of who has the authority to determine the site of treatment once a patient has been found to satisfy the statutory criteria for involuntary commitment. The Georgia Supreme Court decided a case involving a patient who had murdered a deputy sheriff who was transporting her to a hospital under emergency civil commitment (79). She was civilly committed and subsequently petitioned for release. The patient had a long history of behaving violently while not taking medications and a history of stopping medications while in the community. Psychiatric witnesses recommended transfer to a less secure hospital but not outright discharge. The court ruled that the trial court had the sole authority to make such release decisions, and that it was permitted to rely on a "presumption of continued insanity" in doing so.

In *Alabama Dept. of Mental Health and Mental Retardation v. Andres* (80), the trial court found that Andres was mentally retarded and likely to be dangerous to self or others if left in the community. It ordered her committed to a residential facility. The Department of Mental Health appealed, arguing that residential placement was too restrictive for the patient's needs. The appeals court agreed, citing Alabama statutes that authorize the department to make placement decisions. The appeals court ruled that "the court overstepped its authority in attempting to tell the department how to deal with a matter presumptively left to its expertise as the agency charged with administration."

Similarly, in *In the Matter of J.R.R.* (81), two expert witnesses testified in the commitment hearing that J.R.R. met the Wisconsin commitment requirements. One witness testified that involuntary hospitalization was necessary, whereas the other held that placement in a group home was more appropriate. In an attempt at compromise, the trial court committed J.R.R. to a county inpatient facility, but it also expressed a desire to have this patient on an open ward. No open ward space was available, however, and the facility informed the court that it would not accept J.R.R. if he had to be on an open ward. The court concluded that it had no alternative but to place J.R.R. on a locked ward. On appeal by J.R.R., the state appeals court held that the statute was explicit in placing the decisions about the details of treatment in the hands of the county mental health board. The judge had only the authority to determine if involuntary hospitalization was the least restrictive alternative. It therefore affirmed the commitment.

In *Savastano v. Nurnberg* (82), three patients challenged the decision to transfer them from an acute-care city psychiatric hospital in New York to a long-term-care facility over their objections and without a prior court hearing. The trial court ruled that such transfers were a significant change in the nature and length of confinement. The judge concluded that review only by the acute-care facility's director violated state and federal constitutional protections by not providing sufficient protection of patients' due process rights. The judge noted that such transfers frequently are dictated by space considerations, not by medical needs. Arguing that professional judgment rather than administrative convenience should play a major role in transfer and confinement decisions, the court noted that all three patients were discharged shortly after transfer to the long-term facility.

The concept of least restrictive alternative continues to figure in other commitment cases. In *In re Stokes* (83), Stokes was committed to St. Elizabeths Hospital in the District of Columbia as mentally ill and likely to injure herself. The trial court found that she did not need inpatient care and ordered commitment to outpatient treatment. Five months later, Stokes was returned to the hospital, and a hearing was scheduled before a different judge. The appeals court held that less restrictive alternatives to hospitalization had not been sought and that it was the government's obligation to explore those alternatives and to present evidence for its recommendation for disposition before seeking rehospitalization.

In a Vermont case, *In re W.H.* (84), after three unsuccessful attempts to procure an outpatient psychiatric evaluation for involuntary hospitalization because the prospective patient did not show up, the trial court ordered W.H. committed to a state hospital for the evaluation. The order was stayed pending appeal, and the Vermont Supreme Court held that all less restrictive alternatives to inpatient evaluation had not been exhausted and that in the absence of evidence of dangerousness, involuntary hospitalization was not permissible at that stage.

The provision of community services was also addressed by the Georgia Court of Appeals in *Robbins v. Lumpkin* (85). After Lumpkin's initial 6-month commitment for habilitation as a mentally retarded person, the treatment center petitioned for an additional year. Lumpkin's representative argued that Lumpkin did not need inpatient placement. The hearing examiner agreed, but found that no appropriate community facility existed. The examiner therefore ordered the commitment dismissed. Lumpkin appealed, demanding that appropriate facilities be established. The trial court agreed, and ordered the Department of Mental Health and Mental Retardation to purchase adequate services in the community. The appeals court reversed, holding that the trial court exceeded its authority in requiring the department to provide community services.

A number of courts have addressed procedural issues. In an Illinois case, *In re Plank* (86), a recommitment hearing was held, although neither the patient nor his attorney had been given prior notification, as required by state law. Although both were present at the hearing, at which Plank was recommitted, the Illinois appeals court reversed the commitment because of the lack of notice.

In *Curnow v. Yarbrough* (87), Curnow was committed after appointment of counsel and a full-scale adversary hearing. He appealed on the basis of a lack of a probable cause hearing prior to the final commitment hearing, which was not required by the state statute. The Colorado Supreme Court affirmed the commitment, holding that the adversarial hearing satisfied the due process requirements necessary to protect Curnow's rights.

In *Matter of Z.O.* (88), the New Jersey superior court consolidated three similar cases for hearing. The issue was the length of time between hospitalization and the commitment hearing. The court held that the statutory maximum period of 7 days was not impermissibly long, and it affirmed the commitments.

In *Doe ex rel. Doe v. Austin* (89), the federal court for the western district of Kentucky reversed the state court's finding that due process required a judicial hearing. The federal court did, however, affirm the state court's holding that the Kentucky statutes were unconstitutional in that they did not provide the minimal requirements of notice and an adversarial hearing before commitment.

In *In the Matter of the Alleged Mental Illness of Cordie* (90), the Minnesota Court of Appeals dealt with the issue of effective assistance of counsel to represent patients at commitment hearings. The court ruled that appellants had the right to counsel "who shall act as a vigorous advocate on their behalf" (the statutory language) and that the conduct of the attorney should be judged by the same standard as for criminal defense attorneys. Having said that, the appeals court ruled that the procedural problems cited by appellants were insufficient to find ineffective assistance of counsel, and it affirmed the recommitment.

The standard of proof necessary to establish committability has been addressed by several courts. The California Court of Appeals upheld (91) on habeas corpus review, a trial court's use of the standard of preponderance of the evidence (about 51% certainty) for continuing a commitment based on grave disability where the statute did not specify the standard to be used. The statute did specify a probable cause standard (less than preponderance of the evidence) for initial commitment, which had been found constitutionally acceptable by the United States Court of Appeals for the Ninth Circuit (92). The appeals court found that to require a higher standard on habeas corpus review would discriminate against those who could not seek such review because of their disabilities.

In *State v. Casanova* (93), Casanova was found not guilty of arson by reason of insanity. Under the Minnesota statutes, Casanova was initially civilly committed; he appealed the commitment, alleging lack of specificity of the findings that he was in need of treatment, as required by the statutes. The state appeals court held that the trial court erred in committing Casanova based only on general findings of a need for treatment, rather than the statutorily required specific findings. It also held that the trial court erred in not setting a specific period of extended commitment.

In *Lanett v. Texas* (94), Lanett was committed at a jury trial, despite her request for a bench trial (before a judge without jury) and her request to waive counsel and represent herself. The state appeals court affirmed the commitment, holding that state law required a bench trial unless a jury was requested by respondent or counsel, but it was not clear from the record whether counsel had requested a jury or not. The appeals court held any error was legally harmless. In the absence of statutes on waiver of counsel, it also upheld the trial court's determination that Lanett was incompetent to make a voluntary, knowing, and intelligent waiver of counsel because of her mental condition.

Credibility of testimony was a major issue in the case involving the celebrated New York City homeless person known under the pseudonym of Billie Boggs (95). At Boggs's initial commitment hearing, a psychiatrist and a social worker, who had seen Boggs on the streets, and the hospital's treating psychiatrist all testified that Boggs was psychotic and satisfied the criteria for involuntary hospitalization. Three other psychiatrists retained by the Civil Liberties Union, who had seen Boggs only in the hospital after she had been cleaned up, said that she was not dangerous to herself or to others and therefore did not satisfy criteria for commitment under the statute relied on by the state. The trial judge was influenced by Boggs's appropriate appearance in court more than by the testimony of those who had seen her on the streets and released her. The state appellate court disagreed, relying on the detailed testimony about her community behavior, which had been well documented over an extended period. The appellate court reversed the trial court's dismissal of commitment proceedings.

CHANGES IN COMMITMENT STATUTES

Beginning with California's Lanterman–Petris–Short Act in 1969 (96), state legislatures revised their commitment codes to conform with the new dangerousness criteria and procedural reforms that courts were mandating. Although many factors have contributed to deinstitutionalization (24,97), the rejection of clinical standards for commitment has become a focus of criticism from clinicians who feel that dangerousness standards have led to commitment of untreatable patients and to failure to commit others who would benefit from hospitalization.

These critics have increasingly argued for a return to clinically based commitment criteria. In 1975, Alan Stone first articulated the concept of a guardianship model of commitment (98), which was later organized into draft statutory language by Loren Roth (99) and finally approved as policy of the American Psychiatric Association (APA) (100). Under these criteria, dangerousness is irrelevant to commitment. Instead, commitment is based on presence of a severe mental disorder, significant distress or loss of functioning, treatability, incompetence to make treatment decisions, and a risk-benefit analysis favoring treatment.

Supporters of this clinical or guardianship approach argue that such criteria would create a better fit between patients and treaters and would not result in the clinically inappropriate admissions often seen under "dangerousness" standards. Predictably, civil libertarians have opposed "guardianship" criteria, arguing that dangerousness is constitutionally required for commitment (101). Appelbaum (102), defending the guardianship model, has countered that the courts did not rule out commitment based on a need for treatment but rather held that prereform statutes were impermissibly broad and vague.

Critics of need-for-treatment or guardianship standards have argued that such standards inevitably would result in a return to the days of warehousing and abuse (101). Data from Washington State, the first state to broaden its gravely disabled criteria to approach the APA's standard (103), demonstrated that inpatient censuses doubled in a year (104). Critics of the need-for-treatment approach have argued that this confirms that any relaxation of strict commitment criteria would result in a deluge of admissions (105,106). Some of these same critics acknowledge, however, that the pressure to increase admissions in Washington came largely from community response to tragedies involving mental patients and that half the increase in the inpatient census *preceded* the new commitment criteria (105). Maier (107) and Fisher and colleagues (108) identified similar phenomena in Wisconsin and New York State as well as in Washington State; and Fisher and colleagues (108) have concluded that statutory changes may not be required to effect changes in admission patterns, given the inherent flexibility of the existing statutes.

Nevertheless, community pressure and continued criticism from clinicians and advocacy groups such as the Alliance for the Mentally Ill have renewed the debate on commitment criteria in legislatures across the country. North Carolina changed its statutes in 1981 to include a presumption that patients are unable to care for themselves if they engage in grossly emotional or inappropriate behavior or display other signs of severely impaired insight and judgment (109). Similarly, Alaska broadened its definition of grave disability in 1984 to include persons who, as a result of mental illness, will, if not treated, suffer distress that impairs judgment, reason, or behavior, "causing a substantial deterioration of the person's previous ability to function independently" (110). Kansas passed legislation similar to Utah's in 1986, making inability to make treatment decisions necessary to commitment (111).

Legislation in Texas in 1987 created a new criterion for court-ordered temporary or extended mental health services. The statute provides for commitment when, as a result of mental illness, the person will, if not treated, continue to suffer severe and abnormal mental, emotional, or physical distress and will continue to experience deterioration of ability to function independently and is unable to make a rational and informed decision about whether to submit to treatment. For emergency detention or an order of protective custody, the examining physician must determine that the person is mentally ill and represents a substantial risk of serious harm to self or others if not immediately restrained. Risk of harm may be demonstrated either by the person's behavior or by evidence of severe emotional distress and deterioration in mental condition (112).

Montana's 50th legislature introduced need-for-treatment commitment criteria comparable to those proposed by the APA (113). It defined *mentally ill* to mean

> suffering from a mental disorder which has not resulted in self-inflicted injury or injury to others or the imminent threat thereof but which: (a) has resulted in behavior that creates serious difficulty in

> protecting the patient's life or health even with the available assistance of family, friends, or others; (b) is treatable, with a reasonable prospect of success and consistent with the least restrictive course of treatment . . . at or through the facility to which the person is to be committed; (c) has deprived the person of the capacity to make an informed decision concerning treatment; (d) has resulted in the person's refusing or being unable to consent to voluntary admission for treatment; and (e) poses a significant risk of the person's becoming seriously mentally ill [defined as requiring actual threats or dangerous acts], within the meaning of this section, or will, if untreated, predictably result in further serious deterioration in the mental condition of the person. Predictability may be established by the patient's medical history.

Most recently, a joint effort from the Colorado chapter of the Alliance for the Mentally Ill and the Colorado Psychiatric Society led to revisions in the Colorado commitment statutes (114,115). The changes expanded the definition of gravely disabled by providing that a mentally ill person being cared for at home may be hospitalized "if there is notice given that the support given by the family member or other individual who has a similar relationship to the person is to be terminated." To be hospitalized under this standard, patients must have a chronic mental disorder with psychotic features and must have been certified for treatment of the disorder at least twice within the previous 36 months. In addition, the patient must exhibit a "deteriorating course" (116). Jeffrey Metzner, a psychiatrist who co-chaired the task force that developed the revision, stated that the new law will apply only to a small population of chronic patients and will not require additional funds because it applies to patients who would predictably require hospitalization later if they continue to deteriorate, with even longer (and more expensive) hospitalizations (115).

Except for Washington State, the effects of these statutory changes have not yet been studied in any detail. Officials of the Utah Department of Mental Health have stated that they have observed few changes in commitment practice since the requirement for incompetency to make treatment decisions. Reports from the state mental health department in Texas indicate that few changes have been seen as a result of the legislation (personal communication, Legal Division, Texas Division of Mental Health and Mental Retardation, 28 July 1989).

Several researchers have attempted to predict the results of changes in commitment laws. The studies have typically been implemented by asking clinicians evaluating patients for commitment under existing dangerousness criteria also to rate their committability under need-for-treatment criteria. In the first such study (117), admitting psychiatrists were asked to rate patients committed under California's statutes. They reported that 90% of patients met four of the five APA criteria but that only 46% satisfied the requirement for a severe mental disorder. The study design did not permit the authors to estimate the number of patients who were not committable under dangerousness criteria who could have been committed under the APA criteria.

This deficiency has been remedied in two reports from an ongoing collaborative study from Massachusetts. In the first report (118), evaluating clinicians were asked to complete questionnaires on a study sample of both walk-in and emergency room patients. Data were available on 682 walk-in and 378 emergency patients. Of the 199 patients who were felt to meet existing Massachusetts criteria, only 52 met all the Stone-Roth criteria for commitment. The criteria of major distress and incompetent treatment refusal were the most restrictive. Of the 52 patients committable under the Stone-Roth criteria, 46 were also committable under the Massachusetts criteria. The authors acknowledged that in actual practice, clinicians might "fudge" the Stone-Roth criteria, just as they now do with dangerousness criteria.

In a follow-up study (119), the authors asked clinicians to rate prospective patients regarding whether they met the existing Massachusetts dangerousness criteria and regarding whether they would meet a strict interpretation of the Stone-Roth criteria. Of 503 patients evaluated in the emergency room, only 35 (7%) met all the Stone-Roth criteria. In this study, major distress and incompetency to make treatment decisions were the most restrictive criteria. Even if those criteria were eliminated, only 67 patients (13%) met the Stone-Roth criteria. Of patients committable under the Stone-Roth criteria, 32 of 35 also met the Massachusetts dangerousness criteria, whereas only 32 of 296 (11%) patients meeting the Massachusetts criteria also met the Stone-Roth criteria. The authors pointed out that the California study (117) used a narrower definition of severe mental illness that essentially limited it to psychosis, and therefore that this criterion was the most restrictive for them. They also pointed out that the data reported concerning the impact of the revised Washington statute (104,105) did not use the full Stone-Roth criteria because it omitted major distress and incompetence to make treatment decisions—the major factors in rejecting patients in their own studies.

STUDIES OF INVOLUNTARY HOSPITALIZATION

Empirical studies of civil commitment are not new. What is relatively new over the past 5 years is the growing number of studies that are significantly more comprehensive and sophisticated than their predecessors. Most previous studies involved limited investigations of commitment procedures at a single facility. These studies either documented the status quo or attempted to delineate the impact of changes in commitment laws (120). Several trends have been responsible for the advent of studies that provide statewide data and that attempt to consider a wide range of factors that might have affected the specific statutory changes or procedures studied.

One major factor in the change has been a growing interest in commitment procedures by sociologists such as Hiday (121) and Durham (105). Clinicians often have been constrained in their research efforts by limits on time and availability of resources, because research is not a major part of many clinicians' job descriptions. Social scientists, on the other hand, have research as a focus of their professional practice. Appreciating the need for more detailed investigations, social scientists have pursued grants to enable them to carry out such studies. Because sociologists are not usually affiliated with particular treatment facilities, they are more likely than are clinicians to extend their research to more than one site. Another factor has been an apparent increase in interest in research data on the part of state legislators. Although public pressure to revise commitment laws remains a significant antecedent to legislative action, more legislatures are commissioning research and inviting consultants to provide hard data on the impact of changes in statutes in other jurisdictions (106,122) or the results of previous changes in their own state (123) than had been the case.

One problem that has impeded progress in such research is the lack of statistical data available from state mental health departments. Another problem is that the success of deinstitutionalization has shifted the locus of treatment to the local rather than the state level in most jurisdictions, thus making comprehensive data collection more difficult.

Another impetus for the generation of more sophisticated research into constructs relevant to civil commitment has been the expansion of the courts into monitoring clinical practice beyond the decision about commitment. The progressive establishment of a right to refuse psychiatric treatment has generated a significant body of research that is at least a potentially useful data base for courts and legislatures facing the issue for the first time. Although the recognition of the basic right itself usually has been based on constitutional considerations, and thus has not been amenable to data-based decision making, empirical data are more relevant to the procedural regulations necessary to govern the implementation of the right.

Another growth area in research has been in the prediction of dangerousness. Clinicians have been criticized for making such predictions in the context of civil commitment (124) and capital punishment sentencing (125), and they have been held liable for failure to make such predictions in the context of patient harm to third parties. In response to both the criticisms and the potential liability, clinicians have called for more reliable research into the prediction of violence (10), and several groups have responded.

A group of researchers at the University of Oregon have done an excellent job of developing a conceptual framework for analysis of the civil commitment process and for applying that framework to empirical data. Faulkner et al. (126) created a three-step model of commitment to permit comparisons of research findings from different jurisdictions. The steps in the commitment process are *1*) the initial screening phase *2*) the investigation (probable cause) phase, and *3*) the hearing phase. Although involuntary civil commitment can be ordered only at step 3, release can occur at any step. The authors generated equations to depict the percentages of releases at any given step and applied them to data from Oregon from 1977 through 1983. They concluded that in that jurisdiction, the most significant decision-making step was screening, which accounted for 58% of releases, whereas investigation led to 31%, and hearings only to 12%. Of persons entering the system, 84% were released at one step or another. The Oregon model permits comparative research between jurisdictions, and it can serve to guide policymakers when they want to change a system. For example, if policymakers wished to decrease commitments, they would see that changing the hearing would be the least effective way to do so. One weakness of this model, however, is that it assumes that the three phases are independent variables, when in fact it is most probable that decisions at the preliminary stages are based in part on the stricter commitment criteria in effect at the final hearing.

In another application of their method, the University of Oregon research group studied commitment in one Oregon county between 1977–78 and 1982–83 (127). The researchers combined data available from the state with interviews of staff of one community mental health center and investigations of specific changes affecting that center, including changes in staffing, judges, and patient characteristics. Significant changes occurred in 1981–82. The numbers of patients increased at each step of the process except initial holds by police. Changes in judges had little effect. When budget cuts forced less experienced clinical staff to perform the screenings, there were fewer attempts to divert patients to local or outpatient services, and commitments increased. When the state realized that state hospital commitments were increasing significantly from that county, it made strong recommendations that the county go back to diverting more patients. Diversions increased again, and commitments returned to the previous baseline. The authors cite this study as support for their position that changes in commitment rates are highly dependent on system changes and local factors.

In another study, the Oregon group examined the economic costs of commitment (128). They argued that the time before formal commitment must also be considered, because this factor varies widely from jurisdiction to jurisdiction. To examine this factor, they modified the equations from their three-step model to consider detention times and costs of detention. They point out that increasing the prehearing time—at which the greatest number of patients are released—might permit more diversion and thus an overall saving of money. They demonstrate their methodology by making illustrative calculations from Oregon data.

Finally, the Oregon group studied the use of emergency commitment in detail in one Oregon county to analyze the effects of the establishment and then demise of a treatment facility (129). In 1981–82, the study county's commitment rate was half the state average, but the emergency commitment rate was over five times the state average. More than 50% of all commitments were brought under the emergency provisions. There was no local treatment facility that would accept patients detained under the regular commitment process, and the police would not transport patients to the state hospital because it took three trips, due to additional hearings in the referring county. But they would transport patients for emergency hospitalization, which took only one trip. When a local detention and treatment facility was established in 1983, nonemergency detentions rose from 0% to 43%, but then dropped back to 0% when the facility was closed less than a year later because of economic problems. Because emergency commitments to the state hospital tended to be much longer than local commitments (under which most patients were dismissed after fewer than 5 days), the total cost of regular commitment was over four times the cost for emergency hospitalization. The authors emphasize the significant impact of such idiosyncratic local conditions on the commitment system.

Advocacy Services

It is clear from the research on the impact of changes in statutes that the advent of active, adversarial representation of patients facing involuntary civil commitment has had the most significant impact of any of the substantive or procedural changes enacted over the past 20 years (24). Legal changes such as the replacement of need-for-treatment by dangerousness as the major determinant of committability and the provision of most of the rights already afforded criminal defendants have certainly been important. None would have meant much, however, if attorneys had not been available to ensure that the rights established by court decision or statute were in fact provided in court.

Once adversarial representation in commitment hearings was established statutorily (23), if not always effectively in practice (130), it became increasingly apparent that patients' needs for legal services did not end with the commitment hearing. Two major types of advocacy service delivery systems have developed over the past 10–15 years to extend the protections initiated by legal representation at commitment hearings. One has grown from a recognition that protection of patients' rights within treatment facilities cannot be taken for granted without continued advocacy or ombudsman services. Just as states have reformed the procedures governing the process of commitment itself, most have also passed patients' bills of rights guaranteeing, for example, the least restrictive environment necessary for their treatment and the right to appropriate treatment, as well as the civil rights of voting and sending and receiving mail.

Two main types of advocacy programs developed in the 1970s. Wald and Friedman (131) have characterized them as "rights oriented" and "service oriented." Rights-oriented advocates tend to conceptualize the problems facing mental patients in terms of violation of civil rights, and they tend to adopt an adversarial posture toward the mental health bureaucracy, which they typically view as responsible for the deprivations. Rights-oriented rhetoric tends to be "abolitionist" with respect to any type of coerced involvement with mental health service providers. Rights advocates have invested particularly in right-to-refuse-treatment suits. Service-oriented advocates, on the other hand, have been more interested in obtaining adequate treatment and social resources for patients. Their predominant activity has been in the right-to-treatment area.

Scheingold (132) defined the "myth of rights" as an ideology that emphasizes the effectiveness of litigation as a strategy for social change. He criticized this conceptualization of rights because he felt that it leads to overvaluation of the legal process and to a fragmentation of social problems that hinders their solution, and because it discourages examination of the power of the law itself.

Milner (133) further divided the rights-oriented approach as it has been adopted by former mental patient advocacy groups. He contrasted Scheingold's "myth of rights" litigation approach, in which issues are narrowly defined to fit into a legal framework and in which the procedures are under the control of professionals, to the "direction action" or "liberation ideology" approach, in which the issues are broader, institutions are attacked rather than used, and peers rather than professionals are the most important reference group. Lawyers are less central to the direct-action approach, as even the most zealous tend to be pragmatic and willing to compromise rather than to pursue the rigid abolitionist position adopted by militant ex-patients.

Many early advocacy programs were created independently of the facilities to which they were to provide services. Some had considerable difficulty gaining entrance to mental health facilities, and others were expelled after being granted initial access, because they challenged the existing procedures. Programs that undertook only to provide legal services unrelated to the condition of patients' confinement met with considerably less resistance from clinicians and facility administrators.

Brakel (134) studied six such early advocacy programs and concluded that those that adopted a collaborative posture with facility staff were more successful in helping their clients gain their goals. He found that advocates who attempted to work with rather than against the facility staff and administration were able to provide legal services external to the facility and to facilitate changes in the program more effectively.

One program favorably reviewed was the Legal Assistance for Institutionalized Persons (LAIP) program, a pioneering work-study program developed at the University of Wisconsin Law School. In this program, law students under the supervision of practicing attorneys were assigned to provide legal services to clients at state correctional and mental health facilities. The terms of the contract with the Wisconsin Department of Health and Social Services precluded dealing with conditions-of-confinement issues, thus removing the major source of confrontation with the institutional staffs and administration.

In one experimental version of this program, students at two mental health facilities were assigned to the unit treatment teams and did not operate independently of the staff (135). Students thus were given the opportunity to learn firsthand of the complexities of providing direct services and arranging for aftercare for acutely mentally ill clients. The students were expected to abide by team decisions, including those calling for legal action. In their evaluations, the students assigned to this experiment indicated that they felt the in-depth experience helped them place advocacy issues in a broader perspective, enabling them to be more effective with mentally disordered clients.

Lamb (136) also argued in favor of an advocacy program that is collaborative rather than adversarial. He gave examples from his experience in which he felt advocates had lost sight of their goal of providing the most effective services possible to their clients by pursuing a preconceived antagonism toward service providers. Lamb argued that advocates should be *required* to work in mental health treatment facilities to gain personal experience before they are allowed to assume the authority and responsibility of advocacy. He argued that advocates should be supervised by the mental health administration of the facilities to which they provide services; to do otherwise would assume malice on the part of service providers.

Appelbaum (137) made the same point with respect to federal advocacy litigation (138), which also calls for the creation of advocacy programs independent of the mental health system. Ziegenfuss (139) contrasted the external advocacy confrontational approach with the internal advocacy collaborative approach. He argued that if true improvements for patients are to occur, advocates must adopt a systems approach—not a case-by-case approach, which necessarily ignores the effects of a decision on other patients and staff.

These arguments were disputed by two practicing advocates (140), who argued that an adversarial posture is absolutely necessary, both to win the confidence of clients and to effect any significant changes in institutional practices. The practicing advocates pointed to their success in a Massachusetts program in which they used both collaboration with and litigation against the facility to aid their clients. They also disagreed strongly with Lamb's position, holding that advocates must be administratively independent of the mental health facilities to which they provide services lest they be "co-opted" by the clinicians.

The first generation of patient advocacy cases in the 1960s and 1970s involved challenges to a lack of basic civil rights and to appalling conditions in state mental hospitals. Patient advocates had a series of victories in courts and legislatures, but they have had to continue their advocacy in the context of continually decreasing resources for the mentally ill at all levels. Thus, as Rubenstein (141) argued, the conflicts between liberty and paternalism have receded as issues of providing appropriate services have come into the foreground. Rubenstein also argued that the gap between advocates and clinicians has narrowed. That is, most lawyers are likely to accept the efficacy of at least some psychiatric treatments, and most clinicians support most patients' rights except perhaps the right to refuse treatment. The two groups can and have cooperated in various legal and social projects to increase community-based resources for mental patients. Rubenstein also noted that the demonstrable advances in professional practice have increased the vulnerability of individuals and institutions to tort litigation. This increased vulnerability will be a major factor in second-generation legal advocacy. Moreover, although it would seem that everyone could agree that society needs high-quality mental health services, some advocates continue to oppose greater latitude for clinical decision making because it accepts the legitimacy of commitment and mental illness. Other psychiatrists oppose broadening the scope of clinical responsibility because it might increase their liability when they must compromise between ideal standards of care and available resources.

Perlin, speaking in 1982 as the director of New Jersey's advocacy services (130), predicted that the 1980s would see no retrenchment in rights because state courts would take up the mantle of protectiveness abandoned by the federal judiciary. He believed that the courts would continue to examine details, such as definitions of dangerousness, in greater depth and that the courts would continue to explore the right to refuse psychiatric treatment as well as the conditions within treatment facilities. Other areas that he expected to receive attention from advocates included the rights of mentally handicapped inmates in the criminal justice system and criminal aspects of procedures in mental health settings. Finally, Perlin emphasized the importance of advocacy for treatment and of social rights of mental patients in the community.

Freddolino and Appelbaum (142) distinguished *rights protection*—the effort to preserve rights already won—from *advocacy*—the effort to enhance and expand those rights. They reported that 85% of the budgets for rights protectors come from governments, which also are responsible for providing mental health services, a situation that clearly creates potential conflicts of interest. Freddolino and Appelbaum argued that in the current era of diminishing resources for all mental health services—for treatment as well as for advocacy—advocates will need to guard against the squandering of mental health and advocacy resources. They suggest that ex-patient and family advocacy services might rely less on governmental funding and might be encouraged to expand their services. They also urged that cooperation between advocates and service providers without co-optation of either group must increase if resources are not to be wasted in fruitless battles between those charged with the clinical and legal care of patients.

Milner (133) has pointed out, however, that significant ideological differences remain among various groups concerned with the rights of mental patients. Militant patient groups remain committed to total abolition of involuntary commitment and treatment and are strongly opposed to any collaboration with either service providers or advocates whose goals include improvement in psychiatric services. Some advocates and clinicians also support the abolitionist position, and their impact remains out of proportion with their numbers. At the other end of the spectrum, a number of clinicians remain opposed even to the patient rights that have already been established. These clinicians tend to be older and more conservative, and they often have significant power within organized psychiatry. They refuse to cooperate with advocates and refuse to support legal compromises to avoid ending up with even less favorable outcomes.

Commitment to Outpatient Treatment

Since the early case reports from North Carolina (143,144), there has been considerable discussion in the clinical, and more recently the legal, literature concerning the involuntary civil commitment of mentally ill persons to treatment in the community. It has become clear that for a variety of reasons, the focus of the debate in many states has shifted from involuntary hospitalization to outpatient commitment. First, deinstitutionalization has shifted the focus of the controversy concerning compulsory treatment to the community, because that is where the great majority of patients are now found. Initial predictions that involuntary treatment would not be necessary in the community (145) have not been fulfilled. Complicating the issue, fewer than half of the proposed community mental health centers were actually built (146). Moreover, a majority of the centers that were built chose to provide services chiefly for patients other than the deinstitutionalized and the never-hospitalized chronically mentally ill (147). Many of the centers were organized along the lines of traditional private practices, and thus did not place emphasis on services such as transportation to the facility and outreach capabilities, which are essential for patients who are willing to accept services but are unable to take advantage of them for logistical reasons. Finally, it is clear that many patients have been as unwilling to participate in voluntary outpatient treatment as they were to seek hospitalization, even when that outpatient treatment is convenient and effective.

Because of the problems resulting from deinstitutionalization, a number of clinicians and legislators realized that structured treatment in the community would be necessary for some chronically mentally ill persons. Under the doctrine of the least restrictive alternative (148), most states had revised their statutes in the 1970s to include the possibility of commitment to other than inpatient psychiatric facilities.

Patients Suitable for Outpatient Commitment

The major population for which outpatient commitment is clinically appropriate is the group of chronically mentally ill persons with severe psychiatric disorders that result in clinical deterioration satisfying criteria for involuntary hospitalization and who respond well to medication but repeatedly discontinue their medication on discharge. They constitute the majority of the "revolving door" patient population that has led to a significant increase in admissions to hospitals in the face of declining censuses in those hospitals.

Court-ordered outpatient treatment may be necessary for many chronic patients to change the long-established patterns of deterioration and rehospitalization that existed before community mental health centers were established. Many such patients and their families learned to depend on the hospital as a refuge from each other during exacerbations of the patient's psychotic disorder, and these families and patients did not adapt to the availability of community resources created to prevent such problems. Often this lack of response was caused by a lack of transportation to the center or by the fact that centers often have waiting lists, whereas hospitals accept patients 24 hours a day, 7 days a week. Sometimes such families simply waited until the patient became sufficiently ill to warrant hospitalization, and the matter would be out of their hands. Court-ordered commitment to outpatient treatment in such cases may be necessary to educate patients and their families about the availability of community resources and to interrupt cycles of unnecessary hospitalization.

Compulsory medication is obviously the easiest type of compulsory treatment to implement, because medication does not require the active cooperation of patients to be effective. Yet there also are reports in the literature of cases in which commitment has facilitated psychodynamic treatment as well (149). Commitment is bilateral—the facility is as committed to providing treatment as the patient is to receiving it (perhaps the major source of the resistance of many outpatient clinicians to treating committed outpatients). Patients who have experienced repeated rejections and have difficulty in trusting the dedication of their therapists may well be reassured by being committed to a therapist or clinic (147).

The Conditional Release Model

Before the widespread procedural reforms in civil commitment statutes in the 1970s, there was little review of commitments once patients had been involuntarily hospitalized. When patients were considered capable of release from the hospital, they commonly were first placed on "trial visit" status rather than discharged outright. The hospital superintendent thus had the authority to order their rehospitalization without a formal hearing and without having to justify the decision to any external authority. Many hospitals placed all patients on such trial passes rather than discharging them. This system of informal conditional release was the model for the current predominant system of outpatient commitment. Under this system, patients are initially hospitalized. At subsequent hearings, judges have the authority to continue involuntary hospitalization, to commit patients to outpatient treatment, or to release patients outright.

The conditional release model of outpatient commitment has been available statutorily in all states except New York for years (150). Even in New York, informal arrangements, similar to plea bargaining in the criminal justice system, allow outpatient commitment to occur there as well (151). Until recently few states used these provisions as meaningful alternatives to involuntary hospitalization, however. The majority of respondents to a 1984 survey of state mental health program directors and attorneys general demonstrated ignorance of the procedures used in their states (150). Many did not even know that outpatient commitment was statutorily authorized, and few reported that it was used in more than 5% of cases of commitment in their jurisdictions.

Until recently, one major reason for the lack of use of statutes permitting conditional release from hospitalization was the lack of procedural options available to deal with noncompliant patients. Under the old "trial visit" system, patients were technically still on hospital censuses, and rehospitalization was the logical response to deterioration or noncompliance with treatment. After dangerousness became required as a criterion for involuntary commitment, however, conditional release began to receive judicial scrutiny because of the liberty interests involved. One federal district court (152) went so far as to declare that even "trial visit" status was unconstitutional, holding that if patients are sufficiently nondangerous to be released from the hospital, the state no longer has justification for keeping them under commitment.

Other courts have come to different conclusions. The Wisconsin Court of Appeals explicitly upheld that prevention of clinical deterioration and revolving-door admissions justified extended outpatient commitment, even in the absence of overt dangerousness (153). The Idaho Supreme Court upheld the state statutes that directed that all commitments are up to the Department of Health, with the site of that treatment left up to the department (154).

Unfortunately, few statutes have provided adequate procedural regulations to deal with patients who do not comply with court-ordered treatment. Community commitments are far more complex logistically than involuntary hospitalization. There is first a major jurisdictional issue—judges who preside at commitment hearings may not have the authority to authorize or order law enforcement officers in different counties to assume custody of noncompliant patients, unless state statutes specify this clearly. It is still not clear in most states what options are available to deal with noncompliant outpatients. The most frequently used option remains rehospitalization, which of course vitiates the purpose of commitment to outpatient treatment.

Case Law on Outpatient Commitment

Some courts have ruled that revocation of outpatient status presents a sufficient loss of liberty to require a judicial hearing before rehospitalization for patients committed to outpatient treatment under either criminal (155–157) or civil (158–162) statutes. The Rhode Island Supreme Court (163) and a Florida state appeals court (164) have required evidence of dangerousness before revocation of outpatient commitment could be allowed.

The California Court of Appeals held that a prior hearing was necessary unless the patient was dangerous in the community (165). Some courts have required periodic review of the justification for continued outpatient commitment (166,167). Others, however, have held that revocation of outpatient commitment without a prior hearing was acceptable (157,168–172). The Mississippi Supreme

Court, for example, held that the "decision whether to keep a mental patient in a state hospital or to discharge him is not to be decided by a court, but must remain a medical decision, to be decided by medical experts" (173). The Washington Supreme Court (174), the California Court of Appeals (170), and the North Dakota Supreme Court (175) have upheld their state statutes permitting rehospitalization of persons committed to outpatient treatment if they did not comply with their treatment plans. Many of these decisions turned on whether or not outpatient commitment was seen as sufficiently similar to criminal parole to come under the requirements for prior hearings set forth by the U.S. Supreme Court in *Morrissey v. Brewer* (176).

The Court of Appeals for the District of Columbia has taken an intermediate position. It has held that the liberty interests of patients committed to outpatient treatment are qualitatively different from those of patients who have not been committed, and that a temporary rehospitalization for evaluation and stabilization when patients deteriorate *or* are noncompliant is acceptable without a prior hearing (172). In other cases, however, it held that indefinite rehospitalization could not be based on noncompliance alone, but requires a showing of dangerousness, albeit by less than the original clear and convincing evidence standard required for involuntary hospitalization (177,178). It also held that to revoke a commitment to outpatient treatment, the state had to prove that no less restrictive alternative to inpatient treatment existed (178,179).

Another option to deal with noncompliance that has been discussed in several states, and actually attempted in one, is to cite noncompliant patients with contempt of the court order mandating the outpatient treatment. But in one case, a Florida state appellate court ruled that a patient's noncompliance with court-ordered outpatient treatment did not demonstrate "contemptuous intent," and it voided the contempt finding by a trial court (164). However effectual such strategies might be from a legal standpoint, both the legal and therapeutic communities should recognize that a major goal of outpatient commitment is to encourage the eventual development of an effective therapeutic relationship with treatment-resistant patients that will encourage them to accept treatment willingly. Adversarial legal confrontations between therapists and patients generally will undermine this collaborative relationship and hence are to be avoided as much as possible.

A far more clinically effective alternative to rehospitalization would be to authorize local law enforcement officers to take custody of noncompliant patients and take them to the facility to which they were committed for the treatment to be provided. The data, although still largely anecdotal at this stage, indicate that most patients will accept treatment under such conditions. The legal problems involved in this approach can be resolved rather simply in principle, although there has been significant opposition from law enforcement organizations in some jurisdictions because of the prospect of having to spend more of their time in transporting mental patients. One community mental health center in North Carolina has dealt with this problem by having a number of its staff formally deputized, so that they have the authority (as well as the expertise and interest) to provide such transportation. There has been opposition to this proposal from patient advocates, on the grounds that no action involving the assumption of physical custody of outpatients should be taken without a prior court hearing. To date, there are no reported court decisions dealing specifically with this issue.

Committed Outpatients' Right to Refuse Treatment

A major obstacle to successful treatment under outpatient commitment appears to be how to deal with patients who continue to refuse court-ordered treatment with psychotropic medication once they are committed to outpatient centers. Earlier articles suggested that treatment refusal was largely caused by conditions in public mental hospitals, rather than by rejection of treatment as such (145). Later studies have demonstrated convincingly, however, that refusal of treatment largely stemmed from denial of illness (49,180–182) and that the treatment site has little correlation with acceptance or rejection of medication.

No court has yet dealt explicitly with the right of patients committed to outpatient care to refuse court-ordered psychotropic medications. The Massachusetts Supreme Court has held that a legal guardian cannot override a ward's refusal of psychotropic medication without a separate judicial determination that the ward is incompetent to make such treatment decisions (182). Taken together with the court's final decision in the *Rogers* case (58), it appears clear that a judicial determination of incompetency to make treatment decisions would be necessary in Massachusetts before outpatients could be ordered to take medication without their informed consent. The language in other state court decisions concerning the right to refuse treatment would also seem to apply to outpatients as well, particularly as there is an understandable presumption that persons capable of being released from a hospital should be more competent to make treatment decisions than those requiring continued inpatient treatment.

Unlike treatment in inpatient settings, however, where containment is provided and staff are trained in the management of aggressive patients, physical coercion is impractical in most outpatient settings, both for logistical reasons and because of the principled resistance of the majority of outpatient clinicians to using any coercion—much less physical force—in the treatment of their patients. The task force report to the American Psychiatric Association on involuntary outpatient treatment (183) recommends against such force in administration of medication.

This recommendation has been criticized by a psychiatrist at one outpatient facility, who argued that without the capacity to force medication, the court-ordered treatment plan would be impossible to implement in practice (184). This argument ignores the strong resistance from many outpatient clinicians and from civil libertarians. Such resistance has been demonstrated sufficient to defeat outpatient commitment legislation (185).

More substantively, several studies from North Carolina, which has pioneered changes in outpatient commitment, have demonstrated that physical force is seldom necessary in practice to ensure compliance with court-ordered medication. In the first study, Hiday and Goodman (143) reported that even without a comprehensive statute establishing procedures for dealing with noncompliance, the great majority of patients complied with their treatment plans. Miller and Fiddleman (144) reported that although community clinicians remained skeptical of outpatient commitment after reform legislation, they rated a number of cases as successful because patients continued taking medication that they had refused after previous discharges.

Finally, after 1983 statutory revisions that provided for initial commitment to outpatient treatment without a showing of imminent dangerousness, Hiday concluded that physical coercion was unnecessary. Her large-scale study showed that although 80% of patients refused medications at least once during the 6-month study period, 80% were still in treatment at the centers and were generally compliant with medication at the end of the study (186). In conclusion, it appears that a valid court order, even without the provision of practical remedies for noncompliance, is sufficient to persuade the great majority of patients to follow their court-ordered treatment plans, including those requiring psychotropic medications.

Need-for-Treatment Criteria in Outpatient Commitment

In most states, commitment to inpatient or outpatient treatment requires dangerousness. Critics of outpatient commitment, both clinicians (187) and legal scholars (188), have argued that outpatient commitment therefore is impossible, because if persons are as dangerous as the statute requires for commitment, they cannot be safely maintained in the community at all, even under commitment. One successful response to this argument has been to assert that the commitment is justified by the fact that without the continued supervision and treatment promised by the commitment, the patient would rapidly become dangerous again and thus would satisfy the dangerousness criteria for commitment. Such arguments have been accepted by courts in several states (153,165,172).

This argument has also been used as the basis for statutory revisions in several states that codify it into explicitly different criteria for commitment to inpatient and outpatient treatment. Such statutes (189,190) do not permit reliance solely on generalized clinical predictions of deterioration leading to dangerousness but rather require that the prediction be substantiated by the past history of the patient in question. Such criteria limit this type of conditional release to patients who have had previous hospitalizations and unsuccessful attempts at outpatient follow-up, and these criteria thus do not apply to patients new to the system. Data from North Carolina (186) indicate that courts frequently ignore the strict criteria in practice when continued supervision is recommended by the hospital staff. Even if the criteria were strictly applied, however, conditional release would still be available for the population of chronically mentally ill patients for whom the system is chiefly designed.

If need for treatment is the major criterion for commitment to outpatient treatment, and psychotropic medication is a necessary part of that treatment, as it will be for the great majority of such patients, then it is essential that the issue of competency to make treatment decisions be determined at the time of the initial commitment. This will avoid unworkable commitments, which frustrate patients and clinicians and undermine effective delivery of care.

Initial Commitment to Outpatient Treatment

Although most states continue to use outpatient commitment only in the conditional release mode, a few have recently experimented with explicit provisions for initial commitment to outpatient treatment, without going through a phase of hospitalization. Such provisions are designed to avoid hospitalization altogether when it is clinically unnecessary. Under such provisions, pioneered by North Carolina (189) and Hawaii (190), and adopted in some form in Georgia (191), Vermont (192), Montana (193), and Arkansas (194), a hearing is held in the community before any action is taken, and the procedure can lead only to outpatient commitment or release. Patients who meet current dangerousness criteria in most states generally will require hospitalization for effective treatment. For initial outpatient commitment to be possible, therefore, it needs to be based either on need-for-treatment criteria or on predictions that without the proposed treatment the patient would deteriorate to a state of dangerousness that would justify involuntary hospitalization.

Because mandatory outpatient treatment involves a lesser intrusion into personal liberty than does involuntary hospitalization, the arguments in support of need-for-treatment criteria would seem to be even more applicable to outpatient commitment than to involuntary hospitalization. But legal analysis often focuses on the immediate choices—that is, coerced outpatient treatment versus freedom from external control—rather than on the avoidance of greater future restriction and clinical suffering. Thus, to date, no jurisdiction has adopted outpatient commitment criteria based solely on the desire to prevent predictable clinical deterioration. The rather loose definitions of "gravely disabled" in many statutes, however, permit the courts to use a need-for-treatment standard in practice when judges defer to clinical judgment, and such judges are still in the majority at the trial court level.

The revised Georgia statutes (191) provide for outpatient commitment if such treatment is available, if the person is likely to comply with it, and if it will minimize the likelihood of hospitalization. Patients who fail to comply with attendance at the initial hearing or with the treatment ordered are subject to hospitalization. The Vermont statutes (192) provide that the court may order the person to receive whatever treatment other than hospitalization is appropriate for 90 days. If at any time during that period it becomes apparent either that the patient is not complying with the court order or that the alternative treatment has not been adequate, the court may order another hearing. The court may then modify its original order and direct the patient to undergo another program of alternative treatment for the remainder of the 90-day period; alternatively, the court may enter a new order directing that the patient be hospitalized for the remainder of the 90-day period.

Revisions in 1989 to the Montana statutes (193) provide that if a person is found at the hearing to be "mentally ill" (as previously defined to require a prediction of deterioration, but not imminent dangerousness), the patient may be committed for treatment to any facility commensurate with the least-restrictive-alternative principle. The court may order treatment but may not authorize use of physical force to administer medication to an outpatient. The only alternative provided if the court determines that the patient has been noncompliant with treatment is to continue the order for the remainder of the treatment period.

Although still following the conditional release model, Tennessee (195) provides for outpatient commitment under the following criteria: *1*) the patient's condition is likely to deteriorate rapidly to the point where serious harm is likely unless treatment is continued; *2*) the patient is likely to participate in outpatient treatment when under legal obligation to do so and unlikely to participate in outpatient treatment without such an obligation; and *3*) mandatory outpatient treatment is a suitable, less drastic alternative to involuntary hospitalization. The statute provides for communication between hospital and outpatient treater without patient consent and also that the proposed treatment plan must be agreed upon by both hospital and outpatient facility and approved by the court. If the patient is found noncompliant with the treatment and unlikely to immediately comply, the court may order rehospitalization.

Liability Associated With Treating Committed Outpatients

In the post-*Tarasoff* era there is a realistic fear that the risk of civil liability may be increased for clinicians treating committed outpatients. Outpatient clinicians are already expected to exercise a much greater degree of control over their voluntary patients than in the past. It is logical to assume that the courts would hold them to an even higher standard for control of patients committed to their supervision and care. This reasoning has already been adopted by at least one court in the case of an insanity acquittee (196).

Various remedies for this potential liability have been implemented. The Michigan Supreme Court held that state hospital employees have absolute immunity against liability for release decisions (197). However, it is unlikely that such immunity would be extended to clinicians treating committed outpatients, because they are usually employees of local governments. Also, most courts have rejected governmental immunity, even for state employees (198).

Although a number of states have statutorily limited liability for patient harm to third parties, only Arizona has specifically addressed committed outpatients by providing immunity from liability for patient acts toward third parties only for hospital medical directors who place patients on conditional release, as long as the directors act in accordance with the requirements of the statute in deciding to place patients in the community (199). The statute continues the hospital's authority over such patients, including the power to rehospitalize, but it does not provide immunity from liability for the outpatient clinicians treating the patients.

Although a number of jurisdictions still have neither statutes nor case law that clarify clinicians' responsibilities toward potential victims of their patients, it would be prudent to expect that such decisions will be forthcoming and that they will be likely to establish some such duty for outpatient clinicians in general. States wishing to use outpatient commitment as a less restrictive alternative to involuntary hospitalization should consider the policy advantages of providing some specific immunity from liability for those treating committed outpatients.

Field Studies of Outpatient Commitment

A number of empirical studies of outpatient commitment have been recently reviewed (200). Favorable reports have come from North Carolina (143,186,201), Washington, D.C. (202,203), Wisconsin (151), Arizona (204), and New Mexico (205). Anecdotal case reports of effective use of coerced outpatient treatment have also appeared (149,206). Critical reports have appeared from North Carolina (144) and Tennessee (207). From all these studies it appears that the major factor in determining success or failure has been the willingness of the community clinicians to participate actively in the system.

Criticisms of Outpatient Commitment

The response to early reports of outpatient commitment from clinicians and some legal scholars has been generally favorable, with some caveats. Mulvey et al. (208) cautioned against a repetition of past experiences in which the combination of treatment and coercion has too often resulted in the balance shifting toward social control. They concluded that outpatient commitment offers advantages for the chronic, "revolving-door" patient population if the criteria and the procedures are carefully devised and implemented.

Geller (187) pointed out that the absence of effective procedures for dealing with noncompliant patients still characteristic of most outpatient statutes leads clinicians and judges alike to reject the concept as without effective power of implementation or to engage in leading patients to believe that they must comply with the ordered treatment simply because it is ordered by the judge, although in reality nothing will happen if they do not comply. This latter practice requires dishonesty between therapist and patient that, if discovered, may destroy a patient's trust in both therapy and legal justice.

Lamb and Mills (209), in their prescription for needed changes in the provision of treatment for the chronically mentally ill, advocated increased use of outpatient commitment as one method for preventing unnecessary hospitalizations and for preventing clinical deterioration. Brooks (210) identified three classes of patients who might be committed to outpatient treatment: *1*) those who would comply if encouraged, *and* if resources and assertive community clinicians were available; *2*) those who would not comply even if resources were available, because of denial of illness; and *3*) those who realize that medication reduces the symptoms of their illnesses, but find the illness preferable to the side effects of medication. Brooks concluded that outpatient commitment might well be justified for this subset of chronic patients but that the therapeutic community needs to pay careful attention to these patients' rights to avoid the abuses of eras when clinicians were unchecked by legal procedures.

Wilk (211) analyzed the potential impact of initial commitment to outpatient treatment on affected groups, including organized psychiatry, parents of chronic patients, the patients themselves, and nonmedical outpatient clinicians. Balancing liberty and treatment interests of patients, as well as concerns for caseloads and liability of community therapists, Wilk concluded that if adequate resources are provided in addition to appropriate guidelines for commitment, such procedures may provide benefits for a small but clinically and socially significant population of patients.

In the course of his criticisms of the APA's model commitment law (101), Leonard Rubenstein stated that "the most obvious safeguard against improper commitment, a judicial order for outpatient treatment, is nowhere to be found in the model law." This statement is accurate. Alan Stone, a principal author of the model statute, has acknowledged that he considered the issue of "prolonged legally mandated therapeutic intervention outside the hospital in a manner akin to the court-ordered conditional probation or parole allowed in the criminal justice system [but] rejected this as suggestive of the specter of the 'therapeutic state'" (212, p. 988). After initially apparently calling for the establishment of some system of court-ordered outpatient treatment, however, Rubenstein has later opposed it, at least in its prophylactic form (L. Rubenstein, personal communication, 1987).

Several authors have reviewed the embryonic case law on the conditional release model of outpatient commitment. Dougherty (213) simply reviewed decisions and did not comment. Call (214) concluded that courts have gone too far in protecting patients from their therapists and argued that current statutes that permit summary revocation of convalescent leave place clinicians in a legal bind—between allegations of violation of rights without due process and liability for actions of a patient not returned in time. Call argued that the responsibility and authority should reside in the outpatient treatment facility, not in the hospital from which patients are released. Because the decision to revoke outpatient commitment is basically a medical one, a prerevocation hearing in the community may be inappropriate and unnecessary. He suggested that the clinician responsible for the patient's *outpatient* treatment should be able to request that a judge revoke the leave without a hearing if the patient does not comply with the conditions of the outpatient treatment. A full adversarial hearing would be held only after rehospitalization.

Bartholf (215) pointed out that courts have not yet addressed the substantive issue of whether statutes that base outpatient commitment on prevention of deterioration are constitutional. Like some other critics, Bartholf misinterpreted *O'Connor v. Donaldson* (216) by saying that the decision held that "a person may not be involuntarily institutionalized unless he is proven to be dangerous to himself or others, or to be able to survive safely in freedom" (215, p. 13). Bartholf concluded that "unfortunately, while a strong libertarian approach may protect the rights of the mentally ill, it may also ensure that there is little practical utility in the use of mandatory outpatient treatment. . . . The solution, of course, is a sensible balance between the effective treatment of patients and their liberty interests" (215, p. 15).

More substantial criticisms have appeared recently from several attorneys, who concentrate on initial commitment, which they call "preventive commitment." Stefan (217) argued that broader commitment criteria have been justified not only on the basis of provision of treatment for "revolving-door" patients, lower costs of outpatient treatment as compared with hospitalization, and the increasing numbers of chronic patients who refuse voluntary community treatment, but also on the doctrine of least restrictive alternative, the growing number of treatment-refusing chronic patients who cannot be hospitalized under revised dangerousness criteria, a backlash against overlegalization of the mental health system, and advocacy by such groups as the Alliance for the Mentally Ill.

Stefan argued that without evidence of present dangerousness, the state's police power cannot be invoked, and, absent a finding of incompetence, neither should its parens patriae powers. She rejected existing need-for-treatment statutes, arguing that they are circular, defining incompetency in terms of inability to appreciate the need for treatment. Other criticisms include the lack of community resources, the double-agent conflict involved if the same professionals initiate commitment and provide treatment, and a lack of adversarial hearings before initial outpatient commitment. She argued that although preventive detention has been sustained in the federal courts, the decisions involved criminal defendants whose future dangerousness was arguably more predictable than civil committees. She also argued that outpatient commitment might be vulnerable to constitutional challenge on the grounds that the intrusion into privacy involved might not be justified by the state interests served and that there may be an argument against outpatient commitment based on the sufficiency of the incompetency findings justifying coerced treatment.

Stefan also argued that if adequate community treatment were provided, it would add to the roles of community mental health centers without providing additional resources; and, if the resources *are* provided, as they are in North Carolina, the proposed cost savings would not materialize.

The most vehemently negative article comes from Schwartz and Costanzo (188). Its polemical tone, in which sources (including court decisions) are misquoted or misinterpreted, and in which the motives of the proponents of outpatient commitment are impugned, unfortunately detracts from the validity of its analyses, and may serve to polarize those for and against the concept rather than to form the basis of a productive compromise. The authors find nothing acceptable about outpatient commitment, rejecting it as a therapeutic goal and seeing it only in terms of restriction on freedom from external coercion: "Even if it were restricted to those actually incapable of rendering informed treatment decisions, the concept [of outpatient commitment] nevertheless represents a return to the state-sanctioned restriction of nondangerous persons in order to further their supposed interests" (188, p. 1346). The tone of the article is all the more unfortunate because the principal author has demonstrated a far more moderate approach to the subject in verbal presentation than is evident in the article (218).

Although space does not permit a detailed analysis of the lengthy Schwartz and Costanzo article, several of its points need to be addressed. The arguments are made almost entirely from libertarian doctrine, with scant, or incorrect, citations to the existing research literature. For example, it cites Durham and LaFond's analysis of the impact of broadening criteria for involuntary hospitalization in Washington State (105) as the basis for predicting similar problems with outpatient commitment. But it ignores the data from North Carolina (186) that refute that prediction, as well as the fact that the increased hospitalizations in Washington State occurred over the strenuous objections of the clinicians at the hospitals, who had to be ordered by the state supreme court to continue to admit all committed patients.

Despite their partisan introduction, the authors make a number of important points about problems with outpatient commitment. These points include the lack of appropriate community programs to receive committed outpatients, the absence of procedures to regulate involuntary medication, the reluctance of providers to treat their clients involuntarily and to subject themselves to judicial supervision, the absence of judicial mechanisms and personnel to adequately supervise outpatient care, the fears of professionals concerning liability for inadequate treatment or foreseeable harm, and the resistance of neighbors and public officials to accept committed persons in their community. (This last problem, to the extent that it exists, would serve as a check on the inappropriately extensive use of outpatient commitment, a point ignored by the authors.) They also present as an objection that a system of outpatient commitment would require the creation of a governmental obligation to fund a comprehensive system of community services for individuals subject to such commitment, thus contradicting their previous call for increased resources.

The authors then discuss the system of voluntary outpatient care in one part of Massachusetts with which they are familiar, and they claim that this example proves that outpatient commitment is unnecessary. Although admitting that no research studies have been done, the authors cite directors of community mental health centers in the region (who have been demonstrated in other jurisdictions to be resistant to the concept on ideological grounds) as authority for their claim that outpatient commitment would be not only unnecessary but detrimental to patient care.

None of the authors' practical objections invalidate the concept of outpatient commitment, just as the comparable failure of deinstitutionalization does not invalidate the general concept of treatment in the community. But the authors do raise real problems that must be addressed if an outpatient commitment system is to be effective, as the North Carolina experience has demonstrated is possible. Other objections the authors present betray an unfamiliarity with, or distortion of, the research literature. Examples of such flawed scholarship are their allegations that committed individuals cannot effectively be compelled to comply with their treatment, and that few persons would comply with court-ordered treatment and yet be unwilling to voluntarily participate in a community program.

Summary

From the data presently available, it appears that commitment to outpatient treatment can be a very effective method of dealing with patients who respond well to treatment (both pharmacologic and psychodynamic) but who habitually stop treatment at the time of, or shortly after, discharge from hospitalization and deteriorate to the point of requiring rehospitalization. For outpatient commitment to be effective, however, a number of conditions must be satisfied.

First, and most important, there must be sufficient resources available at the outpatient facilities to which commitment is proposed. Such resources must include not only professionals adequately trained to deal with the biological, psychological, and social problems posed by chronic patients but also logistical support services necessary to ensure access to those resources, such as operating hours outside the typical 9 A.M. to 5 P.M. Monday–Friday times, transportation to the facility, and outreach visits to patients and their families in their homes. Many chronic patients have lost, or have never achieved, a level of autonomy that would be necessary for them to keep appointments and follow treatment plans independently (219). Family members often cannot provide transportation or support. Because support and transportation resources are expensive, clinics should not be expected to provide them without some additional governmental financial support. Simply providing these resources will eliminate the necessity for commitment in some cases, but of course some patients and their families will need the additional structure provided by a court order if the mentally ill person is to receive effective services on an outpatient basis and avoid deterioration and hospitalization.

Second, and almost as important, is a willingness—indeed, enthusiasm—on the part of the outpatient clinicians to serve this most difficult population, which by definition is (at least initially) uncooperative with treatment, and which drains clinic resources, usually without providing the financial incentives that clinics are forced to seek in an era of diminishing governmental and third-party support. The decreasing presence of psychiatrists in community mental health centers (220) has exacerbated the problem, because nonmedical clinicians tend to be less authoritarian (221), and therefore less comfortable with coerced treatment, even if they are quite willing to initiate inpatient commitments.

The traditional bipartite system of public mental health care (state hospitals and county outpatient facilities) also encourages "dumping" of patients from one system to the other, rather than continuity of care. This problem is still exacerbated in some states by restrictive confidentiality laws that prohibit effective sharing of information and cooperative treatment planning (222). Unified systems, such as the one that has existed in Washington, D.C., and also in the Veterans Administration system, encourages clinicians to make clinically appropriate placement decisions, because the same clinicians provide the treatment regardless of the site.

A successful system of outpatient commitment also requires procedures for timely hearings in the community for initial commitment and to deal with noncompliant patients, mandatory provisions for community input into court-ordered community treatment, and clear authority for law enforcement to assume custody of outpatients.

Criteria recommended by the APA's Task Force (183) include the following:

1. There must be a severe mental disorder requiring continued treatment in the community.
2. The treating therapist must make the judgment that the patient would survive safely in the community as long as treatment is continued.
3. The therapist must argue convincingly that deterioration is predictable if treatment is not continued (a history of patient noncompliance with treatment after release is useful, but it should not be absolutely required).
4. If sufficient evidence is presented that medication is necessary to prevent deterioration requiring hospitalization, the hearing officer should require medication as part of the treatment plan; medication should not be physically forced on an outpatient.
5. The treatment plan must be explicit about the obligations of the

patient and the treatment provider.

If need-for-treatment criteria are not politically acceptable in a particular jurisdiction, then the criteria should provide for commitment based on a prediction that involuntary outpatient treatment is necessary to prevent the patient from becoming sufficiently dangerous to require involuntary hospitalization. For noncompliant patients, the most effective response would be for the patient to be brought to the outpatient facility for the treatment. Rehospitalization should be a last resort, to be employed only if repeated efforts at community treatment fail.

The criticisms discussed above may have validity if commitments are made without clinical justifications for the proposed treatment and to facilities that lack the necessary resources to provide it. This is a criticism not of the concept of outpatient commitment as it has been outlined here but rather of the implementation by courts, which have often been too ready to order it without clinical justification, and of government, which has been unwilling to provide the necessary resources.

THE INTERNATIONAL PERSPECTIVE

Like the United States, most countries have long histories of paternalistic treatment of the mentally disordered by psychiatrists who are under little or no effective control by the legal system. The increased attention being paid to individual civil rights throughout the world over the past three decades has also had effects on the ways in which mental patients are treated in many countries, although the goals and methods involved in the changes have often differed from those in the United States.

Although there are certainly local variations, the current civil commitment system in the United States is largely rights-driven and is based on judicial interpretations of state and federal constitutions. Because of obvious abuses that occurred under the treatment-driven system in the United States, the need for reform became increasingly apparent. The first substantive challenges to involuntary commitment came from attorneys who conceptualized the problem as the deprivation of civil rights. Many were unalterably opposed to any form of coerced treatment. But realizing that commitment was too entrenched with both organized psychiatry and the public to be eliminated altogether, reformers set out to limit it as much as possible.

The first major approach used in this campaign was a shift from a parens patriae to a police power justification for commitment by the inclusion of dangerousness to self or others as a requirement for commitment. This was followed by the provision of procedural protections for persons facing commitment comparable to those afforded criminal defendants. The emphasis on protection from, rather than facilitation of, treatment dominated judicial and legislative concepts of commitment in the United States from the late 1960s through the 1970s.

Because of the greater integration of the European Economic Community that will occur in 1992, there has been some effort to reconcile the involuntary civil commitment laws of the various countries to conform with the European Declaration of Human Rights. Some of the changes in the European and Commonwealth countries are discussed below.

England

Although other countries have also revised their commitment statutes over the past 30 years in response to the need to correct abuses of public psychiatric hospitals, the rationales and the types of changes have often diverged from those in the United States. In England, for example, changes designed to protect patients from their psychiatrists were enacted well before the 1960s, in response to the lack of treatment provided in public mental hospitals. With the advent of effective treatments for the major psychotic mental disorders, public sentiment changed back toward a medical model and was codified in the 1959 Mental Health Act, which reinstated medical criteria for commitment and returned authority over the admission and discharge processes to psychiatrists.

Over the next 20 years, the United States' experiment with due process as a remedy to institutional abuses affected the debate in England. Led by the "new legalism" arguments of advocate Larry Gostin (223), and influenced by the European Human Rights Convention, proponents of the Mental Health (Amendment) Act of 1982 sought to provide the right to effective mental health services, protection of civil rights, and reduction of the discrimination against the mentally ill (224). In the amendment, dangerousness criteria were replaced by "serious mental illness requiring hospitalization." Patients with less severe disorders (such as personality disorders) also could be committed, but only if they met the requirement for protection of self or others. The authority to decide on admissions and discharges was again largely ceded to psychiatrists, except that powers of the quasi-judicial Mental Health Review Tribunals (which must include a lawyer, a psychiatrist, and a layperson) created under the 1959 Act have been expanded, and it is now required to review commitments at 14 days, 6 months, and every 3 years thereafter. As before, patients can petition for review of their commitment between these specified intervals. The tribunals have the authority to discharge patients against the advice of their treating psychiatrists. Patients may retain counsel for these hearings at their own expense.

A limited right to refuse treatment is recognized under the 1982 act. The right may be overcome without external review in emergency situations, but the definition of emergency, which includes prevention of clinical deterioration, has been criticized as amounting to elimination of the supposed protection (225). In nonemergency situations, patient refusal of psychotropic medications and ECT may be overridden through independent clinical review. The new act provides for patient refusal of treatments that are "hazardous, irreversible, or not fully established." Presently, psychotropic medications are not included in these categories.

Critics of the 1982 act point out that the tribunals have tended to defer to medical opinions (224). With the return to even more medically based criteria for commitment, there is little reason to believe that this will change. There is not yet a well-developed mental health bar in England to provide expert representation, and without a requirement for such representation it would have less impact than it has had in the United States, where such expertise exists.

Canada

Gordon and Verdun-Jones (225) point out that England and the Commonwealth countries traditionally have relied less on courts and constitutional laws than on parliaments for changes in social policy. In addition, the strong federalist traditions and a conservative national supreme court in Canada have left commitment policy largely to the various provinces until the passage of the Charter of Rights in 1982. That federal document addresses many of the same issues as does the United States Bill of Rights, but Canadian common-law tradition still relies more on an informed consent doctrine than a civil rights concept in deciding policy in the area of civil commitment.

The situation concerning the right to refuse treatment in Canada and the Commonwealth countries is similar to that in England (225). There is no national policy; 7 of the 10 provinces grant psychiatrists the explicit authority to treat committed patients, and one

(Prince Edward Island) grants an implicit authority. In Ontario, patients may refuse medications and ECT in nonemergency situations unless the treating psychiatrist appeals to the regional review board for an order authorizing involuntary treatment. However, because the board makes its decisions based on what it considers the "best interests" of the patient—not on whether the patient is competent to make treatment decisions—it is doubtful whether this "right to a second opinion" (226) is effective in providing more than a delay in treatment. In Nova Scotia, patients may refuse psychotropic medications unless the patient is declared incompetent by the treating psychiatrist. Once a patient is declared incompetent, consent for treatment may be given by a guardian, relative, or public trustee. Patients do have the right to appeal the psychiatrist's decision to the Provincial Review Board, where the issue of competency to make treatment decisions is the relevant issue. Similar provisions are found in South Australia. New Zealand, Scotland, and Australia (except for South Australia) appear to have recognized no formal right to refuse treatment at the time of this writing.

Australia

As in Canada, significant local variations in commitment law and practice exist in Australia (227). Because there is no national bill of rights, treatment regulations are established by local statutes. In New South Wales, the 1958 Mental Health Act expressed a preference for voluntary, community-based treatment but provided need-for-treatment commitment criteria and delegated major authority for admission, discharge, and treatment decisions to psychiatrists. Although "mental illness" is not defined in the 1983 revisions, the substantive criteria for the various types of dangerousness are specified in much greater detail than in comparable United States statutes. In addition to the familiar danger of physical harm, manic patients who might endanger their reputations or finances are specifically included under danger to self. Danger to others includes serious harassment as well as physical harm or threats. Physicians have the power to hospitalize patients, but a magistrate must review the process within 24 hours.

Representation by an attorney is mandated at this hearing, but not at subsequent release hearings. Procedural details of the hearing are much stricter under the revised law. The standard of proof has been elevated to "very high probability." Rules for the operation of the Mental Health Tribunal, which reviews commitments, are different under the new law. Representation by counsel is permitted, but not provided by the state; notice to the patient must be provided; the tribunal now has the power to subpoena witnesses; and automatic periodic review of patients' commitments is now required.

The new law establishes a very limited right to refuse psychosurgery and ECT (228). Affirmative consent is required for competent patients, with multidisciplinary review boards created to make the final decisions. In practice, however, clinical determinations of competency to make treatment decisions continue to override refusal of voluntary patients, and the statute still considers involuntary patients incompetent as such to refuse psychosurgery. For patients who are considered by their psychiatrists as incompetent to make treatment decisions, the board may authorize either surgery or ECT if the members are convinced that such treatment is clinically appropriate. The statute does not deal with psychotropic medications; it does state for the first time that such prescriptions must not be "excessive or inappropriate" and must conform to professional standards.

The Mental Health Act of 1986 in Victoria regulates psychosurgery and ECT but does not explicitly deal with psychotropic medications. Clinical determinations of incompetency are usually accepted by multidisciplinary review boards, and the treatments are authorized if the board is convinced that the treatments are appropriate and in the patient's best interests.

The Mental Health Ordinance of 1983 in the Australian Capital Territory provides that psychosurgery may not be performed if the patient refuses it, even if the patient does not appear to be capable of making an informed decision. ECT may be given against the will of an involuntary patient if the local court determines that the patient is incapable of consent, that the treatment will have substantial benefit, and that no effective alternatives exist. Psychotropic medications again are not mentioned.

The Mental Health Act of 1977–1986 in South Australia provides that consent for ECT or psychosurgery must be in writing for competent patients and must be authorized by independent psychiatrists. Patients considered incompetent to give or withhold consent must first be placed under guardianship before either treatment may be administered, except in emergency situations. The act does not specify the considerations that the Guardianship Board must employ in deciding whether or not to authorize involuntary treatment. Medications are not covered.

The Mental Health Act of 1980 in the Northern Territory requires that a hospital's chief medical officer may authorize any involuntary treatment of a mental patient. If the patient is considered competent to consent, the procedure(s) may be carried out without any external review. If the patient does not consent or refuses, the treatment may be applied involuntarily if two independent medical reports indicate that it will not be detrimental to the patient's best interest, or it is not practical to delay it, and it is a "standard medical treatment." The hospital's chief medical officer is automatically appointed as the guardian of all patients who are deemed (presumably by medical certification) incapable of managing themselves.

The current statutes in the remaining jurisdictions in Australia (Queensland's Mental Health Services Act of 1974–1984, Tasmania's Mental Health Act of 1963, and Western Australia's Mental Health Act of 1981) contain no explicit provisions concerning consent for psychiatric treatment. In these jurisdictions, such decisions are governed by common-law principles of consent and the parens patriae powers of the state.

The Eastern Caribbean

Although commitment law in the eastern Caribbean is derived from British legislation (229), different countries have chosen legislation from different periods in English law, reflecting their current views of the balance between treatment and civil liberties. Current statutes in Dominica, Grenada, and St. Lucia are based on the British Lunatics Act of 1890, with no substantive revisions. Jamaican law is also based in the 19th century, under a standard that required such obvious evidence of severe mental disorder that early diagnosis and treatment was almost impossible. The statutes of Antigua, Monserrat, St. Kitts, and St. Vincent were passed in the 1950s and are based on 1931 British mental health legislation that favored provision of treatment over protection of civil rights. All statutes provide explicitly for voluntary as well as for compulsory admissions.

A distinction is made between paupers and private patients. For paupers—those treated in public hospitals, regardless of whether or not the patient's family is paying for the care—magistrates must determine, based on petitions from social workers or police, that the person is of unsound mind and ought to be confined. The magistrate then appoints two physicians (one in Grenada and St. Lucia) to examine the person. There are elaborate provisions to prevent collusion between physicians and any other parties to the process. On receiving the medical certificates, the magistrate may determine that the person is of unsound mind and may order confinement. In emergencies, a relative's petition and a medical certificate are sufficient without the involvement of a magistrate. The emergency process provides for 7 days of hospitalization, during which the regular procedures must be carried out to extend the commitment.

In the case of "nonpaupers," a relative or other person may present a petition and two medical certificates to a justice of the peace to obtain hospitalization. The petitioner must promise to visit the patient every 6 months or to arrange for someone else to do so. If a person suffers from a mental illness, is likely to benefit from treatment, but is incapable of indicating a willingness to receive treatment, a relative may apply to a hospital superintendent and provide two medical certificates. The superintendent has the authority to hospitalize the person for up to 6 months without judicial action. The superintendent may extend the hospitalization for two additional 3-month periods. After that point, judicial certification must be invoked to extend hospitalization. If during those periods the person regains the capacity to make treatment decisions, he or she must be released within 28 days.

Patients hospitalized under magistrates' orders may appeal their detention to the courts and may request a jury trial. Once judicially committed, patients may be released only by the magistrate. Clinicians and relatives must petition for release to the magistrate, the courts, or (in Grenada) the governor general. The hospital superintendent may directly release patients hospitalized under his or her authority.

Trinidad and Tobago passed a Mental Health Act in 1975 that was based on the comparable British Act of 1959. Although more legally detailed than statutes from other area countries, it is still based on medical criteria and provides for significant medical authority. The act provides for voluntary admissions and for five categories of compulsory admissions. First, emergency commitment may be authorized by a hospital medical officer on a petition that alleges that the person ought to be detained in the interests of his or her health, for the safety and protection of others, or both. The petition may be brought by anyone with knowledge of the patient and must be accompanied by one medical certificate. The hospital medical officer may detain the patient until he or she decides either that discharge is in the patient's interest or that the patient is no longer in need of hospitalization. There is no judicial review.

Second, a patient may be admitted for "medically recommended treatment" on the application of a relative or friend, when the application is accompanied by two medical certificates stating that the person is unwilling to express himself or herself as in need of care and treatment. On receipt of such information, the hospital director has the authority to command the police to bring the patient to the hospital. The hospital director also has the authority to release the patient or to place the patient on conditional release for up to 12 months. There is no judicial review.

Third, if a person is found "wandering at large," a mental health officer has the authority to commit the person if the officer believes that "by reason of his appearance, conduct or conversation" the person is mentally ill and in need of hospitalization. On admission, the patient must be examined within 72 hours and must be released unless the hospital director or designee determines that the person is in need of further care and treatment. If such a determination is made, commitment is regulated as noted above.

Fourth, a court may order a person admitted to a hospital for up to 14 days. The law does not specify the circumstances under which a court should take such action, but presumably the person would be before the court for a criminal offense. Once hospitalized, the patient must be examined by the hospital director to determine whether the patient is in need of care and treatment. There is no time limitation for the commitment, but the court must release the patient whenever the hospital director certifies that he or she is no longer in need of care and treatment.

Finally, the minister of national security may order a prisoner transferred to a hospital for appropriate treatment, on the strength of medical certificates from two physicians. The hospitalization continues until the prisoner no longer needs hospital treatment. If the prisoner's sentence expires during the hospitalization, the prisoner may be retained in the hospital under the provisions of "medically recommended treatment" noted above.

South Africa

The Union of South Africa was established in 1910, and its first Mental Disorders Act was passed in 1916 (230). The act provided for the commitment of psychotic mental patients who refused voluntary admission. Disorders satisfying the criteria included schizophrenia, organic brain syndrome with psychosis, epilepsy with psychosis, and mental retardation. Twelve years after South Africa became independent in 1961, the South African Mental Health Act was passed. The revisions were influenced mostly by the advent of antipsychotic medication, and less so by civil rights considerations.

Under the revised statute, any adult may petition a magistrate for a person's commitment if that person appears to be suffering from mental illness to a degree that requires hospitalization. Petitioners must specify their relationship to the patient, and, if they are not related to the patient, they must explain why the petition is not being filed by a family member. The magistrate then appoints two physicians independent of the facility to which commitment is proposed to examine the patient and to record their opinions about the need for hospitalization. Between 2 and 8 days after the patient is admitted to the hospital, a hospital physician must submit a report to the magistrate setting forth his or her opinions on the patient's committability under the statute's medical criteria. If the physician determines that the patient does not meet the commitment criteria, the patient must be released.

The magistrate then submits all the evaluations to a judge for review. Within 42 days after receiving the documents, the judge must issue an order releasing or committing the patient. Commitment is for an indefinite period, but regular review by the treating psychiatrist is required. The reports of the reviews are sent to the commissioner for mental health, who may request further evaluation to justify continued commitment. In addition, the patient may request judicial review through a writ of habeas corpus.

Although dangerousness is not required under the act, physicians who determine as part of the evaluation that a patient is dangerous as a result of mental illness are required to report their findings in writing to a magistrate or police officer.

Pearlman (230) compares the effects of the different commitment criteria in South Africa and the United States. United States criteria, which require dangerousness but define mental illness relatively broadly, result in commitment of a significant number of nontreatable persons. In contrast, South African criteria restrict commitment to psychotic patients, without regard for their dangerousness. South African laws, like those of the Caribbean countries, are concerned with conflict of interest on the part of evaluating physicians. Such considerations are uncommon in commitment statutes in the United States.

The Netherlands

Only 15% of the more than 10,000 annual admissions to Dutch mental hospitals are involuntary (231). This incidence remained relatively constant between 1975 and 1985. Dutch commitment law continues to be governed by the 1884 Lunacy Act, which, despite a number of amendments, delegates most authority to clinicians. Involuntary admission may be ordered by a local court or by a burgomaster. There is no direct appeal to the courts from an order of the burgomaster. Originally designed as emergency proceedings, these orders now account for two-thirds of all commitments. Prospective patients have the right to be heard at the hearing, but the court is not required to appoint counsel to represent them. The criteria for commitment are based on mental illness and need for treatment.

In the past 15 years, a number of forces have converged to make inroads into clinical dominance. These forces include a growing patients' rights movement, a burgeoning professional mental health bar, and the establishment of in-hospital patient advocates. Under pressure from these groups, the government has been drafting reform legislation for a number of years, but the proposed code (BOPZ in Dutch) has been blocked in parliament since 1971 by opposition from clinicians, who objected to judicial interference with psychiatric practice, as well as by opposition from patient advocates who feel that the code does not go far enough. Although the bill has passed one chamber of parliament, its enactment does not seem imminent. The bill would have required evidence of danger to self or others, and it incorporates a least-restrictive-alternative concept. A judicial hearing would be required for commitment, and representation by counsel would be mandated.

The BOPZ also included a patients' bill of rights, including the right to treatment and the right to refuse treatment except to prevent dangerous behavior. Although dangerousness criteria have not yet been enacted into Dutch law, the Supreme Court has begun to require it in individual cases. In addition, a decision by the European Court for Human Rights, which was critical of existing commitment practices, has stimulated interest in changes through the courts.

Although there are currently no statutory provisions for a right to refuse treatment, the Court of Justice at Arnheim ruled in July 1988 that all involuntary treatment is absolutely forbidden, based on a section of the 1988 constitutional revisions guaranteeing the right to bodily integrity. As a result, clinicians who formerly opposed the legalism represented by the BOPZ have begun to support its basic concepts as a way of providing at least some basis for involuntary treatment of committed patients (232).

Belgium

Under the 1850 mental health statute, which still governs commitment in Belgium, decision making for admission and discharge was delegated to psychiatrists (233). No judicial review was required unless the patient appealed the psychiatrist's decision. Involuntary commitment also explicitly established global incompetency. Revisions were proposed as far back as 1969, but they were blocked by disagreements between the Senate and House of Representatives. When similar procedures in The Netherlands were criticized by the European Court for Human Rights (234), the proposals were resurrected and they are now expected to pass both houses.

The revisions would permit commitment either to prevent the person from endangering the life or integrity of someone else, or because the person is dangerous to his or her own sanity. The public prosecutor has the authority to order emergency hospitalization, on the advice of a physician, but the decision must be reviewed by a court within 24 hours of admission. In nonemergency situations, anyone with knowledge of the person can petition for commitment. The petition must be accompanied by a detailed medical certificate. A preliminary judicial hearing must be held within 24 hours, and if the judge determines that there is sufficient evidence to proceed, a full evidentiary hearing must be held within 10 days. The person is informed of the petition and is informed that he or she has the right to representation by counsel, to a medical expert of his or her choosing (appointed by the judge and provided at state expense), as well as to a lay advocate. If the court-appointed psychiatrist disagrees with the treating psychiatrist, both must undergo cross-examination at the hearing.

If the judge determines that the person meets the criteria, the judge may order commitment for up to 40 days. Thereafter, recommitment may be ordered for up to 2 years at a time. Patients may be discharged at any time by the treating psychiatrist, the public prosecutor, or the judge. The patient also may petition for review of the commitment between scheduled hearings.

Austria

Commitment in Austria is still governed by a 1956 Mental Health Act that delegates most decision making to psychiatrists under medical criteria (235). Proposed revisions presently under serious consideration by the Austrian Parliament include both protections for patients before commitment and continuing access to review of the conditions of their confinements if they are involuntarily hospitalized. There are stricter substantive criteria for commitment, as well as increased procedural protections. The admission procedures would be more formal, with increased judicial control over the initial commitment process. An initial judicial hearing would be required within 4 days of admission, with more formal rules and representation by an advocate (but not necessarily a lawyer). There would be continued access to the courts for review of alleged unnecessarily coercive procedures for both voluntary and involuntary patients.

Some critics have argued that the revisions do not go far enough, particularly in the area of representation. The advocates would be employees of established private organizations, which currently supply guardians. These organizations would be responsible for training the new advocates, who must then be licensed and supervised by the ministry of justice and then accepted by the judge in charge of each commitment court. Funds ultimately would come from the state, but would not be under direct state control. The duties of the advocates would be to represent patients at initial hearings and to support patients after commitment if the hospital further restricted their rights. Advocates would be granted unrestricted access to patients and their records and immediate notification of restrictions of patients' rights in the hospitals. In court, however, advocates would have only the same procedural rights as patients, rather than the additional professional privileges and responsibilities characteristic of lawyers.

The advocacy services were field-tested in a pilot project that was begun in 1981. Although an attempt was made to have the advocates function as much as possible as they would under the draft law, of necessity they are still functioning within the framework of the current law. Results of the study cast serious doubts on the realization of the program's goals, because of significant resistance from psychiatrists and frustration of the advocates, who felt that they were having little impact on the system. Advocates succeeded in shaping the commitment hearings, but they failed to gain the appreciation of their clients. Little cohesion or support developed among the advocates themselves, in part because they were hired and trained separately. The advocates were unable to serve the patients without provoking the hospital staff, and thus they could not live up to political expectations. The system has been criticized because advocacy was limited to committed patients, many of whom were indifferent to services, and because it could not address aftercare or conditions within the hospital.

Sweden

Under the 1858 Swedish mental health statute, control over the admissions, treatment, and discharge process was delegated to physicians (236). Revisions in 1967 introduced some legal structure but continued to leave primary control over admissions to physicians. Under this statute, involuntary hospitalization can be effected by two physicians, at least one of whom must be a psychiatrist. Dangerousness to self or others is now a necessary criterion for commitment. In the legislation itself, there was no automatic external review, either of admission or of ongoing hospitalization. Patients have the right to appeal their commitments to an external (nonjudicial) review board, but they are not provided with representation at state expense. Rules promulgated in 1983 require continued hospitalization to be reported to the board at 3 months after admission, and at every 6 months thereafter.

Proposed revisions would make explicit a policy preference for voluntary treatment in home or outpatient settings but would provide emergency involuntary hospitalization for short-term crisis intervention if all other alternatives have been exhausted. Involuntary hospitalization would require a grave mental disorder, essentially equivalent to psychosis, plus a demonstrable need for treatment in an inpatient setting. Dangerousness would no longer be required for commitment. Admission would continue to be under medical control, but there would be automatic judicial review after 8 days of hospitalization, and court authorization would be necessary to continue the hospitalization. Hospitalization beyond 6 months must be reviewed by the Psychiatric Committee of the National Board of Health and Welfare. The revisions would separate the care of senile, demented patients and those committed under the criminal justice system from the care of patients within the civil commitment system. The court is required to appoint a "support person" for patients hospitalized beyond the initial period, but representation by attorneys is not provided. Involuntary medication may be given only if patients' lives or health are in serious danger.

Norway

Under the current Mental Health Act of Norway, involuntary hospitalization requires a serious mental disease, essentially equivalent to psychosis (237). In addition, one of three additional requirements must be fulfilled for commitment: *1*) commitment must be necessary to ensure recovery or considerable improvement of the condition; *2*) hospitalization is required to prevent patients from suffering molestation; or *3*) hospitalization is required to prevent the patient from being dangerous to self or others. Patients may appeal their commitments to a board at each hospital. The Norwegian Supreme

Court held in 1981 that involuntary hospitalization must be considered in relation to the available alternatives. No mention was made of representation by attorneys.

A study of commitment patterns at four psychiatric hospitals between 1976 and 1983 looked at 212 appeals from commitment in which the appeals boards rendered decisions. Sufficient criteria for commitment under the law were listed explicitly in only 81% of the written psychiatric opinions. Need for treatment was alleged in 73% of cases, protection from molestation in 34%, and dangerousness in only 17%. Of the 149 board statements that provided explicit conclusions, release was ordered in only a single case.

France

Only some 20% of patients in French psychiatric hospitals are admitted involuntarily (238). The French commitment system provides two types of "placement" in psychiatric hospitals, *placement officiel,* i.e., overt involuntary hospitalization, and *placement voluntaire,* which requires a petition by a relative or friend, but not the desire of the patient. Only 1% of hospitalized patients are in the *officiel* category. The *voluntaire* commitment is used mostly for the elderly and is comparable to guardianship procedures in the United States. No adequate national statistics concerning the use of commitment are available.

Spain

Although the 1978 Spanish constitution provides a right to refuse treatment for all competent patients (medical as well as psychiatric) under an informed consent analysis, involuntary civil commitment is still governed by the Decree of July 3, 1931, which was more concerned with economic rights and protection of the public than with the civil rights of individual mentally ill persons (239). It granted control over the commitment process to the government, which may (but rarely does) refer cases to courts for judicial review. The criteria include both dangerousness and need-for-treatment standards, although most petitions are brought under the dangerousness standard.

Israel

The current commitment laws in Israel are perhaps the most medically paternalistic in the world (240). The position of district psychiatrist (DP) is endowed with exceptional powers in comparison with those of clinicians in other countries. DPs can authorize involuntary hospitalization and can authorize police to take custody of a person for evaluation or hospitalization. There are relatively few external controls over the decisions of DPs; even hospital directors (if they are not also DPs) cannot make independent decisions about admissions or discharges of involuntary patients without authorization from the regional DP.

Current draft revisions to the mental health law, which are expected to be enacted in the near future, would retain most of the DPs' quasi-judicial powers, with some limitations. There are several criteria for commitment. If the person suffers from a mental illness that results in a recognizable defect in judgment or ability to assess reality, is likely to endanger physically and immediately another person as a result, and does not consent or is incapable of consenting to the requisite treatment, the DP *must* direct the person's admission. Commitment may also occur if the danger is to self or if the dangerousness is defined as likelihood to endanger himself or herself or another person (though the danger is not physical or immediate); if the individual's ability to care for his or her own basic needs is substantially impaired; or if he or she causes serious mental distress to self or to people in the locality or causes serious damage to property. In these cases, the DP *may* order admission. In the last situation (comparable to "grave disability" criteria in the United States), the patient must be informed of his or her right to appeal the hospitalization to the District Psychiatric Board (DPB), which is composed of two psychiatrists and one lawyer. Decisions of the DPB may be appealed to a court.

The DP's commitment order is in effect for 7 days from the time of admission and is extendable for an additional 7 days by the hospital director. Further extensions of up to 3 months at a time must be approved by the DPB. For patients meeting the physical dangerousness to self or others criteria, the DP would also have the option to order compulsory outpatient treatment, with hospitalization as the consequence of noncompliance. There would be no formal right to refuse treatment, but physical force could not be used to administer medication except in an emergency (not yet defined).

Italy

Developments in commitment law and practice in Italy have been unique in many ways compared with European and American experiences (241). The major changes that were incorporated into Law 180 in 1978 came not from legal concerns for liberty and due process but from the social psychiatry movement led by Bisaglia beginning in the 1960s. Bisaglia emphasized the social and political factors that influence the form that mental disorders will take and also the community response to disordered behavior. By "democratizing" the hospitals he directed, Bisaglia sought to remove the pernicious social forces that had led patients to learn that they could not function independently and thus had to rely on psychiatric hospitals to make all their decisions for them. After he succeeded in encouraging patient autonomy within the hospitals, the contrast with the outside became obvious. Bisaglia therefore went into the community to form alliances that would support the dismantling of the asylum. Some who could not live autonomously were given their own apartments in buildings of the former hospitals.

The reformed commitment law eliminated social control aspects by eliminating dangerousness as a criterion and by concentrating on patients' need for treatment. Involuntary treatment could be based only on serious need for treatment, a patient's refusal of that treatment, and the absence of less restrictive means. The Italian reforms have worked best in leftist areas, where Bisaglia's social concepts have taken hold and community support systems have been established independently of the legal system. They have been less effective in conservative areas, which are less receptive to the ideas and less willing to accept the behavior of the deinstitutionalized patients.

The Soviet Union

Although statutes governing the insanity defense had existed for a number of years, before 1988 there were no explicit statutes authorizing or regulating involuntary civil commitment (called "urgent hospitalization") in the Soviet Union. The only procedures were those authorized by the Ministry of Health, which issued instructions in 1971 but limited the distribution of those instructions so that their provisions were generally unknown to the public and frequently not followed in practice. The process of involuntary hospitalization was reported to be largely under psychiatric discretion (242).

In January 1988, the Provisional Guidelines went into effect. They authorize involuntary hospitalization for a person who is a "danger to himself or those around him." They further provide for involuntary psychiatric examination of a "person who commits actions that give sufficient reason to suppose that he has a pronounced mental disorder and at the same time violates public order or the rules of socialist society, and also represents an immediate danger to himself or those around him." As parts of the criminal code define any criminal action (including "violating the rules of socialist society") as sufficient evidence of dangerousness, not unlike the U.S. Supreme Court's decision in a 1983 insanity case (243), the Soviet provisions remain broad enough to permit continued abuse of the procedures. U.S. delegates who surveyed Soviet practices in 1989 found examples of civil commitment of patients who would satisfy neither the mental illness nor the dangerousness criteria of U.S. statutes (242).

The 1988 statute essentially codifies the procedures of the 1971 regulations developed by the Ministry of Health. It requires that involuntary hospitalization be reviewed by a three-member psychiatric commission within 24 hours, every 30 days for the next 6 months, and every 6 months thereafter. It also provides for representation by counsel and for a new level of external review. Patients have the right to defense attorneys. They or their legal representatives now have the rights to include a psychiatrist of their choosing on the review panel, to appeal the commission's decision to the chief psychiatrist of the region, and to appeal those decisions to a court. They also have the right to be placed in the "least restrictive setting" and to confidentiality (244). No data are yet available concerning the implementation of these rights.

In practice, however, most hospitalizations are too brief for these protections to be effective; the average length is 60 days. A 1989 *Pravda* report indicated that of 71,000 urgent hospitalizations in Moscow in 1988, only 10 cases reached the level of court appeal. In addition, few patients appear to be informed of their rights to counsel. Reports to the U.S. delegation also indicated that patients who do not object to hospitalization after the initial 24-hour review are considered "voluntary," and further reviews are not scheduled.

Most of the external review provisions have not yet been fully implemented. In addition, medications (including both depot antipsychotics and aversive drugs such as sulfazine) are still routinely prescribed for violation of hospital rules (245).

There are also explicit provisions in the 1988 statute for commitment to outpatient treatment (244), which states that "persons suffering from chronic mental illness with a tendency toward an unfavorable progression and who are subject to mandatory treatment and dynamic clinical observation are provided with outpatient psychiatric assistance regardless of their consent, and also without the consent of their relatives or legal representatives." No data indicate actual practice in the area of outpatient commitment, however.

The delegation concluded that although the 1988 Provisional Guidelines represent a significant step forward compared with the total psychiatric dominance and lack of independent review characteristic of practices before 1988, much remains to be accomplished in terms both of substantive criteria for commitment and procedural protections for patients facing involuntary hospitalization. They liken the current situation in the Soviet Union to the practices in the United States before the reforms of the 1970s (242).

Final Summary and Conclusions

The practices of involuntary civil commitment continue to change, but in an evolutionary manner, in contrast to the revolutions of the 1970s. It is likely that most of the debates on commitment criteria and procedures will now occur in state legislatures rather than in the courts, although issues that have a major effect on the treatment of committed patients—such as the right to refuse treatment and the duty to protect third parties—will continue to be litigated.

For political and economic as well as legal rights reasons, the major focus will continue to be on treatment in the community. For this reason, the legal debate will continue to shift from the criteria and procedures for involuntary hospitalization to those for involuntary outpatient treatment. Because of community backlash against deinstitutionalization (fueled by occasional tragedies involving mentally ill persons) and the community's reaction to the problem of homelessness, there will continue to be pressure to facilitate admissions to state mental hospitals. The spreading duty to protect third parties will also contribute to an increase in petitions for involuntary hospitalization and to a reluctance to release patients once they are hospitalized.

Psychiatrists have become more active in these debates than they were in the 1970s, and they will need to become even more so if their expertise and viewpoints are to affect the resolution of the controversies. The shift to legislatures should provide psychiatrists with the opportunity to be more effective, because legislators are more likely to be receptive to data than courts have been (72). Legislatures and courts are still ignorant of many relevant aspects of psychiatric practice, such as the effects of medication and clinicians' ability to predict future dangerousness. It will be important to continue the research on these topics to address legal as well as clinical concerns. For example, critics of forced medication claim that medication is ineffective if administered involuntarily. Most psychiatrists would disagree with this statement, but there are no studies in the literature that specifically address the issue.

Finally, psychiatry must continue to advocate for adequate resources for treatment of the mentally ill, both in hospitals and in the community. The major problems that occurred after the 1979 broadening of commitment standards in Washington State were caused by the legislature's failure to anticipate the increased admissions by providing additional resources to the hospitals (105). In contrast, a major reason for the success of the initial outpatient commitment procedures in North Carolina was the allocation of funds to community mental health centers to support the program (186).

NOTES

1. Gutheil TG, Rachlin S, Mills MJ: Differing conceptual models in psychiatry and law, in Legal Encroachments on Psychiatric Practice (New Directions in Mental Health Services, No 25). Edited by Rachlin S. San Francisco, CA, Jossey-Bass, 1985
2. Chodoff P: Paternalism versus autonomy in medicine and psychiatry. Psychiatric Annals 13:318–320, 1983
3. Kaplan LV, Miller RD: Law, psychiatry and rights. Presented at the 14th International Congress of Law and Mental Health, Jerusalem, Israel, June 26, 1989
4. Lévi-Strauss C: Natural Right and History. Chicago, IL, University of Chicago Press, 1953
5. Rachlin S: One right too many. Bull Psychiatry Law 3:99–103, 1975
6. American Medical Association: Principles of Medical Ethics. Washington, DC, American Medical Association, 1957
7. American Psychiatric Association: Principles of Medical Ethics With Annotations Especially Applicable to Psychiatry. Washington, DC, American Psychiatric Association, 1978
8. Tarasoff v Regents of the University of California, 118 Cal Rptr 129, 529 P2d 553 (1974); 17 Cal3d 425, 551 P2d 334 (1976)
9. Huber GA, Roth LH, Appelbaum PS: Hospitalization, arrest or discharge: important legal and clinical issues in the emergency evaluation of persons believed to be dangerous to others. Law and Contemporary Problems 45:99–123, 1982
10. Felthous AR: The Psychotherapist's Duty to Warn or Protect. Springfield, IL, Charles C Thomas, 1989
11. Fleming JD, Maximov B: The patient or his victim: the therapist's dilemma. California Law Review 62:1025–1068, 1974
12. Stone AA: The Tarasoff case and some of its progeny: suing psychotherapists to safeguard society, in Law, Psychiatry and Morality. Edited by Washington, DC, American Psychiatric Press, 1984, pp 161–190

13. Appelbaum PS: The new preventive detention: psychiatry's problematic responsibility for the control of violence. Am J Psychiatry 145:779–785, 1988
14. Schopp RF, Wexler D: Shooting yourself in the foot with due care: psychotherapists and crystallized standards of tort liability. Journal of Psychiatry and Law 17:163–203, 1989
15. Appelbaum PS, Zonana H, Bonnie R, et al: Statutory approaches to limiting psychiatrists' liability for their patients' violent acts. Am J Psychiatry 146:821–828, 1989
16. Currie v United States, No 86-2643 (4th Cir, Dec 28, 1987)
17. Miller RD, Doren DM, Van Rybroek GJ, et al: Emerging problems for staff associated with the release of potentially dangerous forensic patients. Bull Am Acad Psychiatry Law 16:309–320, 1988
18. Segal SP, Watson MA, Goldfinger SM, et al: Dangerousness and civil commitment in the psychiatric emergency room, I: the assessment of dangerousness by emergency room clinicians. Arch Gen Psychiatry 45:748–752, 1988
19. Segal SP, Watson MA, Goldfinger SM, et al: Dangerousness and civil commitment in the psychiatric emergency room, II: mental disorder indicators and three dangerousness criteria. Arch Gen Psychiatry 45:753–758, 1988
20. Segal SP, Watson MA, Goldfinger SM, et al: Dangerousness and civil commitment in the psychiatric emergency room, III: disposition as a function of mental disorder and dangerousness indicators. Arch Gen Psychiatry 45:759–763, 1988
21. McNiel DE, Binder R: Relationship between preadmission threats and later violent behavior by acute psychiatric patients. Hosp Community Psychiatry 40:605–608, 1989
22. Beck JC, Bonnar J: Emergency civil commitment: predicting hospital violence from behavior in the community. Journal of Psychiatry and Law 15:379–388, 1988
23. Brakel SJ, Parry J, Weiner BA: The Mentally Disabled and the Law, 3rd Edition. Chicago, IL, American Bar Foundation, 1985
24. Miller RD: Involuntary Civil Commitment of the Mentally Ill in the Post-Reform Era. Springfield, IL, Charles C Thomas, 1987, pp 65–87
25. Youngberg v Romeo, 457 US 307 (1982)
26. Project Release v Prevost, 551 F Supp 1298 (EDNY, 1982); aff'd, 772 F2d 960 (2d Cir 1983)
27. Stensvad v Reivitz et al, 601 F Supp 128 (WD Wis 1985)
28. Charters v United States, No 86-5568 (4th Cir Sept 18, 1987)
29. Miller RD, Rachlin S, Appelbaum PS: Patients' rights: the action moves to state courts. Hosp Community Psychiatry 38:343–344, 1987
30. Appelbaum PS: The right to refuse treatment with antipsychotic medications: retrospect and prospect. Am J Psychiatry 145:413–419, 1988
31. Appelbaum PS, Hoge SK: The right to refuse treatment: what the research reveals. Behavioral Sciences and the Law 4:279–292, 1986
32. Appelbaum PS, Gutheil TG: Drug refusal: a study of psychiatric inpa-

tients. Am J Psychiatry 137:340–346, 1980
33. Veliz J, James WS: Medicine court: *Rogers* in Practice. Am J Psychiatry 144:62–67, 1987
34. Zito JM, Hendel DD, Mitchell JE, et al: Drug treatment refusal, diagnosis, and length of hospitalization in involuntary psychiatric patients. Behavioral Sciences and the Law 4:327–337, 1986
35. Callahan LA: Changing mental health law: butting heads with a billygoat. Behavioral Sciences and the Law 4:305–314, 1986
36. Rodenhauser P: Treatment refusal in a forensic hospital: ill use of the lasting right. Bull Am Acad Psychiatry Law 12:59–63, 1984
37. Marder SR, Mebane A, Chien C, et al: A comparison of patients who refuse consent to neuroleptic treatment. Am J Psychiatry 140:470–472, 1983
38. Hargreaves WA, Shumway M, Weinstein A: Due process protection for involuntary psychiatric patients treated with psychoactive medication: effects of the Jamison-Farabee consent decree. Presented at the annual meeting of the American Psychiatric Association, Dallas, TX, May 1985
39. Bloom JD, Faulkner LR, Holm VM, et al: An empirical view of patients exercising their right to refuse treatment. Int J Law Psychiatry 7:315–328, 1984
40. Godard SL, Bloom JD, Williams MH, et al: The right to refuse treatment in Oregon: a two-year statewide experience. Behavioral Sciences and the Law 4:293–304, 1986
41. Rivers v Katz, 67 NY 2d 485, 495 NE 2d 337, 504 NYS 2d 74 (1986)
42. Jones et al v Gerhardstein et al, 141 Wis 2d 710, 416 NW 2d 883 (1987)
43. Jarvis v Levine, 403 NW 2d 298 (Minn App 1987)
44. Cournos F, McKinnon K, Adams C: A comparison of clinical and judicial procedures for reviewing requests for involuntary medication in New York. Hosp Community Psychiatry 39:851–855, 1988
45. Rachlin S: Rethinking the right to refuse treatment. Psychiatric Annals 19:213–222, 1989
46. Zito JM, Wanderling J, Haimowitz S, et al: One year under *Rivers*: drug refusal in a New York state psychiatric facility. Presented at the 16th International Congress of Law and Mental Health, Montreal, Canada, June 15–18, 1988
47. Ciccone JR, Tokoli JF, Clements CD, et al: Right to refuse treatment: the impact of *Rivers v Katz*. Presented at the annual meeting of the American Psychiatric Association, Montreal, Canada, May 7–12, 1988
48. Malecha M: *Jarvis*: impact on the public hospitals. Presented at the spring scientific meeting of the Midwestern Chapter of the American Academy of Psychiatry and the Law, Minneapolis, MN, April 9, 1988
49. Miller RD, Bernstein MR, Van Rybroek GJ, et al: The impact of the right to refuse treatment in a forensic patient population: six-month review. Bull Am Acad Psychiatry Law 17:107–119, 1989
50. Miller RD: Unpublished data, 1989

51. Hupfer G: A retrospective study concerning the impact of the *Jones* decision on civil and forensic populations at Winnebago Mental Health Institute. Unpublished study, 1988
52. In re Orr, 531 NE 2d 64 (Ill App Ct 1988)
53. Keyhea v Rushen, 223 Cal Rptr 747 (Cal App 1 Dist 1986)
54. In re K.K.B., 609 P2d 747 (Okla 1980)
55. Harper v State, No 54045-4 (Wash SCt, opinion filed July 7, 1988)
56. People v Medina, 662 P2d 184 (Colo App 1982)
57. Anderson v State, 663 P2d 570 (Ariz App 1982)
58. Rogers v Commissioner, 458 NE 2d 308 (Mass Sup Jud Ct 1983)
59. Opinion of the Justices, 465 A2d 484 (NH SCt 1983)
60. Bentley v State ex rel Rogers, 398 So 2d 992 (Fla 4 Dist Ct App 1981)
61. Dix GE: Realism and drug refusal: a reply to Appelbaum and Gutheil. Bull Am Acad Psychiatry Law 9:180–198, 1981
62. Brooks AD: Law and antipsychotic medications. Behavioral Sciences and the Law 4:247–263, 1986
63. Gutheil TG, Appelbaum PS: "Mind control," "synthetic sanity," "artificial competence," and genuine confusion: legally relevant effects of antipsychotic medication. Hofstra Law Review 12:77–120, 1983
64. Lessard v Schmidt, 340 F Supp 1078 (ED Wis 1972)
65. Suzuki v Quisenberry, 411 F Supp 1113 (D Hawaii 1976)
66. In re Gault, 383 US 541, 86 SCt 1428 (1967)
67. In re Winship, 397 US 358, 90 SCt 1068 (1970)
68. Parham v J.R. and J.L., 442 US 640 (1979)
69. Miller RD: Who's afraid of forensic psychiatry? Bull Am Acad Psychiatry Law (in press)
70. In re DePass, 531 NYS 2d 427 (NY Sup Ct 1988)
71. In re Stefano, 531 NYS 2d 212 (NY Sup Ct 1988)
72. R.J. v Winnebago County, 431 NW 2d 708 (Wis Ct App 1988)
73. Colorado v Stevens, 761 P2d 768 (Colo Sup Ct 1988)
74. In re Harris, 654 P2d 109 (Wash Sup Ct 1982)
75. Reome v Levine, 692 F Supp 1046 (D Minn 1988)
76. Matter of Stewart, 352 NW 2d 811 (Minn App 1984)
77. B.A.A. v Chief Medical Officer, University of Iowa Hospitals, 421 NW 2d 118 (Iowa Sup Ct 1988)
78. In re Lynette H., 368 SE 2d 452 (NC Ct App 1988); rev'd, 374 SE 2d 272 (NC Sup Ct 1988)
79. Butler v Georgia, 369 SE 2d 252 (Ga Sup Ct 1988)
80. Alabama Dept of Mental Health and Mental Retardation v Andres, 515 So 2d 9 (Ala Civ App 1987)
81. In the Matter of J.R.R., 145 Wis 2d 431, 497 NW 2d 137 (Wis Ct App 1988)
82. Savastano v Nurnberg, 529 NYS 2d 403 (NY Sup Ct 1987)
83. In re Stokes, No 85-1249 (DC Cir Ct App July 13, 1988)
84. In re W.H., 144 Vt 595, 481 A2d 22 (1984)
85. Robbins v Lumpkin, 370 SE 2d 635 (Ga Ct App 1988)
86. In re Plank, 523 NE 2d 614 (Ill App Ct 1988)

87. Curnow v Yarbrough, 676 P2d 1177 (Colo 1984)
88. Matter of Z.O., 484 A2d 1287 (NJ Super AD 1984)
89. Doe ex rel. Doe v Austin, 668 F Supp 597 (WD Ky 1986)
90. In the Matter of the Alleged Mental Illness of Cordie, 372 NW 2d 24 (Minn App 1985)
91. In re Grant, 244 Cal Rptr 552 (Cal Ct App 1988)
92. Doe v Gallinot, 657 F2d 1017 (9th Cir 1981)
93. State v Casanova, 359 NW 2d 696 (Minn App 1984)
94. Lanett v Texas, 750 SW 2d 302 (Tex Ct App 1988)
95. Boggs v New York City Health and Hospitals Corp., 523 NYS 2d 71 (NY App Div 1987)
96. California Welfare and Institutions Code §§ 5000–5404 (1967), effective 1969
97. Bachrach LL: Deinstitutionalization: what do the numbers mean? Hosp Community Psychiatry 137:118–119, 121, 1986
98. Stone AA: Mental health and law: a system in transition (DHEW Publ No ADM-76-176). Washington, DC, U.S. Government Printing Office, 1975
99. Roth LH: A commitment law for patients, doctors, and lawyers. Am J Psychiatry 136:1121–1127, 1979
100. American Psychiatric Association: Guidelines for legislation on the psychiatric hospitalization of adults. Am J Psychiatry 140:672–679, 1983
101. Rubenstein LS: APA's Model Law: hurting the people it seeks to help. Hosp Community Psychiatry 36:968–972, 1985
102. Appelbaum PS: Is the need for treatment constitutionally acceptable as a basis for civil commitment? Law, Medicine and Health Care 12:144–149, 1984
103. Washington Revised Code Annotated § 71.05.020(1) West Suppl 1984
104. Pierce GI, Durham ML, Fisher WH: The impact of broadened civil commitment standards on admissions to state mental hospitals. Am J Psychiatry 142:104–107, 1985
105. Durham ML, LaFond JQ: The empirical consequences and policy implications of broadening the statutory criteria for civil commitment. Yale Law and Policy Review 2:395–446, 1985
106. Hirtz R: A multi-state analysis of the adverse impact of broadening involuntary commitment laws for the mentally ill. Report to the members of the Pennsylvania Legislature Select Task Force on Mental Health Care. House of Representatives, Commonwealth of Pennsylvania, Aug 1977
107. Maier GJ: Taking issue: the tyranny of irresponsible freedom. Hosp Community Psychiatry 40:453, 1989
108. Fisher WH, Pierce GL, Appelbaum PS: Law and psychiatry: how flexible are our civil commitment statutes? Hosp Community Psychiatry 39:711–712, 1988
109. North Carolina General Statutes § 122-58.2 (1981)
110. Alaska Statutes § 4730.915(7)(B) (1984)

111. 1986 Kansas Session Laws HB 2050, Kansas Probate Laws, Article 29, §§ 59–2901ff
112. Texas Mental Health Code, as revised by SB 436, 68th Legislature; HB 1256, 69th Legislature, SB 257, SB 245, HB 2031, 70th Legislature, effective Sept 1, 1987 [Texas Statutes annotated art 5547-50(b)(2)(iii)]
113. House Bill No 316, Montana 50th Legislature, amending §§ 51-21-102 through 128. "Act Providing for Involuntary Commitment and Treatment in the Local Community of Persons Who Are Mentally Ill"
114. Metzner JL: "Gravely disabled" redefined. Colorado Psychiatry Newsletter, June 1989, pp 4, 6
115. Hospitalization of mentally ill made easier under new Colorado law Psychiatric News, Aug 18, 1989, p 7
116. Colorado Revised Statutes, Article 10, § 27-10-102 (5) (a), 1989
117. Monahan J, Ruggiero M, Friedlander HD: Stone-Roth model of civil commitment and the California dangerousness standard. Arch Gen Psychiatry 39:1267–1271, 1982
118. Hoge SK, Sachs G, Appelbaum PS, et al: Limitations on psychiatrists' discretionary civil commitment authority by the Stone and dangerousness criteria. Arch Gen Psychiatry 45:764–769, 1988
119. Hoge SK, Appelbaum PS, Greer A: An empirical comparison of the Stone and dangerousness criteria for civil commitment. Am J Psychiatry 146:170–175, 1989
120. Appelbaum PS: Standards for civil commitment: a critical review of empirical research. Int J Law Psychiatry 7:133–144, 1984
121. Hiday VA: Reformed commitment procedures: an empirical study in the courtroom. Law and Society Review 11:652–666, 1977
122. Committee Report No 17 to the [Wisconsin] Legislative Council: Recommendations of the Legislative Council Special Committee on Mental Health Issues. Madison, WI, June 8, 1987
123. ENKI Research Institute: A study of California's new mental health law (1969–1971). Los Angeles, CA, ENKI Corporation, 1972
124. Ennis BJ, Litwack T: Psychiatry and the presumption of expertise: flipping coins in the courtroom. California Law Review 62:693–752, 1974
125. American Psychiatric Association: Amicus brief in *Barefoot v Estelle,* 463 US 878; 103 SCt 3383 (1983)
126. Faulkner LR, McFarland BH, Bloom JD, et al: A method for quantifying and comparing civil commitment processes. Am J Psychiatry 143:744–749, 1986
127. Faulkner LR, Bloom JD, McFarland BH, et al: The effect of mental health system changes on civil commitment. Bull Am Acad Psychiatry Law 13:345–357, 1985
128. Faulkner LR, McFarland BH, Bloom JD, et al: Methodology for the analysis of civil commitment detention times and costs. Bull Am Acad Psychiatry Law 15:359–370, 1987
129. Faulkner LR, McFarland BH, Bloom JD: An empirical study of emergency commitment. Am J Psychiatry 146:182–186, 1989

130. Perlin MJ: Psychiatric hospitalization: some predictions for the eighties, in Critical Issues in American Psychiatry and the Law. Edited by Rosner R. Springfield, IL, Charles C Thomas, 1982, pp 239–262
131. Wald P, Friedman P: The politics of mental health advocacy in the United States. Int J Law Psychiatry 1:137–152, 1978
132. Scheingold SA: The Politics of Rights. New Haven, CT, Yale University Press, 1974
133. Milner N: The dilemmas of legal mobilization: ideologies and strategies of mental patient liberation groups. Law and Policy 8:105–129, 1986
134. Brakel SJ: Legal aid in mental hospitals. American Bar Foundation Research Journal 1981:21–93, 1981
135. Dickey W: The treatment team model of teaching law students in a work study program. Presented at the spring scientific meeting of the Midwestern Chapter of the American Academy of Psychiatry and the Law, Madison, WI, April 15, 1989
136. Lamb HR: Securing patients' rights—responsibly. Hosp Community Psychiatry 32:393–397, 1981
137. Appelbaum PS: The rising tide of patients' rights advocacy. Hosp Community Psychiatry 37:9–10, 1986
138. Public Law 99-319, May 23, 1988: Protection and Advocacy for Mentally Ill Individuals Act of 1986
139. Ziegenfuss JT: Conflict between patients' rights and patients' needs: an organizational systems problem. Hosp Community Psychiatry 37:1086–1087, 1986
140. Schwartz SJ, Fleishner RD: Legal advocacy for persons confined in mental hospitals. Mental Disability Law Reporter 5:264, 277–280, 1981
141. Rubenstein LS: Treatment of the mentally ill: legal advocacy enters the second generation. Am J Psychiatry 143:1264–1269, 1986
142. Freddolino PP, Appelbaum PS: Rights protection and advocacy: the need to do more with less. Hosp Community Psychiatry 35:319–320, 1984
143. Hiday VA, Goodman RR: The least restrictive alternative to involuntary hospitalization, outpatient commitment: its use and effectiveness. Journal of Psychiatry and Law 10:81–96, 1982
144. Miller RD, Fiddleman PB: Outpatient commitment: treatment in the least restrictive environment? Hosp Community Psychiatry 35:147–151, 1983
145. Chambers DL: Alternatives to civil commitment of the mentally ill: practical guides and constitutional imperatives. Michigan Law Review 70:1107–1200, 1972
146. Chu FD, Trotter S: The Madness Establishment. New York, Grossman, 1974
147. Goldman HH, Adams NH, Taube CA: Deinstitutionalization: the data demythologized. Hosp Community Psychiatry 34:129–134, 1983
148. Miller RD: The least restrictive environment: hidden meanings and

agendas. Community Ment Health J 18:46–55, 1982
149. Schneider-Braus K: Civil commitment to outpatient psychotherapy: a case study. Bull Am Acad Psychiatry Law 14:273–279, 1986
150. Miller RD: Commitment to outpatient treatment: a national survey. Hosp Community Psychiatry 36:265–267, 1985
151. Miller RD, Maher R, Fiddleman PB: The use of plea bargaining in civil commitment. Int J Law Psychiatry 7:395–406, 1984
152. Birl v Wallis, 619 F Supp 481 (MD Ala 1985); 633 F Supp 707 (MD Ala 1986)
153. Matter of Mental Condition of W.R.B., 411 NW 2d 142 (Wis App 1987)
154. Glasco v Brassard, 94 Idaho 162, 483 P2d 924 (1971)
155. Ball v Jones, 43 AD 2d 281, 351 NYS 2d 199 (1974); aff'd 36 NY 2d 339, 368 NYS 2d 467, 329 NE 2d 159 (1975)
156. In re Bye, 12 Cal 3d 96, 115 Cal Rptr 382, 524 P2d 854 (1974); cert denied, 420 US 996, 95 SCt 1437 (1975)
157. New Jersey v Carter, 64 NJ 382 (1974)
158. Meisel v Kremens, 405 F Supp 1253 (ED Pa 1975)
159. Lewis v Donahue, 437 F Supp 112 (WD Okla 1977)
160. In re M.M., No 17, 820-CW (La Ct App 2d Cir Dec 13, 1985)
161. In re Commitment of B.H., 212 NJ Super 145 (1986)
162. C.R. v Adams, 649 F2d 625 (8th Cir, 1981)
163. Rhode Island Dept. of Mental Health, Retardation and Hospitals v R.B., 549 A2d 1028 (RI Sup Ct 1988)
164. C.N. v State, 433 So 2d 661 (Fla App 3 Dist 1983)
165. In re Anderson, 73 Cal 3d 98, 140 Cal Rptr 546 (1977)
166. State v Combined Community Services Board, 362 NW 2d 104 (Wis 1985)
167. In re G.K., 514 A2d 1031 (Vt 1986)
168. Dietrich v Brooks, 558 P2d (Or App 1976)
169. Metaxos v People, 76 Colo 264, 230 P 608 (1924)
170. In re McPherson, 176 Cal App 3d 332, 222 Cal Rptr 416 (1985)
171. Application of True, 103 Idaho 151 (Idaho 1982)
172. In re Richardson, 481 A2d 473 (DC App 1984)
173. Hooks v Jacquith, 318 So 2d 860 (Miss 1975)
174. In re Cross, 662 P2d 828 (Wash 1983)
175. Storsteen v Cuypers, 389 NW 2d 812 (ND Sup Ct 1986)
176. Morrissey v Brewer, 408 US 471 (1972)
177. Matter of Mills, 467 A2d 971 (DC App 1983)
178. In re James, 507 A2d 155 (DC App 1986)
179. In re Stokes, No 85-1249 (DC Cir Ct App July 13, 1988)
180. Van Putten T: Why do schizophrenic patients refuse to take their drugs? Arch Gen Psychiatry 31:67–72, 1974
181. Appelbaum PS, Gutheil TG: Drug refusal: a study of psychiatric inpatients. Am J Psychiatry 137:340–346, 1980
182. In re Guardianship of Roe, 383 Mass 415, 421 NE 2d 40 (1981)
183. American Psychiatric Association Task Force Report No 26: Involuntary Commitment to Outpatient Treatment. Washington, DC, Ameri-

can Psychiatric Association, 1987
184. Knoedler W: Outpatient commitment. Hosp Community Psychiatry 39:783–784, 1988
185. Miller RD: In reply (letter). Hosp Community Psychiatry 39:784, 1988
186. Hiday VA, Scheid-Cook TL: The North Carolina experience with outpatient commitment: a critical appraisal. Int J Law Psychiatry 10:215–232, 1987
187. Geller JL: The quandaries of enforced community treatment and unenforceable outpatient commitment statutes. Journal of Psychiatry and Law 14:149–158, 1986
188. Schwartz SJ, Costanzo CE: Compelling treatment in the community: distorted doctrines and violated values. Loyola of Los Angeles Law Review 20:1329–1429, 1987
189. North Carolina General Assembly Session 1983, House Bill No 124
190. State of Hawaii, 12th Legislature, House Bill No 1932-84
191. Georgia Statutes § 88-508
192. Vermont Statutes Annotated Ch 181, § 7618
193. House Bill No 316, Montana 50th Legislature, amending §§ 51-21-102 through 128. "Act Providing for Involuntary Commitment and Treatment in the Local Community of Persons Who Are Mentally Ill"
194. Arkansas Statutes Annotated §§ 59-1415(c), 1409 (Supp 1985)
195. Tennessee Statutes § 33-6-201
196. Cain v Rijken, 717 P2d 140 (Or 1986)
197. Canon v Thumudo, 422 NW 2d 688 (Mich 1988)
198. Felthous AR: Liability of treaters for injuries to others: erosion of three immunities. Bull Am Acad Psychiatry Law 5:115–125, 1987
199. Arizona Revised Statutes § 36-540 (1983)
200. Miller RD: Outpatient civil commitment of the mentally ill: an overview and an update. Behavioral Sciences and the Law 6:99–118, 1988
201. Bernath E, Freeman J, Pickett C: Outpatient involuntary commitment. Presented at the annual meeting of the National Council of Community Mental Health Centers, Las Vegas, NV, April 1986
202. Band D, Heine A, Goldfrank J, et al: Outpatient commitment: a thirteen year experience. Presented at the 15th annual meeting of the American Academy of Psychiatry and the Law, Nassau, Bahamas, Oct 25, 1984
203. Zanni G, deVeau L: A research note on the use of outpatient commitment. Hosp Community Psychiatry 37:941–942, 1986
204. Van Putten RA: Involuntary community treatment: outpatient commitment and its derivatives. Presented at the 38th Hospital and Community Psychiatry Institute, San Diego, CA, Oct 29, 1986
205. Hendrickson K: Outpatient commitment: using an underutilized resource. Presented at the 37th Hospital and Community Psychiatry Institute, Denver, CO, Oct 1985
206. Geller JL: Rights, wrongs, and the dilemma of coerced community treatment. Am J Psychiatry 143:1259–1264, 1986
207. Bursten B: Posthospital mandatory outpatient treatment. Am J Psychi-

atry 143:1255–1258, 1986
208. Mulvey EP, Geller JL, Roth LH: The promise and peril of involuntary outpatient commitment. Am Psychol 42:571–584, 1987
209. Lamb HR, Mills MJ: Needed changes in law and procedure for the chronically mentally ill. Hosp Community Psychiatry 37:475–480, 1986
210. Brooks AD: Outpatient commitment for the chronically mentally ill: law and policy, in Improving Mental Health Services: What the Social Sciences Can Tell Us (New Directions for Mental Health Services No 36). Edited by Mechanic D. San Francisco, CA, Jossey-Bass, 1987, pp 117–128
211. Wilk RJ: Involuntary outpatient commitment of the mentally ill. Social Work 33:133–137, 1986
212. Stone AA: A response to comments on APA's Model Commitment Law. Hosp Community Psychiatry 36:984–989, 1985
213. Dougherty FM: Annotation: right to notice and hearing prior to revocation of conditional release status of mental patient. ALR4th 29:394–400
214. Call JA: Constitutional law: the summary revocation of an involuntary mental patient's convalescent leave: is it unconstitutional? Oklahoma Law Review 33:366–384, 1980
215. Bartholf F: A survey of case law on mandatory outpatient treatment. Developments in Mental Health Law 8:13–15, 1988
216. O'Connor v Donaldson, 422 US 563; 95 S Ct 2486 (1975)
217. Stefan S: Preventive commitment: the concept and its pitfalls. Mental and Physical Disability Law Reporter 11:288–302, 1987
218. Schwartz SJ: Presentation to the Commission to Revise the Mental Health Code of Illinois, Chicago, IL, April 18, 1988
219. Bachrach LL: Asylum and chronically ill psychiatric patients. Am J Psychiatry 141:975–978, 1984
220. Fink PJ, Weinstein SP: Whatever happened to community psychiatry? the deprofessionalization of community mental health centers. Am J Psychiatry 136:406–409, 1979
221. Lindenthal JJ, Thomas CS: A comparative study of the handling of confidentiality. J Nerv Ment Dis 168:361–369, 1980
222. Miller RD: Confidentiality or communication in the treatment of the mentally ill. Bull Am Acad Psychiatry Law 9:54–59, 1981
223. Gostin L: The ideology of entitlement: the application of contemporary legal approaches to psychiatry, in Mental Illness: Changes and Trends. Edited by Bean F. London, John Wiley, 1983, pp 27–54
224. Shapland J, Williams T: Legalism revived: new mental health legislation in England. Int J Law Psychiatry 6:351–369, 1983
225. Gordon R, Verdun-Jones SN: The right to refuse treatment: Commonwealth developments and issues. Int J Law Psychiatry 6:57–73, 1983
226. Verdun-Jones SN: The right to refuse treatment: recent developments in Canadian jurisprudence. Int J Law Psychiatry 11:51–60, 1988
227. Bottomley S: Mental health law reform and psychiatric deinstitu-

tionalization: the issues in New South Wales. Int J Law Psychiatry 10:369–382, 1987
228. Verdun-Jones SN: The dawn of a "new legalism" in Australia? The New South Wales Mental Health Act, 1983, and related legislation. Int J Law Psychiatry 8:95–118, 1986
229. Liverpool N: A survey of mental health legislation in the eastern Caribbean. Int J Law Psychiatry 8:119–131, 1986
230. Pearlman T: Transcultural analysis of civil commitment laws: Texas and South Africa. Presented at the 20th annual meeting of the American Academy of Psychiatry and the Law, Washington, DC, Oct 1989
231. Krul-Steketee: The psychiatric patient in legislation on mental health, in Law and Mental Health, International Perspectives, Vol 3. Edited by Weisstub D. New York, Pergamon Press, 1985
232. Legemaate J: Personal communication, 1989
233. Arteel P: Reform of the commitment law in Belgium. Presented at the 15th International Congress on Law and Mental Health, Jerusalem, June 25–30, 1989
234. Winterwerp v the State of The Netherlands, Nederlandse Jurisprudentie 1980, 114 en Pub ECHR, Series A, Vol 33 (1979)
235. Forster R, Vyslouzil M, Boltzmann L: Patient advocacy: whose and which needs shall prevail? some experiences with a pilot project in Austria. Presented at the 15th International Congress on Law and Mental Health, Jerusalem, June 27, 1989
236. Summary in English. SOU 64:469–482, 1984
237. Hoyer G: Grounds for involuntary hospitalization according to the opinion of Norwegian psychiatrists. Int J Law Psychiatry 11:289–303, 1988
238. Gachnochi G: "Rights of man" and mental health. Presented at the 15th International Congress on Law and Mental Health, Jerusalem, June 28, 1989
239. Calcedo-Ordonez A, Florez JA: Law and psychiatry in Spain. Int J Law Psychiatry 5:413–418, 1982
240. Israeli Draft Law on the Treatment of Mentally Sick Persons, 1988
241. Arata A, Del Brenna AM, Lo Nano D, et al: The therapy of mental disorders in Italy: the role of hospitals after the 1978 reform. Int J Law Psychiatry 7:207–214, 1984
242. Report of the U.S. Delegation to Assess Recent Changes in Soviet Psychiatry to Assistant Secretary of State for Human Rights and Humanitarian Affairs, U.S. Department of State, July 12, 1989
243. Jones v United States, 103 S Ct 3043 (1983)
244. Bonnie RJ: Soviet mental health law and human rights: preliminary observations. Unpublished manuscript, Feb 21, 1989
245. Bonnie RJ: Fifth Samuel and Kathryn Yochelson Lecture, Yale Law School, New Haven, CT, Sept 28, 1989

Section III

Violence by Psychiatric Patients

Kenneth Tardiff, M.D., M.P.H., Section Editor

Chapter 3

Violence by Psychiatric Patients

Kenneth Tardiff, M.D., M.P.H.

Frequency and Patterns of Violence by Patients

This section is a review of studies of descriptive research on the frequency and patterns of violence by psychiatric patients. The frequency of violence by psychiatric patients varies in how studies define violence, the setting, and the types of patients examined. Several studies agree that when violence is narrowly defined as physical aggression directed toward other persons, roughly 10% of patients have manifested violence toward others just before being admitted to psychiatric hospitals—both public (1–3) and private hospitals (4). In studies that have defined violence more broadly to include physical aggression toward persons or objects and verbal aggression, the frequency of violence among patients admitted is approximately 35–45%. Interestingly, even in these broader studies, "attacks on persons" are still roughly 10% (5,6). Likewise, in studies with a narrower focus on types of patients with a greater propensity for violence—for example, schizophrenic patients (7), psychotic adolescents (8), or geriatric patients (7)—the rates of attacks on persons are higher than 10%.

When the setting shifts from preadmission violence to the inpatient unit, the frequency of violence diminishes. In a 1982 study, a colleague and I found that 7% of patients had assaulted other persons at least once in the hospital in a 3-month period preceding a survey we did in state hospitals (10). Among inpatients in private psychiatric hospitals, I found a lower frequency of violence toward other persons (4). When the setting was outpatient clinics, I found that 3% of patients presenting for evaluation in these clinics had been physically violent toward other persons—half of them family members other than children—in the recent past (11).

Age

In all of my studies—public and private admission, long-term hospital, and outpatient studies—young patients were more likely than older patients to have been assaultive (1,4,10,11). The relationship between youth and violence among mental patients had been apparent in other studies of violence (3,12). Although the association of youth and violence is not expected, the association that appeared between violence and older age in admission studies was somewhat surprising (1,4). That is, patients 65 years of age and older were more likely than the middle-aged patients, but not as likely as the younger patients, to have manifested assaultive behavior before admission. Usually gross organic impairment in these older patients and increased impulsivity and disorganization were associated with violence. Most of their violent episodes were not severe in terms of causing injury.

Another study, of patients admitted to the geriatric unit of a state hospital, confirmed the greater risk of violence in older patients (9). Approximately 8% of the patients in this study committed serious violent acts with a weapon, usually a gun, and another 63% were physically assaultive without a weapon or verbally abusive toward other persons. For the geriatric patients who had used a weapon, this usually was their first violent episode and first experience with psychiatric treatment. Often, the violent acts were a result of paranoid delusions and were directed toward imagined persecutors. Those who did not use weapons differed from those using weapons in that a greater proportion of the patients who did not use weapons had organic brain syndrome accompanied by a clouded sensorium. Their violence usually was not dangerous and was reflexive in nature, probably the result of disorganization and frustration rather than paranoid delusions.

Gender

Most studies have shown that men are much more likely than women to be violent (1,2,4,5,8,11,12). There was one exception—a study of patients who had resided in hospitals for long periods (10). That study showed no difference in frequency of assault between male and female patients. Its finding runs counter to what happens in society in general, in that men are responsible for the bulk of violent crime. The predominant result of greater male violence may mean that men are more likely than women to be hospitalized for assaultive behavior in the community. Another explanation is possible, however. Many studies have shown that physical aggression is considered more appropriate for males in our society (13). The absence of sex differences in assaults among long-term patients may suggest that a blurring of sex role differences occurs once a person becomes a chronic patient in a mental hospital. Thus, mental status and age may be relatively more important than sex in determining whether a patient strikes out at other persons in the hospital.

Racial, Socioeconomic, and Cultural Factors

I have not found a disproportionate amount of violence among nonwhite psychiatric patients (4,10,11) except in the public admission study (1). In that study, another analysis that controlled for education as a measure of socioeconomic status did not confirm an increased proportion of violence among blacks (1). On the surface, this contradicts what is seen in society in general—namely, increased rates of homicide and other violence by the nonwhite population. Some social scientists have sought to explain the overall higher level of violence among nonwhites and criminal violence in black ghettos by hypothesizing that the general circumstances of these groups lead them to fight rather than to achieve through legitimate means. Thus, some writers have hypothesized that blacks live in a violent subculture (14–16), whereas others have found that for domestic violence, there is no difference between blacks and whites if socioeconomic status is controlled in the analysis (17).

Some have found that racial inequality and stress were associated with rates of homicide and that the underlying cause was economic inequality (18). Economic inequality was not merely poverty but rather *relative* income differences among individuals. The theory says that violence occurs because of hostility in one person who perceives that he or she is disadvantaged relative to other persons (19). Other studies have found that economic inequality is not related to violence, but that *absolute* poverty is related to violence (20,21).

The contradictory results of these studies are probably caused by their use of large metropolitan areas as units of analysis. To test the hypothesis that economic inequality is related to homicide, Messner and I used small neighborhoods as units of analysis. We found that economic inequality and race were not related to homicide but that the prime determinants were absolute poverty and marital disruption (22).

Thus, the social determinants of violence seem to involve a cycle of poverty and an inability to have basic necessities of life that is marked by disruption of marriages; proliferation of single-parent families; high rates of unemployment; and further difficulties in maintaining interpersonal ties, family structures, and social control. Thus, in evaluating patients, psychiatrists must consider environmental or social factors that may facilitate the expression of violence.

Patients' History of Violence

A history of violence is related to future violence in several respects. People who were abused as children tend to become physically abusive adults, that is, adults who themselves are child abusers or are otherwise violent (23). Reports suggest that 1% of children are physically abused each year (24). This rate reflects actual reports of child abuse. Because only serious physical abuse is reported, the real incidence of child abuse is probably higher. Moreover, children who are not physically abused but who witness intrafamily violence—for example, spouse abuse—tend to have increased rates of and problems with violence among other children. This is especially true of boys, who manifest such symptoms as hyperactivity, cruelty, bullying, and temper tantrums (25).

Child and spouse abuse are significant problems, and, clearly, being abused as a child or being in a family where a spouse is abused may tip the balance toward becoming violent as adults. Of course, childhood and domestic violence are not the primary causes of adult violence, but they are links in a chain of causation. Other such links are also discussed in this section—for example, socioeconomic factors such as poverty, unemployment, education, and culture or the presence of psychiatric disorders, alcohol and drug abuse, and other pathologies.

Whatever the specific antecedents of violent behavior, violent patients admitted to hospitals were more likely than nonviolent patients to have histories of prior arrests and even jail sentences (1). In general, histories of violent behavior are strong predictors of future violent behavior (26). Furthermore, both public and private admission studies show that violent patients also had a greater proportion of suicide attempts than did nonviolent patients (1,4).

Biochemical Factors

Basic research has suggested that suicide and externally directed violence may share the same mechanisms in the brain. Earlier studies have implicated increased levels of norepinephrine and dopamine in aggressive behavior (27). The most promising work has involved the serotonergic system, however. Two studies of men with a history of aggressive behavior found that a history of aggressive behavior and a history of suicidal behavior were both related to decreased cerebrospinal fluid (CSF) 5-HIAA levels (28,29). Altered serotonin metabolism may be a highly significant contributing factor to these behaviors in whatever diagnostic group they occur. A study of CSF 5-HIAA levels in a group of men convicted of criminal homicide and a group of men who attempted suicide found that these groups had lower levels of 5-HIAA in spinal fluid than did control men (30). A study of violent offenders who had killed or attempted to kill with unusual cruelty found that impulsive offenders had significantly lower CSF 5-HIAA concentrations than "nonimpulsive offenders," the latter defined as people who had premeditated their crimes (31). Furthermore, offenders with histories of suicide attempts had lower CSF 5-HIAA levels than those without such histories. These data agree with other studies of suicide and serotonin metabolism (32).

A general conclusion that one may draw from these studies is that low CSF 5-HIAA concentration may be a marker of impulsivity rather than of a specific type of violence—for example, suicide or externally directed aggression. Possibly a history of other impulsive behaviors such as reckless driving, spending, or sexual activity may be relevant to predicting future violence, particularly violence of an impulsive nature.

Psychopathology

My research and studies by others show definite patterns of increased rates of violence among patients with psychopathology. In my public and private hospital admission studies, schizophrenic patients represented a large proportion of patients admitted and were represented in even greater numbers in the groups of violent patients (1,4). Both paranoid and nonparanoid schizophrenic patients were at increased risk of violence just before admission. In the study of private hospitals, adequate numbers of manic patients were admitted to indicate that these patients also were at higher risk of violent behavior just before admission.

In a study of patients residing in hospitals for a long period, only the nonparanoid schizophrenic patients were at increased risk of violence, and those violent patients manifested severe psychotic symptomatology (10). Paranoid schizophrenic patients residing in these hospitals were likely to be in the nonviolent group. Furthermore, a subsequent analysis showed that paranoid schizophrenic patients who had manifested violence in hospitals just before the survey were more likely than other previously violent patients to be deemed appropriate for community placement. It was apparent that the paranoid patients responded to medication and had decreased psychopathology related to violence—or at least they stopped talking about it and controlled themselves (33).

Three other studies found increased verbal or physical aggression in paranoid schizophrenic patients. A fourth study found no statistically significant increase of physical aggression in paranoid schizophrenic patients. Blackburn examined 48 schizophrenic men hospitalized in England and found that 63% of the patients with paranoid schizophrenia and 24% of those with nonparanoid schizophrenia had histories of previous aggressive behavior (34). Planansky and Johnson (35) found that, overall, 58 (29%) of 205 schizophrenic men hospitalized made explicit verbal threats to kill or had attacked people sometime in the past. There was an increased likelihood of a history of homicidal threats or assaultive behavior in the paranoid schizophrenic group, and most of the aggressive threats or behaviors occurred during acute psychotic episodes (35). Addad and colleagues (36) found that of 116 schizophrenic patients in a French hospital, 53 (46%) had a history of previous criminal acts. Of those with a history of criminal activities, paranoid schizophrenic patients had increased rates of crimes against persons—that is, homicide or assault—whereas nonparanoid schizophrenic patients were more likely to have committed nonviolent crimes. Shader and colleagues examined 45 schizophrenic patients on the inpatient unit or in the day hospital of a state hospital who had any recorded episode in which physical aggression was directed toward others. The researchers found that patients diagnosed as the schizoaffective subtype were more likely to have a history of physical aggression, whereas paranoid schizophrenic patients had no increase and other schizophrenic patients had a decreased likelihood of aggression (7).

In a study by Bach-Y-Rita and Veno, 13 of 62 habitually violent patients from a prison population merited a diagnosis of paranoid schizophrenia despite the fact that "psychotic" inmates, as perceived by the correctional authorities, were excluded from the study (37). In another study of 1,241 men remanded to a prison in Britain, Taylor and Gunn found that 9% of the men showed symptoms of a major psychiatric disorder, and most of these were schizophrenic and psychotic when they entered the prison. Offenses among schizophrenic patients commonly involved homicide and arson (38).

A second group of individuals with increased risk of violence among patients admitted to hospitals as well as those in hospitals are patients with organic impairment (1,4,10). Many of the patients had chronic organic impairment of the brain related to chronic alcoholism, trauma, cerebrovascular disease, infection, Alzheimer's disease, and other gross brain disorders. Few cases were associated with seizure disorders, except for patients residing in the hospitals for long periods, and few in any setting were related to partial complex seizures.

The role of gross organic impairment in violence in other populations has been supported. Lewis and colleagues found that among 97 delinquent adolescent boys in correctional schools, 18 had partial complex seizures. They also found that the more violent boys were those with this disorder (39). Although 5 boys committed violent acts during seizures, violence was interictal as well. The violent boys with partial complex seizures were more likely to report impaired or distorted memory and to have low IQs and more frequent histories of head trauma. They also manifested paranoid ideation, hallucinations, or both that were associated with poor impulse control and were not directly related to seizures. Devinsky and Bear have emphasized the importance of epilepsy in violence, and they have illustrated, through the use of case histories, various forms of this violence (40). Devinsky and Bear criticized studies that used patients with generalized seizures in control groups, arguing that a primary limbic focus may be obscured by general seizure activity, or a secondary limbic focus of the seizure activity may result from the generalized seizure activity.

Alcohol and Drug Abuse

In my earlier admission studies (1,4), alcohol and drug abuse were not related to violence among the patients admitted to public or private hospitals other than as etiological factors in chronic organic impairment. This surprising negative finding probably is explained by the small numbers of patients with alcohol or drug abuse included in these studies and, more importantly, by the confounding variable of diagnosis. Schizophrenic patients were less likely to abuse alcohol and drugs. These studies must be updated, however; it is my impression from patients admitted to the hospital now that there is a significant abuse of drugs by schizophrenic patients. A number of epidemiological studies of nonhospitalized populations have found a strong link between alcohol use and violence (41,42). Violence also has been specifically associated with a number of street drugs of abuse, including amphetamines, cocaine, hallucinogens, benzodiazepines, and sedatives (43,44). Phencyclidine (PCP) is particularly virulent in producing bizarre and violent behavior, but the recent rise in heavy crack cocaine use has overshadowed it in the reported incidence of wild psychotic violent states. Of the 2,743 patients who were newly admitted to prison in Britain, 8.6% manifested acute withdrawal from alcohol or drugs, and, of course, many had histories of alcohol abuse, drug abuse, or both (38). Alcohol and drugs are an important factor in violence—either through the pharmacologic effect of disinhibition or during withdrawal, in the case of alcohol, benzodiazepines, and sedatives. Excitement and disorganization as well as delusional thinking occur in the case of cocaine, amphetamines, and some hallucinogens.

Personality and Explosive Disorders

In my studies of patients admitted to hospitals as well as those presenting to outpatient clinics (1,11), assaultive patients were increased proportional to nonassaultive patients in the category of personality disorders. The most solid connection between violence and personality, child, and adolescent disorders was found in the outpatient clinics. Disorders particularly prone to violence include the intermittent explosive disorder and borderline and antisocial personality disorders. With the explosive disorder, there are several discrete episodes of loss of control involving violence toward others or destruction of property. A violent episode may have little apparent precipitating cause or may be linked to predictable patterns of escalation of conflict between the patient and others, usually family members. Violence is out of proportion to any precipitating factors. The violence may occur for a few minutes or an hour and is often associated with alcohol use. Characteristically, it is followed by remorse and feelings of guilt concerning the beating of a spouse, child, or other family member. Between episodes there are few problems with impulse control or violence.

In the antisocial personality there are intermittent episodes of violent behavior; however, between these violent outbursts there is pervasive antisocial behavior without remorse, including thefts, drug dealing, job problems, lying, reckless driving, and other impulsive behaviors. The borderline personality manifests in addition to episodic violence a broad instability of interpersonal relationships as well as profound mood and identity problems. Violence is just one of many impulsive behaviors. Others include sexual acting out, overspending, overeating, suicide attempts, and drug and alcohol abuse.

EVALUATION OF VIOLENT PATIENTS AND RISK OF VIOLENCE

The evaluation of patients who present with problems of violence should be conducted along the same lines as evaluations of patients who present with other symptoms. That is, the psychiatrist should assess the chief complaint and take a history of the present illness, a family history, a personal and developmental history, and a medical history. Also indicated are evaluations of mental status, a physical examination, laboratory tests, and imaging. This section describes the important standards for data collection in the evaluation of violent patients for determining the etiology of the violence, planning for treatment, and predicting short-term potential for violence. Other works provide even more extensive discussions of the evaluation of violent patients (45–47).

The interview and examination of the patient is most important. But the clinician also should turn to other sources of information. For example, police, who may have brought the patient to the hospital; relatives; the patient's therapist; the patient's medical physician; and the patient's past medical records all may provide relevant data. I prefer to interview the violent patient *before* going to these other sources of information, although when police officers bring the patient to the hospital, they should be interviewed before they leave, if at all possible.

The clinician should record the patient's stated reasons for being in the evaluation/treatment setting at that time. Although the patient's stated chief complaint may not agree with other sources of information—for example, the police may say that the patient was brought to the emergency room because he tried to kill his wife with a knife—the clinician should evaluate the complaint as stated by the patient. For example, in this case, the man may say that he came for an evaluation because he was yelling at his wife and not mention a knife. Although the clinician would evaluate fully the violence later, it is important in the early phase of evaluation to let *patients* present their views of their problems so that clinicians may assess the patients' perspective of what the problem is, assess patients' accuracy and reliability, and avoid confrontations that might impede subsequent evaluation.

Assessing the Symptom of Violence

Although clinicians should address all aspects of a patient's present psychiatric illness in the interview, they should put a primary focus on the history of violence as a symptom associated with psychiatric illness. Clinicians should determine the onset of the first violent episode and should develop a chronology of the patient's violence since onset. Clinicians should ask about the frequency and target of violent behavior and should make particular efforts to identify recurring *patterns* of escalation and violence. For example, a husband may arrive home after work after a few drinks, and become very demanding. The patient's wife then typically may counter by pointing out his deficiencies, and hostility may escalate to eventual violence. Clinicians should determine the severity of injury or intended injury. Any associated symptoms either preceding or occurring during the violent episode should be explored—for example, amnesia. The clinician should inquire about prior evaluations the patient may have had of the violent behavior, including tests done—for example, electroencephalogram (EEG) and diagnostic imaging. Likewise, the clinician should compile a detailed history of treatment including medication, hospitalizations related to violence, and other disorders. If necessary, the clinician should request records of evaluations and treatments from other institutions.

The clinician should inquire about other types of violence the patient has manifested, particularly violence of an impulsive nature. This would include past suicidal ideation and behavior as well as behavior such as reckless driving, destruction of property, fire setting, reckless spending, sexual acting out, and any criminal offenses.

Assessing the Family and Culture

In addition to collecting the routine family history—consisting of the names and ages of living relatives and causes of death and any psychiatric illnesses—the clinician should focus on situations in the family and community that can lead to violence. Adolescents and other violent individuals often come from chaotic family situations. Thus, parental psychopathology associated with marital discord, broken homes, and inability to supervise and discipline children adequately often is present in such cases. Furthermore, clinicians should view patients in the context of the patients' familial and cultural values and norms concerning the expression of violence. Often these norms are most clearly related to low socioeconomic status rather than to race. Of utmost importance is the occurrence of violence within the family unit—for example, spouse abuse, child abuse, or other types of violence between family members. Clinicians should determine whether the patient was abused as a child and should inquire into any other domestic violence the patient may have encountered in growing up. Patients' difficulties with reading and other learning disabilities should be assessed in the context of their educational attainment. Finally, the clinician should outline the patient's relationships with his or her peers as well as with family members.

Medical History

Clinicians should conduct an exhaustive review of the patient's medical history and current medical status. A wide range of medical illnesses have been found to be associated with violent behavior. Any medical illnesses should be documented in the record in addition to any past or current medication.

A number of systemic disorders are associated with violence. Many of these are treatable and reversible; thus, recognition is important, and appropriate medical care is necessary. These disorders include hypoxia; electrolyte imbalances; hepatic disease; renal disease; vitamin deficiencies such as B_{12}, folate, or thiamine; systemic infections; hypoglycemia; Cushing's disease; hyperthyroidism; hypothyroidism; systemic lupus erythematosus; poisoning by heavy metals, insecticides, and other substances; porphyria; and other disorders.

A number of primary diseases of the brain can be associated with violent behavior. Violence in temporal lobe epilepsy is not frequent, but when it occurs, it may occur during the ictal period and, if so, is often purposeless. Violence also has been found in the interictal period among patients with temporal lobe epilepsy. In the postictal period, following generalized seizures, violence has been found with encephalopathy. Infections of the brain including viral encephalitis, acquired immunodeficiency syndrome (AIDS), tuberculosis and fungal meningitis, syphilis, and herpes simplex can be associated with violent behavior.

Other primary diseases of the brain associated with violence include head trauma, normal pressure hydrocephalus, cerebrovascular diseases, tumors, Huntington's chorea, multiple sclerosis, Pick's disease, multi-infarct dementia, Alzheimer's disease, Parkinson's disease, Wilson's disease, and postanoxic or posthypoglycemic states with brain damage.

Alcohol and Drugs

Clinicians should make a detailed assessment of the patient's use of alcohol and drugs, because both intoxication and withdrawal may be associated with violence. Ingestion of alcohol often is associated with aggression and violence because of the disinhibitory effect of alcohol, particularly in the initial phase of intoxication. Intoxication is also accompanied by emotional lability and impaired judgment. Violent behavior sometimes is provoked in persons who drink small amounts of alcohol—even amounts that are insufficient to cause intoxication in most people. Violence also may be associated with withdrawal after cessation of heavy ingestion of alcohol for 2 or 3 days. Violence may result from gross disorganization of behavior or in response to threatening auditory hallucinations and delusions in delirium.

Although sedative or anxiolytic substances can produce intoxication and violence, they do so less frequently than does intoxication with alcohol. Nevertheless, the mechanism of action appears in both cases to be the same—that is, disinhibition and acting out of aggressive or sexual impulses with mood lability and impaired judgment. As with alcohol withdrawal, sedative or anxiolytic substance withdrawal may be associated with violence and irritability, particularly after cessation of several weeks or more of moderate or heavy use of these substances. In certain cases, delirium may be present, including vivid hallucinations and delusional thinking with resulting violence.

Cocaine initially produces a feeling of well-being and euphoria. But with continued use, particularly when cocaine is taken intravenously or smoked in the form of crack, the feelings of euphoria can turn to irritability, psychomotor agitation, and suspiciousness and frequently lead to violence. Continued use of cocaine can lead to suspiciousness, paranoid ideation, and subsequently to paranoid delusional thinking. Thus, violence can result from delusional thinking as well as from the effect of cocaine through overall stimulation. Unlike withdrawal from alcohol and the sedative-anxiolytic substances, cocaine withdrawal is not usually associated with violence, but rather with depression. In some cases of prolonged use, cessation of cocaine use can result in profound impairment in thinking, suicidal behavior, and, in some cases, irritability and psychomotor agitation. Likewise, with chronic amphetamine use, there may be paranoid ideation and delusional thinking, agitation, fighting, and other forms of aggression.

Other drugs may cause violence. PCP often produces marked violence, impulsivity, unpredictability, and grossly impaired judgment. In addition, PCP users may manifest delusional thinking, delirium, or both. Inhalants—hydrocarbons found in substances such as gasoline, glue, paint, and paint thinners—are often used by young children and early adolescents to produce an intoxication that may be characterized by belligerence, violence, and impaired judgment.

Prescription drugs may cause violence in excessive doses or through side effects. For example, anticholinergic medication and steroids can produce violence. The agitation of akathisia from neuroleptics may turn to violence.

Mental Status Examination

A careful mental status examination will reveal the presence of psychiatric disorders that are associated with violence. Such disorders include a wide spectrum of organic mental disorders caused by underlying medical illness and alcohol or substance abuse, as discussed above. Other psychiatric disorders associated with a greater risk of violence than are other disorders are schizophrenia, mania, and delusional paranoid disorders. Disorders with violence as part of their diagnostic criteria include organic, antisocial, and borderline personality disorders and conduct and attention-deficit hyperactivity disorders.

Schizophrenia. Paranoid schizophrenia involves delusional thinking in terms of persecution. Such patients feel that people are trying to harm them, that the police or FBI are spying on them, that some unknown mechanism is controlling their minds, or that the therapist is harming them—for example, by "poisoning" them through medication. Paranoid schizophrenic patients may react to these persecutory delusions by retaliating against the presumed source of this persecution. Other types of schizophrenic patients may attempt to kill others because of some form of psychotic identification with the victim, usually a well-known figure or the patient's therapist.

Hallucinations associated with schizophrenia—particularly hallucinations in which the patient is "commanded," for example, by "God" to kill someone—have resulted in violent behavior and homicide. In addition, hallucinations in which patients believe that people are cursing or insulting them may result in retaliation against a supposed source of these insults. Some schizophrenic patients are violent because of their generalized disorganization of thought, lack of impulse control, and purposeless behavior. Excited psychomotor activity may resemble an organic state. Schizophrenic patients have intact orientation and memory, whereas violent patients with organic mental disorders usually do not.

Affective disorders. Manic patients may be violent as a result of their extreme psychomotor agitation, resistance to being contained, or irritable moods associated with angry tirades. Most violence by manic patients is not premeditated. Rarely, a manic patient will become violent as a result of delusional thinking, in which the patient believes he or she is being persecuted because of some special attribute. But more often, manic patients tend to put all impulses into action. If some of these impulses are violent, then they become the sources of violent actions.

Other patients with mood disorders are rarely violent. An exception, although an infrequent one, is the case of the psychotic depressed patient. In this case, extreme hopelessness, feelings that life is not worth living, or delusional feelings of profound guilt may result in violence, usually involving murder, followed by suicide by the patient. If this occurs, it most often involves a woman killing her children and then herself, or a man killing his family and then himself. These cases may result in litigation over whether the depression was adequately recognized and treated.

Delusional disorder. Delusional disorder is uncommon, but it often can be associated with violence. The persistent nonbizarre delusion possessed by these patients may be of the persecutory type, in which patients feel conspired against, cheated, spied upon, poisoned, or otherwise harmed. Such patients are prone to take legal action and to appeal to government agencies. In addition, patients with this disorder often become resentful and angry. They may resort to violence against those they believe are harming them. Delusional disorders of the jealous type involve the persistent belief that the patient's spouse or lover is unfaithful. These patients attempt to restrict the activities of a spouse or lover and often follow the spouse or lover. They may resort to physical attacks on the spouse or lover or someone who is identified as the "other partner" in an imagined infidelity.

Personality and explosive disorders. The intermittent explosive disorder has as a key characteristic an episodic recurrent outburst of aggression and violence that is grossly out of proportion to any precipitating psychosocial stressor. Following this violent episode there is often remorse, as in the case of a husband who has attacked his wife, or a mother who has severely beaten a child. In the intervening period between these violent episodes, there is little evidence of other behavioral problems.

Two other personality disorders are associated with violence—

the borderline personality and the antisocial personality. In the case of borderline personality disorder, in addition to frequently displaying anger and recurrently initiating physical violence toward others, the patient manifests a number of other behavioral problems in addition to and between the violent episodes. These patients often engage in impulsive behaviors, such as suicidal or self-mutilating behaviors, excessive spending, indiscreet sexual behavior, drug abuse, shoplifting, reckless driving, and other self-damaging behaviors. In addition, there is a marked and persistent identity problem manifested by uncertainty about self-image, sexual orientation, career goals, and other values. There often are manipulative attempts to obtain caring from others.

Violence manifested by persons with antisocial personality disorder is just one of many antisocial behaviors. These patients repeatedly get into physical fights and violence involving their spouses, children, and individuals outside of the family. They also display a number of other antisocial behaviors including destroying property, harassing others, stealing, illegal occupations, driving in a reckless or intoxicated manner, and promiscuous sexual relationships. The patient often lies, does not honor financial obligations, and is unable to sustain consistent employment. Alcohol and substance abuse are often a problem. Violence toward others and other antisocial behaviors are not accompanied by remorse or guilt.

Disruptive behavior disorders. Disruptive behavior disorders occur in children and adolescents but they may continue into adulthood as antisocial personality and aggressive violent behavior. Children and adolescents with conduct disorders often are aggressive and display physical violence toward others and cruelty to other people or animals. They also may deliberately destroy property—for example, by fire setting. They may engage in stealing, mugging, purse snatching, robbery, and, later in adolescence, in rape. Often the individuals abuse alcohol and other substances and engage in early sexual behavior. Again, as with borderline personality patients, disruptive antisocial individuals generally do not experience remorse or guilt. They manifest low frustration tolerance and have low self-esteem. Disruptive behavior disorders appear as violence or as other conduct problems in group activities with peers. But disruptive disorders may occur in isolated or solitary situations as well.

Children and adolescents with attention-deficit hyperactivity disorder manifest marked hyperactivity and impulsiveness that may be verbal or physical, but they are less frequently maliciously violent and disruptive than those with disruptive behavior disorders.

Physical Examination

A physical examination will reveal signs of underlying medical disorders that, as noted earlier, sometimes are associated with violence. Signs of alcohol or drug intoxication may be present—slurred speech, incoordination, unsteady gait, nystagmus, dilated or constricted pupils, and elevated blood pressure and heart rate. Withdrawal from alcohol and some drugs may produce autonomic activity, tremors, and even seizures.

Laboratory Testing and Other Procedures

The usual routine laboratory tests are done for violent patients, including complete blood count, blood chemistries (electrolytes, BUN, glucose, creatinine, calcium, phosphate, and liver function tests), thyroid function (T_3RU, T_4, thyroid-stimulating hormone), screening for syphilis, vitamin deficiency testing (B_{12}, folate, thiamine), urinalysis, electrocardiogram, and chest X rays. I believe that EEG should be part of the routine evaluation of the violent patient. The routine EEG should be augmented by nasopharyngeal leads as well as a sleep and sleep-deprived EEG. In addition, blood and urine should be taken at the time of admission for alcohol and drug assay. Because cocaine has a very short half-life—about an hour—it is essential to take blood as soon as possible with a container with fluoride to prevent subsequent breakdown of cocaine in the tube. Any positive drug assay should be confirmed by a different type of assay. For example, radioimmunoassay could be followed by liquid or gas chromatography—mass spectrophotometry.

Clinicians should make liberal use of magnetic resonance imaging (MRI) in assessing violent patients. MRI is superior to computed tomography (CT) in detecting temporal lobe pathology. MRI does not expose the patient to ionizing radiation and can provide several imaging planes—transverse, sagittal, and coronal. MRI is contraindicated in patients with metal surgical clips, metal skull plates, and cardiac pacemakers, however. Another problem in using MRI with violent patients is that it requires the patient's complete cooperation because the MRI subject must not move. CT is superior in terms of its ability to detect intercranial calcifications, tumor margins, and old versus new hemorrhages. CT also does not require the same degree of patient cooperation, and thus it can be used more easily than MRI for agitated, hyperactive patients.

Other laboratory tests are used if a specific disorder is indicated. Such tests would include arterial blood gases (hypoxia); human immunodeficiency virus (HIV) antibodies (AIDS, ARC); glucose tolerance test (hypoglycemia); ceruloplasmin and copper levels in urine and serum (Wilson's disease); urine porphobilinogen (porphyria); heavy-metal screening (poisoning); antinuclear antibodies (systemic lupus erythematosus); and lumbar puncture if intracranial pressure is not elevated (infection, multiple sclerosis, hemorrhage).

Model for Short-term Prediction of Violence

Research studies and clinical experience suggest that a model can be formulated to predict violence in the short term, and that such a model could serve as a standard for what should be asked and considered in decisions involving evaluation of a patient's violence potential. Such decisions include choices to admit or not to admit a patient to a hospital in the emergency room, or they may extend to the outpatient office in *Tarasoff*-like situations—that is, when a duty to protect potential victims of one's patients is involved. Evaluations of potential for violence are made also at the time clinicians are considering discharging a patient from the hospital or deciding about unaccompanied passes. In making any decision on the treatment or placement of potentially violent patients, clinicians should interview family members, police, and other persons with information about the patient and violent incidents involving the patient. This will give the clinician some baselines against which to measure the clinician's own data about the patient and will help the clinician guard against being misled by patients who minimize their own dangerousness.

The evaluation of homicide potential is analogous to that of suicide potential. Even if the patient does not express thoughts of violence, clinicians should routinely ask as part of every evaluation the subtle question, "Have you ever lost your temper?" If the answer is yes, the evaluator should proceed in terms of how, when, and so on, in the same manner one would check for suicide potential with, "Have you ever felt that life was not worth living?"

The *appearance* of the patient may alert the clinician to the potential for violence. This includes the loud, agitated, angry-appearing patient who is impatient and refuses to comply with the usual intake procedures in the emergency room or clinic as well as the quiet, guarded patient who requires careful listening to for subtle violent ideation. Dysarthria, unsteady gait, dilated pupils, tremors, and other signs of acute drug or alcohol intoxication dictate caution and serious consideration of the patient's potential for violence, even though threats of violence may not be expressed.

As with the evaluation of suicide potential, evaluating violence potential includes assessing the question, *How well planned is the threat?* Vague threats of killing someone are not as serious—all other things being equal—as are specific, well-formulated threats against a specific person.

As with suicide, the *availability of a means of inflicting injury* is important. For example, if the patient has recently purchased or owns a gun, one should obviously take the threat more seriously.

A past history of violence or other impulsive behavior is often predictive of future violence, as in destruction of property, suicide attempts, reckless driving, reckless spending, criminal offenses, sexual acting out, and other impulsive behavior. Clinicians should assess the *degree of past injuries*—for example, broken bones and lacerations—as well as *toward whom* violence has been directed and *under what circumstances*. Often there is a pattern of past violent behavior in specific circumstances. For example, such a pattern might involve escalation of a dispute between a husband and wife or a child and parent about issues of money, esteem, or sexuality.

Clinicians should find out whether patients have a history of being *abused as a child* or were in families in which physical abuse occurred. Likewise, a history of *obstetrical complications or head injury* should be explored.

Alcohol and drug abuse should be assessed. Substances that can produce violent behavior as a result of the intoxicated state as well as during withdrawal include alcohol, barbiturates, other sedatives, and benzodiazepines. Other substances can produce violence when the patient is intoxicated—cocaine, hallucinogens, and amphetamines.

Organicity increases the risk of violence. Central nervous system disorders have been associated with violent behavior and have been described earlier, as have some systemic disorders affecting the central nervous system.

As with suicide, the presence of *psychosis* should make one take threats of violence very seriously and makes the assessment of violence potential essential, even if threats are not apparent. The paranoid schizophrenic patient poses a number of problems. First of all, paranoid delusions may be subtle, or a patient may attempt to hide them. Therefore, the evaluator must listen for nuances and should follow up regarding the assessment of violence toward others. Another problem with violent paranoid schizophrenic patients is noncompliance with medication once the patient has been stabilized. Compliance with treatment is an important factor in the assessment of violence potential. Patients with other types of schizophrenia have more disorganized symptomatology, and violence may be the result of that or of delusional or hallucinatory symptoms, particularly command hallucinations. Manic patients are also disorganized and less goal oriented in their violent behavior. Depressed patients are rarely violent. Patients who have psychotic depressions, however, may murder spouse, children, or both and then commit suicide.

Last, *demographic characteristics* of patients should be considered, with increased risk of violence among the young, among males, and among persons coming from environments of poverty, disrupted families, and decreased social control where violence is frequently resorted to as a means of attaining a goal.

All of these factors are weighed in the final assessment of whether the patient poses such a significant risk to others that some action is necessary on the part of the evaluator. Action may include changing the treatment plan; hospitalizing the patient; or warning the intended victim, the police, or both. All of the data on which the decision that the patient is or is not at risk for violence is based should be documented in writing, and the rationale used in arriving at the decision should be evident in the *written documentation*. Reassessment of violence potential should be made at short intervals, for example, on a visit-to-visit basis, within a few days, if the patient is to continue to be treated outside of a hospital or other institution. Clinicians have not been faulted as much for inaccurate prediction as for failure to collect data necessary for the prediction of violence and to logically use that data to make a prediction.

Standards in the Use of Seclusion and Restraint

The psychiatric use of seclusion, restraint, or both has become the subject of lawsuits in two arenas. The first involves malpractice cases in which a hospital, physicians, or both are sued for damages in relation to physical injury or death of a patient because of the use of seclusion or restraint or in relation to prolonged use of seclusion or restraint. The second area involves class-action suits against hospitals and departments of health or correction aimed at improving quality of care, the number of staff, and education of staff in the use of seclusion, restraint, and nonphysical means of managing violent behavior.

Success of the plaintiff or the defense in these cases rests on whether there are written guidelines on the use of seclusion and restraint in the hospital, whether these guidelines meet national standards, and whether there is written evidence in the clinical records that the guidelines were followed. This section describes a reasonable clinical standard of care in regard to seclusion and restraint.

Youngberg v. Romeo

The landmark case in the use of seclusion and restraint is the 1982 U.S. Supreme Court case of *Youngberg v. Romeo* (48). Mr. Romeo was a profoundly retarded man who was committed to a state hospital in Pennsylvania. He was often violent toward other patients and staff as well as self-injurious and the victim of violence from others. He sued the hospital for damages on the basis of his constitutional rights. In this decision the Court acknowledged the patient's right to liberty, but indicated that this should be balanced by the institution's duty to protect the patient and others from acts of violence. In deciding whether the patient should be deprived of liberty—that is secluded or restrained—the Court deferred to clinical judgment, in that the Court's role should be to make certain that *professional* judgment was exercised. The Court indicated that in the seclusion or restraint of a patient, "the decision if made by a professional is presumably valid" and "liability may be imposed only when the decision by a professional is such a substantial departure from accepted professional judgment, practice or standard as to demonstrate the person responsible actually did not base the decision on such a judgment."

The importance of this case is that the Court deferred to professional judgment rather than itself prescribing a rigid hierarchy of restrictiveness in the management of violence by patients. At the time the Court's decision was rendered, I was chairing a task force of the American Psychiatric Association (APA) to develop guidelines for the psychiatric uses of seclusion and restraint. The guidelines have been approved by the APA and have set reasonable minimal clinical standards for management of violence using seclusion and restraint in the context of verbal intervention, medication, and other factors in the treatment environment (49). These guidelines, expanded upon in a book (50), represent a minimal standard and have stimulated and served as a model for guidelines at a local level for hospitals.

Wexler points out that in emergency situations the clinician has flexibility in the use of seclusion and restraint (51). In cases of imminent physical violence or escalating aggression, most clinicians' decisions to use seclusion or restraint can be supported. With adherence to APA or appropriate local hospital guidelines for indications, contraindications, assessment by a physician, monitoring, and care of the patient in seclusion and restraint, the clinician can be reassured that liability will not be imposed even if a patient is inadvertently injured or even killed during these procedures. In the use of seclusion and restraint for behavior therapy, Wexler observed that when restrictive behavioral techniques, such as locked timeout or restraint, are used as part of a behavioral treatment program, these are usually applied in response to severe, dangerous, disruptive, or destructive behavior. This is supported under *Romeo*'s principles of emergency management in the use of seclusion and restraint. If restrictive procedures are used after the violence has occurred, and when the patient does not pose a substantial danger, then the emergency rationale would not apply. Use of seclusion or restraint in these cases would then raise the question of informed consent and the ability of a patient to give it and presumably the patient's ability, if competent, to withdraw informed consent at any time.

Prevention

The ward environment, treatment program, and staff should be structured to prevent violence and thus to limit the use of seclusion and restraint as much as possible. The staff should be caring and nonauthoritarian, yet in control of the patient's behavior. Attention should be given to preventing violence by being available to talk with and listen to the patient. The staff should talk with the patient in a calm, nonprovocative manner. The staff should be alert, however, to warning signs of violence for an individual patient—that is, signs that have preceded violence in the past. For example, a patient may have manifested a specific pattern of behavior or speech before an explosive episode. This may be in the form of pacing in front of the nursing station or some other warning sign known to have preceded violence in the past. As escalation begins, medication may be offered, and increased staff attention and support is indicated. There should be an ongoing program of treatment and activity aimed at promoting social behavior. As the subsequent section discusses, the proper type and dose of medication should be used to treat the underlying disorder without excessive sedation or side effects.

To prevent inappropriate seclusion or restraint or, on the other hand, not using these techniques when they should be used, ward staff should know their own feelings about violent patients based on countertransference or other emotional reactions to patients (52). The staff should be constantly monitoring the ward dynamics, particularly staff conflict that may result in inappropriate patient care in the management of violence. Staff members should think about their own past experiences with violence and about how such experiences may affect their treatment of patients. Anger toward a patient for a particular act may be justified, or it may be the result of countertransference or inappropriate emotional reactions toward the patient.

Educational programs should be provided for staff, not only in the use of physical restraints but for the sensitive, nonprovocative use of verbal means of dealing with violence or impending violence. Educational programs should not be merely didactic. Instead, they should be interactional and should make use of small-group discussions and even role-playing. In addition to scheduled in-service meetings and classes, staff and patients also should discuss a violent episode once it has occurred. The violent episode should be discussed in terms of what happened, what could have prevented it, why seclusion or restraint was used (if it was), and how the patient or the staff felt about the use of seclusion and restraint. It is important to recognize that most patients will have negative reactions to being secluded and restrained. Among other patients on the ward, it is important to talk about the violent episode and why seclusion and restraint were used for that particular patient. Open discussion can help allay patients' fears that they could be secluded or restrained for no apparent reason in the future.

Indications for Seclusion, Restraint, or Both

Indications for seclusion and restraint are, first, to prevent imminent harm to the patient or other persons when other means of control are not effective or appropriate; second, to prevent serious disruption of the treatment program or significant damage to the physical environment; and third, to assist in treatment as part of ongoing behavior therapy. In addition, seclusion may be used to decrease the stimulation a patient receives and may be at the patient's request. The decision about whether to use seclusion, restraint, medication, or any combination of these controls is made on the basis of the clinical needs of the individual patient—not on any hierarchy of which control is considered least restrictive. For example, if the etiology of a patient's violent behavior is unknown, restraint may be indicated to maintain the patient in the drug-free period for evaluation. Restraint permits clinicians to observe the patient over time and to differentiate toxic from functional states. In addition, the treating professional may prefer to seclude or restrain a violent patient if the patient has or might have a medical illness or drug allergies that would preclude using certain medications to control violent behavior. Under certain circumstances, seclusion of a patient may be indicated for both the patient's benefit and that of the environment. Certain events, such as destruction of property, uncontrollable screaming or abuse, uncontrolled intrusiveness on others, or fecal smearing, may constitute treatment indications for seclusion or restraint based on environmental needs, but clearly such actions must be undertaken in conjunction with continued consideration of the patient's own needs.

Another issue concerning seclusion and restraint is whether the staff should use these measures only when a patient is actually manifesting dangerous behavior or whether the staff may use these procedures in anticipation of imminent dangerous behavior by the patient. There is no hard-and-fast rule here. Rather, such decisions depend on the staff's professional knowledge of the individual patient. Staff who are thoroughly familiar with a patient's history may rely on past patterns of verbal or nonverbal phenomena that have occurred before previous violent episodes. Note, however, that staff must cite and document specific previous patterns of behavior to justify seclusion or restraint.

Seclusion may be used for decreasing stimulation, usually for psychotic patients. The quiet atmosphere of a seclusion room is a relief from sensory stimulation that may worsen a manic state or contribute to delusional ideas in schizophrenia before medication is effective. Again, there must be adequate and continuing documentation to justify seclusion.

Contraindications for Seclusion and Restraint

Seclusion and restraint are contraindicated as treatment modalities for punishment—that is, they should never be used to seek retribution for an act when no danger exists to the patient or others. Seclusion or restraint also may be contraindicated because of a patient's clinical or medical condition. The patient with an unstable medical status, resulting from infection, cardiac illness, disorders of thermoregulation, or metabolic illness, may require close monitoring and close physical proximity of staff, so that seclusion is not indicated. Restraint alone may be particularly valuable in neurologic problems such as delirium and dementia, where the patient's vulnerability to the reduced sensory input caused by seclusion may lead to worsening of the total clinical state. Seclusion is also relatively contraindicated for patients experiencing a paradoxical reaction to phenothiazine medications; patients who have just taken overdoses and require close monitoring; patients presenting with symptoms of serious and uncontrollable self-abuse and self-mutilation; and when seclusion rooms cannot be sufficiently cooled on hot days for patients receiving drugs such as neuroleptics, which impair thermoregulation.

A patient should never be secluded or restrained for the pure convenience of the staff. Although protection of other patients from harm is a valid indication for seclusion, mere mild obnoxiousness, rudeness, or other unpleasantness to others is not. If prolonged seclusion or restraint occurs for such a reason, the treatment plan, setting, or both should be questioned.

With physical restraint, one must guard against circulatory obstruction, which can be minimized by temporarily releasing one of four-point restraints every 15 minutes. Another adverse effect with restraints is the possibility of aspiration of foreign matter into the lungs. If a patient is lying on his or her back or is obstructed while restrained, one must guard against aspiration by constant monitoring. Last, deaths from strangulation have resulted from camisole and vest restraints.

Emergency Use

Initiation of an episode of seclusion or restraint is usually an emergency procedure carried out by the nursing staff on an inpatient unit. Continued seclusion or restraint requires a physician's review, however. Each institution has specific time parameters regarding review, and psychiatrists should be familiar with them. A physician's order for seclusion or restraint is generally valid for 12 hours and in many hospitals for shorter periods. The following parameters come from the APA Task Force Report (49). The physician should be notified as soon as possible that a patient has been put in seclusion or under restraint. When notified by telephone, the physician should indicate approval pending personal examination of the patient. At least for the first episode of seclusion or restraint the physician should see the patient preferably within 1 hour or less after the beginning of the seclusion or restraint episode. During the initial visit the physician should document the evaluation in the patient's record. The episode should be reviewed by the patient's physician and treatment team. For each subsequent seclusion or restraint episode for that patient, the physician should be notified. In cases of subsequent episodes physicians can exercise professional judgment about whether an actual visit is indicated, but they should be careful to indicate any special precautions that must be taken or monitoring that must be done by the nursing staff.

The Physician's Subsequent Role

A physician should see the secluded or restrained patient as frequently as is necessary to monitor any changes in the patient's mental or physical status. The frequency of these visits may vary. A minimum of two visits a day, approximately 12 hours apart, is recommended. Some patients will require more frequent visits—for example, patients with concurrent medical problems, patients receiving medical treatment that may complicate seclusion or restraint, patients with organic brain syndrome, and situations in which hyperthermia may occur so that the patient should be closely monitored. When the physician sees the patient, any order for seclusion or restraint should be reaffirmed in the patient's record. During the visit, the physician also should review the frequent nursing observations of the patient in seclusion or restraint.

During the visit a physician should examine the patient and document in the patient's record the reason for continued seclusion or restraint, taking into account the patient's mental and physical status, the degree of agitation, physical and emotional adverse effects of seclusion, and other factors such as staffing and the ability to handle the patient on the open inpatient unit.

It should be emphasized that the guidelines for a specific hospital may and, one hopes, will be more restrictive than time parameters indicated in this book and that the clinician must adhere to hospital guidelines. The guidelines for seclusion and restraint within a specific hospital should be rehearsed and approved by the hospital staff as well as the legal staff. This includes specific techniques for putting a patient into seclusion, specific time parameters for physicians visiting the patient and for staff monitoring, and restraint devices such as four-point leather restraints or other devices.

Carrying Out Seclusion and Restraint

Once a decision has been made to begin seclusion or restraint of an agitated patient, a seclusion or restraint leader should be chosen among the clinical staff. The leader should indicate the roles to be played by the remaining staff in the seclusion and restraint process. There should be adequate staff to control the patient's behavior if the patient refuses to comply with requests to go into seclusion. This consists of at least five staff members, one for each extremity and one, who can be the seclusion leader, to control the patient's head. This standard for the number of staff needed to safely manage violence has been used as the basis of lawsuits and labor negotiations. At night, or when the units have low staffing patterns, there must be a mechanism to rapidly summon staff from other units in case of an emergency that requires seclusion or restraint.

The staff should gather around the seclusion leader at the time of first contact with the violent patient. The area should be cleared of all other patients and physical obstructions leading to the seclusion room. Ideally there should be someone who will observe the procedure and note any injuries or difficulties with physical technique. This will make possible a critique of the seclusion or restraint procedure after the episode.

At the time of the first contact with the patient and throughout the procedure, the staff must not humiliate or threaten the patient. They must maintain the patient's dignity and self-esteem. Physical force begins after a prearranged signal from the seclusion leader. Each staff member grabs and controls one of the patient's extremities. Careful not to injure the patient, the staff bring the patient to the ground through a backward motion, and each extremity is restrained at the joint by a member of the team. The patient's head should be controlled to prevent the patient from biting or from sustaining a neck injury. The staff should be cautious to avoid injuring the patient or causing pain. After the patient is restrained on the ground, additional staff may be called to assist in moving the patient to the seclusion room or to help apply physical restraints. Safe lift techniques and the use of restraints must be practiced routinely. Once the patient is in the seclusion room, his or her street clothes are removed, and special attention is paid to removing rings, belts, shoes, matches, and other potentially destructive objects. If indicated, medication may be injected at this time—that is, while the patient is physically restrained.

After a patient has been placed in seclusion or has been restrained, the staff should discuss the episode among themselves to critique the technique and to verbalize any conflicting feelings. The staff should also consider, especially on units where violence is rare, discussing the behavior that led to the seclusion or restraint episode at community meetings with patients.

Monitoring and Care by Staff

While the patient is in seclusion or restraint, the nursing staff should observe him or her at least every 15 minutes. Observations may be done by looking through the window of the seclusion room, especially for severely violent patients. Staff should record their detailed observations in a written log. These visual checks are important to minimize the possibility that patients might harm themselves in the seclusion room. Of course, if self-mutilation is a concern, seclusion may not be indicated for the patient, or constant observation of such patients is indicated.

A direct visit to the seclusion room is indicated at least every 2 hours. In the case of very violent patients, it is advisable that an adequate number of staff accompany the nursing staff. During these visits, vital signs should be taken and meals, fluids, toileting, and other care of the patient should be provided. All observations and recordings should be documented in the patient's record. The patient should be allowed to go to the bathroom at least every 4 hours. Again, for very violent patients, adequate staff should be present at that time. With patients in restraints, the restraints will probably have to be removed while the patient is allowed to go to the bathroom.

Meals should be brought to the patient at regular intervals when the ward meals are served. Eating utensils, if any, should be blunt—even plastic knives and forks can be used as weapons. The patient should be instructed to sit at one corner of the seclusion room while the meal tray is placed in the seclusion room. If possible, the staff should be present with the patient while the meal is being eaten. This is to allow interpersonal contact with the patient as well as to make observations about the patient's degree of self-control. If the patient eats alone, the reason should be documented in the patient's record. There should be adequate attention to fluid intake to prevent dehydration. Documentation of fluid intake is necessary in the patient's record.

The environment of the seclusion room should be free of hazards. Seclusion rooms are usually empty except for a mattress. The mattress should be constructed of durable foam and not of fiber or other materials that patients could use to hang or suffocate themselves. The mattress should not be flammable, and patients should be searched for matches before being placed in seclusion. The ceiling of the seclusion room should be high, with recessed light fixtures. All walls and ceilings should be made of material that cannot be gouged out by patients. There should be no sharp edges to windows and no protuberances such as oxygen jets. Staff should be able to observe every portion of the seclusion room; this may require reflectors. Staff must be able to monitor patients to prevent self-mutilation and other injuries.

If patients are very hyperactive and there is concern about exhaustion, then restraint with or without seclusion should be considered. If it appears that a patient's psychosis has become worse in the seclusion room, the psychiatrist should consider the impact of sensory deprivation. In this case, restraint alone or constant attention by the staff may be indicated.

Release From Seclusion and Restraint

A patient may be released from seclusion or restraint when the patient's behavior is under control and no longer poses a danger to self or others or further disruption of the treatment environment. The ability of a patient to control his or her behavior and to cooperate is evaluated throughout the seclusion episode. For example, during each visit, the patient's ability to respond to a verbal request should be judged. A patient may be asked to sit in a particular part of the seclusion room, or cooperation may be reflected in the patient's increasing willingness to take oral medication rather than having to have injections. At a higher level, the patient will be able to cooperate with physical examinations, interviews, bathing, toileting, and other procedures.

Release from seclusion is a gradual process. The steps may involve opening the seclusion room door for brief periods of time, followed by continued opening of the seclusion room door, to spending time alone in the patient's room, until the patient can be released to the general ward environment. Any evidence of loss of control or lack of cooperation should result in movement back to more restrictive steps in the procedure.

Following an episode of seclusion or restraint, the patient should be allowed to voice his or her feelings about the episode and should be questioned about what led up to the behavior requiring seclusion or restraint as well as what could have been done to prevent the escalation.

Medication

Medication for patients in seclusion or restraint is indicated in cases of severe agitation or psychotic psychopathology. Physicians should be cautioned, however, about overmedicating patients so that they become lethargic, disorganized, or violent as a result of organic impairment. Injections of as-needed (PRN) medication should be avoided if the patient is in seclusion, because this may cause the patient to receive varying doses of medication across nursing shifts and may make assessment of the patient difficult. Instead, a fixed-dose regimen is preferable, and frequent evaluation by the physician is indicated.

Restraint on Open Wards

Some types of restraint devices may be used to allow the patient to remain in the open ward setting. These devices include binding of the wrists to a belt around the patient's waist or binding patients to a wheelchair. These strategies allow restrained patients to participate in group meetings and other activities of the ward. Attention should be given, however, to protecting restrained patients from being injured by other patients on the unit.

BEHAVIORAL TREATMENT

Behavioral treatment programs have been used for the management of violent behavior in severely impaired institutional populations. This approach may be used in conjunction with other treatment approaches for severely impaired patients such as chronic schizophrenic or mentally retarded patients. The basic principles have been described elsewhere (53,54). The goal of the behavior treatment program is to convert an unstructured hospital setting that may promote violent behavior among patients into a structured setting that will provide stimuli aimed at decreasing violent behavior and promoting social behavior.

Setting up a behavioral treatment program on an inpatient unit requires the services of a trained, experienced behavioral analyst. The behavioral analyst plans the treatment program in conjunction with the interdisciplinary staff and trains and supervises staff in the implementation of the treatment program. Behavioral treatment programs should be reviewed periodically by persons other than the ward personnel to ensure their quality and ethical standards. In addition, patients should be involved as much as possible in the formulation of the plans involving them, and they should provide written consent if they are competent to do so. The goals and process of the treatment program should be discussed with patients, and an assessment should be made of each patient's desires in considering privileges and rewards that may be used to motivate positive behavior.

The first part of the behavioral program should be the specification of target behaviors that will be addressed. These behaviors must be specifically stated. "Physical aggression" is too nonspecific, and the behavior should be defined more precisely, as, for example, "pulling other person's hair, biting, kicking, punching, scratching, and so on." For each target behavior there should be a clearly specified response by the staff to the behavior.

Behavioral responses or techniques can be arranged on a continuum of degree of restrictiveness. Unlike their use in emergency situations, seclusion and restraint–like techniques are considered most restrictive compared with other behavioral techniques available in a structured treatment unit. These include, from least to most restrictive, *1*) positive reinforcement (token economies, differential reinforcement of other behaviors, low rates of behavior); *2*) teaching social skills as alternatives to violence; *3*) negative reinforcement (withdrawing positive reinforcement, ignoring undesirable behavior; sensory extinction with physical devices such as using a helmet to prevent patients from engaging in self-stimulating head banging); *4*) contingent observation; and *5*) seclusionary time-out, contingent restraint, or both.

Positive Techniques

Positive behavioral techniques are described clearly and in detail by Liberman and Wong (53,54). A few comments about behavioral techniques—particularly seclusion and restraint procedures in behavioral programs—are warranted nonetheless, because some lawsuits have hinged on whether seclusion or restraint of the patient is part of a valid behavioral treatment program or is abuse.

Token economies have been used to promote social behavior and decrease antisocial behavior in institutions. Patients are expected to perform at a higher level of functioning to earn tokens that can be exchanged for cigarettes, food, and other privileges. In the management of violence, token economies usually require the patient to go for a certain period without physical aggression toward others to be promoted to a higher level of the program—that is, to a level with more privileges.

Frequently for violent patients, reinforcement of nonviolent behavior must be given in the early phase of treatment and at very short intervals—for example, every few seconds or every few minutes. One type of program is *differential reinforcement of other behavior.* This involves delivering reinforcement after a specific period during which the patient has not manifested inappropriate behavior or violence. At the end of each period, which may be in seconds or minutes, a patient receives reinforcement—such as praise, attention, food, or cigarettes—for abstaining from assaultive or destructive behavior. As the program continues, and the patient becomes more cooperative, reinforcement can be spaced over longer periods, eventually leading to a token economy program.

A variant of this is *differential reinforcement of low-rate behavior.* This type of program provides positive reinforcement if the rate of violent behavior or other undesirable behavior falls below a particular level—for example, two violent episodes per hour. That is, the patient would be scheduled to receive reinforcement if he or she was aggressive once per hour or less.

With these positive reinforcement approaches, the patient, once under control, may be taught social skills as alternatives to aggressive and destructive behavior. Clearly disturbed patients may become violent because they are unable to use social skills such as solicitation, persuasion, and negotiation. Behavior therapists may embark on training patients in how to use these alternatives to violence *1*) by giving instructions describing and providing the rationale for the behavior being taught, *2*) by modeling or demonstrating the desired behavior, *3*) by rehearsing or acting the behavior with the patient, and *4*) by giving positive reinforcement for the performance of the correct behavior. Social skills training can teach alternatives to violent behavior that include appropriate affect, appropriate expression of frustration, and requests for the listener to change his or her behavior. Success in these social skills learned in the role-playing situation should be translated to the natural setting of the inpatient unit of the ward.

Other Techniques

Some programs use negative stimuli or the withholding or withdrawing of positive stimuli to decrease violent behavior and other undesirable behaviors. The first type of program is *social extinction,* which is useful if the aggressive behavior is harmless and does not lead to more serious violent behavior. This approach involves deliberately not responding to the patient's inappropriate behavior by ignoring or turning away from the patient. In this type of program it is important that all staff are consistent in their response to the patient's inappropriate behavior. Another type of approach involves withdrawing positive reinforcement when the patient manifests violent or other inappropriate behavior. For example, staff may restrict the patient's privileges or impose a fine of tokens. A related program is *sensory extinction,* in which self-injurious behavior is self-stimulatory. For example, a patient who engages in head banging can be fitted with a protective helmet and padded gloves, which decrease the stimulation from such behavior. A patient who scratches his or her own face may be required to wear rubber gloves.

Other programs remove the patient from the environment or treatment program for varying periods. *Contingent observation* removes the patient from participating in an activity for a short period following violence or other inappropriate behavior, usually of a minor nature. The patient may be instructed to leave the activity and sit in a chair nearby for a few minutes while watching the appropriate behavior of other patients. After 5–15 minutes of watching others, the patient can rejoin the activity.

Seclusionary time-out or *time-out from reinforcement* involves placing the patient in a special area and depriving the patient of reinforcements following violent or other inappropriate behavior. This may actually involve a seclusion room. Unlike seclusion used for the emergency situations described earlier in this chapter, however, seclusionary time-out in behavioral programs is administered immediately following display of a specific target behavior, whether it is of immediate danger to others or not. Unlike the use of seclusion in the emergency situation, it is *brief*—as little as 5 minutes and rarely longer than 1 hour. Also unlike the emergency use of seclusion, the physician need not see patients each time they are placed in seclusionary time-out.

Contingent restraint involves immobilizing some part of a patient's body by some device such as soft ties, a restraint chair, cuffs, or a posey jacket after the patient has committed a specific violent act. The patient is in time-out from reinforcement, and the staff give no attention to the patient other than what is necessary for medical reasons. Contingent restraint may be preferred to seclusionary time-out if the patient has demonstrated self-injurious behaviors that would recur if the patient was left alone in seclusion. Treatment teams should be alert to the possibility that the patient may enjoy being restrained or secluded—that is, as a way of avoiding the activities of the ward and becoming isolated.

These seclusion and restraint–like procedures are used as part of an overall plan with less restrictive and positive reinforcements in behavioral treatment programs planned and implemented by professionals trained in behavioral therapy. These programs should be reviewed initially and periodically by staff not involved with the patient's direct treatment.

PSYCHOPHARMACOLOGY

In managing violent behavior, clinicians must be knowledgeable about psychopharmacology. Such knowledge is essential in treating the psychiatric disorders underlying violence as well as in controlling acute violent episodes. Lawsuits claiming excessive seclusion or restraint or related to injuries inflicted in seclusion or on inpatient units often involve the question of whether the right medication or medications in adequate doses were used. If an ineffective type or dose of medication is used, the risk of violence grows, and the need to use other physical means of control is increased. Patients should not be in prolonged seclusion or restraint because of inadequate medication. Yet patients should not be anesthetized to keep them out of seclusion or restraint. Instead, the treatment plan must be reviewed with an eye to changing the medication, adding other treatment such as behavioral therapy, or both. This section describes the standard approaches to the pharmacologic management of violence in the emergency situation. It also describes the use of neuroleptics and other drugs in the chronic management of the violent patient.

Emergency Medication

The use of medication in emergency situations is legally at the clinician's discretion, because it is to prevent injury to others or the patient. Emergency medication is useful for psychotic violent patients, where it is often used in conjunction with seclusion or restraint. Emergency medication is indicated for nonpsychotic, violent patients when verbal intervention is not appropriate or effective. It may be used instead of seclusion or restraint, or, it may be used with seclusion or restraint when the patient is severely agitated or violent to minimize the detrimental effects violence may have on the patient—even though the patient is secluded or restrained.

I believe that neuroleptic medication should be used primarily for the management of violent patients who manifest psychotic symptomatology. Occasionally it may be indicated for patients who are not psychotic but who are violent, as in the case of patients with organic brain dysfunction where anxiolytic agents or sedatives may worsen the clinical picture. In the emergency situation neuroleptic medication is often given intramuscularly; however, it may be offered by mouth with the clear stipulation that if the patient does not take the medication, it will be given intramuscularly.

Rapid neuroleptization. Soloff (55) has reviewed the literature on the use of rapid neuroleptization and the acute management of the violent patient. He indicates that a range of drugs can be used in this procedure and that there is general safety and efficacy with rapid neuroleptization. It has been demonstrated effective with schizophrenic and manic patients and lessens delusions, hallucinations, and disorganized thought. Rapid neuroleptization also reduces agitation and violence. There are two basic strategies here. One is to use high-potency neuroleptic drugs with an anxiolytic or other drug for sedation if necessary. The other is low-potency neuroleptic drugs for their antipsychotic effects and their sedative side effects. The choice of strategy also should take into consideration the patient's history and physical status. Clinicians should review the patient's previous responses to medication as well as the presence of medical illnesses that may predispose to or be exacerbated by extrapyramidal side effects or orthostatic hypotension. If extrapyramidal side effects are less acceptable, low-potency neuroleptics should be used. If orthostatic hypotension and related side effects are less acceptable, then high-potency neuroleptics are indicated. The physician should feel free to change strategy if the patient's medical condition changes.

The use of high-potency drugs with rapid neuroleptization often involves haloperidol. With the high-potency neuroleptic strategy there are two approaches. The first is a low-dose approach using haloperidol 5 mg (1 ml) im every 4–8 hours for a maximum dose of 15–30 mg a day. The high-dose approach uses haloperidol 10 mg (2 ml) im every 30 minutes with a 24-hour maximum dose of 45–100 mg. Most patients treated for violence and acute psychosis usually will need 15–60 mg per day. Improvement in terms of decreased violence and hostility is rapid, often within 20 minutes of the initial injection of haloperidol 10 mg im.

With rapid neuroleptization one should be cautious to exclude patients who are delirious or otherwise organically impaired, because the sedative or anticholinergic effects of the neuroleptics may exacerbate such conditions. Likewise, intoxication with alcohol or other sedative drugs is a contraindication to rapid neuroleptization, because the patient's level of consciousness may be impaired. Use of these medications in alcohol withdrawal is also contraindicated because they decrease the seizure threshold. Extrapyramidal symptoms such as akathisia may produce a paradoxical reaction with an increase of agitation and violence. Other serious side effects include neuroleptic malignant syndrome and, very rarely, laryngeal dystonic reaction.

Low-potency neuroleptic medications are used less frequently than are high-potency neuroleptics because of the association of low-potency neuroleptics with orthostatic hypotension and because the sedation obtained by the use of low-potency neuroleptics can also be obtained through the use of lorazepam with high-potency neuroleptic medication. If the low-potency neuroleptic strategy is to be used, chlorpromazine is usually the drug of choice. A test dose of 10–25 mg im of chlorpromazine is recommended, and the patient is observed for orthostatic hypotension. If this is not a problem, chlorpromazine should be given 25 mg im (1 ml) every 4 hours in a low-dose approach or up to 75 mg (3 ml) every 4 hours for the high-dose approach. The maximum daily dose for intramuscular chlorpromazine is 400 mg a day. No more than 3 ml should be injected at each injection site, because local tissue irritation may result. Vital signs should be monitored. If there is an extreme hypotensive crisis—that is, the systolic blood pressure is less than 80 mm/Hg on rising—the patient will require treatment with vasopressors such as metaraminol bitartrate or levarterenol bitartrate. Epinephrine is contraindicated, because it may lower blood pressure further in neuroleptic-induced orthostatic hypotension.

Once the patient's violence is under control, either by the low- or high-potency strategy, clinicians may begin oral medication using a milligram-for-milligram translation on a 24-hour basis and allowing for further intramuscular doses in case of recurrence of violent behavior. Other clinicians suggest oral doses 1.5 times the intramuscular dose administered in the first 24 hours. Oral medication should be given in liquid form and should be divided into two or more doses depending on the clinical situation.

Benzodiazepines. The benzodiazepines can be used very effectively in emergencies when violence is occurring or imminent. Benzodiazepines may be used with the neuroleptic medications for schizophrenic patients, manic patients, and patients in other psychotic states. Or, benzodiazepines may be used alone for the management of nonpsychotic patients. Patients who appear to have some degree of control may be offered benzodiazepines as an oral medication. In most emergency situations, however, benzodiazepines are used intramuscularly or intravenously. A number of clinicians have become cautious about using benzodiazepines because there have been reports of paradoxical violence. Aggressive dyscontrol in patients treated with benzodiazepines appears to be overstated, however, and is infrequent, with the possible exception of treatment with clonazepam and alprazolam (56).

The safest and most rapid method of administering the benzodiazepines is by injection intramuscularly rather than intravenously. I prefer lorazepam for intramuscular injection because it is reliably and rapidly absorbed from injection sites, unlike diazepam or chlordiazepoxide. Lorazepam also is useful because it produces sedation for a longer period than diazepam, since it remains in the circulation rather than being absorbed into tissues. On the other hand, the half-life of lorazepam is 12 hours—much shorter than that for diazepam—so that accumulation is not as problematic as it is with diazepam. Given by intramuscular injection, lorazepam rapidly begins to enter the circulation and produces sedation within an hour. Oral administration of the drug produces more gradual effects—sedation occurs usually between 1 and 4 hours. The dose is 2–4 mg by mouth or intramuscularly. A subsequent 2- to 4-mg dose can be repeated if there is continued agitation and aggression at a time depending on the routine of administration—that is, in 1 hour or so if administered intramuscularly or in 4–6 hours if by mouth. Often this is sufficient to manage violence in the emergency situation. After the emergency has subsided, lower maintenance levels of lorazepam, with or without neuroleptics, to a maximum of 10 mg a day in three divided doses can be given. Lorazepam up to 4 mg for an average-sized person could be given intravenously, but slowly at the rate of 2 mg (1 ml) per minute to avoid respiratory depression. This can be repeated in 10 minutes if needed (57). This route of administration should be used only in severe violence, and resuscitation equipment with staff trained in its use should be nearby because laryngospasm or respiratory depression are potential side effects.

Barbiturates. The barbiturate usually used for violent patients in the emergency situation is sodium amobarbital, administered intravenously in 10% aqueous solution. The total dose used is 200–500 mg, and the rate of administration should not exceed 1 ml per minute (57). While administering the medication, one should attempt to achieve sedation or sleep without depressing respiration. Respiratory depression and laryngospasm are possible side effects, so again resuscitation equipment and staff able to use this equipment must be nearby. The effect of this medication occurs within a few minutes, and the dose may be repeated if the patient becomes more agitated and aggressive later. Recurrent dosing must be used only in extreme emergencies and usually requires concurrent restraint of the patient while administration of sodium amobarbital is taking place.

Informed Consent for Medication

The use of medication other than in emergencies must be done with the patient's consent, or the right to refuse treatment must be overridden. Appelbaum has presented different models of the right to refuse treatment (58). He points out that the legal right to refuse neuroleptic medication is now more than a decade old, beginning with a series of decisions in the *Rogers* case in Massachusetts. He notes that judicial decisions on the right to refuse treatment have fallen into two types—treatment-driven and rights-driven models. Treatment-driven models defer to the physician's decision about whether medication is appropriate even if the patient refuses it. Many states provide for independent clinical reviews of the appropriateness of the medication, usually by professionals not involved with the patient's daily care. The basic principle is that the professionals' responsibility for caring for patients is to be balanced against patients' civil and therapeutic needs for individual autonomy.

The rights-driven model reaffirms the individual's rights to liberty and to control intrusions on one's body. In this model, there are judicial reviews of the patient's competency, the appropriateness of the medication, and the patient's best interest if the patient is incompetent. This has been the long-standing model in Massachusetts. More recently, New York has adopted this model except that court-substituted consent is used. In a persuasive article, Shaw maintains that the balance has tipped too far in the direction of patients' rights and that the legal profession has underestimated the personal and social consequences—including homicide—resulting from patients' exercise of the right to refuse medication (59).

Wettstein advises on how to proceed if a patient refuses treatment (60). The clinician should assess why the patient is refusing medication or other treatment. First, the clinician should assess the competence of the patient to give informed consent. If the patient is functionally incompetent, it is appropriate in most jurisdictions to use judicial-type proceedings to establish a substituted judgment of consent or ruling on the best interest of the patient.

If the patient is competent to refuse medication, the clinician should assess reasons for the refusal. The patient may not understand the benefits versus the risks of treatment, may be denying the severity of the illness or violence potential, or may have cultural or religious grounds for refusing medication. As noted about the use of seclusion and restraint, the clinician also should assess the dynamics of the ward environment, or, if the patient is an outpatient, the dynamics of the family and other significant persons in the patient's life. The clinician should attempt to clarify with the competent patient any problems or reasons for refusing medication.

Long-term Medication

In long-term pharmacologic management, there is no one drug for the treatment of violence, because the etiology for violence differs among patients. Thus, several drugs have some proven efficacy in the management of violent behavior.

Neuroleptics. Neuroleptics are used to address delusional thinking and to control violence in schizophrenia, mania, and some organic disorders. Paranoid schizophrenic patients who have manifested violent behavior or have made threats of violence tend not to comply with medication, so for them clinicians should consider the use of long-acting depot forms of neuroleptic medication. Violent mentally retarded patients should not be treated with neuroleptics, however, unless psychotic symptomatology is part of the clinical picture, because use of long-term neuroleptics for retarded patients raises the risk of side effects such as tardive dyskinesia and may impair learning in a group for which learning is a major problem.

Haloperidol and fluphenazine are popular because they can be administered rapidly in high doses on inpatient units, have minimal side effects, and do not decrease the seizure threshold in epileptic patients as much as low-potency neuroleptics. This last safety point is important in cases where subictal activity may coexist with schizophrenia. Also advantageous in combating patients' noncompliance, clinicians may make a smooth transition from use of oral or short-acting intramuscular haloperidol or fluphenazine in the acute state to the long-acting depot intramuscular forms of these drugs.

If the clinician wishes to choose a neuroleptic with more sedative side effects, or if extrapyramidal side effects are problematic, the clinician may use chlorpromazine or other low-potency neuroleptics. I do not recommend thioridazine for violent psychotic patients because the clinician may want to use propranolol for these patients and, as is discussed later, propranolol increases blood levels of thioridazine and the risk of pigmentary retinopathy. This chapter does not describe details of doses and administration of neuroleptics or describe the numerous side effects, because psychiatrists should possess this general knowledge or review it readily elsewhere (57).

If compliance is a problem, and depot medication is not indicated or desired, then blood levels of neuroleptics should be monitored to see if any drug is present. Analytical methods preferred are gas chromatography with mass spectrophotometry, and high-pressure liquid chromatography for measurement of plasma concentrations.

For the refractory violent schizophrenic patient who has not responded to adequate trials of standard neuroleptic medications and is often in seclusion, restraint, or both, a new drug, clozapine, should be considered. Clozapine should be reserved for such patients, and informed consent must be obtained, because there is a risk of agranulocytosis in roughly 1% of patients taking the drug. I have seen dramatic improvement in approximately one-third of refractory violent patients on clozapine. Clozapine should be started at 25 mg twice a day for 2 days and then given at 50 mg three times a day for several days, and then gradually increased over a week or so until the dose is in the therapeutic range of 300–450 mg per day in divided doses (61). Extrapyramidal side effects are rare. Postural hypotension may be avoided in most patients by using this gradual increase in dosage. Seizures have been reported with clozapine, usually only at levels exceeding the therapeutic range.

Anxiolytics and sedatives. The use of anxiolytic drugs and sedatives for the control of violence over a long period is not recommended because these medications are associated with drug abuse, dependency, and tolerance, particularly in patients with personality disorders and violence. In addition, they can produce sedation, confusion, and depression. There should be clear-cut indications, namely an anxiety disorder, for the long-term use of anxiolytic agents. This is in distinction to their short-term emergency use where sedative side effects are sought in the management of violence. Physical dependence results in a withdrawal reaction if these medications are discontinued rapidly. This withdrawal reaction may involve aggression and violent or suicidal behavior as well as other symptoms including anxiety, irritability, insomnia, tremors, headache, dizziness, anorexia, nausea, vomiting, diarrhea, incoordination, seizures, and depression. The onset of the withdrawal reaction depends on the particular medication and may be anywhere from a day for a short-acting drug such as lorazepam to as long as a week following cessation of other longer-acting drugs. A gradual reduction of dosage is recommended: 5–10% a day for 10–14 days (57) with a long-acting benzodiazepine substituted for shorter-acting benzodiazepines. Patients with a history of seizures, alcohol abuse, or abuse of other drugs should be hospitalized for detoxification.

Carbamazepine. Carbamazepine is approved as an anticonvulsant medication for complex partial seizures and generalized clonic-tonic seizures and other types of partial seizures. It has fewer side effects such as sedation when compared with phenytoin and barbiturates (62). A number of case studies and open drug trials have indicated that carbamazepine is effective for the management of aggression in several types of psychiatric patients. In a double-blind, crossover study of 13 chronic psychiatric patients, 10 of whom were schizophrenic, there were beneficial effects in decreasing aggressive episodes (63). Although the patients were not epileptic, they did have temporal lobe EEG abnormalities. The patients were treated with neuroleptics, anticholinergics, antidepressants, and benzodiazepines. The dose of carbamazepine was 200 mg, 3 times a day.

Luchins reported on an open carbamazepine trial in seven chronic psychiatric inpatients, six of whom had schizophrenia (64). None of the patients had EEG abnormalities. He reported that six of the seven patients had fewer aggressive episodes while on carbamazepine than either before or after treatment with the drug. All the patients were concurrently treated with neuroleptic drugs.

Carbamazepine has been found effective in decreasing aggression in patients with psychiatric diagnoses other than schizophrenia (65). These include personality disorders, conduct disorders, and some organic disorders. Caution should be given to the use of carbamazepine in patients with gross brain damage, mental retardation, or both, because of reports of paradoxical worsening of aggression in these patients. Thus, carbamazepine may be effective in managing aggression and irritability in patients with overt seizures, both partial and complex seizures and generalized seizures, in schizophrenic patients with and without EEG abnormalities, and in other types of patients with episodic violence without gross brain damage or mental retardation.

Early reports about carbamazepine causing thrombocytopenia, agranulocytosis, and aplastic anemia have not been supported, and these side effects appear to be rare. Nevertheless, monitoring of hematologic and liver functioning is essential in addition to a complete medical evaluation. Complete blood count and platelet count are recommended before treatment and every 2 weeks for the first 2 months of treatment and every 3 months thereafter. Liver function tests should include SGOT, SGPT, LDH, and alkaline phosphatase. These tests should be repeated every month early in treatment and every 3 months thereafter. Patients should be monitored clinically —for example, to detect respiratory infections or other manifestations of agranulocytosis. Patients with leukopenia, thrombocytopenia, or liver disease should *not* be treated with carbamazepine (66).

Some patients treated with carbamazepine report side effects such as nausea, drowsiness, vertigo, ataxia, blurred vision, and diplopia, which are usually mild and decrease when the dosage is decreased. There are other less frequent toxic consequences of treatment such as jaundice, renal effects, nystagmus, skin reactions, and thyroid effects. In approximately 5% of patients, carbamazepine must be discontinued because of toxic reactions. Dyskinetic movements such as dystonia, dyskinesias, and other extrapyramidal reactions are rare and self-limited if the medication is withdrawn or the dosage is decreased.

For an anticonvulsant response with carbamazepine, the therapeutic serum levels are 8–12 ng/ml. The usual method for treatment of seizures is to prescribe 100–200 mg twice a day for 1 week, and then to increase the dose by 100- to 200-mg increments and to measure serum levels when daily doses of 400–600 mg are achieved. It is not uncommon for patients with seizure disorders to take up to 1,200 mg a day. The onset of therapeutic effects is within the first days or weeks after treatment is initiated (62). Patients without seizure disorders have benefited from carbamazepine at doses of approximately 600 mg a day. Once the therapeutic level is reached and a response is obtained, clinicians should monitor blood levels of carbamazepine every month for the first 3 months and every 3 months thereafter.

Propranolol. Silver and Yudofsky have reviewed a number of control studies, open trials, and case reports on the effectiveness of propranolol in the management of aggressive behavior (67). Most of the patients studied and responding to propranolol were those with organic brain disease, often with gross impairment secondary to trauma, tumor, alcoholism, encephalitis, Huntington's disease, dementia, Wilson's disease, Korsakoff's psychosis, and mental retardation. In addition, some patients with minimal brain dysfunction or attention-deficit disorder also have been reported to respond to propranolol. Nearly all the patients in these studies were refractory to other medications including neuroleptics, anxiolytic agents, anticonvulsants, and lithium. In a number of cases concurrent neuroleptic medication was used.

Before using propranolol, clinicians should make a thorough medical evaluation of the patient. Patients with the following diseases should be excluded from treatment with propranolol: bronchial asthma, chronic obstructive pulmonary disease, cardiac diseases including angina or congestive heart failure, diabetes mellitus, significant peripheral vascular disease, severe renal disease, and hyperthyroidism. Hypertensive patients should be given propranolol with caution, because sudden discontinuation of propranolol may result in rebound hypertension.

The initial dose of propranolol is 20 mg, three times a day. The dosage is increased by 60 mg every 3–4 days. A test dose of 20 mg may be given if there are clinical concerns about hypotension or bradycardia. Propranolol is increased unless the pulse rate is reduced below 50 beats per minute or if the systolic blood pressure is less than 90 mmHg. If the patient experiences severe dizziness, ataxia, or wheezing, the medication should be held and then reduced or discontinued if the symptoms persist. Doses of greater than 800 mg are usually not required to control aggressive behavior. Although a therapeutic effect may be seen in several days, it usually takes longer. Clinicians should maintain patients on the highest dose of propranolol for at least 8 weeks before determining that the patient is not responding to the medication. If the patient is on neuroleptic medication or anticonvulsant medication, clinicians should monitor plasma blood levels of neuroleptics carefully. Propranolol has been shown to increase plasma blood levels of neuroleptic medications, particularly thioridazine, which could result in pigmentary retinopathy.

To withdraw the patient from propranolol, clinicians should decrease the dosage gradually by 60 mg per day until the patient is on a daily dose of 60 mg per day. Then the medication should be decreased at the rate of 20 mg every other day. In patients with hypertension, propranolol should be decreased even more gradually to prevent rebound hypertension.

Side effects found with propranolol include hypotension and bradycardia, although these may be managed by decreasing the dose of the drug. Above 300 mg per day there is usually no worsening of bradycardia or hypotension. Depression has been reported rarely by patients receiving propranolol, and sedation is sometimes reported as a side effect.

Other beta-blockers. Silver and Yudofsky have reviewed other case studies using beta-blockers other than propranolol (67). These include the use of nadolol in doses of 80–160 mg per day in the treatment of aggressive patients with chronic paranoid schizophrenia. Pindolol has been reported to be effective in the treatment of aggressive patients with chronic paranoid schizophrenia or organic brain syndrome. Metoprolol has been reported effective with two patients, one with intermittent explosive disorder related to meningitis and alcohol abuse, and the other with a penetrating brain trauma with temporal lobe epilepsy. The control of aggressive outbursts was reported with 200–300 mg per day of metoprolol.

Lithium. Long-term use of lithium is useful to prevent manic episodes and associated hyperactive aggressive behavior. The use of lithium for disorders other than bipolar disorders for the management of aggression has been much more controversial. In a recent double-blind trial testing the effectiveness of lithium in the treatment of aggression in adult mentally retarded patients, Craft et al. found that 73% of patients showed a reduction in aggression during treatment (68). A serum lithium concentration of 0.7–1.0 meq/L was necessary for a clinical effect. The use of lithium was the same as that for the management of bipolar patients. Although there have been other reports of the use of lithium in other disorders, there is a paucity of double-blind controlled studies. These disorders include patients suffering from organic brain syndrome and head injury; aggressive schizophrenic patients; nonpsychotic, aggressive prisoners and delinquents; and children with conduct disorders and attention deficit. Some researchers contend that lithium can increase interictal aggression in patients with temporal lobe epilepsy and can cause other adverse effects in patients with other seizure disorders and other abnormal EEG changes.

Because lithium affects many organ systems in the body, an extensive medical examination is recommended before beginning lithium and during the course of treatment (66). The medical evaluation includes ascertaining whether there is a history of familial kidney disease and whether there are symptoms of disorders, particularly related to the kidney—that is, diabetes mellitus, hypertension, and the use of renal toxins. Evaluation for thyroid disease should include family history of thyroid disease as well as eliciting current symptoms related to thyroid disease. Evaluation of hyperparathyroidism should include measurement of serum calcium. If the serum calcium is elevated, the patient should be referred for further evaluation. Evaluation of cardiac function should include a history of symptoms of cardiac disease and an electrocardiogram if the patient is more than 40 years of age or if there is a suspicion of cardiac disease. Laboratory tests should be repeated every 3–6 months for renal and thyroid dysfunction, 1 month after serum level is stable, and every year thereafter for cardiac dysfunction. The fasting glucose level should be monitored every year.

The therapeutic plasma levels for patients on lithium to control aggression range from 0.7 to 1.0 meq/L. Plasma levels should be obtained 12 hours after the last lithium dose. Once the therapeutic lithium level has been stabilized, levels should be monitored every month for the first 6 months and every 2–3 months afterward. Lithium should not be used during pregnancy, because congenital abnormalities, particularly heart defects, have been reported. It should be used with caution in women of childbearing age.

As one approaches the toxic range of serum lithium levels (1.5–2.0 meq/L), drowsiness, vomiting, muscle weakness, ataxia, dryness of mouth, abdominal pain, lethargy, dizziness, slurred speech, and nystagmus are early signs of intoxication. At levels above 2 meq/L, symptoms include anorexia, severe nausea and vomiting, blurred vision, fasciculations, clonic movements of the whole body and limbs, hyperactive tendon reflexes, choreoathetoid movements, toxic psychosis, syncope, EEG changes, acute circulatory failure, stupor, and coma. The last stages of lithium toxicity are manifested by generalized convulsions, oliguria, and death.

Long-term administration of lithium has resulted in impaired renal function and, rarely, persistent neurological deficits. Thus, long-term lithium treatment for violence should be undertaken only after serious consideration. Because lithium is excreted by the kidneys, it should be used cautiously in patients receiving diuretics or who are on low-salt diets. If lithium is used concurrently with neuroleptic medications, blood levels of the neuroleptic medication should be monitored. Clinicians should take precautions in using lithium in the elderly because renal function usually declines with age.

Psychostimulants. Brizer has reviewed the literature on the use of psychostimulants for the treatment of violent behavior (69). The use of amphetamines is accepted in controlling aggressive behavior associated with attention-deficit disorder and hyperactivity. There have been some reports of the successful use of amphetamines to control aggression in adults with a history of this disorder as well. In addition, two studies reported successful use of amphetamines in delinquent youths—one in controlling aggression in a group of hospitalized aggressive black delinquents, and the other to decrease violence in the classroom for a group of aggressive outpatient boys with antisocial behavior. Further studies are indicated, and clinicians should prescribe amphetamines only with caution because there is great potential for addiction and abuse. Psychostimulant abuse may exacerbate or cause violent behavior through hyperactivity, emotional lability, or delusional thinking.

Clinician Safety and Protection of Potential Victims

Most of what has been said in the preceding sections of this chapter has focused on the evaluation and treatment of the violent patient with emphasis on the proper standard of care and the welfare of the patient. The last section shifts attention to the safety and welfare of persons around the patient—that is, the persons treating the violent patient and other potential victims of violence by the patient. A review of the literature on attacks on clinicians and the protection of other potential victims is followed by guidelines proposed to address these concerns.

Studies on Risk of Attacks by Patients

Violence by patients toward mental health professionals is not uncommon. Surveys on this subject have been conducted with psychiatrists practicing predominantly in outpatient settings in large cities such as San Diego, Philadelphia, Baltimore, Vancouver, and Cincinnati (70–74). Despite their differing methodologies and geographic areas, these studies have found that roughly 40% of psychiatrists have been physically attacked by patients at least once in their careers, and a greater number have been threatened by their patients. Some of these surveys included other mental health professionals and found that the rates of physical violence were less than for psychiatrists—roughly 10% for psychologists and 20% for social workers (70,74). Surveys of inpatient units showed that nurses have the highest rates of being attacked. For example, 80% reported being attacked by patients in a Veterans Administration hospital (75). Younger, more inexperienced staff and psychiatric residents are attacked more frequently than older, experienced clinicians (70–72,76). Note that the higher number of attacks is for staff who have fewer years "at risk" in their professional careers. It is unclear whether the increased frequency of attacks is caused by a lack of education and experience or by the possibility that younger clinicians—for example, psychiatric residents on inpatient units or in aftercare clinics—are more likely to be assigned to work with violent patients.

It is important to note that attacks on psychiatrists by patients can occur in all types of treatment settings—in private offices and outpatient clinics as well as in inpatient units and emergency rooms. Although assaults in offices are less frequent, they are more likely to involve guns, knives, and other weapons (71,77).

The diagnostic group most likely to attack clinicians in inpatient and outpatient settings is schizophrenic patients (70,72,77,78). Some surveys have found, however, that other groups also frequently attack clinicians, such as patients with personality disorders (71) and those who are depressed and have a history of suicide attempts (70). The circumstances surrounding assaults on clinicians often involve admissions to a hospital, giving of medication against the patient's wishes, clinicians' refusal to discharge a patient, or setting of limits in some other manner. Other high-risk situations include evaluation of unknown patients, custody cases, and denial of compensation. Some violence is unrelated to treatment, however, and clinicians have been attacked even by patients who are not their own. Clinicians who were threatened or attacked report that they had not considered a wide range of possible means of dealing with the situations (71,74).

The Emergency Situation

Clinicians, particularly those who serve in inpatient units or emergency rooms, ultimately will face a situation in which a patient has attacked someone or is threatening to attack people. Often it is the psychiatrist or senior nurse who is called on to take charge and to assess, contain, or defuse the violent confrontation. The responsible clinician must make a rapid decision about using physical controls, medication, or verbal intervention. Practices and procedures for using seclusion, restraint, and medication have been discussed above. But whether to use these controls or to talk to the patient without physical controls remains an important issue. In making such decisions, clinicians should first consider the clinical state of the patient. Patients known to have organic mental disorders are unlikely to be influenced by verbal means. But here, clinicians should concentrate on treating the underlying medical or other physical disorder rather than giving neuroleptics to control violence. If the patient's etiology is unknown, the patient probably should be restrained while laboratory tests and evaluation proceed if there is actual violence or imminent violence.

Violent schizophrenic or manic patients are also unlikely to be influenced by verbal means. Here, neuroleptic medication rapidly administered is usually the treatment of choice, although these patients may have to be restrained or secluded until the neuroleptic takes effect. Patients who are not psychotic and not affected by organic disorder are often amenable to verbal intervention and may not require seclusion or restraint. The clinician may want to offer medication, thus giving the patient an option or at least a sense of some control in the situation.

Talking With a Violent Patient

If one decides to talk with a violent patient, the next question is where—in an open place or a private place? A wide range of options should be considered. The most private one is to be with the patient with the door to the office closed. The clinician should sit between the patient and the door in case escape is necessary. The next option is to interview the patient alone in an office with the door open. Or, the clinician can interview the patient in the office with the door open and the staff outside the door. The next option is to interview the patient in an office with staff present. Finally, the clinician can interview the patient in an open space with staff nearby. The clinician should feel safe in the setting chosen, because clinicians who are unduly fearful may not be able to make a full evaluation of the patient. In addition to ensuring that they meet their own concerns about safety, clinicians should recognize and prepare for the possibility that they will experience countertransference or other inappropriate reactions such as denial that may interfere with their effective management of a particular patient.

Clinicians should consider the following recommendations about how to talk with someone who has been or may be violent. Approach the patient in a calm manner with the appearance of being in control. Speak softly, in a nonprovocative, nonjudgmental manner. Begin by commenting in a neutral but concrete manner about the obvious—for example, "You look angry." Do not make emotional or pejorative comments, which are provocative and probably will result in further violence. Make sure there is adequate space between the clinician and the patient. Also ensure that doctor and patient are both either sitting or standing because the clinician must not tower over the patient or be intimidating in any way. Show respect for the patient. It is best to avoid continued direct eye contact with the patient, because this may be interpreted as a challenge. The clinician should attempt to project a state of passivity, yet also a sense of being in control of the situation.

When the patient begins to talk, listen and be empathic, concerned, and uncritical. Try not to interrupt the patient, because often patients with personality disorders manifesting violence have difficulty in expressing their concerns verbally. The initial phase is not the time for interpretations or attempts at psychodynamic formulations or insights that may only result in provoking the patient. The clinician should try to obtain the patient's view of the situation and what led up to the violent episode. Once this has been elicited, the clinician may subtly and gently attempt to state his or her perception of what the situation is and attempt to correct a misperception by the patient. The clinician should not promise something that may not be possible. For example, the emergency room clinician should not promise not to admit the patient to the hospital, and the inpatient clinician should not promise not to restrict or seclude the patient.

Physical Aspects of Safety

The clinician should consider the physical aspects of the office or other setting in which violent patients will be interviewed. There should be solid, heavy furniture that would be difficult to move or throw. A lightweight chair that can be used as a shield against sharp weapons may be advisable. I prefer to sit between the patient and the door. Ideally, there should be two exits to the clinical setting so that the clinician may use one to exit if the patient enters the other with a weapon. Private offices should contain no heavy objects, such as ashtrays, that can be thrown. Pillows or other soft objects are useful as shields in case of attack. Clinicians should have a method for indicating that they are in danger. This may be in the form of a "panic button" or in a prearranged message, such as, "Please cancel my appointment . . ." for a time later in the day. Likewise, there should be some way for the receptionist or person outside of the office to indicate a potentially dangerous situation to the clinician before the patient enters the office.

When interviewing patients who have been violent or who are potentially explosive, clinicians should pay attention to their own attire for safety reasons. Glasses should be removed before interviewing these patients. Men should remove their neckties or tuck them into their shirt. Women should remove jewelry such as necklaces and earrings. Likewise, if the patient has been violent and is to be put into seclusion, clinicians should ensure that dangerous clothing such as belts or neckties has been taken from the patient, and that the patient is not carrying or proximate to dangerous objects such as pens, jewelry, or matches.

Thackrey has described and illustrated a number of physical maneuvers that clinicians may use in response to violence by patients (79). Although practice of the maneuvers is essential if they are to be effective in emergencies, the brief review that follows is intended to make clinicians aware of the range of possibilities that they may confront and of the range of alternatives they may use to deal with potentially violent patients—for example, how to deflect blows and knives and how to effect release from holds on various positions of one's body, including choke holds and biting. These maneuvers are defensive rather than "martial arts" movements and are not intended to hurt patients.

Weapons

A controversial issue is whether patients should be screened routinely for weapons in emergency rooms. Residents in psychiatry and other specialties and other frontline staff are becoming increasingly vocal about the number of patients carrying guns and knives because of drug dealing and other violent aspects of the urban environment. McNeil and Binder reported that 4% of patients were found to be carrying weapons during a routine search in an emergency service in San Francisco (80). Their procedure involves a sign in an emergency room that states that for the safety of patients and staff, all persons entering the emergency room will be screened for weapons. Staff must repeat this information orally to patients before the screening. The procedure involves clinical staff supervision of security personnel who search patients' jackets and purses. Patients may be asked to display the contents of their pockets, and a more thorough search may be instituted, if clinically indicated. Advocates of routine searches believe that they are better than searching only if there is a suspicion of weapons. The routine-search procedure has been received well, and patients have expressed positive feelings about increased safety in the emergency room. If a patient feels that a search is an invasion of privacy, the patient can seek treatment elsewhere unless the patient appears to meet criteria for involuntary hospitalization, in which case the patient would not be allowed to leave the emergency room.

If the patient appears in a treatment setting with a weapon such as a gun, responsible clinicians should ensure exposure of as few staff as possible to the situation. For example, if a psychiatrist is aware of an armed patient who is in the reception area, the psychiatrist should immediately retreat to the office rather than engaging the patient in the treatment area. As many staff as possible should be removed from the treatment area where the patient appears with the gun. The first few minutes in this situation are crucial. If trapped, the clinician should acknowledge the patient with something obvious, such as, "I see you have a gun." The clinician should appear calm and should not be intimidating, confrontational, obnoxious, or argumentative. The clinician should encourage the patient to talk during the initial phases and to repeat the patient's concerns back to him or her. No attempt should be made to take the weapon from the patient. A suggestion may be made that the patient put the weapon down on a desk. The clinician should not reach for the gun or tell the patient to drop the gun because this could result in discharge of the weapon.

Attention should be given beforehand to ways of warning persons outside of the room that the clinician is in danger. Again, this may be achieved by an actual "panic button" that alerts staff in a central location or through some prearranged message by the telephone in which the receptionist outside of the office can be alerted that a dangerous situation exists. There should be a specific written plan as to a course of action—for example, alerting the police and clearing the area of patients and staff. If a hostage situation develops, obviously this calls for a professional hostage negotiator. Once the hostage negotiator is in charge, a clinician who is held hostage should relinquish any leadership role among the other hostages, because serving as a leader may make the clinician the target of the hostage-taker's violence.

Turner has made specific recommendations concerning such situations (81). He advises to do exactly as the hostage-taker says and to avoid an open display of despair or loss of control such as crying or begging. Hostages should remain observant. Note that in cases where there were a number of hostages, and one was killed, the hostage killed was often the one who behaved in a manner different from the rest. Do not attempt to escape or overpower the hostage-taker unless absolutely certain of success.

Transference and Countertransference

Turning to less dramatic but equally important issues, the ongoing treatment of the violent patient as an inpatient or outpatient requires constant attention to transference and countertransference (82). The therapist must continually monitor the patient's feelings, because they can change as a function of the patient's illness. Paranoid and borderline patients, or those with a history of psychotic illness, cannot handle the intimacy of treatment and respond with threats of violence or actual violent or destructive acts. Therapists should discuss with patients any comments, letters, notes, or messages on answering machines that can be interpreted as threatening or indicative of aggressive thoughts on the part of the patient. A patient's purchase of any weapon should be monitored. The therapist must constantly assess whether the patient poses a danger to him or her.

Therapists must take any threat seriously, because there is no such thing as a harmless threat. Clinicians threatened by former patients or those in treatment must respond. A therapist should meet in a safe place with the threatening patient, with colleagues or security personnel available and alerted. The therapist can state that the threats are frightening, but that the therapist wishes to resolve what is going on between himself or herself and the patient. Clinicians may admit fear to a patient, but an appropriate response about the threat also should involve an acknowledgment or affirmation of its illegality and of the intervention the therapist will take. Violent patients who make verbal threats may wish for intervention, and controls provide this.

Therapists must evaluate their countertransference and other feelings constantly. Aggression usually mobilizes fear in the clinician, who can respond by projecting anxieties onto the patient or by seeing the latter as more violent and threatening than the patient really is. On the other hand, denial of fear can lead to the false perception of the patient as "interesting" instead of potentially dangerous. Therapists have experienced a wide variety of defense mechanisms with violent patients—for example, projection of anger at a patient for lack of progress and exaggeration of the patient's violence potential. Therapists may displace fear of one violent patient to another who may not pose a danger. Therapists also are subject to reaction formation or identification with the aggressor in treating attractive patients, who then are viewed as not as dangerous as they really may be.

Clinicians must avoid denial. Questions need to be asked about the ownership of weapons, about the existence of a victim, about previous violence toward the victim, about the patient's attitude toward his or her children, pets, and spouse, and about the level of destructiveness within the household. Patients who indicate that they "lost their temper," should be questioned in-depth.

Use of a Consultant

One way of guarding against errors in denying or exaggerating a patient's potential for violence is to have the patient seen in consultation. Forensic institutions operate on the principle of shared responsibility, whereby several clinicians make judgments about a patient's violent propensities. In general clinical practice, the therapist likewise should think about having a violent patient seen in consultation with another therapist. This is particularly important when the clinician is worried about the risks the patient poses to society, or when the clinician becomes frightened for his or her own safety. Consultation also has legal implications in the more formal assessment of risk and the duty to protect intended victims.

Duty to Protect Intended Victims

The physician or other therapist has a legal and ethical duty to protect intended victims from violence from patients if the therapist has a professional relationship with the patient. The depth of this relationship is not as important as the fact that the relationship exists. For example, a clinician may be very involved with a patient's treatment, as in the case of treatment on an inpatient unit or in outpatient psychotherapy. Or, the relationship may not be as intense, as when clinicians provide medical coverage or prescribe medication for patients treated by nonmedical therapists.

Physicians have always had an *ethical* duty to protect others. The *legal* precedent for the duty to protect began with the *Tarasoff* decision in California more than a decade ago (83). A brief summary of this well-known case should suffice. Mr. Poddar was a graduate student at the University of California at Berkeley. There he met Ms. Tarasoff. After a brief and superficial relationship with him, Ms. Tarasoff ended the relationship. Mr. Poddar was very distraught and was seen and treated in outpatient psychotherapy at the University of California. He told his therapist that he had thoughts of killing Ms. Tarasoff, and the therapist was also told by a friend of the patient that Mr. Poddar had purchased a gun. The therapist and his supervisor decided that Mr. Poddar posed a danger to Ms. Tarasoff and decided to hospitalize him. They contacted the university police for assistance in hospitalizing him. The university police spoke to Mr. Poddar, who denied any homicidal ideation. No further action was taken. When Ms. Tarasoff returned from a trip out of the country, Mr. Poddar murdered her.

Ms. Tarasoff's parents sued the University of California for negligence for failing to *protect* Ms. Tarasoff by confining Mr. Poddar and for failing to warn Ms. Tarasoff of Mr. Poddar's threats. The Supreme Court of California ruled that the therapist should have warned the intended victim. The psychiatric profession was very concerned that this duty to warn would pose a broad threat to patient confidentiality. The California Supreme Court agreed to rehear the case, this time deciding that the duty of a professional is to protect and *not* necessarily to warn an intended victim of violence. In most states this is now the responsibility of the clinician—that is, to protect and not necessarily to warn an intended victim. Ironically, California has recently passed a law that requires clinicians to protect *and* warn intended victims.

Beck has indicated in a review with an excellent presentation of cases from recent court decisions that most cases have been decided in favor of the defendant—that is, the clinician (84). A few cases decided in favor of the plaintiff have appeared in retrospect not to have been completely justified. These cases have involved failure of one clinician to communicate a history of violence to a subsequent clinician or a failure of a clinician to obtain past records indicating that a patient had a history of violence and might be a danger in the future. Another case involving release of a patient who subsequently killed his mother was decided against the defendants because a note was found in which the patient threatened to kill his mother. In another case involving release of an inpatient, the clinicians were held liable for not keeping a patient who abused PCP in the hospital longer because of the patient's history of violence, despite the fact there were no grounds that justified continued commitment of the patient. In retrospect, the hospital should have petitioned the courts and thus shifted the responsibility for continued hospitalization or discharge to the legal system.

Appelbaum has presented a three-stage model of how the clinician can satisfy the *Tarasoff* obligation to protect intended victims from violence by one's patients (85). The first stage, assessment, has two components. In the first component, the therapist must gather data relevant to an evaluation of dangerousness, and a determination of dangerousness must be made on the basis of that data. Earlier in this review I presented data necessary for the determination of a patient's violence potential. This includes information on past history of violence including frequency, victims, and severity as well as a history of other impulsive behaviors. This information should be sought not only from the patient but also from the patient's family, the police, and prior clinical and criminal records. Information should be sought about the patient's developmental history as well as medical history, including alcohol and substance abuse and other illnesses related to violence. In the second component of this stage, the clinician should assess in-depth and record the patient's mental status and physical status and any relevant laboratory results, particularly those reflecting alcohol or drug abuse. A model for the short-term prediction of violence has been presented earlier that involves using the data collected and assessing how well planned a threat of violence is and how available are the means of inflicting injury.

The second stage of Appelbaum's model involves selecting a course of action if the clinician decides that the patient poses a serious threat of violence. The clinician may consider a wide range of alternatives to protect intended victims short of warning them. For example, the clinician may decide to intensify treatment by increasing the number of visits or by instituting or increasing medication. Particularly in the case of psychotic patients, the clinician may decide to increase compliance by the use of depot neuroleptic medications or to involve the family in efforts to control the patient or prevent access to weapons. The clinician may decide to consult with a colleague about the patient's dangerousness and about alternatives to control the patient. This process may lead the clinician to seek more information on the past history of violence by the patient. Police may be warned about the patient's intent to harm intended victims. Finally, the clinician may hospitalize the patient.

If clinicians decide to warn an intended victim, they should not do this unilaterally or in an insensitive way. Instead, they should involve the patient in decision making. If the victim is to be warned it may be advisable to have the patient listen while the clinician discusses the situation with the intended victim. Further, it may be advisable to bring the victim into treatment if the victim is an intimate of the patient or a family member.

Once the decision has been made that a patient is dangerous and a plan of action has been formulated, the third stage of Appelbaum's model requires therapists to implement their plan appropriately, in an effective and timely manner. Furthermore, therapists must continue to monitor the course of action they have taken, particularly if it does not involve warning the victim or hospitalizing the patient. Note that all these efforts will not protect the clinician against liability when a patient injures or kills someone, if the process of assessing, selecting a course of action, and implementing that course is not documented in detail in the patient's record.

NOTES

1. Tardiff K, Sweillam A: Assault, suicide and mental illness. Arch Gen Psychiatry 37:164–169, 1980
2. Craig TJ: An epidemiological study of problems associated with violence among psychiatric inpatients. Am J Psychiatry 139:1262–1266, 1982
3. Zitrin A, Hardesty AS, Burdock EU, et al: Crime and violence among mental patients. Am J Psychiatry 133:142–149, 1976

4. Tardiff K: Characteristics of assaultive patients in private psychiatric hospitals. Am J Psychiatry 141:1232–1235, 1984
5. Rossi AM, Jacob M, Monteleone M, et al: Violent or fear-inducing behavior associated with hospital admission. Hosp Community Psychiatry 36:643–647, 1985
6. McNeil DE, Binder RL: Violence, civil commitment and hospitalization. J Nerv Ment Dis 174:107–111, 1986
7. Shader RI, Jackson AH, Harmatz JS, et al: Patterns of violent behavior among schizophrenic inpatients. Diseases of the Nervous System 38:13–16, 1977
8. Inamdar SC, Lewis DO, Siomopoulos G, et al: Violent and suicidal behavior in psychotic adolescents. Am J Psychiatry 139:932–935, 1982
9. Petrie J: Violence in geriatric patients. JAMA 248:443–448, 1982
10. Tardiff K, Sweillam A: The occurrence of assaultive behavior among chronic psychiatric inpatients. Am J Psychiatry 139:212–215, 1982
11. Tardiff K, Koenigsberg HW: Assaultive behavior among psychiatric outpatients. Am J Psychiatry 142:960–963, 1985
12. Evenson RC, Altman HI, Sletten IW, et al: Disturbing behavior: a study of incident reports. Psychiatric Q 48:266–279, 1974
13. Maccoby EM, Jacklin CN: The Psychology of Sex Differences. Stanford, CA, Stanford University Press, 1974
14. Wolfgang ME, Ferracuti F: The Subculture of Violence: Toward an Integrated Theory in Criminology. New York, Methuen, 1967
15. Wolfgang ME: Sociocultural Overview of Criminal Violence, in Violence and the Violent Individual. Edited by Hays JR, Roberts TK, Solway KS. New York, SP Medical and Scientific, 1981, pp 151–178
16. Silberman CE: Criminal Violence, Criminal Justice. New York, Vintage, 1980
17. Centerwall BS: Race, socioeconomic status and domestic homicide: Atlanta, 1971–1972. Am J Public Health 74:813–815, 1984
18. Blau JR, Blau PM: The cost of inequality: metropolitan structure and violent crime. American Sociological Review 47:114–129, 1982
19. Vold GV: Theoretical Criminology. New York, Oxford University Press, 1979
20. Defronzo J: Economic assistance to impoverished Americans: relationship to incidence of crime. Criminology 21:119–136, 1983
21. Williams K: Economic sources of homicide: reestimating the effects of poverty and inequality. American Sociological Review 49:283–289, 1984
22. Messner S, Tardiff K: Economic inequality and levels of homicide: an analysis of urban neighborhoods. Criminology 23:241–267, 1985
23. Kempe CH, Helfer R (eds): The Battered Child Syndrome, 3rd Edition. Chicago, IL, University of Chicago Press, 1980
24. Heins M: "The Battered Child" revisited. JAMA 251:3295–3300, 1984
25. Jaffe P, Wolfe D, Wilson SK, et al: Family violence and child adjustment: a comparative analysis of girls' and boys' behavioral symptoms. Am J Psychiatry 143:74–77, 1986

26. Monahan J: The Clinical Prediction of Violent Behavior. Rockville, MD, U.S. Department of Health and Human Services, 1981
27. Eichelman B, Elliott GR, Barchas J: Biomedical, pharmacological and genetic aspects of aggression, in Biobehavioral Aspects of Aggression. Edited by Hamburg DA, Trudeau MB. New York, Alan R Liss, 1981, pp 165–179
28. Brown GL, Goodwin FK, Ballenger JC, et al: Aggression in human correlates with cerebrospinal fluid amine metabolites. Psychiatry Res 1:131–139, 1979
29. Brown GL, Elbert MH, Goyer PF, et al: Aggression, suicide and serotonin: relationship to CSF amine metabolites. Am J Psychiatry 136:741–746, 1982
30. Lidberg L, Tuck JR, Asberg M, et al: Homicide, suicide and CSF 5-HIAA. Acta Psychiatr Scand 71:230–236, 1985
31. Linnola M, Virkkunen M, Scheinin M, et al: Low cerebrospinal fluid 5-hydroxyindoleacetic acid concentration differentiates impulsive from nonimpulsive violent behavior. Life Sci 33:2609–2614, 1983
32. Linkowski P: Editorial: Suicide and biochemistry. Biol Psychiatry 20:123–124, 1985
33. Tardiff K: Assault in hospitals and placement in the community. Bull Am Acad Psychiatry Law 9:33–39, 1981
34. Blackburn R: Emotionality, extraversion and aggression of paranoid and non-paranoid schizophrenic offenders. Br J Psychiatry 115:1301–1302, 1968
35. Planansky K, Johnson R: Homicidal aggression in schizophrenic men. Acta Psychiatr Scand 55:65–73, 1977
36. Addad M, Benezech M, Bourgeois M, et al: Criminal acts among schizophrenics in French mental hospitals. J Nerv Ment Dis 169:289–293, 1981
37. Bach-Y-Rita G, Veno A: Habitual violence: a profile of 62 men. Am J Psychiatry 131:1015–1017, 1974
38. Taylor PJ, Gunn J: Violence and psychosis. Br Med J 288:1945–1949, 1984
39. Lewis DO, Pincus JH, Shanok SS, et al: Psychomotor epilepsy and violence in a group of incarcerated adolescent boys. Am J Psychiatry 139:882–887, 1982
40. Devinsky O, Bear D: Varieties of aggressive behavior in temporal lobe epilepsy. Am J Psychiatry 141:651–656, 1984
41. Goodman RA, Mercy JA, Loya F, et al: Alcohol use and interpersonal violence: alcohol detected in homicide victims. Am J Public Health 76:144–149, 1986
42. Tardiff K, Gross E, Messner SL: A study of homicide in Manhattan, 1981. Am J Public Health 76:139–143, 1986
43. Menuck M: Clinical aspects of dangerous behavior. Journal of Psychiatry and Law 11:277–304, 1983
44. Nurco DN, Ball JC, Shaffer JW, et al: The criminality of narcotic addicts. J Nerv Ment Dis 173:94–102, 1985

45. Tardiff K: Assessment and Management of Violent Patients. Washington, DC, American Psychiatric Press, 1989
46. Reid WH: Clinical evaluation of the violent patient. Psychiatr Clin North Am 11:527–537, 1988
47. Tardiff K: A model for the short-term prediction of violence potential, in Current Approaches to the Prediction of Violence. Edited by Brizer DA, Crowner M. Washington, DC, American Psychiatric Press, 1989, pp 1–12
48. Youngberg v Romeo, 102 Sup Ct 2452 (1982)
49. American Psychiatric Association: Seclusion and restraint: the psychiatric uses (Task Force Report No 22). Washington, DC, American Psychiatric Association, 1985
50. Tardiff K (ed): The Psychiatric Uses of Seclusion and Restraint. Washington, DC, American Psychiatric Press, 1984
51. Wexler DB: Legal aspects of seclusion and restraint, in The Psychiatric Uses of Seclusion and Restraint. Edited by Tardiff K. Washington, DC, American Psychiatric Press, 1984, pp 111–124
52. Lion JR, Pasternak SA: Counter-transference reactions to violent patients. Am J Psychiatry 130:207–210, 1973
53. Liberman RP, Wong SE: Behavioral analysis and therapy procedures related to seclusion and restraint, in The Psychiatric Uses of Seclusion and Restraint. Edited by Tardiff K. Washington, DC, American Psychiatric Press, 1984
54. Wong SE, Woolsey JE, Innocent AJ, et al: Behavioral treatment of violent psychiatric patients, in The Violent Patient. Edited by Tardiff K. Philadelphia, PA, WB Saunders, 1988
55. Soloff PH: Emergency management of the violent patient, in Psychiatry Update: American Psychiatric Association Annual Review, Vol 6. Edited by Hales RE, Frances AJ. Washington, DC, American Psychiatric Press, 1987, pp 510–564
56. Dietch JT, Jennings RK: Aggressive dyscontrol in patients treated with benzodiazepines. J Clin Psychiatry 49:184–188, 1988
57. American Medical Association: Drug Evaluations. Chicago, IL, American Medical Association, 1986
58. Appelbaum PS: The right to refuse treatment with antipsychotic medication: retrospect and prospect. Am J Psychiatry 145:413–419, 1988
59. Shaw MR: Professional responsibility of attorneys representing institutionalized mental patients in relation to psychiatric medication. Journal of Health and Hospital Law 22:186–194, 1989
60. Wettstein RM: Psychiatry and the Law, in The American Psychiatric Press Textbook of Psychiatry. Edited by Talbott JA, Hales RE, Yudofsky SC. Washington, DC, American Psychiatric Press, 1988, pp 1059–1083
61. Davis JM, Barter JT, Kane JM: Antipsychotic drugs, in The Comprehensive Textbook of Psychiatry. Edited by Kaplan HI, Sadock BJ. Baltimore, MD, Williams & Wilkins, 1989
62. Evans RW, Gaualtieri CT: Carbamazepine: a neuropsychological and psychiatric profile. Clin Neuropharmacol 8:221–241, 1985

63. Neppe VM: Carbamazepine as adjunctive treatment in nonepileptic chronic inpatients with EEG temporal lobe abnormalities. J Clin Psychiatry 44:326–331, 1981
64. Luchins DI: Carbamazepine in psychiatric syndromes: clinical and neuropharmacological properties. Psychopharmacol Bull 20:569–571, 1984
65. Mattes JA, Rosenberg J, Mays D: Carbamazepine versus propranolol in patients with uncontrolled rage outbursts: a random assignment study. Psychopharmacol Bull 20:98–100, 1984
66. Silver JM, Yudofsky SC: Psychopharmacology and electroconvulsive therapy, in The American Psychiatric Press Textbook of Psychiatry. Edited by Talbott JA, Hales RE, Yudofsky SC. Washington, DC, American Psychiatric Press, 1988, pp 767–853
67. Silver JM, Yudofsky S: Propranolol for aggression: literature review and clinical guidelines. International Drug Newsletter 20:9–12, 1985
68. Craft M, Ismail IA, Krishnamarti D, et al: Lithium in the treatment of aggression in mentally handicapped patients. Br J Psychiatry 150:685–689, 1987
69. Brizer DA: Psychopharmacology and the management of violent patients. Psychiatr Clin North Am 11:551–558, 1988
70. Bernstein HA: Survey of threats and assaults directed toward therapists. Am J Psychother 35:542–549, 1981
71. Dubin WR, Wilson SJ, Mercer C: Assaults against psychiatrists in outpatient settings. J Clin Psychiatry 49:338–345, 1988
72. Madden DJ, Lion JR, Penna MW: Assaults on psychiatrists by patients. Am J Psychiatry 133:422–425, 1976
73. Tardiff K, Maurice WL: The care of violent patients by psychiatrists: a tale of two cities. Canadian Psychiatric Association Journal 22:83–86, 1977
74. Whitman RM, Armao BB, Dent OB: Assault on the therapist. Am J Psychiatry 133:426–431, 1976
75. Lanza ML: How nurses react to patient assault. J Psychosoc Nurs Ment Health Serv 23:6–11, 1985
76. Carmel H, Hunter M: Staff injuries from inpatient violence. Hosp Community Psychiatry 40:41–46, 1989
77. Hatti S, Dubin WR, Weiss KJ: A study of circumstances surrounding patient assaults on psychiatrists. Hosp Community Psychiatry 33:660–661, 1982
78. Ruben I, Wolkon G, Yamamoto J: Physical attacks on psychiatric residents by patients. J Nerv Ment Dis 168:243–245, 1980
79. Thackrey M: Therapeutics for Aggression: Psychological/Physical Crisis Intervention. New York, Human Sciences Press, 1987
80. McNeil DE, Binder RL: Patients who bring weapons to the psychiatric emergency room. J Clin Psychiatry 48:230–233, 1987
81. Turner JT (ed): Violence in the Medical Care Setting: A Survival Guide. Rockville, MD, Aspen, 1984

82. Lion JR, Tardiff K: The long-term treatment of the violent patient, in Psychiatry Update: American Psychiatric Association Annual Review, Vol 6. Edited by Hales RE, Frances AJ. Washington, DC, American Psychiatric Press, 1987, pp 537–548
83. Tarasoff v Regents of the University of California, 118 Cal Rptr 129, 529 P2d 553 (1974)
84. Beck JC: The therapist's legal duty when the patient may be violent. Psychiatr Clin North Am 32:665–679, 1988
85. Appelbaum PS: *Tarasoff* and the clinician: problems in fulfilling the duty to protect. Am J Psychiatry 142:425–429, 1985

Section IV

Psychiatrists' Relationships With Nonmedical Professionals

Carol C. Kleinman, M.D., J.D., Section Editor

Chapter 4

Introduction

Carol C. Kleinman, M.D., J.D.

Many, if not most, physicians practicing today entered medical school motivated by an ideal of the physician as a healer. In medical school that ideal was tempered by the knowledge that our ability to effect cures is really very limited. Perhaps our greatest disillusionment, however, has come not from the limitations of medical science but from the increasing constraints imposed on us by the society in which we practice our profession.

Psychiatry, perhaps more than any other medical specialty, has had to cope with an increasingly complex environment. Psychiatrists are called on to fulfill many roles. We must justify our existence to the public and defend our profession from those who doubt its efficacy and who would curtail the public's ability to use our services. Although psychiatrists are assumed to be experts in communicating with others, unfortunately, because today's training programs emphasize biological psychiatry, the art of communication is often neglected. To operate successfully in the public arena, psychiatrists must become more adept at making their case to decision makers and at mobilizing public opinion in support of preserving the quality of mental health care. Among other things, this means that our profession must become more comfortable in dealing with and in using the communications media.

Increasingly, psychiatrists are faced with conflicts between their responsibilities to their patients and their duty to the institution or the society of which they are a part. How, for example, should psychiatrists employed by a health maintenance organization deal with the treatment limitations imposed by the institution for which they work, when they believe that these limitations interfere with or even prevent proper patient care? Hitherto sacrosanct principles —such as the preservation of patient confidentiality—are being challenged today by competing and sometimes compelling obliga-

I thank my husband, Ted, without whose love, technical support, and editorial assistance this section would not have been possible.

tions the psychiatrist owes to the public. For example, what duty do psychiatrists have to disclose patient confidences when their failure to do so may result in injury to others? This issue can arise in a wide variety of contexts, such as cases involving patients with AIDS, patients engaged in criminal activities, and patients engaged in occupations in which their illnesses could endanger public safety or national security. Despite *Tarasoff* (1), its progeny cases, and new statutes enacted in many states, questions are left unanswered (2). The innate difficulties of coping with these conflicts are compounded by the legal liability that can result from making decisions that are subsequently judged incorrect.

The interactions between psychiatry and the law also complicate our lives. Because ours is a highly litigious society, it is increasingly difficult for those of us in private practice to avoid contact with lawyers and with the courts. In a nation in which nearly 50% of marriages end in divorce, psychiatrists more and more frequently find themselves involved in litigation involving matrimonial and child custody issues. We are also called on to testify regarding the mental condition of patients who have suffered tortious injury of one sort or another. The wide range of these cases includes women who have been victimized by sexual harassment in the workplace, accident victims suffering from posttraumatic stress disorders, and those who seek compensation for mental and emotional suffering. Finally, some of us are called on in criminal cases to provide either factual or expert testimony regarding the competency or the state of mind and responsibility of the defendant. Involvement in legal proceedings frequently is difficult for psychiatrists both because the "rules of the game" are so unfamiliar and because the adversarial nature of the legal process is alien to the collegial environment in which most of us, both by temperament and training, are used to functioning.

Also complicating modern psychiatric practice are the increasingly difficult relationships between psychiatrists and other mental health professionals. The traditional notion of the mental health team "headed" by the psychiatrist is being widely challenged. Increasingly, psychologists and to a lesser extent psychiatric nurses and social workers are seeking to expand their traditional areas of responsibility. Some see this as a battle for "turf." Whatever the motives involved, attempts to expand the roles of nonphysician mental health professionals must be judged by their impact on the quality and availability of mental health care within our society. The stakes in these contests are high, both for the future of psychiatry as a profession and for the treatment of people with mental health problems. If psychiatrists abdicate their responsibility to actively participate in the resolution of these issues, they do so not only at their own peril but at the risk of compromising the quality of care available to patients.

The five articles in this section explore the diverse roles and issues described above that today confront practicing psychiatrists. They are offered in the hope that they will help us all to function more effectively in the increasingly difficult environment in which we work.

Much as one might wish otherwise, psychiatrists practice a difficult profession in a complex world. The price of successfully functioning in such a world is that psychiatrists must educate themselves about the issues affecting them and must act to shape the future of their profession. Only by doing these things can psychiatrists keep faith with psychiatry as a discipline and with those whom they have taken an oath to help.

NOTES

1. *Tarasoff v Regents of the University of California*, 17 Cal3d 425, 131 Cal Rptr 14, 551 P2d 334 (1976)
2. Simon RI: Clinical Psychiatry and the Law. Washington, DC, American Psychiatric Press, 1984, pp 306–336

Chapter 5

Psychiatrists' Relationships With Nonmedical Mental Health Professionals

Carol C. Kleinman, M.D., J.D.

The past 50 years have seen significant changes in the way mental health care is delivered in our country. Participation by nonmedical professionals in the delivery of mental health services has significantly increased. Consequently, it has become more and more difficult to know who has authority—over what and over whom. Psychiatrists who have been trained to think of themselves as the leaders of a mental health team are discovering that their traditional roles and responsibilities are continuously being challenged.

Over the past 10 years, the competition among medical and nonmedical professionals for a shrinking number of mental health dollars has grown increasingly fierce. Government, business, and insurance companies often seem less concerned with quality of care than with purchasing services at the lowest possible price. New "delivery concepts," such as managed mental health care, preferred provider organizations, and health maintenance organizations have emerged in response to pressures for lower costs. Traditional methods for delivering mental health services thus are in flux.

Licensing laws, codes, and regulations stipulate the limits within which each of the mental health professions is authorized to practice. Increasingly, however, nonmedical professionals are trying to obtain privileges, beyond those granted by their state licenses, by going to the courts and to state legislatures and engaging in "turf" battles with psychiatrists. Psychologists are demanding independent hospital admitting privileges, prescription-writing privileges, and reimbursement under Medicare provisions. In some states, social workers are lobbying for the independent right to diagnose patients. Mental health nurses and marriage counselors are lobbying for increased recognition, responsibility, and autonomy. This year, after a 3-year lawsuit, four psychologists were successful in getting the American Psychoanalytic Association to agree to relax the requirements for admission of psychologists as full-fledged psychoanalysts.

The American Psychiatric Association and its district branches are learning that to protect the traditional role of psychiatrists in the practice of medicine and to protect the public, they must fund and organize political action committees; keep up with local legislation and hearings; write letters to elected officials; and testify before local, state, and federal decision-making bodies.

THE PSYCHIATRIST'S TRADITIONAL RELATIONSHIP WITH NONMEDICAL THERAPISTS

Good patient care frequently requires the skills of both psychiatrists and nonmedical professionals. For the psychiatrist, these interprofessional relationships, at various times, may be supervisory, consultative, or collaborative. It is important that psychiatrists understand the different roles they are expected to play and the responsibilities they assume in each of these relationships (1).

Collaborative Relationships

In a collaborative relationship, responsibility for the patient's care is shared, but each therapist's responsibilities are determined by the standards that apply to his or her particular discipline (2). The patient should be informed of the responsibilities assumed by each therapist. Frequently there are areas of overlap, because the assumption of responsibilities by a therapist representing one discipline does not diminish the normal responsibilities of collaborating therapists belonging to other disciplines. Psychiatrists and nonmedical therapists need to periodically evaluate the patient's clinical condition to ensure that the treatment plan is appropriate, and when participating therapists determine that termination of their collaborative relationship is appropriate, they must inform the patient.

Consultative Relationships

When psychiatrists are consulted by another mental health professional, they do not have a treatment relationship with the patient and assume no responsibility for the patient's care. The psychiatrist's only relationship is with the consulting therapist. The psychiatrist relies on information provided by the therapist and offers a medical opinion that the therapist may or may not accept. As a consequence, even where the psychiatrist is negligent in rendering advice, he or she may nevertheless be found not responsible for causing the patient harm (3). The result in such a situation may depend on whether the therapist to whom the advice is given is judged capable of evaluating the information and opinion received. Therefore, when a nonmedical therapist seeks an opinion, it is important for consulting psychiatrists to determine whether that therapist has met professional standards of independent functioning in his or her own discipline (2).

Supervisory Relationships

Supervisory relationships entail the greatest risk of liability. Here, psychiatrists assume direct responsibility for the care of the patient and active guidance of the therapists they are supervising. A psychiatrist supervising nonmedical professionals is responsible for the patient's initial workup, diagnosis, and physical status, and for developing a treatment plan.

Under traditional tort law, psychiatrists are directly responsible for the wrongful acts of employees who are acting within the scope of their employment. The psychiatrist-employer is held vicariously liable for negligent acts of nurses and other employees even when the psychiatrist is totally without fault (3).

Because supervising psychiatrists assume medical responsibility for the patient, just as though they were sole providers, psychiatrists should not allow themselves to be used as a means of obtaining insurance payment for nonmedical providers (4). It is unethical for psychiatrists to continue a collaborative, consultative, or supervisory relationship in which their role is being misrepresented or in which the care provided by a nonmedical therapist is inadequate or inappropriate, unless the psychiatrist's purpose is to raise the quality of care. Psychiatrists who assume responsibility for a patient's treatment must ensure that they are appropriately informed about the nature of the treatment and the clinical course of the patient. The frequency of collaboration, consultation, and supervision must be sufficient to ensure that the psychiatrist's medical, ethical, and legal responsibilities to the patient are being fulfilled in accordance with local and state government guidelines (4). Psychiatrists must also be careful when making referrals that they are not referring the patient to a nonmedical person any matter that requires the exercise of professional medical judgment (5).

Courts have addressed the issue of negligent supervision and negligent institutional policies governing patient management (6–8). Although a supervisor may not be held directly responsible for the negligent acts of a supervised individual who is on a "frolic of his own," the supervisor can be held responsible for damages resulting from negligent supervision (4,9).

Courts have made use of the doctrine of vicarious liability and the "borrowed servant" rule to hold psychiatrists responsible for the negligence of others. Under the doctrine of vicarious liability, psychiatrists may be held liable for harm negligently caused by an individual over whom they have control. Accordingly, a psychiatrist directing a therapeutic team may be held vicariously liable for the negligent acts of members of the team. Similarly, a psychiatrist who employs nonmedical therapists is vicariously liable for their negligent acts (10).

Under the "borrowed servant" doctrine, psychiatrists seeing patients in a clinic or hospital setting may be held responsible for the negligent acts of nonmedical therapists who are not their employees but who are present to assist in the treatment of those patients. The "borrowed servant" rule (11) states that a servant directed or permitted by one master to perform services for another may become the servant of that other person in performing those services. Therefore, a critical question is, When does a master-servant relationship arise between a psychiatrist and a nonmedical therapist employed by a person or institution other than the psychiatrist? Certainly, in a hospital setting, where psychiatrists direct a team in the treatment of patients, they are likely to be viewed as possessing sufficient control over other therapists to warrant being held vicariously liable for the "servant" therapists' negligent acts (4).

Special problems arise for psychiatrists when they consider signing insurance and treatment-plan forms for nonmedical therapists. The supervisory role of psychiatrists with nonmedical mental health professionals carries with it very specific responsibilities. If a form contains a signature line for a "supervising position" or a treatment-plan signature line labeled "reviewed and approved by," the psychiatrist must be certain that the services described were in fact provided. It is both unethical and fraudulent for psychiatrists to represent on a form that specific tasks have been performed if they know that these tasks have not been performed (4,12). When signing an insurance form for therapy performed by a nonmedical therapist, psychiatrists must indicate who actually performed the therapy (5). If psychiatrists bring a nonmedical mental health professional into their office as a colleague, they must be very careful to avoid sharing in the fees received for services performed by the nonmedical professional. Section 2, Annotation 7, of the American Psychiatric Association's *Principles of Medical Ethics With Annotations Especially Applicable to Psychiatry* specifically states that "an arrangement in which a psychiatrist provides supervision or administration to other physicians or nonmedical persons for a percentage of their fees or gross income is not acceptable; this would constitute fee-splitting. In a team of practitioners, or a multidisciplinary team, it is ethical for the psychiatrist to receive income for administration, research, education, or consultation. This should be based upon a mutually agreed upon and set fee or salary, open to renegotiation when a change in the time demand occurs" (13). Psychiatrists may only charge nonmedical practitioners an appropriate amount for services provided—for example, space, secretarial support, supervision, and consultation (5,13).

A question has arisen about whether it is proper for a psychiatrist to be the "medical director" of a private psychiatric clinic—the rest of whose staff consists of nonmedical professionals—when the psychiatrist spends very little time at the clinic. It is *not* ethical for psychiatrists to lend their name to a clinic merely to legitimize it. Psychiatrists must spend sufficient time there to ensure that proper care is being given and that nonmedical staff are not assuming responsibilities requiring medical training (5).

Antitrust Issues

For many years a variety of defenses limited the application of federal antitrust laws to the provision of health care services. Recent Supreme Court decisions have eroded these defenses, however, so that today health care providers can be held accountable for anticompetitive behavior (14).

The basic objective of the antitrust laws is to eliminate practices that inhibit free competition based on *price, quality,* and *service*:

> The Sherman Act was designated to be a comprehensive charter of economic liberty aimed at preserving free and unfettered competition as the rule of trade. It rests on the premise that the unrestrained interaction of competitive forces will yield the best allocation of our economic resources, the lowest prices, the highest quality, and the greatest material progress, while at the same time providing an environment conducive to the preservation of our democratic, political and social institutions. (15)

Under federal antitrust laws, conduct that clearly harms the interest of America's health care consumers, and thus violates antitrust laws, can have serious consequences. These can include heavy fines and even jail terms.

In a recent address before the American Medical Association (AMA) House of Delegates meeting in Dallas, Assistant Attorney General Charles F. Rule stated three rules for physicians to follow to avoid violation of antitrust laws:

> First do not agree with competing independent doctors in terms of price, quantity or quality—including fee schedules and relative value skills; second, do not agree with competing independent doctors on the patients that you are willing to serve, the locations from which you are permitted to draw patients, or where you will locate your offices; and third, do not agree with competing independent doctors to refuse to offer your services to alternative delivery systems.

Mr. Rule warned that each violation of the antitrust laws is punishable by up to 3 years in jail and fines of $250,000 (16).

Although the federal government and state attorneys general have responsibilities for enforcing antitrust laws, private parties also can bring suits in federal court either to recover threefold damages suffered or to enjoin a violation of antitrust laws (17). Many private treble-damage actions are brought as class actions under Rule 23 of the Federal Rules of Civil Procedure. As a consequence, the federal courts have been deluged with antitrust complaints brought against health care providers.

Psychoanalysis and the Antitrust Laws

Psychologists have made effective use of the antitrust laws to expand their rights. More than 3 years ago, four Ph.D. psychologists filed suit against the American Psychoanalytic Association, the New York Psychoanalytic Institute, the Columbia University Center for Psychoanalytic Training and Research, and the International Psychoanalytic Association.

The plaintiffs alleged that by maintaining admissions policies limiting psychoanalytic training to physicians, psychoanalysts had conspired to restrain trade and to develop a monopoly over the practice of psychoanalysis, in violation of the antitrust laws. The four psychologists contended that if the barriers to the practice of psychoanalysis were removed, the cost of this treatment to patients, the government, and third-party payers would decrease drastically. They also claimed that more people would be able to take advantage of psychoanalysis, because many geographical areas have few or no psychiatrists. The plaintiffs maintained that the advanced training required of doctoral-level clinical psychologists provides them with adequate knowledge and background to engage in psychoanalytic practice. In addition, the psychologists maintained that excluding them from psychoanalytic training and practice limits competition in the health care market and disrupts the quality and efficiency of care afforded the public.

Until recently, only physicians were eligible for psychoanalytic training, although a small number of psychologists were accepted into the institutes after they signed a waiver stating that they would not practice as psychoanalysts once they completed their training. Two years ago, however, the American Psychoanalytic Association did formally change its admissions policy to accept well-qualified therapists regardless of the degree they held.

In October 1988, the antitrust suit against the American Psychoanalytic Association was settled out of court (18). The psychologists called the settlement an end to the "anticompetitive practices that have ill-served the public." They stated that it will "serve as an example" to psychiatrists and other physicians that "restrictions" on the types of professionals who practice in the mental health area "cannot be sustained" (18).

In addition to assuring psychologists that it would continue to train psychologists and other nonmedical clinicians in its institutes, the American Psychoanalytic Association agreed, as part of the settlement, to allow teachers in these institutes to teach in new psychoanalytic institutes being established by psychologists. The suit also opened up membership in the International Psychoanalytic Association and its training institutes to psychologists and other qualified nonmedical clinicians. Because the litigation was settled on a class-action basis, the settlement precludes any future suits by psychologists against psychoanalysts on the same grounds (18).

The psychologists' antitrust suit did not just occur "out of the blue." Observers had warned that something akin to what has happened would be the ultimate result of the demedicalization of psychiatry that began in the 1960s and continued throughout the ensuing decade. During the 1970s American psychiatry changed its course radically. There was a marked swing back toward the neurosciences and biological psychiatry; a renewal of bonds with the rest of medicine; sharp confrontations between psychiatry and other mental health disciplines; a struggle for power in medical school departments of psychiatry between psychoanalysts, dynamically oriented psychiatrists, and biological psychiatrists; and an overall weakening of psychoanalysis in institutional psychiatric systems (19).

The reversal of the 1970 decision terminating the internship requirement for psychiatrists symbolized the reassertion by psychiatrists of their medical identity. The "remedicalization" of psychiatry also was profoundly influenced by

> socioeconomic and political forces, including the escalating role of third-party insurance, the drying up of federal funds for training and research, competition from nonmedical mental health disciplines, and enormous pressure for accountability in order for the cost of treatment to be reimbursed. The economic recession of the early 1980's had an enormous impact on all of medical practice; we are now enmeshed in one of the most radical (perhaps revolutionary) periods in the history of medicine . . . [C]oping with economic realities in psychiatric and psychoanalytic practice has become the dominant adaptive task of the 1980's. (19)

The settlement between the psychologists and the American Psychoanalytic Association has given rise to a variety of concerns. Some have expressed fear that the new policy of even-handed admissions would end the close ties between organized psychiatry and the American Psychoanalytic Association. Others have voiced concern that the number of M.D.'s entering psychoanalytic training may dwindle.

Dr. Melvin Sabshin, Medical Director of the American Psychiatric Association, wrote in 1985 that "[t]he broad institutionalization of nonmedical candidates would convey the message that psychoanalysis is not a medical field per se" (24). Although many non-M.D.'s have conducted analysis with good technique, in Dr. Sabshin's view the issue of their technical competence is outweighed by diagnostic and triage questions. Can the nonmedical graduate competently decide whether a patient should be treated by psychotherapy or psychoanalysis? Would consultation with a family practitioner or other medical specialist suffice to permit combined use of psychotherapy and pharmacotherapy (24)?

Underlying much of the rhetoric is the fear that psychoanalysis will become less of a medical subspecialty as psychologists assume increasing responsibility for carrying out treatment. Dr. Sabshin believes that the most important area of struggle today is whether psychologists should be allowed to make diagnoses and determine appropriate treatment modalities. Certainly, he argues, the more nonmedical people become involved in psychoanalysis, the harder it will be to argue in favor of medical reimbursement (Melvin Sabshin, personal communication).

From the other side of the battlefield, predictions are now heard: "Psychologists will be the leaders in the psychoanalytic fields for the next five decades. The medical monopoly is over in psychoanalysis." Or, "Winning the lawsuit is like the establishment of World War II Victory Gardens, we have set aside a plot of land for ourselves so we can start to work." One psychologist asserted that with the favorable settlement of the lawsuits, psychologists have "emancipated [them]selves from psychological and professional bondage."

Brian Welch, J.D., Ph.D., Executive Director for Professional Practice of the American Psychological Association, assesses the impact of the settlement by observing that "psychologists as a group have been reluctant to assert their rights and psychiatrists have traditionally had a sense of entitlement. I hope [the settlement] will help psychologists—particularly young psychologists—appreciate the enormous contribution they have to make to the mental health delivery system, in particular, and to society as a whole." Welch believes that within 10 years, 50% of the candidates in any psychoanalytic institute will be psychologists (20).

Clearly, there is a strong sense of militancy and some strident rhetoric emanating from the psychologists' camp. In the words of one psychologist, the settlement of the lawsuit begins a new phase in the history of psychoanalysis,

> not just the history of psychoanalytic psychology in the United States, nor just that of psychoanalysis in the United States: I mean the history of all psychoanalysis. The historical record warrants my making this sweeping judgment, for it shows the United States to be particularly fertile soil for psychoanalytic thought, practice and research and it shows clinical psychology in the United States to be a particularly fertile source of new and good ideas. (21)

However, the warfare between psychologists and psychiatrists continues.

CAPP v. Rank—The Right of Psychologists to Admit Patients

In 1984, the California Association of Psychology Providers (CAPP) sued the California Department of Health Services and its Director, Peter Rank, for restraint of trade, claiming that the state discriminated against psychologists by denying them the right to admit and discharge patients independently and the right to treat them in hospitals without the supervision of a psychiatrist. The CAPP suit challenged two state regulations (22) providing that in acute-care psychiatric hospitals or in psychiatric units of acute-care general hospitals, psychiatrists must be responsible for the "diagnostic formulation for each patient and the development and implementation of the individual patient's treatment plan." The psychologists maintained that these activities were within the scope of their licensure (23).

The California Superior Court found in favor of the psychologists but was overturned by the California Court of Appeals in June 1988 (24). The appeals court held that although a physician's function may encompass the practice of psychology, a psychologist may *not* practice medicine. It found that

> [o]nly a physician is authorized to render diagnosis concerning a mental disorder, organic in origin and nature. Similarly, to the extent that a mental disorder is susceptible to treatment by drugs, surgery or electroconvulsive therapy, only a physician is authorized to create and implement such a treatment plan therefor. Psychologists cannot make a medical diagnosis or devise and implement a treatment plan utilizing such means since those matters are not "consistent with the scope of their licensure." A gap in patient care arises if the physician does not have the initial and ultimate responsibility for a patient suffering from a mental disorder under those circumstances. If the psychologist were accorded unfettered discretion to admit his or her patient to a health facility and to implement a nonmedical treatment based on a nonmedical diagnosis without the supervision of a physician, then the patient's health may be at risk. Such was not the Legislature's intent.

The court of appeals also held that the

> legislature intended to require health facilities to allow their appointed clinical psychologists the right to diagnose and treat their patients without interference or hindrance from a physician, only in those instances where a physician has initially ruled out a medical basis for the patient's mental disorder and determined that it is not subject to medical treatment, and where the patient's mental disorder does not subsequently become susceptible to medical treatment after admission to the health facility. Under such circumstances the functions of the psychologist and physician become coextensive in that either would be authorized to practice psychology . . . [T]o require a patient to be diagnosed and treated by a psychiatrist, or the psychologist to be supervised by a psychiatrist, after a medical diagnosis and medical treatment have been ruled out, would constitute discrimination against the psychologist as prescribed by the legislature. (25)

CAPP appealed the appellate court's decision to the California Supreme Court, which has agreed to hear the case. In their brief to the California Supreme Court, CAPP argues that the question for decision is whether the California legislature intended for patients who need hospital care for mental disorders to "continue to receive care from the therapist of their choice? Or, alternatively, did the

Legislature intend to deprive patients of this right if their therapist is a clinical psychologist?" The psychologists contend that the core issue is really economic. "[F]ewer patients and less responsibility for psychiatrists necessarily affects the income of psychiatrists" (26). The psychologists conclude by urging that they be permitted to independently "admit, diagnose, and treat patients in health facilities so long as *1*) they function within the scope of their license and competence; *2*) they function in accordance with the facility's rules; and *3*) backup medical care is available to the extent that a patient needs services that only a physician can provide" (26).

The essence of the psychiatrists' response to these arguments is that diagnosing an illness and formulating and implementing a treatment plan for hospitalized patients are services that "only a physician can provide and are therefore outside of the psychologist's scope of license and competence" (27). The psychiatrists point out that in today's world, patients who require hospital treatment are usually suffering from severe mental illness such as schizophrenia or a major depressive disorder that is in its active, acute phase. Usually the patient has to be in serious medical jeopardy and in a position where he or she is posing a danger to self or others. Psychiatrists disagree with the psychologists' attempt to portray the typical hospital patient as someone receiving outpatient therapy whose condition worsens, thereby requiring a more structured environment and continued psychotherapy from a "familiar helper." The psychiatrists argue that taking diagnostic responsibility and formulating a treatment plan for a hospitalized patient require *1*) a familiarity with the physical factors that can lead to and affect the course of mental illness; *2*) an understanding of when it is appropriate to secure medical tests and consultations and how to interpret their results; and *3*) the ability to understand and administer basic medical treatments, such as the large variety of psychotropic medications that are a routine part of hospital care (27).

Fighting continual lawsuits against an array of nonmedical mental health professionals exacts a tremendous emotional, financial, and time cost from psychiatrists. A victory for psychologists on the hospital privilege issue in the nation's most populous state would provide a precedent for use by nonphysician providers in other states. Recognizing the potential significance of the CAPP case, local American Psychiatric Association (APA) branches outside of California and individual APA members have sent financial contributions to the California Psychiatric Association to help defray the expenses of the lawsuit. The APA Board of Trustees has voted to file an amicus brief in the case because it has national implications for the treatment of the mentally ill (24).

MEDICARE REIMBURSEMENT FOR PSYCHOLOGISTS' SERVICES

Another area in which psychiatrists' relationships with nonmedical professionals has come under review is reimbursement under Medicare. Medicare is the largest federal health insurance program both in terms of benefit payments (approximately $77.7 billion in 1986) and persons served (approximately 28.8 million older Americans) (27).

In light of the *CAPP* case, it is worth noting that Congress explicitly conditioned hospital coverage under Medicare on the "requirement that every patient must be under the care of a physician" (28). Treatment by a psychologist is authorized only when "patients are referred by a physician, who establishes a plan for the patient's total care and retains overall responsibility for patient management" (29). Looking at the delivery of outpatient mental health services, however, Congress has recently changed Medicare to permit direct reimbursement to psychologists and social workers, rather than indirect reimbursement through a doctor or a clinic.

Before these recent changes, direct payment to psychologists or social workers could be made only if they practiced in a community mental health center or a rural clinic. The new law does require these nonphysician providers to "agree to consult with a patient's attending physician" in accordance with criteria to be developed by the Department of Health and Human Services. The conference report accompanying the legislation indicates that the conferees intended to require that nonphysician providers tell their patients that it is desirable to consult with the patient's primary-care physician for the purpose of considering potential contributing medical conditions. Unless the patient objects, the primary-care physician also is to be consulted about the services being provided by the nonmedical professionals. These consultations must be documented (30).

The position of the APA was that the psychologist should be reimbursed only after a physician has provided a medical differential diagnosis. The APA believes that this requirement would protect the large group of elderly patients who have coexisting mental and physical illnesses and whose conditions may be exacerbated by drug interactions (31,32).

Psychologists lobbied for a change in the present reimbursement rules, framing their arguments in favor of coverage in terms of access to care, a subject that disturbs many members of Congress very much. They noted that Medicare is the only existing health care plan that does not provide beneficiaries with direct access to psychological care except in community mental health care centers and rural clinics. National Institute of Mental Health data show that 50–70% of the mental health needs of the elderly go unmet.

Moreover, elderly people who do gain access to the health care system often receive inappropriate and poor treatment. Between 75 and 85% of all mental health services received by this segment of the population are rendered by general physicians "who typically have less than three months of mental health training and are poorly equipped to detect, diagnose, or treat the mental health needs of the elderly" (33). Psychologists claimed that maldistribution of psychiatrists is seriously impeding access to mental health care among the elderly. They argued that their own increased numbers are more equitably distributed across the country, and their lower fees make modifying the Medicare law to allow the elderly easier access to psychologists a logical solution (33). What they do not address is the stigma that deters the elderly from consulting any mental health professional in the first place.

Responding to the psychologists' arguments before the House Energy and Commerce Subcommittee on Health, APA Deputy Medical Director Carolyn B. Robinowitz noted that despite claims to the contrary, most doctoral-level psychologists in independent practice work in areas where psychiatrists already practice. Dr. Robinowitz also took issue with the contention that making nonphysician providers eligible for Medicare reimbursement would lead to substantial cost savings because they have lower fees than physicians. Not only are clinical psychologists' fees quite close to those charged by psychiatrists, she argued, but once psychologists are eligible for insurance reimbursement, their fees tend to creep up even closer to those of psychiatrists. Whatever small savings would accrue to the Medicare fund by adding a class of nonphysician providers soon would be wiped out by the cost of their failure to diagnose physical illnesses that aggravate or cause mental disorders. If Congress makes additional funds available for mental health treatment under Medicare, the APA prefers that they be used to reduce, to the customary 20%, the 50% copayment that is currently required from beneficiaries receiving mental health services (31).

PRESCRIPTION PRIVILEGES

The latest challenge to psychiatrists comes in the area of the right of psychologists to prescribe psychotropic drugs. This fight is spearheaded by Patrick H. DeLeon, Ph.D., a clinical psychologist and lawyer, who wields considerable power as a staff assistant to Senator Daniel K. Inouye of Hawaii. Using that power, DeLeon is now demanding that the military give its psychologists prescription rights. In his view, "prescribing is a little function which is really no big deal—except for turf reasons" (34).

Dr. DeLeon has predicted that prescription privileges for psychologists will evolve in stages over several years. At Congress's request, the Pentagon has promised a demonstration training program in which military psychologists will be permitted to prescribe drugs. Action also has begun at the state level. A first-ever bill, introduced this year in the Hawaii legislature, would license qualified psychologists to prescribe psychotropic drugs. Dr. DeLeon also anticipates that in about 10 years, psychiatric social workers also will demand prescription privileges. He trivializes a psychiatrist's 12-year education process, contending that medical school is largely irrelevant to psychiatric practice and that most of what well-trained psychiatrists know about prescribing psychotropic drugs is learned in residency (34).

Both the APA and the AMA have publicly stated their opposition to the prescribing of medication by persons who have not had the appropriate medical education, orientation, training, and experience (35, 36). Complaints made by the APA to the Indian Health Service (IHS) led IHS to discontinue its policy of permitting psychologists to prescribe medications independently of physician supervision (37). The issue is far from settled, however.

CONCLUSION

This review of the battles over access to psychoanalytic training, hospital admitting privileges, rights to prescribe drugs, and Medicare reimbursement makes it clear that psychologists and psychiatrists are today at war. Like most wars, this one is fueled by misunderstandings, past resentments, extremism, and the normal human drives for power and turf. The principal cause, however, probably lies in the competition for the shrinking number of dollars that society is willing to spend on mental health care. Like any war waged in our courts and our legislatures, a side's strength comes as much from the amount of money it has to spend and from the number and militancy of its adherents as from the force of its arguments. Viewed in these terms, psychiatry as we know it today is in serious trouble. The real tragedy of this little war, however, is that it ignores the larger events that are taking place in our health care system.

Despite the efforts of the federal government and private payers and health insurers, health care costs have continued to increase at an unacceptable rate. As many as 37 million Americans may lack any health care coverage at all (Office of Senator Edward Kennedy, personal communication). The likelihood is increasing that rather than continuing to tinker with the present system, Congress will radically overhaul it within the next few years. If this happens, a critical issue will be the extent to which mental health services are covered under the new system. This is an issue about which psychologists and psychiatrists can make common cause. The fight for an adequate share of the pool of dollars dedicated to the health care system will not be an easy one. Congress will need to be convinced that psychotherapeutic treatment is both efficacious and cost-effective (i.e., that its availability offsets the need for more expensive medical treatment in large numbers of cases). If psychologists and psychiatrists continue to battle one another rather than uniting to fight the battle for adequate mental health coverage in the years ahead, both professions and, indeed, society as a whole will lose.

NOTES

1. American Psychiatric Association: Position statement on psychiatrists' relationships with nonmedical mental health professionals. Am J Psychiatry 130:386–390, 1973
2. American Psychiatric Association: Guidelines for psychiatrists in consultative, supervisory, or collaborative relationships with nonmedical therapists (official actions). Am J Psychiatry 137:1489–1491, 1980
3. Klein JI, Macbeth JE, Onek JN: Legal Issues in the Private Practice of Psychiatry. Washington, DC, American Psychiatric Press, 1984
4. Simon RI: Clinical Psychiatry and the Law. Washington, DC, American Psychiatric Press, 1984, pp 378–390
5. American Psychiatric Association: Opinions of the Ethics Committee on the Principles of Medical Ethics With Annotations Especially Applicable to Psychiatry. Washington, DC, American Psychiatric Association, 1985
6. Cohen v State of New York, 51 AD 2d 494, 382 NYS 2d 128 (1976)
7. Andrews v United States, 732 F2d 366 (4th Cir 1984)
8. Peck v The Counseling Service of Addison County, Inc., 146 Vt 61, 499 A2d 422 (Vt Sup Ct 1985)
9. Kuder AV: Psychiatric supervision: a legal business. The Washington Psychiatric Society Newsletter, Sept 1984, p 3
10. Quimby CW: Law for the Medical Practitioner. Washington, DC, Aupha Press, 1979
11. Restatement (Second) of Agency § 227 (1957)
12. When not to sign insurance and treatment plan forms. American Psy-

chiatric Association Legal Consultation Plan Newsletter, Nov 1985, pp 4–5
13. American Psychiatric Association: The Principles of Medical Ethics With Annotations Especially Applicable to Psychiatry. Washington, DC, American Psychiatric Association, 1989
14. Proger PA: Antitrust primer. Presented at the National Health Lawyers Association: Antitrust in the Health Care Field, Washington, DC, Jan 1989, pp 25–27
15. Northern Pacific Railway v United States, 356 US 1, 4–5 (1958)
16. Bianco EA: Antitrust violations can mean jail. Legal Aspects of Medical Practice, April 17, 1989, p 7
17. 15 USC §§ 15, 26
18. Psychologists to be admitted to psychoanalytic institutes. Psychiatric News, Nov 18, 1988, p 7
19. Sabshin M: Psychoanalysis and psychiatry: models for potential future relations. J Am Psychoanal Assoc 33:473–491, 1985
20. DeAngelis T: Suit opens doors to analysis training. Monitor, June 1989, p 16
21. Schafer R: After the settlement. The Round Robin 5(1):14, 1989
22. Cal Admin Code, tit 22, §§ 70577 (d)(1) and 71203 (a)(1)(A)
23. Cal Health and Safety Code § 1316.5
24. California privilege case draws support from other APA DB's. Psychiatric News, Jan 6, 1989, p 7
25. California Association of Psychology Providers (CAPP) v Rank, No B020113, slip op, Calif Ct of App (2d D June 2, 1988), pp 12–13
26. Plaintiffs-Respondents' California Supreme Court Brief, CAPP v Rank, No S002524
27. Amici Curiae California Supreme Court Brief in Support of the Moving Parties-Appellants, CAPP v Rank, No S0025524
28. 42 USC, § 1395 x(e)(4)
29. Department of Health, Education and Welfare, Independent Practitioners Under Medicare: Report to Congress ii, 1968
30. Herrington BS: Breakthrough heralded in mental health benefits. Psychiatric News, Dec 15, 1989, pp 2, 12–13
31. APA testifies on Medicare payments to psychologists. Psychiatric News, July 7, 1989, pp 1, 22
32. Sabshin M: Coverage of psychologists' services under the Medicare program, including HR 774. Testimony of the American Psychiatric Association before the House Ways and Means Subcommittee, March 6, 1989
33. Welch BL: Mental health needs of older adults, HR 477. Testimony of the American Psychological Association before the House Energy and Commerce Subcommittee on Health, June 1989
34. Jancin B: Says psychologists will win prescribing privileges fight. Clinical Psychiatry News, June 1989, pp 1, 18
35. AMA backs APA position of denying prescription privileges to psychologists. Psychiatric News, July 7, 1989, p 17

36. Report of the Committee on Psychiatric Services in the Military to the Joint Reference Committee. June 1989, p 16
37. Prescribing privileges for IHS psychologists. Memorandum from John Porvaznik, M.D., Asst. Surgeon General to the Chief Medical Officer, Dec 9, 1988

Chapter 6

Managed Health Care and the Evolution of Psychiatric Practice

Stephen W. Siebert, M.D.
Stuart B. Silver, M.D.

Freud, the originator of psychotherapy as we know it, practiced in a mode that can be described as individual, entrepreneurial, and unregulated by outside agencies. Fees were for service rendered and came from the pocket of the patient or a family member. . . . There was no requirement to make medical diagnoses, to define a medical necessity, to establish criteria for "cure" or an endpoint of treatment, or to differentiate between the qualifications of physicians and other purveyors of psychotherapy. . . . This kind of individualistic therapeutic relationship continued for several decades after psychotherapy by psychiatrists took hold in the United States, but it has been altered irrevocably by the different conditions under which psychotherapeutic psychiatry now operates. (1)

CASE VIGNETTE

When I first began working with Joe, he was a 32-year-old, recently divorced, public service employee in a low-level position. He then had traditional third-party insurance with a $100 deductible; his insurance covered 80% of my fee. Although initially Joe sought treatment for unhappiness about his divorce, he evidenced features of a borderline personality disorder, with a history of alcohol and mixed substance abuse. Making a diligent commitment to weekly psychotherapy, Joe gained insight into his long-standing social introversion by exploring certain extremely painful experiences from his adolescence.

Unfortunately, Joe's insurance plan limited payment for psychotherapy to 20 sessions. He was unable to pay for additional sessions out of pocket because of substantial debt incurred during protracted divorce proceedings. Joe transferred his care to a community mental health center that offered a sliding-scale fee schedule, but the center was unable to provide insight-oriented psychotherapy. He became dissatisfied with the mental health center, which provided shorter, less frequent visits of supportive psychotherapy. Further, his therapist was a "mental health counselor" with whom he was unable to establish rapport.

One year later, after joining a health maintenance organization (HMO) plan that his employer offered at a lower cost than his previous insurance plan, Joe contacted me to resume his psychotherapy. The HMO offered a maximum of 40 psychotherapy sessions with a $2 copayment, but the treatment was limited to brief psychotherapy or crisis intervention. To continue to treat Joe, I abandoned my previous analytically oriented psychotherapy and adopted a problem-oriented, time-limited approach. Joe subsequently identified and worked toward well-defined social and occupational goals. Although I continued to see Joe weekly, the HMO allowed this because of our medical group's low total expenditure for mental health services.

The next year, the HMO benefits changed through an increase in copayment to $20. Joe's psychotherapy evolved into monthly supportive sessions with discussion of termination, although clinically this seemed premature. Several months later, the HMO defined ongoing weekly visits to be "nonacute," which almost eliminated the prospect of continuing our psychotherapy sessions under his insurance plan. Also, the plan allowed "medication management" visits, because the HMO was concerned that patients taking medication might show increased rates of hospitalization without regular outpatient contact. Because Joe was receiving a low-dose psychotropic, we continued our weekly visits, albeit for 20- to 30-minute sessions. Curiously, because this was a "medical" visit, neither the mental health copayment nor limitation on total visits applied. Fortunately, through this arrangement Joe concluded his psychotherapy, and I now see him infrequently, primarily for medication renewals. He is considering returning to a traditional insurance plan to regain some autonomy over his total health care. What he may not know is that his employer's insurer has recently signed a contract with a mental health care utilization review company that will require preauthorization for all mental health evaluation and treatment services.

GENERAL CONSIDERATIONS

The interplay between mental health care financing and psychiatric treatment has become increasingly complex. During the last decade, profound changes have occurred in the economic and organizational aspects of mental health care delivery (2). The total cost of mental health care increases at an alarming and disproportionate rate compared with other health care costs. In 1987, corporate expenditures for psychiatric care rose by 34%; costs for chemical dependency treatment rose by 53%. In 1990, the total cost for mental health and chemical dependency treatment is estimated to exceed $80 billion, up from $35 billion in 1980 and $50 billion in 1983. To the dismay of economists, there has been no reduction in cost despite the proliferation of less expensive mental health care providers. Over the past 5 years the total number of mental health practitioners has increased from 50,000 to 250,000, yet the average cost of an outpatient visit increased by more than twice the rate of the consumer price index (3). This massive inflation of health care cost has led to ever-expanding participation in health care decisions by corporate and governmental forces that move primarily toward cost containment (4). In this chapter we examine the various aspects of this issue and their effects on current and future psychiatric practice.

Two features of mental health care contribute substantially to its vulnerability to insurance cost-containment strategies. The first such feature, unique to psychiatric practice, is the existence of an extensively developed public mental health care system. Through tireless campaigning in the mid-nineteenth century, Dorothea Dix convinced legislatures that the care of the mentally ill was horrendous and could only be remedied if state governments took responsibility. Subsequently, large public mental hospitals proliferated throughout the country. The existence of these state institutions has created a dependable economic and programmatic safety valve for the insurance industry and most private hospitals.

A major problem for the psychiatric profession and the community at large has been the deterioration of quality at state-run institutions. At the beginning of the twentieth century, the efforts of Clifford Beers and Adolf Meyer mobilized the "mental hygiene" movement. They aroused hope for the curability of mental illness through early recognition and treatment. Meyer emphasized the importance of environmental influences on the development of psychiatric disorders and advocated a public health approach. Responding to the mental hygiene forces, the federal government created the National Institute of Mental Health (NIMH) in 1946. Subsequently, the NIMH became the catalyst for public policy to form community mental health centers. Thus, a highly developed system of care has evolved in the public sector offering publicly subsidized inpatient and outpatient services (5). Therefore, neither inpatient nor outpatient mental health coverage by insurers is absolutely necessary in any jurisdiction.

The second characteristic of psychiatric practice rendering it vulnerable to insurance limitation is that it deals with mental symptoms and "functional" illness. In the past, there has been much criticism that psychiatric problems tend to be subjective; that psychiatric treatment is indeterminate and variable. Often there is no definable pathologic lesion, no telltale X ray or laboratory test, no fever or other reproducible physiologic finding. An economic corollary is that psychiatric costs do not correlate well with diagnosis (6–8). The psychiatrist must accept the current presumption by most third-party payers that, historically, psychiatric services have been excessive, inappropriate, low in quality, unregulated, and poorly monitored by the profession. The stark reality is that every year we see more restriction and exclusion of existing services in the name of providing more cost-efficient programs. Advocates of regulation claim that it can be done without lowering the quality of services. Some even claim that regulation can effect lower costs with higher quality of service.

Most prospective purchasers of health insurance do not anticipate contracting a mental disease. Insurance companies consider any individual with a mental disorder who seeks an insurance plan with generous mental health benefits as an "adverse selection." Restrictions in health insurance further stigmatize the person who has a mental illness. Many ill individuals delay seeking treatment until the pathologic picture becomes so severe that it requires hospitalization. Thus, a prevalent view has developed that most mental disorders are poorly defined and that mental health care is nonessential.

Other social forces tend to discourage patients from seeking the treatment that is available. These barriers promote popular pessimism about the treatability of serious mental illness and the popular skepticism about the necessity of ambulatory care (9). A consequence of these trends is the continual redefinition of essential versus nonessential mental health services. The lack of agreement among responsible psychiatrists about the proper management of patients with a given diagnosis provides much latitude for third-party payers to "doctor shop." Economic incentives may lead providers to avoid effective but more costly approaches to care. Where professional consensus is lacking, financial incentives have exerted powerful influences over clinical judgment.

Private health insurance for the treatment of mental disorders is more restrictive than is coverage for other medical problems. This trend may be on the verge of a major upheaval. The Court of Appeals of Arkansas has ruled that a patient with bipolar affective disorder has a physical illness under the terms of his or her Blue Cross and Blue Shield policy and is entitled to the same benefits provided to patients with any other physical illness (10). Still, at present, fewer than half of employee health plans have equivalent inpatient coverage, and fewer than 10% have equivalent outpatient benefits (11).

Third-party insurers have taken steps to contain health care costs by introducing greater "cost sharing" by patients (via increased deductibles and coinsurance) and greater "risk sharing" by providers via a variety of management schemes. Coverage for mental health services usually limits days of care or amount of eligible fees, or requires copayments. After insurers apply total benefit caps, high copayments, and larger deductibles, they seek professional review to satisfy themselves that only "medically necessary" services are rendered (12). Psychiatrists range in their responses from those who express bitter opposition even to the idea of "managed care" to others who embrace the concept with entrepreneurial zeal.

Some managed-care firms operate nationally, and this represents a new, multimillion dollar industry. In 1988, 5 million persons with indemnity insurance had their mental health care reviewed by case managers, and by 1993, this number will increase to 50 million. More than 80% of the population with traditional insurance will be subject to some element of managed care (3).

Many large corporations and employers are abandoning traditional indemnity insurance plans entirely. Health Maintenance Organizations (HMOs) use an entirely opposite economic principle. Because managers of health services are "prepaid" via capitation, their financial incentive is to minimize total expense. The provider's income thus may increase in proportion to the length of time the patient stays out of treatment. The HMO provides economically attractive, comprehensive health coverage to consumer "subscribers" in exchange for limiting their choice to a group of contracted physicians. The plan manager limits medical services to those deemed "necessary" within the limitations of the contract. HMO membership has grown by more than 15% annually since 1983. In 1987, there were approximately 400 HMOs with 20 million enrollees. It is predicted that within 2 years, this figure will increase to more than 50 million (13). Unfortunately, HMOs target large employers and are "skimming off" the healthiest consumers. This leaves indemnity insurers with sicker patients who have to pay higher and higher insurance premiums, copayments, and deductibles.

The model of the future is called a "triple option," "point of service," or "time of need/choice plan." At the time an employee needs a medical service, a choice can be made to use either a managed-care option or go outside the plan. In the latter case, the subscriber would pay an "equity copayment" equivalent to the difference between the managed-care plan cost and the amount charged by the outside provider. This is estimated to be about half the average professional fee or one-third the daily hospital rate (14). Many Preferred Provider Organizations (PPOs) or Networks (PPNs) provide some of these features.

CURRENT TRENDS

Several readily identifiable strategies characterize managed-care approaches, whether applied to standard indemnity plans or integrated into an HMO. There is accumulating evidence that these mechanisms can have a significant effect on total mental health care costs and practices. The RAND Health Insurance Study, which randomly assigned patients to different systems and then followed them for several years, showed that incentives operate in the predicted direction. The population assigned to the HMO received 40% less inpatient care. Whereas twice as many HMO patients received outpatient mental health services, psychiatrists provided only 30% of their care compared with 62% of care for fee-for-service patients (15).

Preauthorization

A primary care or "gatekeeper" physician must authorize psychiatric evaluation and any subsequent treatment. This authorization functions to confirm that the stated service is medically necessary and will be provided at a previously negotiated, often discounted rate. Eligible services may be authorized or denied based on a telephone conversation. The sequential process of authorization can become onerous. Consider an acutely psychotic patient who presents to an approved hospital emergency room. Authorization is required both for the patient to be seen by the primary-care physician and again for the psychiatric consultation. Additional authorization is required for inpatient hospitalization, at an authorized psychiatric inpatient unit, or to hospitalize outside the plan if the psychiatrist is unable to locate an inpatient bed from a list of approved facilities. Many plans exclude specific diagnoses from coverage—for example, substance abuse, which may be a "rider" in the health plan contract. Some categorically exclude psychological testing as a diagnostic modality.

Intake/Triage Interviews

A triage interview will selectively refer the patient to a mental health provider who can provide the required service. Insurers will seek ways to direct their policyholders to the least costly provider, most of whom are not psychiatrists (16).

Difficulties for the practicing psychiatrist arise from the unique professional milieu of mental health care in which several professions offer overlapping services. In most jurisdictions, psychologists, psychiatric nurses, social workers, and other counselors can provide mental health services directly to patients and often may practice independently. In some jurisdictions, these allied professionals may receive third-party reimbursement. Consequently, organized psychiatry has been struggling to define both the unique characteristics of its professional domain and appropriate interaction with these other disciplines. No other medical specialty faces this magnitude of nonphysician providers who compete within the private sector.

One likely effect of insurance company cost-saving and the ready availability of allied professionals providing therapy will be a further pressure toward separating evaluation from treatment functions. Psychiatrists increasingly will render only diagnostic evaluations, order medications and relevant testing, and provide consultation. They then will prescribe treatment programs that are carried out by others. An alternative approach might be the mandate for second opinions before an insurer authorizes care, much as in the surgical field. These may be required by the manager before authorization for further evaluation or treatment.

In the future, we will likely see historical profiling of provider by inpatient mean length of stay, or mean number of outpatient sessions, with selective referral to the most "cost-effective" providers. Similarly, the most popular providers of therapeutic services will be those who can consistently deliver a "completed case" within the requisite limits initially set for the treatment contract.

"Approved" Treatment Plans

Increasingly, "approved" treatment plans are restricted to crisis intervention or brief (e.g., time-limited), diagnosis-specific, empirically validated methods. Psychiatrists will be called on for services limited to rapid stabilization of inpatients experiencing episodes of acute illness in which prompt hospital discharge is expected. Such treatment plans use a traditional medical model rather than the biopsychosocial model of many current treatment plans. Psychiatrists will need education in new methodologies, and many will have to make attitudinal changes to become comfortable with scrutiny of their work (17).

Chronic mental conditions, or any condition not likely to respond to short-term treatment, may be categorically excluded (18).

Thus, inefficient or inadequate treatment may lead, alarmingly, to reclassification of the disorder, in the midst of an approved treatment plan, to a "chronic" condition that is no longer covered.

Concurrent Treatment Plan Review

If providers can successfully negotiate the steps of preauthorization, intake/triage, and use of "approved" plans, they may receive approval for 5 days of hospitalization, six outpatient visits, or fewer, after which the whole cycle begins anew. Therapists must now submit data for utilization review, and these data are compared with aggregate norms. The data will become more burdensome to produce and also will be scrutinized for the degree to which the referring agent's prescriptive plan is fulfilled.

Many potential problems exist in the relationship that will de velop between psychiatrist-providers and managed-care reviewers. Utilization reviews will stiffen the adversarial postures of psychiatrists and managers. Although the profession may argue strenuously for true peer reviewers, physicians are more expensive than nonmedical reviewers, who now are and may well remain the norm. Thus, any managed-care system will need to address and resolve the inevitable disputes involving the provider, the patient, and the reviewer.

Most private psychiatric hospitals must have preadmission reviews and continued-stay reviews. In a recent survey of private psychiatric hospitals by the National Association of Private Psychiatric Hospitals (NAPPH), most respondents were critical of outside reviewers for interfering with clinical care. There were many complaints about unqualified (frequently nonmedical) reviewers making arbitrary and inconsistent decisions (19).

Limitations on Total Number of Visits

HMOs are marketed as "total care packages," and many consumers are unaware of the fine-print limitations on treatment until an authorization is denied. This can be particularly difficult for the provider when plan benefits change and the *provider* rather than the patient is notified first. Physicians who work through HMOs are no longer working solely for the patient and become an agent of the insurer as well. When providers let patients know of changes, they may find themselves the focus of their patient's feelings of anger, loss, and abandonment.

Legal and Ethical Issues

The American Psychiatric Association Ethics Committee recently addressed the changes in the economic environment of psychiatric practice and their impact on the ethics of practice (20). The committee raised several specific concerns that have only recently appeared within the legal arena:

1. The present modes of health care reimbursement and cost-cutting initiatives will leave an increasing portion of the mentally ill population without adequate health care coverage.
2. Abandonment of patients who exhaust their health insurance coverage is a threat. Currently, once a treatment plan is recommended, the psychiatrist has the responsibility to complete the treatment or arrange a suitable treatment alternative. The California appeals court ruled in *Wickline v. California* (21) that the responsibility for hospital discharge remains with the physician despite the decision of the utilization reviewer. Physicians are not immune from malpractice liability by going along with such decisions and can be criticized for not appealing the utilization reviewer's decision.
3. Many psychiatrists sign agreements and contracts that they poorly understand. As they become aware of limitations, the resultant demoralization may lead to lower professional standards and to greed. In *Varol v. Blue Cross and Blue Shield of Michigan* (22), the court ruled that when psychiatrists voluntarily agree to a program's requirements and criteria, they are subsequently obligated to abide by them.
4. Erosion of confidentiality by reviewers and insurance managers through intrusion into the doctor-patient relationship is another ethical issue raised by current trends in mental health care finance. Utilization reviewers are strongly criticized on this point when they request direct patient interviews. Unfortunately, doctors are likely to be equally critical of reviewers' "inadequate data base" when reviewers decide to limit services based solely on their perusal of a patient's chart.
5. Financial exploitation of patients may result from the overt incentives present in an HMO. Sabin argues that if a clinician is not prepared to describe the terms under which he is treating the patient, including financial incentives and restrictions on refer-

rals, the system in which he is working is not ethical (23).

6. The last important ethical issue regarding HMOs is the potential that considerations of cost will lead to inadequate supervision of nonmedical providers or to assignment of patients to unqualified providers.

RECOMMENDATIONS

Webb argues for a new dimension of informed consent that includes discussion of economic as well as medical aspects of treatment. He recommends that the psychiatrist discuss the nature of any insurance coverage and the means by which the physician is reimbursed, including the presence of incentives to provide the least costly forms of treatment (24).

The few legal decisions in this area suggest that the psychiatrist may be left with responsibility and liability, despite the erosion of authority. Psychiatrists are urged to demand the basis for managed-care decisions and to aggressively appeal when any decision is likely to affect the patient's condition adversely. The psychiatrist should keep in mind that the cost of unreimbursed patient care is small when compared with potential malpractice liability. There is legal precedent for recovery of reimbursement when the physician can prove the care provided was medically indicated. In *Hughes v. Blue Cross of Northern California* (25), a patient was awarded punitive damages for the retrospective denial of reimbursement when he showed that the denial was based on inadequate information and an arbitrary standard of care. Psychiatrists are strongly advised to monitor carefully all court decisions in this evolving medicolegal arena (26).

The subtleties of the art of medicine may be submerged by pressures for standardization at the cheapest denominator. This formalization of the structure of evaluation, diagnosis, and therapeutic approach constitutes a major shift from much current psychiatric practice, in which these functions occur in parallel over the course of the initial phase of treatment. There is also an unfortunate trend toward denigrating the importance to the healing process of the early relationships patients form with their doctors. Large areas of psychoanalytic knowledge are bypassed in what has become a mechanized approach to medical care. Reexpressing this clinical experience in a manner perceivable as relevant in the economic and political debate of cost containment will be a major challenge for the psychiatric profession in the coming years (27,28).

NOTES

1. Chodoff P: Effects of the new economic climate on psychotherapeutic practice. Am J Psychiatry 144:1293–1297, 1987
2. Staton D: Mental health care economics and the future of psychiatric practice. Psychiatric Annals 19:421–427, 1989
3. Boom in managed psychiatric care will continue. Clinical Psychiatry News 17:6, 1989
4. Caldwell B: As costs rise employers alter MH plans. Employee Benefit Plan Review 43:76–88, 1988
5. Modlin HC: A history of mental health services prior to World War II, in Psychiatric Administration. Edited by Talbott JA, Kaplan SR. Orlando, FL, Grune & Stratton, 1983
6. English JT, Sharfstein SS, Scherl DJ, et al: Diagnosis-related groups and general hospital psychiatry: the APA study. Am J Psychiatry 143:131–139, 1986
7. Taube CA, Goldman HH, Lee ES: Use of specialty psychiatric settings in constructing DRGs. Arch Gen Psychiatry 45:1037–1040, 1988
8. Essock SM, Norquist GS: Toward a fairer prospective payment system. Arch Gen Psychiatry 45:1041–1044, 1988
9. Feldman DB: Insurance coverage of mental health care (letter). Am J Psychiatry 144:829–830, 1987
10. Arkansas appeals court rules bipolar disorder a physical illness under health insurance policy. Hosp Community Psychiatry 9:453–454, 1988
11. Brady J, Sharfstein SS, Muszynski IL: Trends in private insurance coverage for mental illness. Am J Psychiatry 143:1276–1279, 1986
12. Lehman AF: Capitation payment and mental health care: a review of the opportunities and risks. Hosp Community Psychiatry 38:31–38, 1987
13. Martinsons JN: Are HMOs slamming the door on psychiatric treatment? Hospitals 50:56, 1988
14. Carving out mental health: a new way to provide care. Psychiatric News 24:9, 1989
15. Manning WG, Wells KB, Benjamin B: Use of outpatient mental health services over time in a health maintenance organization and fee-for-service plans. Am J Psychiatry 144:283–287, 1987
16. Rinella V: Ethical issues and psychiatric cost-containment strategies. Int J Law Psychiatry 9:125–136, 1986
17. Schneider-Braus K: A practical guide to HMO psychiatry. Hosp Community Psychiatry 38:876–879, 1987
18. Seltzer DA: Limitations on HMO services and the emerging redefinition of chronic mental illness. Hosp Community Psychiatry 39:137–139, 1988
19. Cost containment measures impede patient care, results of NAPPH survey indicate. Psychiatric News 24:9, 1989
20. Ethics Committee of the American Psychiatric Association: New Men-

tal health economics and the impact on the ethics of psychiatric practice: a report of the Hastings Center conference on psychiatric ethics and new economics. Ethics Newsletter, April/May 1988, pp 1–7

21. Wickline v California, 192 Cal App 3d 1630, 238 Cal Rptr 810 (1986)
22. Varol v Blue Cross and Blue Shield of Michigan, 88-CV-40095, US Dist Ct, E Dist Mich, So Div/Flint, March 2, 1989
23. Sabin JE: Psychiatrists face tough ethical questions in managed care settings. Psychiatric Times 6:9, 1989
24. Webb WL: Ethical psychiatric practice in a new economic climate. Psychiatric Annals 19:443–447, 1989
25. Hughes v Blue Cross of Northern California, 199 Cal App 3d 318, 245 Cal Rptr 273 (1988)
26. Managed care court decisions reveal disturbing pattern. Psychiatric News 24:10, 1989
27. Holder HD, Blose JO: Changes in health care costs and utilization associated with mental health treatment. Hosp Community Psychiatry 38:1070–1075, 1987
28. Wells KB, Manning WG, Valdez RB: The effect of insurance generosity on the psychological distress and psychological well-being of a general population. Arch Gen Psychiatry 46:315–320, 1989

Chapter 7

Psychiatrists' Relationships With the General Public

Ellen G. McDaniel, M.D.

Since its professional beginnings, psychiatry has had an ambivalent relationship with the general public. At times, the public has viewed psychiatry with skepticism, anger, and disappointment, such as following the trial of John W. Hinckley, Jr. At other times, the public overvalues psychiatry, looking to the field for answers to questions that will not be solved for years—if at all. Psychiatry may overreach in its desire to please the public and may respond with inappropriate defensiveness when it fails to meet all expectations. On occasion, it has behaved naively or with callous indifference, as when the American Psychiatric Association conducted a nationwide poll of its members to evaluate the mental health of a presidential candidate. Psychiatry is not unique in lapsing in its effort to find a healthy relationship with the public, as evidenced by the questions of ethical violations that were raised when four psychologists discussed Kitty Dukakis's recent mental illness in the *Boston Globe*. This chapter, however, focuses specifically on the relationship of *psychiatrists* with the public.

The Public's Negative Impressions

The Individual

Part of the public's vacillation in viewing psychiatry is unavoidable. Individuals displace their irrational fears and primitive yearnings onto available objects—people, money, food, races, and religions—which provide symbolic representation for intense conflictual feel-

I thank Mr. John Blamphin, Director of Public Affairs, American Psychiatric Association, for his assistance.

ings. This displacement,which is useful as transference in a carefully managed psychoanalytic psychotherapy, forms the basis of all kinds of maladaptive stereotyping in society. Occupational groups certainly are not exempt from this.

Physicians, previously exalted as highly valued and respected professionals, in recent years have been criticized for being insufficiently compassionate or competent and for being more concerned with economics and technology than with the humans under their care. Psychiatry as a specialty has been particularly subject to attack. The scientific foundations of the specialty, the mental health of its practitioners—"But you're so normal for a psychiatrist"—the cost of treatment, the chronicity of many mental disorders—all are listed in the general public's indictment of psychiatrists and psychiatry.

For centuries, mental illness has been viewed with a particular kind of fear, a fear qualitatively different from fear of a terminal illness. In the mentally ill, one sees the part of one's own identity that is irrational and frightening. Experientially, only sleep separates the dreams of a nonpsychotic person from the hallucinations of a schizophrenic. Good clinicians will appreciate the threads of similarity and use that recognition to understand the patient. Projection and denial, however, are often strategies the public uses to distance itself from the mentally ill, and distance can be enhanced by criticizing. The fear of one's psyche is seen in the discomfort expressed by some people when introduced to a psychiatrist in a nonprofessional setting—"I'd better not talk. You might read my mind"—implying both that the psychiatrist is so powerful that he or she can read one's thoughts, and that if those thoughts were read, something terrible would be seen.

Mental illness has been stigmatized in this society. Although this social stigmatization has decreased in recent years, most individuals who are involved in mental health treatment still typically do not make their experiences public. The silence of patients has added to the mysteriousness of psychiatry, because it has constricted the general public's understanding of the range of problems treated and the therapeutic approaches used. Unsophisticated people often view patients with mental illnesses as "crazy," as violent, or conversely, as "the worried well" who "indulge" themselves in treatment.

The Media

The public's perception of psychiatry has been molded partially by the portrayal of psychiatrists in the media—in newspapers, magazine articles, novels and short stories, films, and cartoons. Although fiction and film can present characters with mental illness (and the psychotherapists who treat them) in a fairly realistic and compassionate manner (1,2), the misuse and abuse of psychiatry has been the subject of very popular books and movies (3), the object of scathing articles (4,5), and the target of popular jokes and cartoons. In the novel *August*, the female psychoanalyst treats a very difficult borderline patient with an appropriate and useful mixture of analytic neutrality and subdued empathy, against the background of her own personal problems. Dr. Berger, in the novel and film *Ordinary People*, helps a suicidal adolescent come to terms with his past and his family by using compassion and active interventions. In contrast, the psychiatrist who insists that his state mental hospital patients conform and submit to him in *One Flew Over the Cuckoo's Nest* appears as a stupid, self-serving, and ruthless tyrant.

The Judicial System

Psychiatry has been severely criticized for its involvement in the judicial system. An extreme point of view might be that if the image of psychiatry is to be improved, psychiatrists should stay out of the courtroom. How can psychiatry avoid being on the defensive when the public is offered such tantalizing headlines as "When Psychiatrists Take the Stand, Science Itself Goes on Trial" (6) or "Doctors Seek Crackdown on Colleagues Paid for Testimony in Malpractice Suits" (7)? The battle of the experts in the Hinckley trial has been examined and interpreted so many times (8) that it has become part of the popular American culture. What displacements are being foisted on the psychiatric experts in that event?

Smith (9), in an excellent review of mental health expert witnesses, describes the several roles of the mental health experts in the courtroom: teacher, priest, wizard, magician, decision maker, scapegoat, advocate, informal advisor, and smoke screen. Each role invites criticism. Psychiatrists argue among themselves whether their role in the courtroom should be that of an impartial, objective scientist or that of an advocate, albeit one who maintains his or her intellectual integrity (10).

Expert witnesses have been accused of transgressing their functions as teachers and scientists when they become advocates. The expert is criticized for practicing magic when he or she makes predictions about such matters as the ultimate outcome of therapy for an offender or the offender's future dangerousness, neither of which can be forecast precisely (11). This criticism gains intensity when psychiatrists predict dangerousness without ever seeing the individual (12) or when psychiatric experts err by incorrectly concluding that an individual is not dangerous (13). Interestingly, much less attention is paid to false-positive predictions—for example, when an individual who is deemed "dangerous" by a psychiatrist turns out to be innocuous.

When the courts appear to defer to the expert as a decision maker—for example, in court rulings that uphold a professional judgment standard in right-to-refuse-treatment cases, in involuntary commitment hearings, in an insanity-defense case, or in a child-custody battle—psychiatrists are castigated for usurping patients' rights to liberty and privacy or for being "hired guns" who speak from the viewpoint of whichever side pays the bill. Finally, mental health experts have been used (and let themselves be used) to serve ends other than those dictated by their role as experts; this is the smokescreen role. Examples include using experts to introduce otherwise impermissible evidence into the court or to give testimony that allows a patient to get needed treatment by being involuntarily committed as dangerous, when in fact the patient is ill but not a threat.

There is a role for psychiatric expertise in the judicial system, just as there is a role for any other expert testimony (14). Criticisms of psychiatric testimony inevitably will continue, however, because the justice system in the United States is based on an adversarial resolution of conflict in which disagreement is implicit. Physicians are humans first, and are fallible and idiosyncratic. Some experts inevitably will receive unfavorable local, if not national, attention for questionable conduct in the courtroom. Controversy continues over whether psychiatrists should limit themselves to testimony about an individual's mental condition or should offer testimony on ultimate issues of fact (15). The American Psychiatric Association (APA) supports the former position (16), but this is by no means a unanimous view among forensic psychiatrists. The profession is still struggling to establish ethical codes and specialized training for psychiatrists who partake in forensic psychiatry (17,18).

Criticism of psychiatry in the courtroom will continue. Still, criticism helps to ensure that the profession constantly examines its own behavior. The real problem may not be the fact that there is criticism but rather how the profession handles it.

The Culture

The first amendment right to freedom of speech, which includes the right to privacy—a major constitutional issue in recent court decisions (19,20)—is cherished in the United States, although the public has been very critical of contemporary court decisions in which this right has been extended. Psychiatric treatment has been referred to by some as a form of mind control. For example, the public has a misperception that when a patient is under hypnosis, the hypnotist can obtain accurate information about anything known to the subject, regardless of the subject's wish to maintain secrecy. The courts know better and have not accepted material obtained under hypnosis at face value (21, 22). Advocates of the right to refuse treatment have referred to the use of major tranquilizers in treating psychosis as a form of thought control (23). Legal scholars and practitioners, concerned about the abuse of commitment statutes to contain deviant behavior, have implied that psychiatry uses mental illness as a label to ensure social control in a community (24, 25).

American culture nourishes individualism. Extended families live a continent apart. So-called bedroom communities are populated by families who move every 3–5 years in their climb up corporate or institutional ladders. Class structure, relative to other cultures, is loosely defined, and mobility up and down the socioeconomic ladder is part of the American culture's folklore and very much a reality of present-day life. Hard work, drive, education, and of course, luck seem to be the ingredients considered necessary for success.

This cultural background has made the public wary of psychiatry as potentially capable of changing one's individualistic stamp to satisfy a political, institutional, or other cultural goal at the expense of individual liberty interests. Psychiatry's presence in the correctional system, justice system, political system, educational system, and other cultural institutions is suspect to the degree that the population being served worries about the profession's ulterior motives and its ability to influence social institutions.

The Profession's Contribution

Psychiatry, unfortunately and inadvertently, has contributed to the negative stereotyping of the profession. It has struggled for years to establish a valid and reliable diagnostic nomenclature. The profession's past follies in this area have made headlines and have not encouraged admiration. In Rosenhan's often-quoted article (26), the author concluded that professionals cannot distinguish the sane from the insane in psychiatric hospitals. Critics (27) of this study never achieved the recognition that Rosenhan was given, perhaps because bad news always makes better press than good news. In a speech to the Public Affairs Network Institute (28), APA Public

Affairs Director John Blamphin stated that the media likes news in the "Big C" categories: "Crime, Controversy, Conflict, Catastrophe, Crisis, and Color." Scholarly revisions and retorts are not "media events."

The inexactness of psychiatry's diagnostic terms and categories has generated criticism from civil libertarians and from conscientious legislators. Well-intentioned individuals find this lack of diagnostic precision frustrating when they are involved in drafting a state's commitment statutes or a Patients' Bill of Rights, or in setting up review and appeal procedures for patients who refuse treatment. Legislation and administrative regulations often are compromises and are somewhat vague as written, leading to inevitable difficulties and inviting professional criticism.

Commitment statutes are one category of legislation that illustrates the problem of definitions. These statutes often use elusive terminology in defining who should be committed (e.g., who is "dangerous" or "in need of treatment"). There is a tendency to overdiagnose human behavior (29), and presenting oneself to a psychiatrist with a complaint sometimes will ensure a diagnosis of a mental disorder—especially if reimbursement for the visit is sought from a third-party payer and a diagnosis is required.

Psychiatry's visible expansion into legal matters has spurred the public to resist "medicalization" of civil behavior. For example, critics charge that psychiatrists are overliberally committing people to mental hospitals who should go to prison instead, thus treating deviant behavior as mental illness rather than as criminality (30). Criticisms run in the opposite direction as well: psychiatrists are sometimes held responsible for illiberal civil commitments that put a patient's potential for dangerousness and the psychiatrist's own liability for a failure to warn or protect above the patient's rights to personal liberty. Psychiatry's inexactness has made it all the more difficult to respond to the resulting criticism—that psychiatry is either "too soft" on crime or "too tough" on individual rights (31).

Psychiatry has damaged its own image in several public fiascoes, for example, when the profession had a vote on whether to call homosexuality a mental disorder and when it conducted a nationwide poll of its membership to "diagnose" a presidential candidate. Although these blunders occurred several years ago, they are still recalled to illustrate the profession's shortcomings.

The mental health and motivations of those entering the field of psychiatry have been the subject of much speculation and joking. In a recent cover article in the *Atlantic* (32), all mental health therapists were grouped together. This is a problem in itself, because to help preserve its public image, psychiatry not only has to answer criticisms leveled at it but also has to fend off attacks aimed at other mental health workers whom the lay public does not regularly differentiate from psychiatrists in terms of education, ethical standards, and scientific foundations. The author of the *Atlantic* article attacked all mental health workers for being pathologically attracted to helping professions and for using patients to satisfy their own disturbed needs. The article itself drew a fair amount of criticism for using unscientific methods, for displaying conceptual confusions, and for indulging in the same "psychobabble" that it attacked (33). Yet, again, the provocative "bad news" disseminated by such articles usually affects people far more than do the defensive retorts.

The profession does not help to disprove the long-standing belief that psychiatrists are to be mistrusted when individual psychiatrists are brought to court for having sex with patients and mount defenses calling such ethical lapses "treatment in the interest of the patient" (34). The public relations problem is compounded, of course, when television movies are made about such cases.

Psychiatry stayed out of the mainstream of medicine for many years, especially when psychoanalysis reached its zenith. This isolation did not lend credibility to psychiatry as a medical specialty based on scientific principles. It also discouraged colleagues in other medical specialties from offering their support. Thus, psychiatry often is grouped with all other mental health therapies because psychiatrists themselves have made no real effort to distinguish their profession as a *medical* specialty.

POSITIVE DIRECTIONS IN PSYCHIATRY

Given the wealth of new research findings, publications, and scientific advances that are pouring forth, today's physicians must struggle to keep current in their own area of expertise. Medical school educators estimate that 5 years after they graduate, physicians will be out of touch with current medical school curricula. Medical school admissions committees, in fact, are reluctant to accept transfer applicants who have been away from the basic sciences for more than a year.

Psychiatry has had its own explosion in knowledge and in career opportunities. Exciting advances are taking place in the field. These include significant discoveries in psychopharmacology, increased use of sophisticated technology to diagnose disorders, rapid increases in understanding of the biochemical basis of behavior, unfolding of the genetic basis of specific mental illnesses, elaboration of brain physiology, and development of new treatment modalities.

More recently graduating resident psychiatrists also have a wider range of career possibilities. For example, they can treat the homeless mentally ill in an urban shelter, administer psychiatric care for a health maintenance organization, organize a vertically integrated state system of mental health services for juveniles, treat adults in a private outpatient practice, and conduct research in a basic science laboratory.

When the civil rights movement began in the early 1960s, advocacy groups began to escalate in both size and effectiveness. The growth of patient and citizen advocacy groups involved with mental health issues, on the national as well as on the local level, has been of tremendous benefit to psychiatry. Among the larger organizations are the National Mental Health Association, the National Alliance for the Mentally Ill, the National Depressive and Manic Depressive Association, the American Mental Health Fund, and the National Alliance for Research on Schizophrenia and Depression. Some of these organizations are geared toward developing research opportunities for a particular disorder; some are more oriented toward serving as advocates for patients and their families; some are primarily interested in educating the general public about mental illness. Respected internationally known figures, addressing audiences through these groups, have revealed their own struggles with mental illness. This contributes to the demystification of mental illness and reduces the likelihood that the public will stereotype the mentally ill in exclusively negative terms (35).

Because of increasing economic competition, the scientific explosion in the basic and clinical sciences, and the changing ethics about advertising, psychiatrists are becoming less isolated and are establishing themselves as physicians first, and as specialists in psychiatry second. This "remedicalization" of psychiatry has had a positive effect on the public image of psychiatry and potentially can help to destigmatize the profession, psychiatric treatment, and mental illness itself.

THE AMERICAN PSYCHIATRIC ASSOCIATION'S DIVISION OF PUBLIC AFFAIRS

APA's Division of Public Affairs has three main areas of function: media relations; public information and education; and public relations projects such as the Annual Campaign, which is an educational and not a fund-raising endeavor.

Media relations includes tasks such as establishing a wide network of personal contacts in the media, giving appropriate sources interesting and timely information of importance to psychiatry, and responding to a crisis or opportunity that involves psychiatry. The profession is most aware of the reactive position that the national organization has taken in response to media issues that involve mental health issues—for example, the attempted assassination of a public figure or the bombing of a commercial airline. Active media involvement also involves creating opportunities to explain, inform, and educate the public about the field of psychiatry.

Examples of the Division of Public Affairs' efforts to educate the public about mental illness demonstrate the complexity of the public relations effort. Factors such as age, education, socioeconomic status, ethnic identification, and region of the country must influence the type of material used to reach a designated audience. The profession still must define or refine its conception of the approaches and media that are most useful in getting a clear image of psychiatry across to disparate public audiences.

The APA Joint Commission on Public Affairs and the Division of Public Affairs designed a series of pamphlets to promote informed, factual discussion of mental disorders and their treatments. These pamphlets were distributed to all APA psychiatrists, nonpsychiatrist physicians, and mental health facilities. The topics covered include substance abuse (36), teen suicide (37), anxiety disorders (38), schizophrenia (39), phobias (40), mental health of the elderly (41), posttraumatic stress disorder (42), manic-depressive disorder (43), obsessive-compulsive disorder (44), depression (45), and an overview of mental illness (46). The pamphlets describe the disorders, offer theories on etiology, give epidemiologic data, and describe a range of treatment options. The vocabulary, although free of jargon, is directed toward readers with at least a high school education. In addition, the Division of Public Affairs advertises books written for the general public that have been published by the American Psychiatric Press, including books on depression (47), cocaine abuse (48), phobias (49), and a guidebook for relatives of hospitalized psychiatric patients (50).

The Division of Public Affairs is in the process of producing a comic book, targeted for children and adolescents, on mental disorders more frequently found in those age-groups (e.g., eating disorders, depression, suicide) but with information on other problems as well, because family members of the designated audience may be the ones with the mental disorder. The target date for distribution is 1990, and the intent of the book is to educate the audience with the hope of destigmatizing mental illness and encouraging those in need to seek help. Distribution will be made to schools, clinics, and mental health associations.

The APA received an education grant from The Upjohn Company to produce three films dealing with panic disorders, anxiety disorders, and depression. These films, along with workshop materials, will be directed primarily toward educating emergency room physicians but also will be appropriate for physicians in the fields of family practice, internal medicine, and pediatrics. These public information films will be available through APA's district branches, from community mental health centers, and from patient advocacy groups. Presently, only the film on panic has been made. All future films will probably have some child psychiatry content.

The Division of Public Affairs used to focus its attention on Mental Illness Awareness Week as its special yearly project. Recently, however, the division has conducted year-long campaigns on topics related to the general heading "Let's Talk About Mental Illness," as well as continuing its Mental Illness Awareness Week activities. The topic for the 1989 campaign was "It's More Than What You Think." This campaign was designed to educate the public about the magnitude of the problem of mental illness, what it costs society, the availability of new and more effective treatments, the problems of health insurance coverage, and the need to maintain substantial support for research. The 1990 campaign slogan is "A Matter of Fact." This campaign focuses public attention on the facts that effective treatment provides improved health and quality of life for those suffering from mental illnesses, and that research efforts will aid in diagnosis and treatment and will help measure the effectiveness of certain treatments. Each year, each of the 76 district branches receives a campaign kit (51,52) that explains in detail how to conduct a public relations effort.

Several years ago, the APA began a Public Affairs Network Institute that serves as a training ground for psychiatrists involved in work with the public and with legislators. The Institute is organized and staffed by the Division of Public Affairs. The members participate in workshops designed to help them become more effective advocates for psychiatry. Sessions at the 1989 meeting covered on-camera media training, public-speaking techniques, developing films and public service announcements, coordinating successful district branch Mental Illness Awareness Week campaigns, and building local public affairs coalitions.

The American Academy of Child Psychiatry also has been actively involved in media relations. The organization has its own series of fact sheets available to professionals for use with parents, the media, and schools.

MEDIA RELATIONS

To promote effective relations with the media, a psychiatrist needs some appreciation of the tasks, problems, and ethics of reporters. Unfortunate misunderstandings and some hostility have arisen between psychiatrists and the media because of a lack of appreciation of the reporter's role.

Professionals in the news media decide what is news, just as psychiatrists decide what is mental illness, designers decide what is fashion, and environmentalists decide what is pollution. Generally, the task of a reporter is to find and communicate news to the general public in an interesting, accurate, and prompt manner. Reporters are usually not advocates for a position but attempt to take a neutral and objective stance in conveying information to their audience.

In 1977, the American Psychiatric Association published guidelines for psychiatrists who interact with the media (53). An addendum was published in 1982 (54). Of course, psychiatrists should be professional and should use good common sense in dealing with the media. Several specific areas of interaction deserve attention here.

First, note that the public will tend to look at what a psychiatrist says to the media as reflecting an opinion of the profession rather than that of the individual speaking—even when the psychiatrist emphasizes the distinction. Nonetheless, it often is important to state the distinction for the record.

In answering a question on the treatment of a disorder, the speaker should list the variety of accepted approaches and then discuss the particular one the speaker prefers. Because the psychiatrist being interviewed will be perceived as an expert, he or she should avoid answering questions that are outside his or her field of expertise. Not all questions must be answered. The psychiatrist can tactfully and sometimes with humor defer an answer by saying, "The research isn't advanced enough to know the answer," or "My friends in the field of allergy would be better equipped to answer that." An interview should not be a platform to advance one's personal biases and beliefs. Criticizing a professionally accepted treatment approach can undermine acceptable treatment of patients listening to the program and can lead to "broadcast suits."

All of the ethical guidelines used in everyday practice apply to media communications. Psychiatrists should never violate patient confidentiality. They should never reveal the content of interviews or records obtained in the process of conducting a forensic evaluation. If a psychiatrist testifies in court, everything explicitly stated in the courtroom under oath becomes public information, but other material must remain confidential.

Psychiatrists should never offer comments that can be construed as making a diagnosis or offering therapy to a listening audience. This becomes particularly important on call-in talk shows. The psychiatrist may use comments from listeners as a prompt for a general discussion about a mental disorder or a course of treatment and may offer suggestions on how to get an evaluation and treatment for those who think they may have that problem. A connecting link between specific complaints and a general discussion can be made—for example, "those symptoms can be found in many disorders, including depression," and a discussion about depression may ensue.

The psychiatrist who is communicating with the media must *assume that everything said to a reporter is on the record.* If a communication should not be published, it should not be made. Because of deadlines and because the reporter—not the psychiatrist—is the author of any story, the psychiatrist will rarely if ever see a draft of a story before it goes to press.

The following summarizes tips for a successful media interview:

1. When you are contacted by the media, find out what the reporter wants. Even though the interview may be very brief, prepare for it carefully or refer the reporter to someone with more expertise.
2. Don't confine your responses to single-word answers but do keep strictly to the point, and be as concise as possible. A radio or television interview that might take 15 minutes may result in only 30 seconds on the air, so make your words count.
3. Speak in everyday language. Avoid technical terms and professional jargon. Avoid the typical pitfalls of public speaking ("uh," "you know"). Try to be animated.
4. Maintain eye contact with the reporter, even in radio appearances. When you move your gaze away from a focus, your voice may fade because of subtle shifts in your head movement.
5. Avoid picking up on the negative innuendos of a reporter. Answer by giving as many positive points as possible. Do not become defensive. Psychiatry in general and psychiatrists in particular do not have to have all of the answers.
6. Correct misinformation and tell the truth. Don't speculate. If the answer is not known, don't guess.
7. Humor has its place, but its use should not undermine the seriousness of the topic being discussed or the gravity of the situation being examined.

8. Relax, enjoy, and come across as an interesting professional and human.
9. Because television is a visual medium, you will need to consider your attire and nonverbal behavior.

Forensic psychiatrists will recognize that many of the suggestions for relating to the media apply equally to testifying in the courtroom.

FUTURE NEEDS

For psychiatry to improve its relations with the general public, psychiatrists need to become much more involved in public affairs. This involvement can take place at the national, state, county, and community levels. Active involvement with the media, with the district branches' public affairs efforts, and with the local and state medical and specialty societies is essential. Look for opportunities to inform and educate the public about mental illness and psychiatry.

Psychiatrists need to express greater professional pride in their chosen specialty without becoming fanatical about a particular theory, training program, or treatment approach. A little more knowledge about the respect for the breadth of the field's accomplishments, a little more sensitivity in communications to patients and their families, and a little less "psychobabble" all would be tonics for the public relations of the profession.

Psychiatry needs to continue moving into the mainstream of medicine. This would heighten the awareness of the scientific foundation of psychiatry; it would make seeking an evaluation and treatment by a psychiatrist more acceptable; and it would prompt medical colleagues in other fields to support psychiatry. It also would help the public to differentiate psychiatrists from other mental health workers.

Criticism is inevitable. Mastering the art of dealing with criticism—that is, hearing, acknowledging, and appraising it without getting defensive—is something every clinician hopes his or her patients achieve. Because criticism of the psychiatrist's role as an expert witness in court, of the insanity defense, and of the use of psychoactive drugs is certain to continue, psychiatrists must become familiar with these and other controversial psychiatric issues. They must develop answers that give a balanced picture, and they must find broader strategies to educate the public about the issues.

NOTES

1. Rosner J: August. New York, Houghton Mifflin, 1983
2. Guest J: Ordinary People. New York, Viking Penguin, 1976
3. Kesey K: One Flew Over the Cuckoo's Nest. New York, Penguin, 1975
4. Maeder T: Wounded healers. The Atlantic, Jan 1989, pp 37–47
5. Faust D, Ziskin J: The expert witness in psychology and psychiatry. Science 241:31–36, 1988
6. Englade K: When Psychiatrists Take the Stand Science Itself Goes on Trial. The Scientist 1:24–25, 1988
7. Richards B: Doctors seek crackdown on colleagues paid for testimony in malpractice suits. Wall Street Journal, Nov 7, 1988, p B1
8. Caplan L: The Insanity Defense and the Trial of John W. Hinckley, Jr. Boston, MA, David R Godine, 1987
9. Smith SR: Mental health expert witnesses: of science and crystal balls. Behavioral Sciences and the Law 7:145–180, 1989
10. Perlin ML: The Supreme Court, the mentally disabled defendant, psychiatric testimony in death penalty cases, and the power of symbolism: dulling the ache in Barefoot's Achilles heel. New York University Law School Human Rights Annual 3:91–169, 1985
11. Barefoot v Estelle, 463 US 880 (1983)
12. Dix G: Participation by mental health professionals in capital murder sentencing. Int J Law Psychiatry 1:238, 1978
13. Meyer RG, Landis ER, Hays JR: Law for the Psychotherapist. New York, WW Norton, 1988
14. Slovenko R: The lawyer and the forensic expert: boundaries of ethical practice. Behavioral Sciences and the Law 5:119–147, 1987
15. Slobogin C: The "ultimate issue" issue. Behavioral Sciences and the Law 7:259–266, 1989
16. Insanity Defense Work Group: American Psychiatric Association Statement on the Insanity Defense. Am J Psychiatry 140:681–688, 1983
17. Rogers R: Ethical dilemmas in forensic evaluations. Behavioral Sciences and the Law 5:149–160, 1987
18. Weinstock R: Perceptions of ethical problems by forensic psychiatrists. Bull Am Acad Psychiatry Law 17:189–202, 1989
19. Griswold v Conn, 381 US 479 (1962)
20. Roe v Wade, 410 US 113 (1973)
21. State of New Jersey v Paul Hurd, 173 NJ Superior Court 333 (1980)
22. The People v Donald Lee Shirley, 31 Cal 3rd 18 (1982)
23. Harper v Washington, 110 Wash 2d 873, 759 P2d 358, 361 (1988)
24. Monahan J: The psychiatrization of criminal behavior: a reply. Hosp Community Psychiatry 24:105–107, 1973
25. Shah SA: Some interactions of law and mental health in the handling of social deviance. Catholic University Law Review 23:674–719, 1974
26. Rosenhan DL: On being sane in insane places. Science 179:250–258, 1973

27. Spitzer RL: On pseudoscience in science, logic in remission and psychiatric diagnosis: a critique of Rosenhan's "On Being Sane in Insane Places." J Abnorm Psychol 84:442–452, 1975
28. APA members learn secrets of public affairs to help mentally ill, promote psychiatry. Psychiatric News, May 19, 1989, p 3
29. Miller DJ: Involuntary mental hospitalization. Compr Psychiatry 9:187–192, 1968
30. Melick ME, Steadman HJ: The medicalization of criminal behavior among mental patients. J Health Soc Behav 20:228–237, 1979
31. Appelbaum PS, Zonana H, Bonnie R, et al: Statutory approaches to limiting psychiatrists' liability for their patients' violent acts. Am J Psychiatry 146:821–828, 1989
32. Maeder T: Wounded healers. The Atlantic, Jan 1989, p 37
33. Vatz RE, Weinberg LS: In defense of the motivation of therapists. Baltimore Sun, Feb 26, 1989, Pespective 5M
34. Julie Roy v Renatus Hartogs, MD, 85 Misc 2nd 891 (1976)
35. Frenkiel N: Again, a star gazer. Baltimore Sun, May 8, 1989, pp B1–2
36. APA Joint Commission on Public Affairs and the Division of Public Affairs: Let's Talk About Substance Abuse. Washington, DC, American Psychiatric Association, 1988
37. APA Joint Commission on Public Affairs and the Division of Public Affairs: Let's Talk Facts About Teen Suicide. Washington, DC, American Psychiatric Association, 1988
38. APA Joint Commission on Public Affairs and the Division of Public Affairs: Let's Talk Facts About Anxiety Disorders. Washington, DC, American Psychiatric Association, 1988
39. APA Joint Commission on Public Affairs and the Division of Public Affairs: Let's Talk Facts About Schizophrenia. Washington, DC, American Psychiatric Association, 1988
40. APA Joint Commission on Public Affairs and the Division of Public Affairs: Let's Talk Facts About Phobias. Washington, DC, American Psychiatric Association, 1988
41. APA Joint Commission on Public Affairs and the Division of Public Affairs: Let's Talk Facts About Mental Health of the Elderly. Washington, DC, American Psychiatric Association, 1988
42. APA Joint Commission on Public Affairs and the Division of Public Affairs: Let's Talk Facts About Post-Traumatic Stress Disorder. Washington, DC, American Psychiatric Association, 1988
43. APA Joint Commission on Public Affairs and the Division of Public Affairs: Let's Talk Facts About Manic-Depressive Disorder. Washington, DC, American Psychiatric Association, 1988
44. APA Joint Commission on Public Affairs and the Division of Public Affairs: Let's Talk Facts About Obsessive-Compulsive Disorder. Washington, DC, American Psychiatric Association, 1988
45. APA Joint Commission on Public Affairs and the Division of Public Affairs: Let's Talk Facts About Depression. Washington, DC, American Psychiatric Association, 1988

46. APA Joint Commission on Public Affairs and the Division of Public Affairs: Let's Talk Facts About an Overview of Mental Illness. Washington, DC, American Psychiatric Association, 1988
47. Greist JH, Jefferson WJ: Depression and Its Treatment. Washington, DC, American Psychiatric Press, 1984
48. Weiss RD, Mirin SM: Cocaine. Washington, DC, American Psychiatric Press, 1987
49. Zane MD, Milt H: Your Phobia: Understanding Your Fears Through Contextual Therapy. Washington, DC, American Psychiatric Press, 1984
50. Korpell HS: How You Can Help: A Guide for Families of Psychiatric Hospital Patients. Washington, DC, American Psychiatric Press, 1984
51. Division of Public Affairs, American Psychiatric Association: Campaign Kit 1989. Washington, DC, American Psychiatric Association, 1989
52 Division of Public Affairs, American Psychiatric Association: Campaign Kit 1990. Washington, DC, American Psychiatric Association, 1990
53. 1989 Joint Commission on Public Affairs, American Psychiatric Association: Guidelines for psychiatrists working with the communications media. Am J Psychiatry 134:609–611, 1977
54. American Psychiatric Association: Addendum to Public Affairs Guidelines, March 13, 1982. Washington, DC, American Psychiatric Association, 1982

Chapter 8

The Role of the Psychiatric Expert: How to Work With Attorneys

Neil Blumberg, M.D.

Whether or not clinical psychiatrists have an interest in psychiatry and the law, they are likely to be brought into the legal arena at some point in their careers. Because between 50 and 85% of all trials utilize medical reports or testimony, psychiatrists eventually will have to deal with lawyers and the legal system, most probably as treating psychiatrists or as expert witnesses (1). Despite the controversy about whether psychiatrists *should* be in the courtroom, the reality is that we *are* there and have been since the 14th century (2). There is no sign that the demand for medical or psychiatric testimony in the courtroom is lessening. This chapter thus seeks to provide psychiatrists with information and a framework for dealing with lawyers and for providing testimony. This framework should help to minimize the anxiety that psychiatrists who are forensic neophytes may experience and hopefully will transform potentially traumatic events into ones that are challenging and emotionally satisfying.

The psychiatrist may be involved with the legal system in one of four ways: *1*) as a fact witness, *2*) as an expert witness, *3*) as an amicus curiae, or *4*) as a litigant. Only the first two—the roles of the psychiatrist as fact witness (i.e., treating doctor) and as expert witness—are discussed in this chapter. The primary focus is on the psychiatrist as an expert witness and on his or her relationships as such with lawyers.

The Psychiatrist as Fact Witness

Psychiatrists may become involved in legal proceedings because they have treated a patient who is or becomes involved in either criminal or civil litigation. Such situations may arise where psychiatrists treat patients who later commit a criminal offense or become involved in a civil lawsuit. Or, situations may arise where an individual who is already involved in some type of litigation seeks psychiatric treatment.

If a psychiatrist has been treating a patient and the patient subsequently commits a criminal offense or sustains a personal injury, the psychiatrist may have information about the patient's psychiatric condition that may be important to all parties involved. It is a doctor's duty to maintain the confidences given by a patient during psychiatric treatment. But when the patient and the patient's attorney decide to raise the issue of the patient's mental state in a legal proceeding, they are generally considered to be waiving the confidential relationship between psychiatrist and patient. The doctor then may disclose confidential information. Moreover, it is not a doctor's right to selectively release information about a patient. A patient will either sign a release authorizing disclosure of information or the court may order the disclosure of that information. The decision about who are the appropriate parties to receive such information passes out of the psychiatrist's hands. Psychiatrists who receive a signed order from the court to release information must make that disclosure or suffer possible legal consequences.

Occasionally, psychiatrists may receive a subpoena duces tecum instructing them to produce certain records. Attorneys may obtain a subpoena duces tecum from the clerk of the court merely by making an appropriate request. But unless this subpoena is accompanied by a court order, or the patient has authorized the release of records, the psychiatrist should not disclose the patient's records. A subpoena is a legal document and appears authoritative, but it does not carry the authority of an actual court order. Remembering the adage, "Lawyers demand, but only judges command," should keep this issue clear.

When psychiatrists begin treating patients who inform them that they are already involved in a legal proceeding, the psychiatrist should advise the patient that the information generated during psychiatric treatment may not be confidential. Waiver of the patient's privilege to confidentiality may occur if the patient makes the waiver or if the court determines that such information may be essential to the litigation. A frequently encountered situation is when one of the participants in a divorce seeks psychiatric treatment to cope with the emotional trauma of the divorce. The issue of that patient's emotional condition may be raised in the proceeding, and, instead of helping the patient, the information a psychiatrist obtains in psychiatric treatment may be used against the patient—for example, to prevent the person from obtaining custody of the children. Thus, psychiatrists should consider it imperative to inform patients who are legally entangled of this potential pitfall.

As a fact witness, a psychiatrist is compelled to present information based on his or her direct observation and knowledge of the patient. This includes discussions, observations, and medical conclusions made during the course of treatment. Because their information is not substantially different from that given by other fact witnesses, psychiatrists who are called as fact witnesses are paid as such—a fee substantially less than what they might receive as expert witnesses. Psychiatrists who appear as fact witnesses are asked about their direct observations of the patient only and are not called on for medical-legal opinions.

In fact, a major difference between a fact witness and an expert witness is that the latter's testimony includes forensic opinions. Issues that go beyond the observation required of the fact witness and involve the opinion testimony of the expert witness include causation of a particular emotional problem and questions of sanity and competency. Yet, although the testimony of fact witnesses clearly is more limited than that of expert witnesses, it may be of greater potential benefit to the client, because treating psychiatrists generally are viewed as more credible than experts who may be seen as the "hired guns" of parties in litigation.

The Psychiatrist as Expert Witness

The primary focus of this chapter is on psychiatrists' relationships with lawyers when psychiatrists serve as expert witnesses. Legal situations often may require attorneys to call on psychiatrists for expert testimony in both the civil and criminal arenas. The increased prominence of psychiatrists in the courtroom is confirmed by a correspondingly rapid growth in the subspecialty of forensic psychiatry. This subspecialty now has some 24 fellowship programs, several national organizations, and a board certification process to identify psychiatrists who have particular knowledge, training, and experience in the law. In the civil area, forensic consultations may involve *1*) malpractice, *2*) personal injury (liability and/or damages), *3*) workers' compensation, *4*) divorce and custody litigation, *5*) competency and guardianship, and *6*) civil commitment. In the criminal area, psychiatrists are regularly consulted on *1*) competency to stand trial and other competency-related matters, *2*) criminal responsibility, *3*) waiver of *Miranda* rights and voluntariness of confessions, *4*) intoxication, *5*) mens rea defenses and diminished capacity, *6*) presentence evaluations, *7*) juvenile waivers, and *8*) mitigation in sentencing in capital cases.

The role of a psychiatrist in consultation with a lawyer may vary depending on the needs of the attorney and the issues involved. Generally, such consultations involve one or a combination of the following: direct consultation with the attorney, comprehensive written evaluations, and expert testimony.

Some psychiatrists delineate a variety of different "roles" that the psychiatric expert may play, including *1*) educator, *2*) investigator, *3*) clinical evaluator, *4*) interpreter, *5*) trial strategy adviser, *6*) drama coach, *7*) drama critic, *8*) rewrite editor of hypothetical questions, and *9*) personal emotional support or therapist to legal counsel or the parties involved (3). Observers who are more critical of psychiatrists' presence in the courtroom have cast them in more questionable roles, such as *1*) priest; *2*) wizard, astrologer, and psychic; *3*) magician; *4*) decision maker; *5*) scapegoat; *6*) advocate; and *7*) smoke screen (2).

My view of the role of the psychiatric expert is consistent with that of Tanay (4). That is, the psychiatric expert functions basically as a teacher of the lawyer and the trier of fact. Psychiatrists as expert witnesses use their special knowledge of mental illness and human behavior to shed light on issues that otherwise might confuse or confound the legal process.

The major difference between the fact witness and the expert witness is that the expert witness, based on his or her knowledge, training, and experience, is found by the court to be able to provide relevant information beyond the scope of the layperson. Thus, the expert witness may testify not only about facts and observations but may also render his or her professional opinion.

Expert witnesses are entitled to expert-witness fees, which are usually based on an hourly rate. Experts may be required to review records, consult with attorneys, examine litigants, prepare reports, prepare testimony, and actually provide testimony—activities that frequently require extensive time and energy commitments. Hence, it is appropriate for psychiatrists to bill at their usual and customary hourly rates for any and all time spent on a case. It is unethical—and in some states illegal—to accept a contingency percentage of a case. The appearance of bias in such situations is apparent if a fee is based on the outcome of a case.

On occasion, situations arise in which after completing a forensic evaluation a psychiatrist determines that the person being evaluated is in need of treatment. If possible, it is best to keep the roles of evaluating and treating psychiatrist separate. Although treating physicians are generally viewed in court as more credible, psychiatrists who become both the treating doctor and the expert witness may encounter several pitfalls. First, treating doctors *should* have a bias toward their patients, because their role is to help the patients. But expert witnesses must maintain an objective view of the individual and the legal situation. Second, the impact of providing testimony about a patient may significantly distort and interfere with the psychotherapeutic process, especially in more dynamically oriented psychotherapy. Last, psychiatrists who are recommending and providing treatment for a patient after the patient experiences some type of personal injury cannot avoid the appearance of feeding their own pockets. That is, juries will be skeptical of "experts" who render the opinion that Mr. A will require 2 years of twice-weekly psychotherapy, administered by the expert, as a result of the injury the patient sustained. Even though such treatment might be perfectly appropriate and situations may arise when it is impossible to refrain from playing both roles, it is best to choose one or the other role when possible.

Steps Toward Becoming an Expert Witness

Assuming that psychiatrists are willing to provide expert assistance to an attorney, they should carefully follow several steps when an attorney asks for their assistance in a particular case.

Clarify the issue. This is probably the most basic but overlooked point in a forensic consultation. Lack of clarification of what the attorney needs from the psychiatrist is also one of the major sources of dissatisfaction with legal psychiatric consultations.

Typically, the attorney calls and says he or she needs the client evaluated. The client then arrives, and the psychiatrist takes a history and does a mental status examination. The psychiatrist may have no idea about whether the issue is disability, liability, emotional damages, need for treatment, or a means by which an attorney hopes to delay going to trial.

Psychiatrists can save time and aggravation by finding out why the client is being evaluated and what specifically the attorney wants addressed in the psychiatrist's report.

Should one do it? Once psychiatrists understand what the attorney wants, they should decide whether to take on the consultation. One factor involved should be whether the psychiatrist is knowledgeable in this particular area. For example, psychiatrists with training in treating adults might be asked to evaluate a 6-year-old child. Some may and others may not be willing or competent to do so.

Psychiatrists should determine whether they have any personal biases that may affect their ability to render a fair assessment. For example, if the psychiatrist or a close family member was the victim of a violent crime, will this skew an assessment of a criminal defendant?

Psychiatrists should think about whether they have any conflicts of interest in taking on the case—such as having a personal or business relationship with one of the litigants.

Skeletons in the closet. Psychiatrists also must consider whether there may be any areas of their background, training, or experience that if discovered will jeopardize the attorney's case. If so, lawyers should know this from the outset to make an informed decision about the usefulness of particular experts in particular cases. For example, if a psychiatrist who is to testify about malpractice has had judgments for malpractice rendered against him or her, the psychiatrist will lose all credibility when this is discovered. If a psychiatrist's license has ever been suspended or revoked, if the psychiatrist has been the subject of any medical disciplinary proceeding, or if the psychiatrist has ever been convicted of a criminal offense, these facts and any others that may impugn the psychiatrist's credibility as an expert witness should be discussed with the attorney before any involvement is finalized.

Fees. Although doctors do not like to acknowledge that they work, in part, to make money, this is a basic reality and a potential major source of conflict in dealing with lawyers. Psychiatrists who become involved in forensic cases should clarify fee arrangements at the outset. Practitioners should let the attorney know their hourly fee and whether that fee will apply to all time spent on the case or will vary according to different services, such as reviewing records, giving court testimony, traveling, preparing for court appearances, and so on. I charge one hourly rate for all time spent on a case, which helps keep things simple when billing time comes, but other practices are common and acceptable.

It is appropriate and ethical to request a retainer in a private forensic case. This is a means by which a psychiatrist-witness is assured of payment regardless of the outcome of the case. It is never pleasant or particularly fruitful to attempt to collect from a client who has lost a case. Where the "operation" (testimony) was a success, but the "patient" (client's lawsuit) died, psychiatrists who have rendered services without payment are unlikely to get paid. Professionals who consult for government agencies, insurance companies, or attorneys they trust may not need to ask for retainers. Even so, as Slovenko (5) notes, "The expert at times may be a 'hired gun' but, quite often, he may need a gun to get paid."

Psychiatrists who serve as expert witnesses should determine by whom they will be paid—whether the client or the attorney—and who will be responsible for any charges in excess of the retainer. There is no hard and fast rule in this area. However, if the client is of questionable reliability or means, the psychiatrist may want to more strongly consider receiving payment through the attorney. Last, as noted earlier, avoid contingency fees.

Defining roles. Expert witnesses should clarify the particular service that will be required of them. The forensic "consultation" may range from translating a medical record for the attorney to doing a complete evaluation of the client, preparing a report, and testifying in court. By understanding the attorney's needs in a case, psychiatrists can then provide the appropriate intervention.

Clinical evaluation. When an evaluation of a litigant based on direct interview is required, psychiatrists should address several issues. Before conducting any interviews, psychiatrists should request and review all materials that provide relevant information about the individual and situation. Although in therapy situations psychiatrists may not want to be "contaminated" by external information, in forensic cases psychiatrists will use their time most productively if they have the data beforehand. In criminal cases, psychiatrists as expert witnesses should obtain records such as police reports; witnesses' statements; the defendant's confession; the defendant's FBI "rap sheet"; and the subject's mental health records, school records, and other institutional records. In addition, in civil cases, the expert witness should review the deposition testimony of the evaluee or other witnesses, answers to interrogatories, and any other relevant documentation that might be available. The rule of thumb is that the more information one has, the better founded will be one's ultimate opinion. There is nothing more unnerving than becoming aware of important and decisive data on the witness stand.

After reviewing all available materials the psychiatrist should be in a position to conduct a clinical examination. Although there is no definite rule about how long the interview should be or about the number of interviews necessary, clearly the more time psychiatrists spend with the client, the more reliable are their conclusions. Knowledge and thoroughness translate into greater credibility before a judge or jury. Although external factors may limit the number of interviews one can conduct, and the length of those interviews, it is useful to see the client on more than one occasion. In that way, psychiatrists can compare the individual's mental status during all interviews, ask certain questions again to check for consistency of responses, and follow up on issues that emerged only during the first interview. In a relatively uncomplicated case, from 2 to 6 hours of interview time with a client should allow psychiatrists sufficient time to complete a comprehensive history and mental status examination.

Depending on the nature of the forensic issue and the diagnostic uncertainty, psychiatrists who serve in legal cases may want to have the client undergo a psychological or neuropsychological evaluation. Although it is not a necessity, psychological testing may be useful in a forensic psychiatric evaluation in providing another source of data to confirm or refute your opinion. Tests, such as the Minnesota Multiphasic Personality Inventory (MMPI), that have scales that suggest when individuals are exaggerating their emotional difficulties may be helpful in supporting a diagnosis of malingering. Although finances may be a consideration, and most cases can be resolved with thorough interviewing and reviewing all materials, psychological testing may provide even more data and a firmer ground on which to base conclusions.

Reports. Once psychiatrists have completed interviews and reviews of records, they should be in a position to prepare a report of findings. When consulting for an attorney, *never* prepare a report without discussing with the attorney what you have found and what kind of report, if any, is required. Attorneys who have retained psychiatrists' services either directly or through their client have a right to know what the expert witness thinks before the witness prepares a report. Attorneys do not have a right to dictate the conclusions of such reports. But, in most jurisdictions, once a report is prepared, that information is discoverable. Thus, if expert witnesses have come to a conclusion unfavorable to the party that has retained them, the party may not want to provide more ammunition to the other side by asking the psychiatrist for a formal report. To quash such a report before it is prepared is entirely ethical behavior, because it is the attorney's job to present the best case for the client. Because the expert witness is a consultant to the attorney and because whether or not a report is prepared in no way influences the psychiatrist's conclusions, there is no compromise of the psychiatrist's position.

Reports, when prepared, may vary in length and detail required. Psychiatrists should discuss the length and detail of the report with the attorney. At a minimum, however, the psychiatrist's evaluation should include opinions and the bases for those opinions. In many instances, a thorough review of all aspects of the history; mental status examination; review of records; and diagnoses, opinions, and their bases will be required.

However complex or simple the report, it will be scrutinized carefully. In most instances psychiatrists are known to attorneys and the court only through this report, because actual psychiatric testimony is required in only a small percentage of cases. Reports that are well organized, easily understood, comprehensive yet concise, neat, and jargon-free will generate further referrals.

Psychiatrists who are subsequently requested to provide testimony will be cross-examined on the information in the report. Thus, the report must say essentially what one would say in court. A slipshod report containing errors, misinformation, and unsupported conclusions will undermine the effectiveness of the psychiatrist's testimony.

Some attorneys may request a draft of the report. Preparing a draft report can be a useful way of refining one's writing style, checking the accuracy of factual material reviewed, and deleting extraneous material. Although there is controversy concerning the use of drafts (6), I have prepared such reports on occasion and have generally found the process useful. But note that such drafts are discoverable and that some attorneys may seek to offer suggestions that alter conclusions, remove essential information, or otherwise compromise the integrity of the report. For example, I completed a draft of an evaluation in a personal injury case, and the attorney suggested that because I found a psychiatric disturbance, it really was "not essential" to include that the illness was also present before the accident.

Depositions. A deposition is an official recording of a witness's testimony under oath. Generally, a psychiatrist is "deposed" when he or she is involved in a civil case. Although depositions are not required, they may be used to preserve the testimony of psychiatrists who cannot be present for in-court testimony. Frequently, such depositions are videotaped and played at the time of trial. The deposition thus proceeds exactly as the expert's testimony would in trial. The psychiatrist is sworn in, qualified as an expert, presents direct testimony, and then undergoes cross-examination by opposing counsel. Objections are made during questioning but are ruled on later by the judge. If an objection is sustained, the expert's answer may be edited from the tape.

Depositions are more common for discovery purposes. They are requested by the opposing counsel to discover what facts the expert relied on and what opinions the expert is going to render at trial. Discovery depositions also give the opposing attorney an opportunity to assess the expert as a witness, to learn the strengths and weaknesses of the evaluation, and to get the expert to commit to a position under oath.

Depositions generally take place in either the office of the psychiatrist or that of one of the attorneys. The psychiatrist usually is required to bring all of the materials reviewed and all notes. All of these may be reviewed by opposing counsel.

Arrangements for the deposition should be clarified beforehand. "When" and "where" are the easiest to decide. Fees for deposition testimony, predeposition preparation, and review of the deposition transcript should be agreed on in advance, as should which party will pay for what time. Usually, the side requesting the deposition pays for the expert's time during the deposition. The parties should clarify beforehand how long the deposition will be, and if experts clear their schedules for the requested time, the responsible party should bring payment for the entire time. Whoever is responsible for the time spent in deposition preparation and in review of the transcript after the deposition should be informed of those expenses.

A predeposition attorney conference is a must. Psychiatrists should use this time to learn what to expect from opposing counsel, the nature of the questions, potential pitfalls, and the various tactics that may be used against them. Prospective experts may wish to have the attorney run them through a cross-examination if they are relatively inexperienced as witnesses. Attorneys should review the psychiatrist's file on the client. Certain materials in the file may be considered "work product" and should not be made available to opposing counsel. If asked during the deposition, psychiatrists should acknowledge that such materials have been removed as "work product." If opposing counsel disagree on the admissibility of work-product materials, a judge will decide what should and should not be produced. Psychiatrists must not compromise their own credibility by not acknowledging the existence of work-product material.

Depositions can be treacherous. In the relaxed and informal

atmosphere of one's office, following casual conversation with attorneys, one may lower one's guard and say things that one would never say in court. Thus, the psychiatrist must prepare for a deposition as if preparing for court. Psychiatrists will be held to their deposition testimony, and what they say during the deposition will be used against them if possible. If at trial the expert says something that varies from the deposition testimony, the cross-examination may go like this:

> Q: Well doctor, didn't you just testify that Mr. X never had a history of psychiatric difficulties before his injury?
> A: Yes.
> Q: Doctor, on page 153 of your deposition, didn't you state, "Mr. X became severely depressed following the death of his father last year"?
> A. Yes, but . . .
> Q: Tell us doctor, are you lying under oath now or were you lying under oath at your deposition?

At the conclusion of any deposition, psychiatrists will be asked if they are waiving their signature of the deposition. By waiving signature of the deposition, the psychiatrist is attesting to its accuracy without actually reading the deposition. Psychiatrists should not waive their signature unless specifically advised to do so by the attorney. By not waiving signature, the psychiatrist will receive a copy of the deposition transcript and will have an opportunity to review it for accuracy. Although one cannot *change* one's answers, the expert on occasion may catch small typographical errors or omissions in transcription that can make gigantic differences to testimony and credibility. On one occasion my transcribed testimony omitted the word "not" and changed my opinion to "for these reasons Mr. C was [not] a high suicide risk."

Trial testimony. Providing psychiatric testimony in court can range from emotionally exhilarating to devastating. The key to making a day in court emotionally rewarding is *preparation.* Expert witnesses who have done a thorough workup, know their case, plan their direct testimony, and anticipate potential areas of cross-examination should be able to leave the courtroom with a feeling of confidence and pride in a job well done, regardless of the outcome of the case.

As before depositions, psychiatrists should insist on a pretrial conference with the attorney. The attorney probably will require some background on the psychiatric concepts and terms that will emerge in court. Once the psychiatrist has "taught" the attorney

"Psychiatry 101" with reference to the case, together they should plan out the direct examination. Regardless of one's experience in court, "winging it" on the witness stand usually looks just like it sounds. Use the pretrial conference to discover the potential pitfalls of the case that undoubtedly will be explored on cross-examination. Should one deal with negative aspects of the evaluation on direct examination or wait until cross-examination? These issues and more need to be resolved before one goes on the witness stand.

Direct examination. When one is called to the witness stand after being sworn in and identified to the court, one's qualifications will be reviewed to determine whether the court will accept one as an expert witness. This part of the direct examination, conducted by the attorney whom the expert is assisting, is called *voir dire*. Psychiatrists will want to describe their academic background, training, work experience, licensure, board certification, awards, publications, and any other relevant information. The attorney will want to show the court that the witness indeed is an expert in the area the witness is addressing. Naturally, one should be humble in reciting one's achievements, but nonetheless one must document one's expertise in psychiatry. If one has qualified previously as an expert witness in court and has worked for plaintiffs and defendants, or for the prosecution and the defense, let the court know this; it enhances one's credibility.

Once the attorney has offered a psychiatrist as an expert, the opposing side may challenge one's credentials or question areas of one's background. Although attacks of this nature may feel personal, they usually are not. It is the opposing counsel's job to diminish the credibility of the other side's witnesses, and what better place to start than here? If the information has not been obtained during deposition, or if it has and is helpful to the other side, one should expect questions aimed at showing how little experience one has had in the particular area to be addressed. If one is not board certified and the opposing doctor is, this will be brought out. If one is board certified one may be asked how many times one had to take the boards. If one has ever been the subject of a professional disciplinary proceeding, been successfully sued in professional practice, or been denied hospital privileges, these areas will be probed by a thorough examiner. If experienced expert witnesses have tended to testify more for one side than another, an attempt will be made to make the witness appear biased. This is why it is essential to let the attorney know areas of vulnerability in one's background *before* taking the stand, so that the attorney can determine whether the strength of one's opinion and other factors outweigh potentially "negative" areas of one's qualifications. This may save the client's case and may relieve the psychiatrist of unnecessary embarrassment.

Once psychiatrists have been qualified as expert witnesses, they are at the heart of the direct examination. Although direct examination by one's attorney may seem easier than the following cross-examination, presenting psychiatric testimony can be difficult. In response to questions from the attorney the witness will describe the purpose of the examination, who requested the services, the materials reviewed, who was interviewed, where the interviews took place, how long the interviews lasted, and what other tests or procedures were administered.

Depending on the nature of the case and the style of the attorney, either one may give an opinion in the case and then explain the basis or reasoning supporting that opinion, or one may describe the findings and conclude with an opinion. In either case, one should avoid using psychiatric jargon. Explain all terms so that the judge and jury will clearly understand. One's reasoning should be sound and easy to follow step by step.

Any opinions that the expert renders must be to a reasonable degree of medical certainty or probability. It is not enough to say that something is possible. But what is reasonable medical certainty? Rappeport (7) admits that he has "discovered that the status of reasonable medical certainty is quite uncertain." He advises, however, that psychiatrists should ask the attorneys "how it is supposed to be told and then tell it as close to what they want within the limits of your honesty and integrity." Diamond (8) suggests that reasonable medical certainty "should express the psychiatrist's highest level of confidence in the validity and reliability of his opinion."

There has been much discussion, both for and against, about whether an expert should be an advocate of a particular side or position (9–13). Proposals for impartial psychiatric experts have been made, although this has been described as an "ideal fiction" (12). According to Slovenko (13), "An expert who takes a neutral role does his party a disservice, for the opposing party's expert will undoubtedly assume his role as advocate and his advocacy would go without challenge. Hence, when a witness chooses to testify as an expert for a party, he is expected to do so under the terms of the adversary system or he should not participate." A lawyer expressed a more picturesque version of the same sentiment: "I would go into a lawsuit with an objective, uncommitted, independent expert about as willingly as I would occupy a foxhole with a couple of noncombatant soldiers" (2).

I agree with the approach of Shapiro (9), who suggests that one should maintain as much objectivity as possible during the evaluation. Once one has reached an opinion, however, one should become an advocate of that opinion and not of a particular "side."

One should be careful not to overstate one's case. Doing so will increase one's vulnerability during cross-examination. One should be aware of countertransference in the courtroom (14). Unconscious distortions of findings and impairment in the quality of a presentation may occur if one is not aware of this potential danger.

One should maintain eye contact with the judge or jury—whoever is the trier of fact—when responding to questions. They, not the attorney, are the decision makers.

The use of visual aids is also helpful in presenting testimony. Charts may help to clarify a point and may help the jury to recall testimony more easily. In addition, it will allow the expert witness to leave the stand and approach the jury. This will increase the jurors' attentiveness to one's testimony. One may be reawakening jurors' childhood trauma of falling asleep in class and being approached by the teacher, but one certainly will focus the jurors' attention and renew their sense of responsibility. Avoiding long, rambling discourses and having an active give and take with the attorney also will aid in this goal. Lengthy testimony necessarily may be dull, so keeping jurors alert is essential.

Using direct quotes is also effective in illustrating a point. Instead of saying that the patient had loose associations, provide an excerpt of what the patient actually said.

In rendering diagnoses, one should refer to generally accepted psychiatric diagnoses, as described in DSM-III-R. Try to avoid lengthy lectures on one's theoretical orientation. Psychoanalytical hypotheses may be wonderful for case conferences, but they tend to confuse laypeople.

Last, there has been some debate as to one's appearance and attire in court. Resnick (1) discusses at some length research concerning different aspects of one's appearance in court. The basic tenet is to maximize the likelihood that the jury is paying attention to what one says and not to how one looks. Dressing conservatively, limiting jewelry, and presenting a neat yet attractive appearance should help accomplish that goal.

Cross-examination. Once an expert witness has finished direct examination, the witness should feel confident and comfortable in the role of expert. One may wonder why one was so anxious beforehand, because the testimony went so smoothly and everyone was paying such close attention. On occasion, I have seen neophyte experts testifying, and after direct examination, they have actually gotten up to leave the witness stand, believing that their "day in court" was over. They were then reminded that opposing counsel had "a few questions" as part of their cross-examination.

The purpose of cross-examination is to discredit adverse testimony. The manner of cross-examination varies with the style of the attorney. Some are polite but persistent, some are angry and intimidating, and some take on the avuncular role of the "country lawyer." Regardless of approach, the goal of cross-examination is the same—to make the expert look bad.

Attacks in cross-examination are directed at either the expert, the expert's opinion, or both. Shapiro (9) identifies the progression of attack from the opinion to the credentials to the person. He advises that when the attack is focused primarily on the expert as an individual, one should actually feel confident, because one's opinion and credentials were unassailable.

Early in my career, I presented testimony that was extremely effective in a criminal case. Moreover, my credentials were unassailable. The cross-examination consisted of one question. In a condescending and sneering voice, the attorney asked me, "Well, Doctor, how old are you"? I responded. He said, in a similarly condescending tone of voice, "No further questions."

Another sort of personal attack is attributed to the unidentified trial lawyer who, after failing to refute or undermine the opposing expert witness, stated, "Gentlemen of the jury, there are three kinds of liars—the common liar, the damned liar, and the scientific expert" (15).

If not questioned on voir dire about one's credentials, one still may encounter such questions on cross-examination. Because the opposing attorney may have believed that you would be admitted as an expert anyway, he may have withheld questions about your professional background and credentials for cross-examination. The purpose of this area of inquiry is to assault one's credibility as an expert.

When engaging in a "witness attack," opposing counsel will try to expose one's inexperience and lack of credentials. If an expert who testifies often is retained primarily by one side or another, this will be brought out, suggesting bias.

One's fee may be questioned in an attempt to portray one as a "hired gun" whose opinion can be bought. Questions such as, "Doctor, how much are you being paid for your opinion?" should be responded to by clarifying that experts are not paid for their *opinion* but for their *time*. If one is not questioned about fees, this usually means that the opposing attorney believes that attacking the expert's character will be fruitless or that opposing counsel have had to pay their expert even more.

The most effective cross-examination must address and discredit an expert's opinion. The adequacy of the psychiatrist's examination of the subject will be reviewed. How long did you actually meet with the client? How often did you see the client? Did you review all available materials? Did you interview family members or witnesses? Were the interviews done in private? Were others present during the interviews? How soon after the offense or injury did you examine the client?

Regardless of how thorough one might have been, it can always be made to seem that one could have done more. In one criminal case for which I had spent many hours with the defendant and had interviewed more than 20 material witnesses, opposing counsel still brought out the fact that I had not interviewed Mr. X, who in actuality had no additional information to provide.

Other areas of inquiry may focus on whether the expert formed an opinion before having all the facts. If one did not know an important fact, does knowing it now change one's opinion? On occasion this may occur, either by accident or deliberately. If the new data might change one's opinion, one should acknowledge it. It will be the job of one's attorney either to object to the new information or to provide a fuller picture of the information or to clarify cross-examination questions on redirect examination.

Inconsistencies or inaccuracies within one's report will be attacked, as will inconsistencies between one's court testimony and deposition testimony and court testimony and report. Even conversations about a case outside any professional setting may be questioned if they differ from one's testimony. A colleague of mine who was testifying for the defense in a criminal case was waiting in the hallway to come into court and made an offhand remark to the prosecution that despite his own firmly held opinion, "this was a real close case and could go either way." After my colleague presented his direct testimony in court and affirmed that he held his opinion "to a reasonable degree of medical certainty," the first and last question the prosecutor asked him on cross-examination was, "Well, Doctor, didn't you just tell me in the hallway that . . ."

Ziskin and Faust (16) have written extensively on how to discredit psychiatric and psychological testimony. Some familiarity with this work and the criticisms of it may be helpful in anticipating attacks on psychiatry and the psychiatric literature (17,18).

While testifying, in addition to the previously noted suggestions, one should take one's time responding to questions. Water should be handy in case one's throat gets dry. If one is misquoted—which might be done deliberately—one should correct the attorney before going further. If one does not understand a question, one should ask the attorney to rephrase it.

If one is being interrupted or badgered, one should say so to the attorney and to the judge. This will enable one to more fully answer the questions.

If one does not know an answer, one should admit it. An opposing attorney once asked me if I was familiar with a particular text. I said I was, and the attorney then asked me what color the book's cover was. At that time, I could not recall, and I said so. The attorney then suggested that the cover was red. I repeated that I just could not recall. When I returned to my office, I found the book and noted that the cover was black. No doubt, the attorney had the book with him and was just waiting for me to fall into the trap, so that he could embarrass me with my "lack of knowledge" about the book.

If one needs to refresh one's memory while testifying by referring to notes, do so. This is certainly better than making an inaccurate statement.

Expert witnesses should make an effort not to be defensive or lose their temper, despite the considerable tension that may build up in court. Opposing attorneys score points if they are able to unsettle a witness.

It is generally a good idea to avoid humor in the courtroom. Making light of a serious situation impairs credibility.

Last, one should try to enjoy an experience as an expert witness. Remember, psychiatrists know more about psychiatry than opposing counsel. With careful preparation, one should be able to convert what might be a nerve-racking experience into a stimulating and rewarding challenge that serves the interest of justice.

NOTES

1. Resnick P: The psychiatrist as an expert witness. Lecture presentation-course presented at the 139th annual meeting of the American Psychiatric Association, Washington, DC, May 10–16, 1986
2. Smith S: Mental health expert witnesses: of science and crystal balls. Behavioral Sciences and the Law 7:145–180, 1989
3. Curran W, McGarry AL, Shah S: Forensic Psychiatry and Psychology. Philadelphia, PA, FA Davis, 1986
4. Tanay E: The expert witness as a teacher. Bull Am Acad Psychiatry Law 8:401–411, 1980

5. Slovenko R: The lawyer and the forensic expert: boundaries of ethical practice. Behavioral Sciences and the Law 5:119–148, 1987
6. ABA Criminal Justice Mental Health Standards, Chicago, IL, American Bar Association, 1989
7. Rappeport J: Reasonable medical certainty. Bull Am Acad Psychiatry Law 13:5–15, 1985
8. Diamond B: Reasonable medical certainty, diagnostic thresholds, and definitions of mental illness in the legal context. Bull Am Acad Psychiatry Law 13:121–128, 1985
9. Shapiro D: Psychological Evaluation and Expert Testimony: A Practical Guide to Forensic Work. New York, Van Nostrand Reinhold, 1984
10. Otto R: Bias and expert testimony of mental health professionals in adversarial proceedings: a preliminary investigation. Behavioral Sciences and the Law 7:267–273, 1989
11. Diamond B: The fallacy of the impartial expert. Archives of Criminal Psychodynamics 3:221–236, 1959
12. Gorman W: Are there impartial expert psychiatric witnesses? Bull Am Acad Psychiatry Law 11:379–382, 1983
13. Slovenko R: Psychiatry and Law. Boston, MA, Little, Brown, 1973
14. Schetky D, Coleback E: Countertransference on the witness stand: a flight from self? Bull Am Acad Psychiatry Law 10:115–121, 1982
15. Foster W: Expert testimony—prevalent complaints and proposed remedies. Harvard Law Review 11:169–186, 1987
16. Ziskin J, Faust D: Coping With Psychiatric and Psychological Testimony, 4th Edition, Vols 1–3. Venice, CA, Law and Psychology Press, 1988
17. Buck O: The question of validity and reliability in forensic evaluations. Presented at the annual meeting of the American Academy of Psychiatry and Law, Portland, OR, Oct 28, 1983
18. Hoge S, Grisso T: Fryeing Faust and Ziskin: expert opinion. Massachusetts 2:1, 4–7, 1988

Chapter 9

Special Problems for Military Psychiatrists

Edmund G. Howe, M.D., J.D.

The principle of confidentiality is highly regarded in the military (1), but military physicians face obligations regarding confidentiality that differ from those of their civilian colleagues (2). In this chapter, I discuss three situations in which military psychiatrists encounter conflicts between military obligations and confidentiality: when they treat servicepersons who abuse alcohol or drugs, servicepersons who are gay, and servicepersons who have human immunodeficiency virus (HIV) infection.

Initially, this chapter describes the impact of military regulations because this impact is often misunderstood, even perhaps by some military physicians. Then, the chapter enumerates the conflicts just described. Because military psychiatrists can warn servicepersons in all these situations about the special limitations on confidentiality—that is, that psychiatrists might report their patients—the chapter then discusses psychiatrists' legal obligation to do so. The chapter details psychiatrist-patient privilege in the military, and ends with a recent survey of Army psychiatrists' views of the effects of limited confidentiality and privilege on their practice.

The Impact of Regulations

Military regulations direct military physicians, as they do all servicepersons, to report known violations of military law. When these regulations are general, such as the articles in the Uniform Code of

---

I express my appreciation to Marie L. Lofty for her patience and extraordinary help in preparing this manuscript and Harry C. Holloway, Col., M.C., U.S.A. (Retired), Robert J. Ursano, M.C., U.S.A.F., Simon L. Auster, M.D., Carol C. Kleinman, M.D., J.D., and Theodore Kleinman, L.L.B., M.B.A., L.L.M., for their most helpful comments.

The views expressed in this chapter are entirely the views of the author and do not in any way represent the views of the Department of Defense.

Military Justice (UCMJ) concerning dereliction of performance of duty (3) and conduct prejudicial to good order and discipline (4), they connote an ethos, and under exceptional circumstances, as when servicepersons show a consistent or flagrant disregard of military interests, the articles of the UCMJ provide grounds for criminal sanctions (5). As a basis for criminal prosecution, however, they are inherently problematic. As one judge stated in a recent military court of appeals case, "We have serious doubts about the propriety of using this particular regulation as a basis for criminal prosecution" (5).

There are several reasons for caution in using military regulations when they imply or involve legal action. First, their scope is overly encompassing. Navy Regulation Article 1139, for instance, requires persons in the Department of the Navy to *report offenses* (italics mine) committed by Navy personnel to proper authority (5). If taken literally, this regulation would require reporting of violations of federal civilian law, federal military law, state law, administrative regulations, honor codes, and religious tenets (5).

Second, servicepersons would have an "absolute, all-inclusive" duty to report such offenses (5). If all servicepersons believed that they should comply with this requirement, the results could be disadvantageous to servicepersons' morale, in addition to flooding military courts and prisons. As Military Appellate Court Chief Judge Everett stated, "I certainly would not wish to live in a country like Nazi Germany, where children were motivated to report any seemingly disloyal thought or action of family members" (5). Third, when the circumstances that would trigger servicepersons' obligation to report are ambiguous or absent, servicepersons may lack notice regarding when and whether they must comply (5,6).

When regulations are specific, as they are in requiring military personnel to report servicepersons who use marijuana (1,7) the problem of scope is eliminated, but the problems of duty and compliance remain. More importantly for military physicians, general and specific reporting requirements may conflict with other, overriding military and professional obligations to give servicepersons optimal medical care.

Most commanders neither want nor expect servicepersons to report all offenses, particularly when servicepersons are military physicians. Unless military physicians can maintain servicepersons' trust, they may be unable to perform their primary functions—keeping servicepersons healthy and reporting their medical conditions accurately. As a retired line officer stated, "You deal with . . . situations differently. With the recruit, you have to consider the importance of your relationship as a physician with that recruit, and how the effectiveness of the physician in the military depends on his having the confidence of the patients that they can safely be open and truthful with their physicians" (1).

As I have suggested elsewhere (8), the military's strict regulations against homosexual acts and the use of marijuana, but its latitude in not requiring physicians to report these particular behaviors, may further contradictory ends. Strict regulations and threats of criminal sanctions are intended to deter these behaviors. Yet the fact that military physicians are not being required in practice to report these behaviors may further the likelihood that servicepersons engaging in such acts will come to physicians for care and speak to them truthfully.

Commanders generally do not want physicians to report servicepersons, and probably because of this, no military physician ever has been prosecuted for not reporting a serviceperson who committed an offense (1). Army psychiatrist Dr. Matthew Parrish stated in 1972 that "in over 20 years of psychiatric practice in the military, I was never forced to reveal anything a patient told me in confidence —though I was a witness at many court-martials and boards. Furthermore, I know of no other psychiatrist in the military who was so forced" (9). His statement is representative of the experience of other military psychiatrists.

Though such regulations may, then, be binding if taken at face value, for most servicepersons and especially military physicians, they primarily are directive. Consequently, when military physicians encounter servicepersons who have violated military regulations, under most circumstances, physicians can use their discretion to decide whether or not to report the violation. This freedom has the merit of allowing military physicians to take into account factors affecting individual servicepersons. Yet it also allows inequity when military physicians assess similar circumstances differently. More importantly, perhaps, it allows the possibility that military physicians will abuse their discretion to further personal prejudices, as I show later in this chapter.

Confidentiality Regarding Drug and Alcohol Abuse

Joseph A. Pursch, M.C., U.S.N., formerly the Chief of Neuropsychiatry at the Naval Dispensary in Washington, DC, asserted in 1972 that servicepersons who abused drugs fell into one of three categories (10). The first group tended to decompensate emotionally, even under minor stress, and used psychoactive drugs in the hope that drugs would help them feel better. For this group, psychiatric help was rarely successful, and such individuals usually were discharged from service through administrative channels. A second group had strong antisocial tendencies and used drugs primarily to escape their service obligation. In possible support of this assertion, Pursch noted that discharges for homosexuality in the Navy had declined over the same period that discharges for drug abuse had increased. This suggests that those seeking discharge from military service have turned from feigning homosexuality to feigning drug use. A third group experienced adolescent turmoil, but, unlike servicepersons in the first two categories, were ashamed of their drug abuse and wanted to complete their tour of duty. "The key to successful rehabilitation, . . ." Pursch concluded, "is the selection of suitable candidates."

Pursch's analysis illustrates different tasks of military psychiatrists that may come into conflict when they encounter servicepersons who abuse drugs or alcohol. These tasks include the need to discharge servicepersons who are emotionally unsuited for the military; to discern if servicepersons are attempting to use the medical system to obtain some goal other than medical care and, if so, to manage them appropriately; and to treat servicepersons, whenever possible, so that they can perform adequately and remain on active duty.

THE ALCOHOL AND DRUG ABUSE PREVENTION PROGRAM

The military recently adopted new regulations regarding alcohol and drug abuse in response to a congressional statute that was designed to combat the national drug problem (11,12). In 1986, for example, the Army adopted Army Regulation 600-85, which established the current Alcohol and Drug Abuse Prevention and Control Program (ADAPCP) (13). This regulation outlines a "limited use" category of alcohol- and drug-dependent servicepersons that is designed to increase the number of servicepersons who will seek treatment voluntarily. The limited-use policy prohibits commanders from taking administrative or disciplinary actions against soldiers who enroll in ADAPCP on evidence obtained through mandatory urine or alcohol breath tests; or who refer themselves to ADAPCP, and who possess drugs for personal use at the time they present themselves for treatment. The policy does not extend such "immunity," however, to criminal acts committed by such servicepersons while they are under the influence of illegal drugs or alcohol or to illegal use or possession of drugs after they enter the program.

The congressional statute that fostered these regulations emphasized the importance of confidentiality. In the legislative history, conferees stressed that "the strictest adherence to the [confidentiality] provisions . . . is absolutely essential to the success of all drug abuse prevention programs" (12). The statute requires that records of the identity, prognosis, and treatment of patients by any department or agency of the United States be disclosed only for these following purposes, expressly authorized by the statute: No one, other than the serviceperson's commander and immediate supervisor, must know that the soldier is in an alcohol or drug rehabilitation program. Officers above the unit level, with rare exceptions, are to know only the number of abusers in a program within their commands, but not their specific identities. Servicepersons' confidentiality is not protected, however, if doing so could adversely affect the welfare of other persons, the military, or national security. Counselors and other medical personnel must advise their commander immediately of information that might affect patients' performance in a sensitive duty position. If the need to release information is in doubt, the counselor must release this information to the serviceperson's commander, so that the commander can decide what action, if any, he or she deems necessary (14).

The importance placed on protecting servicepersons' confidentiality is illustrated by a recent case in which the military court of appeals overturned a serviceperson's conviction on the ground that the government had violated its own regulations prohibiting the disclosure of information (12). The court held that the prosecution had violated confidentiality provisions of the Army's alcohol and drug regulation when the prosecution presented evidence of the accused's involvement in the Army's alcohol and drug abuse program to rebut the accused's statement that he had "never been in trouble" before.

A commander may directly order servicemembers to report for evaluation or treatment, and both the serviceperson's participation and success may be a condition for his or her remaining on active duty. If servicepersons fail to meet these obligations in an alcohol or drug rehabilitation program, they may be administratively discharged or barred from certain military roles. As an example of the latter, servicepersons in the Navy who do not demonstrate freedom from alcohol and drugs after they have completed a treatment program may be kept in the military but disqualified from duties on submarines or at plants involving nuclear materials (14).

CONFIDENTIALITY REGARDING HOMOSEXUAL SERVICEPERSONS

Homosexual acts are illegal in the military under the UCMJ (15). Oral and anal sexual acts between *heterosexual* partners are also illegal. Military physicians who report these acts between homosexual partners, but not heterosexual partners, discriminate against servicepersons who are homosexual. They may be doing so because they believe that this will further the military's best interests (16) or, as suggested previously, because of personal prejudice.

Historically, homosexual persons have been excluded from the military primarily on the basis of two rationales: that homosexual servicepersons pose a risk to national security and that they disrupt troop morale (17).

The first assertion has been eroded by several court decisions. Recently, for instance, a class action was brought by civilians in a U.S. District Court against the Department of Defense for subjecting homosexual applicants for positions requiring security clearance to expanded investigations (18). The court cited a recent Senate subcommittee finding that in approximately 40 "significant" cases of espionage, only two involved persons were homosexual and neither of these persons was "blackmailed" because of homosexuality (19). The court concluded, "[These] stereotypes have no basis in reality and represent outmoded notions about homosexuality, analogous to 'outmoded notions' [regarding] . . . gender" (18).

In another case just decided, the U.S. Court of Appeals for the Ninth Circuit ruled that Perry Watkins, a sergeant in the Army, could not be precluded from reenlisting (20). Watkins had acknowledged in 1967, when he first entered the service, that he was homosexual, and he had been permitted to reenlist thereafter until the case in question. One judge, concurring with the result but differing in his rationale, stated that the Army's denying Watkins reenlistment solely because he was homosexual violated the equal protection clause of the Fifth Amendment and therefore was unconstitutional.

When, if ever, military physicians should report homosexual servicepersons on the basis of "threats to national security" or "disruption of troop morale" is open to question (21). In any case, most physicians have not reported homosexual servicepersons, as the survey of Army psychiatrists (22), which will be described shortly, exemplifies.

Some military psychiatrists who have not reported homosexual servicepersons have, however, written notes in these patients' charts using some euphemism, such as "the patient shows psychosexual confusion." Such statements appear so nonspecific that they would have little meaning to persons other than care providers, but this is not necessarily the case.

Investigators in the Air Force, if not the other services, who have had independent grounds for suspecting that servicepersons were homosexual sometimes have obtained such servicepersons' medical charts, perhaps by convincing military psychiatrists that they should release them, and then confronted servicepersons with these entries in the hope that they could induce them to acknowledge their homosexuality. Strict regulations in all three services, however, govern this situation (23), and even in the Air Force, the only service in which a regulation explicitly grants investigators access to health records (24), an authority, such as the hospital commander, must determine the legitimacy of such requests (1).

Military psychiatrists who understand these requirements therefore can refuse to release medical records unless they are ordered to do so. Because investigators who request medical records may be on "fishing expeditions," and the confidentiality of records is of prima facie importance, it is unclear when, if ever, authorities would grant their request.

Confidentiality Regarding Servicepersons With HIV Infection

When cases involving HIV first appeared, the military had no specific policy regarding military physicians' obligations when they encountered infected servicepersons. Because such servicepersons—whether homosexual, heterosexual, or intravenous-drug users—pose a potential danger of spreading the virus to third parties, military physicians had an additional reason for reporting infected servicepersons who were homosexual or who used intravenous drugs. Before the promulgation of specific regulations, Navy physicians, for example, reported the homosexuality of three infected servicepersons who had disclosed to the physicians that they were homosexual. Administrative discharge proceedings were initiated, and these servicepersons felt "betrayed" (25).

Because adverse sanctions could be taken against infected servicepersons who acknowledged intravenous-drug abuse or homosexual acts as the likely source of their infection, such individuals would be far less likely to seek help or be frank about their behavior. Therefore, in 1985, to obtain more accurate epidemiological data, the military enunciated a policy providing servicepersons immunity from criminal sanctions brought against them on the basis of information obtained during epidemiological assessment (26). This policy was intended not to offer servicepersons with HIV who used intravenous drugs or were homosexual complete immunity from prosecution, but rather to balance the military's need for information with its previous policy of prohibiting homosexuality and nonmedical drug use (27). Servicepersons still could be administratively discharged or, if evidence of homosexual acts was obtained from an independent source, prosecuted on the basis of this information.

The Army responded differently to this new policy than the Navy and Air Force. Army physicians obtained epidemiological data from soldiers with HIV and, instead of reporting them, in most instances allowed them to remain on active duty. In the Air Force and Navy, on the other hand, few servicepersons with HIV divulged that they were homosexual or used drugs, but it was understood that if they so disclosed, they would be subject to administrative discharge (28).

The degree to which infected servicepersons with HIV in the Army were willing to disclose that they were homosexual is controversial. Military investigators reported that 15 of 41 patients with HIV at Walter Reed Army Medical Center were heterosexual (29) and also stated that they were unaware of "any evidence" that soldiers were more likely than civilians to lie to their personal physicians (30). Others, however, questioned both claims, because they believed that the percentage of homosexual persons in the military was likely to be similar to that in civilian populations (31).

On October 14, 1986, Congress extended the protection afforded infected servicepersons by prohibiting the military from taking any adverse actions, including involuntary separation, against them on the basis of information obtained from these servicepersons during epidemiological assessment (32). Servicepersons still could be prosecuted if evidence of homosexual activity was obtained independently, and under this law they also could be denied security status on the basis of disclosures that they were homosexual or used intravenous drugs.

The latter exception was controversial. Deputy Defense Secretary William H. Taft IV considered this exception the "least intrusive means" of protecting the national interest. Senior members of the House Judiciary Committee, however, felt that denying servicepersons security status on the basis of their disclosures "guaranteed" that information necessary to save lives would not be available (33).

On April 20, 1987, the military addressed an additional important issue and enacted a memorandum delineating military physicians' responsibilities to protect third parties (34). Military physicians who encountered servicepersons with HIV were required under this memorandum to inform people with whom the infected individuals shared needles or had sex if these contacts were both identified and beneficiaries of military medical care. If either condition was absent, military physicians were required only to pursue actions required by state law.

Issues of disclosure and epidemiology also arise, of course, in civilian settings (35). Some considerations differ in the military, however, such as the military's need to maintain servicepersons' health and battle-readiness and its obligations to provide dependents with medical care.

In an effort to protect third parties further, the Department of Defense issued a directive on August 4, 1988, requiring commanders to counsel servicepersons with HIV and to order them to avoid infecting others. The directive stated: "It will be made clear to the individual that ignoring counseling, and knowingly risking the transmission of HIV to others at a later time, may result in administrative or disciplinary action" (36).

The Air Force implemented this directive by issuing a policy on December 13, 1988, that required Air Force servicepersons with HIV to sign this statement:

> Although I may have no symptoms presently, I may still transmit this infection to others through sexual intercourse, sharing of needles, donated blood products, and possibly exposure of others through saliva, oral genital contact, or intimate kissing. I have been informed the transmission of HIV infection through intercourse can be avoided only through abstinence. If I cannot abstain, then I must engage only in protected sexual relationships, i.e., using a condom. (37)

At this time, at least six servicepersons with HIV have been prosecuted for engaging in unsafe sex (38). Three of these cases have had appellate review (38–40). In one case, *U.S. v. Woods* (39), the court addressed the legal relevance, if any, of victims "consenting" to unprotected sex. The court decided that victims could not consent:

> Where conduct constitutes a crime because it causes or threatens bodily harm, the law as a matter of public policy will allow a victim's consent to be effective only if the conduct to which the consent refers does not cause or threaten serious bodily harm or death. . . . [As in] prosecution for statutory rape, the apparent consent of the female is no defense. In order to protect the female victim, even from herself, the law regards her as incapable of giving effective consent.

In a second case, *U.S. v. Johnson* (38), the court addressed the question of what charge(s) would be appropriate when a serviceperson with HIV knowingly engaged in unsafe sex. In a footnote, the court, quoting from a legal treatise (41), cited this analogy: "The victim of an HIV assault [is comparable] to an individual handcuffed to a briefcase full of explosives. The briefcase may never explode or it may explode and maim the victim or it may kill." The court then noted that "the analogy can be extended a step further. If the assailant does not inform the victim of his infection, it is as if the victim is handcuffed to the briefcase but does not even know the potentially lethal briefcase is there!"

Addressing the "proper charging of AIDS-related misconduct," this court declared:

> The range of possibilities is wide, from attempted murder to assault, and it encompasses the possibility of pleading AIDS as an aggravating factor in such crimes as sodomy or adultery. . . . In military law, such disparate items as a meat fork, tape recorder, cowboy belt, or a United States Marine recruit are means [likely to produce death or dangerous harm] if used in the requisite way. Viewed in light of these precedents we are convinced that semen carrying the HIV virus indeed can be a means to commit aggravated assault.

MILITARY PSYCHIATRISTS' OBLIGATION TO GIVE SERVICEPERSONS ADVANCED WARNINGS

In all of the situations described above, military psychiatrists could give servicepersons advance warning that they might violate their confidentiality (35). It could be assumed that because all servicepersons know that military doctors *might* violate their confidentiality, no warning is necessary. Yet, because military physicians to such an overwhelming extent have respected servicepersons' confidentiality in the past, servicepersons have at least this reason for believing that military psychiatrists will continue to maintain it.

Legally, it is unclear when, if ever, military psychiatrists must warn servicepersons that they might report them. Under specific, exceptional circumstances, which shortly will be discussed, psychiatrists, as all military authorities, probably are required to warn servicepersons under Article 31(b) of the UCMJ, the military equivalent of civilians' *Miranda* warning. This article states:

> No person subject to this code may interrogate or request any statement from an accused or a person suspected of an offense

> without first informing them of the nature of the accusation and advising them that they do not have to make any statement regarding the offense of which they are accused or suspected and that any statement they make may be used as evidence against them in a trial by court martial. (42)

The rationale for establishing Article 31(b) is important to understanding its present application. It was enacted at a time when the *Miranda* warning was "almost unknown in American courts" (43), because there was concern that servicepersons were exceptionally subject to responding to what they believed their military superiors would want them to say. The warning was primarily intended to remind servicepersons that when they faced circumstances of "presumptive coercion, implicit in military discipline and authority," they could remain silent (43).

However, the drafters intentionally left the question of who was required to give Article 31(b) warnings unresolved, so that military courts subsequently could determine these requirements (43). In 1981, the Court of Military Appeals provided two tests for deciding when a person must give Article 31(b) warnings. Warnings were required when a person subject to the code is acting in an official capacity and when the person who would be warned perceives that the inquiry involves more than a casual conversation (44).

In *U.S. v. McClelland* (45), the court applied these two tests in a case involving a military social worker. It held that the social worker was acting not to assist a family but rather as an investigator when he met with the accused and his wife and inquired about alleged sexual abuse. The serviceperson's wife had called the psychiatry clinic and described a problem of child sexual abuse or words to that effect. The social worker then made an appointment with the couple and, when he saw them, asked the serviceperson to tell him about the problem. The serviceperson, believing that the discussion was confidential, replied that he had "fondled his daughter's genitals." The social worker then did not pursue the matter further but suggested that the serviceperson seek legal counsel and notified military law enforcement personnel of the serviceperson's "confession."

The court, applying the first part of the above test, stated, "We believe that any reasonable person given the same information would have concluded that the appellee was suspected of having committed a criminal offense." Applying the second part, the court declared, "The dichotomy of rank between the parties coupled with the tenor of the meeting indicate that the appellee's perception of the event was considerably more than that of a casual conversation." Accordingly, the court ruled that the social worker's failure to warn the serviceperson of his Article 31(b) rights warranted suppression of the serviceperson's confession.

In an earlier case, *U.S. v. Hill* (46), the court also held that the statements of the accused to a social worker were not admissible because the record failed to establish that the social worker had warned the serviceperson of his Article 31(b) rights before questioning him about the alleged offense.

Military psychiatrists probably are required to give Article 31(b) warnings, then, in any instance in which they are acting in an official capacity and when the conversation may be perceived as investigatory, therapeutic, or confidential, as opposed to casual. Psychiatrists and others may be excused from the requirement, however, if, by not giving a warning to the patient, they might save a third person's life or ensure the public safety. The rationale underlying this exception is similar in principle to the *Tarasoff* case (47) and its progeny (48). That is, the psychiatrist may violate the patient's confidentiality without warning the patient when this is necessary to protect a third party.

The Military Court of Appeals, citing a Supreme Court holding (49), articulated this exception in *U.S. v. Jones* (50). In this case, a serviceperson had just killed a man and told a desk sergeant in a military police station, "I stabbed him." The sergeant, thinking that the serviceperson wanted to get the victim medical attention, asked the serviceperson the victim's location without advising the serviceperson of his Article 31(b) rights. The evidence obtained as a result of the serviceperson's disclosure was admissible on the basis of this exception.

In light of the case precedents regarding military social workers (45,46), servicepersons who engage in illegal acts and come to military psychiatrists for treatment have rights to *Miranda*-like warnings that civilian patients under comparable circumstances lack. Military psychiatrists who know of these precedents and value confidentiality absolutely, as when they do not report servicepersons, could protect such servicepersons from effective prosecution by *not* warning them. Thus, a military psychiatrist can undermine the validity of a case by *failing* to issue a warning.

PRIVILEGE

Psychotherapist-patient privilege is limited in the military. Servicepersons' communications to psychiatrists may have to be disclosed in court in several situations, such as when servicepersons undergo compulsory forensic examinations and when servicepersons have been treated under circumstances unrelated to the court proceeding but that later become relevant (22).

When military psychiatrists conduct forensic examinations to determine whether servicepersons were sane when they committed a crime, servicepersons cannot raise the insanity defense and then remain silent. The rationale for requiring servicepersons who claim insanity to waive the right against self-incrimination is that if offenders raised this defense but refused to cooperate with government-appointed psychiatrists, it would place the prosecution at too great a disadvantage.

This solution, referred to as the *forfeiture sanction,* is more "harsh" than the approaches taken by most civilian courts (51). More "mild" solutions in civilian practice include barring testimony from a defendant's own psychiatrist or permitting a defendant's psychiatrist to testify, but allowing the prosecution to comment on the defendant's noncooperation (51).

When military doctors testify, however, they can only divulge information necessary to show the basis for their psychiatric conclusions (52). This limitation on psychiatrists' disclosures, common also in civilian settings (53), is intended to limit the disadvantage to defendants resulting from their waiving of the right against self-incrimination.

These "compromise" resolutions to the conflicting interests of prosecutors and criminal defendants are controversial, however. In *U.S. v. Babbidge* (54), a 1969 military case, the U.S. Military Court of Appeals held that once the accused "opened his mind to prove insanity, . . . this action constituted a qualified waiver of his right to remain silent." Judge Ferguson, dissenting, stated: "I believe the privilege of self-incrimination, guaranteed by the Fifth Amendment of the Constitution, is *unqualified* and transcends any needs of the government to enhance its prosecutorial evidence."

Impact of Military Rules on Confidentiality and Privilege

A study recently has been conducted on Army psychiatrists' views of the impact of limited confidentiality and privilege on their practices (22). These psychiatrists first were given a hypothetical case involving a male patient who admitted to sexually abusing his daughter and were asked whether they would report it. This offense is the same crime for which the court required military care providers to give an Article 31(b) warning in the two cases previously discussed. Of the respondents, 98% indicated that they would report the incident; only 80% would report it, however, if the child was no longer at risk.

The doctors also were asked the degree, if any, to which they warned servicepersons regarding the limits of confidentiality. Twenty-five percent told servicepersons they saw for medical reasons that commanders had access to their psychiatric records if they had a need to know. Ten percent gave servicepersons a preprinted form explaining the limits of confidentiality before beginning treatment, but 20% gave no advice at all unless an issue involving confidentiality arose.

The psychiatrists also were asked how, generally, they thought the limitations on confidentiality and privilege affected psychotherapy. Seventy-four percent said that they saw little or no effect on their ability to treat patients, although some among this group indicated that as a result of these limitations, they reduced some of their inquiries, particularly regarding homosexuality. Others stated that limited confidentiality and privilege seriously impaired effective psychotherapy and that servicepersons—especially officers—avoided seeking help because they understood that confidentiality was limited.

On the basis of these findings, the study's authors argued that a limited-use policy, like the one for servicepersons with problems of substance abuse, should be extended to all servicepersons seeking psychiatric care, except for those suspected of child abuse and those who posed a threat to national security. To be consistent, these authors probably should have added, along with the first exception, servicepersons who pose a serious threat of harm or death to any third party.

The conclusions that can be drawn on the basis of this study are limited, however. Child abuse also must be reported, for example, in civilian settings, but comparable data from civilian psychiatrists are missing. The authors reported two studies involving civilian psychiatrists' views, but neither study is closely analogous.

In one of the studies, however, therapists in California, describing the effects of *Tarasoff*, suggested that limited confidentiality would inhibit patients' disclosures. This speculation is similar to Army psychiatrists' belief that limited confidentiality in the military inhibits servicepersons from coming for treatment. Yet it is unclear that this effect must occur in the military. As already indicated, in the vast majority of clinical interactions, military psychiatrists *can* protect their patients' confidentiality.

Conclusion

Military regulations, if taken literally, would appear to require military psychiatrists to report all illegal conduct of servicepersons that comes to their attention. Yet, in view of the military's nonaction against any military physician for not reporting such servicepersons, in actuality, the obligation is more theoretical than real. Military psychiatrists may misinterpret their obligations and warn servicepersons, needlessly, that if servicepersons disclose illegal behavior such as homosexual acts, they would have to report them. It is not necessary for the military to extend its limited-use policy, which applies to substance abuse, to all servicepersons receiving psychotherapy to create a more trusting atmosphere. In fact, it can be accomplished now, where it does not exist already—at little cost to servicepersons' autonomy—if military physicians clearly understand that they lack an actual obligation to report and inform servicepersons accordingly.

Extending the limited-use policy to servicepersons with psychiatric problems other than substance abuse would not significantly change most military psychiatrists' practices. Even under the current limited-use policy, care providers must violate a patient's confidentiality whenever there is a significant risk to third parties or to the military. Furthermore, if the limited-use policy regarding substance abuse were extended to cover all psychotherapy, reporting requirements would be more explicit. It could be argued that this change would be beneficial because these decisions are too important to be left to a psychiatrist's individual discretion (55). However, the absence of explicit reporting requirements, as exists under the current system, allows military psychiatrists greater freedom and flexibility to tailor their responses to individual servicepersons' needs.

When servicepersons pose a serious threat to third parties or to the military, and when the limited-use policy (which does require reporting) does not apply, military physicians face a genuine quandary. If they give these servicepersons advance warning that they might report them, the servicepersons would be less likely to incriminate themselves and more likely to cause serious harm. For example, if an HIV infected serviceperson was having unprotected sex without informing his or her partner, by warning the serviceperson the military psychiatrist might lose the opportunity to contact and protect the third party.

In some cases, for military psychiatrists to lose this opportunity would be tragic. Yet, their only other choice would be to deceive patients knowingly. If military psychiatrists deceive these servicepersons, they would violate the servicepersons' dignity. This practice would seem to conflict with the intent of those who drafted Article 31(b), as previously discussed. The drafters of Article 31(b) established the protection against self-incrimination to enhance servicepersons' dignity, despite the obvious cost to prosecutors' interests.

Further, by providing advance warning rather than deceiving servicepersons in this situation, military psychiatrists might not only meet these servicepersons' best interests, but, in net effect, the military's overall good as well. Military psychiatrists' primary functions, as noted, are to maintain a unit's health and to have accurate information regarding it—not to serve as informants. They can accomplish these objectives only if they preserve servicepersons' trust. This would best be achieved if military psychiatrists tell serviceperson/patients when they will not report them and warn them when they might.

NOTES

1. Auster SL: Confidentiality in military medicine. Milit Med 150:341–346, 1985
2. Ursano RJ, Jones DR: The individual's vs. the organization's doctor? Value conflict in psychiatric aeromedical evaluation. Aviat Space Environ Med 11:704–706, 1981
3. Uniform Code of Military Justice, Article 92
4. Uniform Code of Military Justice, Article 134
5. U.S. v Reed, 24 MJ 80 (CMA 1987); see also U.S. v Tyson, 2 MJ 583 (NCMR 1976) and Laws Applicable to All Department of Defense Personnel, AFR 30-30, Attachment 3, n3, 21 June 1983, regarding the 18 USC 4 (misprision of a felony). This crime is applied to the military in U.S. v Assey, 9 CMR 732 (1952) and U.S. v Maclin, 27 CMR 590 (1958).
6. cf, United States v Thompson, 22 MJ 40 (CMA 1986), in which the court addressed the duty of a noncommissioned officer to prevent the crime of another serviceperson's smoking marijuana. The court concluded, "in the absence of an identifiable regulation, directive, or custom of the service which would provide notice to noncommissioned officers of the *legal* requirements to which they are subject, we are reluctant to approve criminal sanctions under Article 92(3) for failure to perform a general unspecified duty to 'prevent' crime" (at 41); and United States v Delaney, 16 MLR 2241 (AFCMR 1988), in which the court addressed the failure of an Air Force woman to report homosexual conduct between two other women in her apartment. The court declared, "Suspicion that

perhaps some offense was taking place behind closed doors is not enough to place a duty on appellant that she report this equivocal relationship to higher authority" (at 2242).
7. U.S. v Heyward, 22 MJ 35 (CMA 1986)
8. Howe EG: Medical ethics—are they different for the military physician? Milit Med 146:837–841, 1981
9. Parrish MD: A veteran of three wars looks at psychiatry in the military. Psychiatric Opinion 9:6–11, 1972
10. Pursch JA: Drug abuse in the armed forces: an indicator of suitability, fitness or motivation for duty. Milit Med 137: 188–190, 1972
11. 21 USC § 1175, transferred by Pub L 98-24, § 2(b) (16) (B), 97 Stat 182, (April 26, 1983) to 42 USC § 290ee–3(a)
12. United States v Howes, 22 MJ 704 (ACMR 1986)
13. Alcohol and Drug Abuse Prevention and Control Program. Army Regulation 600-85, Washington, DC, Hdqs Dept of the Army, Nov 3, 1986
14. Kallen LH, Grodin DM, Vinet RG: Legal aspects of alcohol abuse in the Navy. Behavioral Sciences and the Law 7:355–377, 1989
15. Uniform Code of Military Justice, Article 125
16. In Gayer v Schlesinger, 490 F2d 740, 747 n14, an official of a security clearance program was asked "whether [the] criminality of other kinds of sexual activity proscribed by statute—such as fornication, heterosexual sodomy, adultery—were offered the same treatment [as homosexual conduct]." He answered that they were not unless there was specific reason to suspect the activity might render the individual susceptible to blackmail.
17. C4 AR 635-200, Sept 1, 1981, Chapter 15, Separation for Homosexuality, § 1. 15-2 Policy a
18. High Tech Gays v Defense Industrial Security Clearance Office, 668 F Supp 1361 (ND Cal 1987)
19. Hearings before the Permanent Subcommittee on Investigations of the Committee on Governmental Affairs, U.S. Senate, 99th Cong, 1st Sess, Federal Government Security Clearance Programs, Appendix: FBI testimony before Senate Permanent Subcommittee on Investigations/Financial distress/Greed, pp 171–178, and United States Memorandum, Dec 3, 1984, Espionage directed against the United States, pp 913–926, 1985
20. Watkins v United States Army, No 85-4006, U.S. Ct App 9th Cir, May 3, 1989; summarized in The gay sergeant, American Bar Association Journal 79:92, 1989. But see Army can deny admitted homosexuals the right to re-enlist. The United States Law Week 58:1034, 1989; and Armed forces/re-enlistment, Ben-Shalom v Marsh, CA7, No 88-2771, Aug 7, 1989. The United States Law Week 58:2118–2119, 1989. See also Watkins v United States Army, 837 F2d 1428 (9th Cir 1988).
21. Howe EG: Ethical issues regarding mixed agency of military physicians. Soc Sci Med 23:803–813, 1986
22. Hayden DL: Should there be a psychotherapist privilege in military court-martials? Military Law Review 123:31–107, 1989
23. U.S. Air Force Regulation 168-4, Administration of Medical Activities,

Section D, Safeguarding and Releasing Medical Information, and Laws Affecting Disclosure, Chapter 12.6, Art 12-35, April 1987; U.S. Army Regulation 40-66, Medical Research and Quality Assurance Administration, Chapter 2, Confidentiality of Medical Information, Jan 31, 1985, Update; and NAVMED U.S. Navy Medical Command P-117 Manual of the Medical Department, Chapter 23: Reports, Forms, and Records, Section III, Release of Information From Records, Art 70-79, Nov 25, 1980

24. U.S. Air Force Regulation 168-4, Chapter 12-28: "Release to OSI:. . . . (c.) Before providing access to the records, they are reviewed by DBMS or his designee"
25. Smith P: Navy forces out victims who admit homosexual contact. Navy Times, Aug 26, 1985 at 4. cf, Howe EG: Trust between military physicians and servicepersons with HIV: implications for civilian medicine. Biolaw 2:5:101–112, 1988; and Howe EG: Confidentiality in the military. Behavioral Sciences and the Law 7:317–338, 1989
26. Memorandum from the Secretary of Defense, Policy on Identification, Surveillance and Disposition of Military Personnel Affected with HTLV-III (Oct 24, 1985)
27. Norman C: Military AIDS testing offers research bonus. Science 232:818–820, 1986
28. Howe EG: Ethical problems in treating military patients with human immunodeficiency diseases. Journal of Contemporary Health Law and Policy 3:111–149, 1987
29. Redfield RR, Markham PD, Salahuddin SZ, et al: Heterosexually acquired HTLV-III/LAV disease (AIDS)–related complex and AIDS: epidemiologic evidence for female-to-male transmission. JAMA 254:2094–2096, 1985
30. Redfield RR, Wright DC, Markham PD, et al: Letters/female-to-male transmission of HTLV-III. JAMA 255:1705–1706, 1986
31. Potterat JJ, Phillips L, Muth JB: Letters: lying to military physicians about risk factors for HIV infections. JAMA 257:1727, 1987. See, generally, Forde RJ: Letters: homosexuality, confidentiality and the military. JAMA 258:202–203, 1987.
32. National Defense Authorization Act for Fiscal Year 1987, PL 99-661, Division A, Title 7, § 705c (1986) codified in 10 USC 1074
33. Maze R: Hill, services debate [adverse actions] after confidential interviews. Navy Times, June 29, 1987 at 3; cf, in a case just decided by the United States Court of Appeals Sixth Circuit: the wife of an Air Force Sergeant who held a high-security position sought psychological advice from a civilian psychologist employed at an Air Force base regarding her husband's excessive use of alcohol and marijuana. After the psychologist sought advice from a military psychiatrist, the psychiatrist informed the spouse that the psychiatrist must report known or suspected drug use to military authorities, and subsequently did so. The wife sued for breach of confidentiality. The court stated, as dicta, that "[t]he risk that a person in such a position may be compromised would likely

override the requirement of confidentiality in this case. Howes v U.S. (U.S. Court of App, 6th Cir) No 88-4168; decided Oct 19, 1989 at 9.

34. Secretary of Defense Memorandum, Policy on Identification, Surveillance and Administration of Personnel Infected With Human Immunodeficiency Virus (HIV), April 20, 1987
35. Howe EG: Military physicians' legal and ethical obligations to third parties when treating servicepersons infected with HIV (human immunodeficiency virus). AIDS and Public Policy Journal 2:46–62, 1987; see also Howe EG: Ethical aspects of military physicians treating patients with HIV, Part 3: the duty to protect third parties. Milit Med 153:140–144, 1988.
36. Secretary of Defense Memorandum, Policy on Identification, Surveillance and Disposition of Military Personnel Affected With Human Immunodeficiency Virus (HIV), Aug 4, 1988
37. Policy on Identification, Surveillance, and Administration of Personnel Infected With Human Immunodeficiency Virus (HIV), Department of the Air Force, Dec 13, 1988
38. U.S. v Johnson, 27 MJ 798 (AFCMR 1988)
39. U.S. v Woods, 27, MJ 749 (NMCMR 1988)
40. U.S. v Womack, 27 MJ 630 (AFCMR 1988)
41. Wells-Petry M: Anatomy of an AIDS case: deadly disease as an aspect of deadly crime. Army Lawyer, Jan 1988, pp 17–26
42. Uniform Code of Military Justice, Art 31
43. United States v Gibson, 3 USC MA 746, 14 CMR 164 (1954). See, generally, Morris JR: Rights warnings in the military: an article 31(b) update. Military Law Review 115:261–294, 1987; and Supervielle MEF: Article 31(b): who should be required to give warnings? Military Law Review 123:151–214, 1989.
44. U.S. v Duqa, 10 MJ 206 (CMA 1981)
45. U.S. v McClelland, 26 MJ (CMA 1988)
46. U.S. v Hill, 13 MJ 882 (ACMR 1982)
47. Tarasoff v Regents of University of California, 17 Cal 3d 425, 551 P2d 334, 131 Cal Rptr 14 (1976)
48. McCarty CB: Patient threats against third parties: the psychotherapist's duty of reasonable care. Journal of Contemporary Health Law and Policy 5:119–140, 1989 at 130–133, and particularly 130, n. 74
49. New York v Quarles, 467 US 649, 104 S Ct 2626, 81 L Ed 2d 550 (1984)
50. U.S. v Jones, 19 MJ 961 (ACMR 1985)
51. Brooks AD: Law and Psychiatry in the Criminal Justice System. Boston, MA, Little, Brown (in press)
52. Rule 302—Privilege concerning mental examination of an accused, in Manual for Courts-Martial. Washington, DC, U.S. Government Printing Office, 1984, at A22-7-9. See also Saltzburg SA, Schinasi LD, Schlueter DA: Military Rules of Evidence Manual. Charlottesville, VA, The Michie Co, 1981, at 89–101. Communications between psychiatrists and serviceperson/patients may, however, be protected under the attorney-client privilege if psychiatrists are used by the defense only to assist in

preparation of an insanity defense. U.S. v Toledo, 25 MJ 270 (CMA 1987) at 275.

53. U.S. v Parker, 15 MJ 146 (CMA 1983)
54. U.S. v Babbidge, 18 USCMA 327, 40 CMR 39 (1969)
55. Beauchamp T, Childress J: Principles of Biomedical Ethics, 2nd Edition. New York, Oxford University Press, 1982, at 233

Features

Recent Legal Developments and Psychiatry

Steven B. Bisbing, Psy.D., J.D.

The Canadian Connection: A Canadian Perspective on Clinical Psychiatry and the Law

Selwyn M. Smith, M.D.

Expert Opinion: A Case of Tardive Dyskinesia

Thomas G. Gutheil, M.D.
Robert L. Sadoff, M.D.

The Psychiatrist in the Courtroom: Suicide Litigation

Jeffrey D. Robertson, J.D.
Robert I. Simon, M.D.

Chapter 10

Recent Legal Developments and Psychiatry

Steven B. Bisbing, Psy.D., J.D.

The law is constantly changing to reflect current social attitudes; to incorporate developments by professional bodies, such as psychiatry and medicine; and to redress outdated ideas, theories, and mores. This chapter is intended to identify some of the recent legal cases and statutes that are either of national or regional significance to psychiatric practice or of general interest to psychiatrists.

Although few landmark decisions in general are rendered each year, let alone in mental health law, some cases significant to psychiatric practice do not involve psychiatrists as parties. For example, cases involving surgeons, family physicians, or psychologists may address a rule of law, a clinical issue, or a medicolegal topic that is similar to or applicable to an area of psychiatric practice. Because of the general "cross-application" of cases to many health care providers, knowledge of these cases is of value to the psychiatric practitioner. I have included some cases in this chapter because they represent an interesting "twist" in judicial thinking, because the underlying facts of the case are unusual, or because the decision is particularly well written and thought-provoking.

In terms of the application of the cases and statutes listed and their "authoritative value" across the country, the following rule of thumb applies: *Only* cases rendered by the United States Supreme Court must be followed by the courts in every jurisdiction. *All other* cases, state and federal, have precedential value only in the jurisdiction they cover. In other words, courts not within the jurisdiction of the court in which a case opinion is published *may* choose to—but are not required to—follow its conclusions. The cases selected in this chapter, unless otherwise noted, generally have legal authority only in the state or federal jurisdiction in which the decision was rendered. Still, all of the cases selected do illustrate some medicolegal principle or issue typically applicable to the common laws of most states, unless otherwise noted.

Consistent with my practice in Volume 1 of this series, I have organized the case law and statutes under subheadings:

I. Civil law—professional practice
II. Civil law—liability and standard of care
III. Criminal law
IV. Ethics and professional conduct
V. Hospitals/institutional care
VI. Patient rights
VII. Expert testimony
VIII. Legislation (see Appendix)

Because of page constraints, only a selection of cases can be reported. Readers are welcome to submit cases or legislation reported in 1989–90 for consideration in Volume 3 of the *American Psychiatric Press Review of Clinical Psychiatry and the Law.* Also, comments regarding any aspect of this chapter would be appreciated.

I. CIVIL LAW—PROFESSIONAL PRACTICE

Various private and inpatient practice measures concerning hospital privileges, Medicaid reimbursement rights, medication prescription rights, and the legal right to diagnose and treat organic disorders dominate the health care agendas of at least 12 states and Congress. The debate, lobbying, and aggressive public advocacy conducted by psychiatrists and psychologists before state legislatures, state regulatory agencies, and the courts seem to have risen to a fever pitch.

At the heart of the controversy is the contention by members of the medical community—particularly the American Psychiatric Association—that the diagnosis and treatment of mental disorders, especially those of an organic origin, should be provided only by professionals trained in medicine. Psychiatrists maintain that to allow other professional groups, such as psychologists, to provide such services would deprive patients of competent care or at least impede delivery of such care. This conclusion is well illustrated in a recent complaint filed by psychiatrists with the Florida State Board of Psychological Examiners. The complaint challenged psychologists' right to diagnose, stating, in part, that

> Authorizing psychologists to perform the medical acts included within the terms "diagnosis and treatment" will seriously, materi-

> ally and substantially impair the ability of psychiatric physicians to deliver qualified and competent medical care for their patients and to the general public by delaying consultations with competent physicians or totally avoiding such consultations. The result will be less competent delivery of care to those patients, greater incidence of misdiagnosis of mental illness and emotional disorders, as well as organic disorders that manifest as mental and emotional disorders, all to the detriment of those patients and the general public.(1)

Yet according to a spokesperson for the American Psychological Association, the case represents a lot more than a concern for quality patient care. An equally significant issue, the psychology association alleged, was that psychiatrists are trying to narrow the economic market regarding who can provide mental health services (2). Whether or not this conclusion is accurate, the stakes are high, particularly for psychologists who wish to gain a measure of parity with their psychiatric and medical colleagues in hospitals and other inpatient settings. In no fewer than 12 states, bills or court decisions are pending on the scope of mental health patient practice and whether it involves psychologists (3). The states involved and a summary of the pending actions are listed and discussed below.

Alabama

A bill has been introduced allowing psychologists to admit patients into hospitals, with the provision that requires "effective communications between psychologists and physicians." At stake is the receipt of insurance reimbursement (by psychologists) for the work they do with these patients.

California

Probably nowhere else is the controversy over the parameters of clinical practice between psychiatrists and psychologists being more contested than it is in California. In *California Association of Psychology Providers (CAPP) v. Rank,* the state's Department of Health Services issued regulations in 1983 that conflicted with a state law (4) that had established the rights of hospitals to extend staff privileges to psychologists. The psychologists promptly challenged the department's regulations (5), and a trial court ruled in favor of CAPP. The state medical association and local psychiatric groups appealed that ruling.

From a practical standpoint, the legal issue was whether psychologists were permitted, under a new California statute, to exercise extensive inpatient hospital practice privileges. The case, interestingly, was first brought because some hospitals were granting psychologists privileges and others were not, and CAPP maintained that the code required that all hospitals in the state permit psychologists practice privileges. A significant issue in the case was the meanings of *diagnose* and *diagnosis* according to the state code. Although the state health and safety code authorized psychologists to "diagnose" psychological problems and mental disorders, the appeals court, in overturning the initial decision, concluded that these words were not defined in that context. The appeals court concluded that psychologists were not competent to make "organic diagnoses." Accordingly, the court held that psychologists could only work with patients after psychiatrists had determined that there was no possibility of "organic involvement" in the condition being treated and that there was no probability of need for somatic treatments during the course of a patient's illness.

In essence, this opinion can be interpreted as stating that psychologists are not qualified to diagnose or treat organic problems, and therefore should not be allowed to practice independently in hospitals. The California Supreme Court has decided to hear the CAPP case, with a decision to be rendered sometime during the summer of 1990. Commentators following this case are fairly well agreed that although the case technically has authority only in California, it is likely to be a harbinger of hospital privilege trends elsewhere.

Connecticut

A bill was introduced earlier this year requiring that anyone who "diagnoses and treats illness" have a medical degree. This bill was killed in committee and is not expected to be reintroduced.

Florida

A challenge by the state psychiatric association regarding psychology licensing law permitting psychologists to diagnose and treat organic complaints was made in early 1989. It is reported that this issue has been before the psychology regulatory board for months without any sign of resolution (3).

Hawaii

A bill, supported by the state medical association, has been introduced in the legislature requiring that individuals in workers' compensation cases be referred by a physician to receive psychological services. This bill was strongly opposed by the state's psychological association and apparently has died in committee.

In a similar action, some Hawaii state legislators failed in 1988 in an attempt to make their state the first to grant psychologists the right to prescribe psychoactive medication for treating mental illness (6). It is notable that in Hawaii all bills have a 2-year life, and therefore this bill or an amended version of it could be reintroduced.

Maryland

A bill permitting psychologists to practice in Maryland hospitals passed the state Senate but died when the House failed to vote on it before adjournment for 1989. The bill was written to give psychologists the right to practice independently in a hospital so long as physicians do not object. If, in a particular hospital, physicians were to object to the independent practice of psychologists, a "collaborative" team would then be established. This bill is given an excellent chance of passing in the 1990 legislative session.

Massachusetts

State psychiatric and psychological associations are negotiating a provision in a bill that would allow psychologists to co-admit patients with psychiatrists.

New Jersey

A hospital privilege bill for psychologists has been introduced but is given little chance of passage this year.

New York

In an effort to trim the state budget, the governor sought to eliminate psychologists from private Medicaid reimbursement. This proposal was defeated, leaving intact an existing system that allows both psychiatrists and psychologists to provide reimbursable mental health services.

Pennsylvania

A bill authorizing hospitals to allow psychologists on their staffs has been introduced but is given little chance of passing this year.

Tennessee

The state psychiatric association sought to exclude psychologists from diagnosing and treating a wide range of "medical mental disorders" but later dropped that provision from a mental health benefits bill. The existing bill still divides a whole range of mental disorders into three "medical" categories, despite psychologists' continued participation.

Texas

The state medical association is fighting a bill that would give hospitals the right to allow psychologists on their medical staffs. The medical association contends that psychologists should not practice in hospitals without the supervision of a physician. The legislature is said to be fairly evenly split on this bill.

State Cases

Numerous cases of lesser note but of state and regional appeal that illustrate some of the time-honored legal principles in medical jurisprudence continue to be decided annually. In *Chizmadia v. Smiley's Point Clinic* (7), the Minnesota Court of Appeals held that once physicians at an eye clinic had referred a patient to a specialist, the doctor-patient relationship between the clinic doctors and the patient had ceased. This case provides a good example of one of the rules underlying the doctor-patient relationship. That is, there must be a reasonable manifestation of the existence of a doctor-patient relationship for it to be deemed "established" for purposes of a malpractice action. This manifestation may be explicit (e.g., verbal exchange of expectation of reconvening treatment next week) or implicit (e.g., a prescription that will require monitoring). In the eye clinic case, the referral to another physician for more specialized treatment, without a reasonable indication by the referring doctor that additional care would later be provided by him, was held to signal that the relationship with the original provider was terminated.

Another issue that poses an occasional problem for the courts and malpractice litigants is determining what constitutes the "standard of care" by which the defendant's (e.g., physician's, psychiatrist) conduct will be assessed. For most psychiatrists and other's physicians, the standard by which their conduct is measured is in terms of the "average" practitioner in the professional class to which the defendant belongs (8). Other courts apply similar descriptions, such as "reasonably competent" (9) or "ordinary" (10) psychiatrist.

Problems can arise in determining "standard of care" when the practitioner—because of differences in experience, training, or education—is not an ordinary psychiatrist or physician. For example, in medicine, as in many professions, some specialists are considered "expert." Generally, the courts have held such specialists to the professional standards of other similarly situated members of the specialty or field in which they practice (11). For example, in *Justari v. Nappi* (12), a Pennsylvania appellate court ruled that a resident who was training to be a specialist should be held to an intermediate standard of care somewhere between that of a general practitioner and that of a specialist in the field for which the resident was training.

Another problem area—more of a historical anecdote today but still occasionally arising in the case law—is the evaluation of the standard of care in terms of the defendant's "geographical area." Using the "locality rule," courts years ago would narrowly formulate the standard of care in terms of the practices and procedures typical of the defendant's actual area of residence. Today only a handful of states still cling to this practice (13). The most common successor to the strict locality rule is a simple variation on the theme. That is, courts and legislatures hold that the standard of care should be based on the practice in the "same or similar locality" (14). A growing number of courts, however, reflective of a national trend, have attacked the locality rule and its variations directly and have concluded that there should be no geographic limitations on the standard of care, especially for specialists such as psychiatrists. Professionals—especially specialists, many courts contend—should be held to the level of care of members of the same specialty generally because their practice, education, and training are based on a national standard. A recent example of this thinking is reflected in *Shamburger v. Behrens* (15), in which the South Dakota Supreme Court adopted a national standard of care for medical specialists.

One area of medical practice, regardless of specialty, that historically has caused physicians problems with the law is when patient records are demanded by parties involved in litigation. This frequently comes up in some form of legal proceeding in which a psychiatrist's patient is involved, and the psychiatrist is issued a subpoena to release certain records, to testify, or to do both. As aptly explained in *Legal Issues in the Private Practice of Psychiatry* (16), psychiatrists or physicians sometimes have a legal responsibility to release certain patient records. This responsibility, as codified in the

American Psychiatric Association's *Principles of Medical Ethics With Annotations Especially Applicable to Psychiatry* (17), is clearly sanctioned when a competent patient provides an informed authorization or the psychiatrist is "under proper legal compulsion." The question for many psychiatrists is, What constitutes proper legal compulsion? "Although it issues from a court, a subpoena is not itself 'proper legal compulsion'" (18). A subpoena *compels* the designee to *appear,* not to testify. Similarly, in the case of a *subpoena duces tecum,* the designee is required to *bring* the designated records, but without an informed authorization from a competent patient or an order from the court (e.g., the judge), disclosure of patient records should be resisted (19).

The limits to which third parties (e.g., parties not related to litigation) may have access to a patient's records is another issue increasingly being addressed in the case law. For example, in an investigation of a psychiatrist's professional conduct, a New York trial court ruled that a subpoena issued by the Board of Professional Medical Conduct for the records of a second psychiatrist and a psychologist was improper (20). The court quashed the subpoena on the grounds that the requested records were not critical to the investigation, that the alleged misconduct was remote in time to the subsequent treatment, and that no relationship was established between the records sought and the allegation being investigated. A general rule of thumb governing the release of records in these situations is that without a patient's authorization, the need for the records must *outweigh* a patient's right to continued, confidential communications with the professional of his or her choice. This has historically been considered to weigh heavily in favor of confidentiality and to limit the circumstances in which it may be breached. Even in such circumstances, it is the psychiatrist's duty and within the authority of the court to *narrowly restrict* the release of confidential information to only that information directly relevant to the issues precipitating disclosure (21).

A recent case illustrating two of the legal exceptions to the physician-patient privilege is *New York v. Hawkrigg* (22). In it, the defendant, who was aware that he had AIDS, was charged with having sexual relations with a child. The court refused to dismiss a grand jury indictment against him based in part on his assertion that the submission of his medical records was a violation of the physician-patient privilege. The court ruled that even if the privilege existed, and despite an exception to the privilege in child abuse matters, it was waived by the defendant's disclosure of his condition to a number of third parties before the alleged act of deviant sexual intercourse.

In another case of unusual circumstance involving privilege, a federal district court held that a social worker's brief statements in a state court regarding his client's mental condition were absolutely protected (23). In this case, the social worker had treated a police officer and his wife in four marital counseling sessions. The social worker sued in small claims court for the payment of his professional fees, and the parties reached a settlement in which the officer agreed to pay $220 at a rate of $10 per month. A dispute over payment ensued, however, and the social worker requested a disclosure hearing to determine the officer's assets and ability to pay the debt. During the hearing in open court, the social worker revealed that he had diagnosed the officer as having depression. The officer then sued in federal court alleging that the social worker's comments constituted, among other things, slander and invasion of privacy. In granting the social worker's motion for summary judgment, the federal court ruled that the utterance of this diagnosis was protected from suit, as generally are all statements made in judicial proceedings. The court elaborated that any privilege that the officer might have had—such as withholding authorization to disclose confidential information—was superseded by judicial proceedings privilege from subsequent lawsuit or other adverse action.

II. Civil Law—Liability and Standard of Care

In 1987, the *Wall Street Journal* reported an attorney for the American Psychiatric Association as stating "lawyers for psychiatric and psychological groups advise members to consider *Tarasoff*-type lawsuits as an ever-present possibility" and that it was estimated that well over 100 such cases are pending, "two or three in every state" (24). Currently, this prediction has fallen far short in terms of the number of published and unpublished cases concerning malpractice involving the duty to warn. There is growing evidence, however, that the "duty to warn" *is* becoming more "ever present." For example, since 1987, there have been no fewer than 18 published or cited cases and 12 new statutes. Moreover, in tracking the development of duty to warn case and statutory law involving Tarasoff-like scenarios with mental health professionals, I have found to date no fewer than 48 published or cited opinions and 14 states with relevant statutes. This tally indicates that 31 jurisdictions have made some form of ruling regarding a mental health professional's duty to warn or protect endangered third parties from the potential risks posed by their patients (25) (see Appendix).

Between June 1988 and September 1989, several new cases and

statutes interpreting and applying the foundational tenets of *Tarasoff v. Regents of the University of California* (26) according to the laws of their jurisdiction were published.

Thirteen years of case law after the 1976 *Tarasoff* decision, courts and legislatures continue to add twists and turns to what has frequently been described as the most vexing psycholegal doctrine confronting therapists today. For example, in a recent Arizona case, *Hamman v. County of Maricopa*, the state supreme court refused to limit a psychiatrist's duty to protect third parties to only those instances in which a specific threat was made (27). Instead, the court expanded the scope of protection to include foreseeable victims that are in the "zone of danger" that is subject to probable risk of the patient's violent conduct. This case has been remanded (sent down to a lower court) for further proceedings to determine whether the defendant psychiatrist owed a duty to protect the patient's stepfather from an attack by the patient 2 days after the patient was sent home by the defendant.

In Colorado, the state supreme court, as in *Hamman*, rejected the relatively narrow identifiable threat–identifiable victim standard and concluded that a psychiatrist had a duty to exercise due care in determining whether an involuntarily committed psychiatric patient had a propensity for violence and would present an unreasonable risk of serious bodily harm to *others* if released (28). The court's opinion appears to expand the duty not only to identifiable victims but to the much broader "foreseeable" public if it is determined that the patient poses an "unreasonable risk of serious bodily harm" in general.

The *Hamman* opinion and others like it (29) ignore the well-documented fact that psychiatrists can neither "predict" future dangerousness nor "read" the thoughts and motives or "guarantee" the actions of their patients especially as time passes following discharge. In addition, expansive decisions such as *Hamman* and *Perreira* place professionals working in inpatient facilities in conflict with their ethical, clinical, and legal duty not to unreasonably confine a patient. The Colorado court appears to skirt these considerations in its conclusion that due weight should be given to extending the term of a patient's commitment or to placing appropriate conditions and restrictions on the patient's release. These options ignore the reality that there are scant resources or options for "conditioning and restricting" patients' release once they are discharged from a hospital.

A South Carolina appeals court, in a more reasonable and realistic opinion, concluded that a state psychiatrist did not owe a duty to warn a hospital patient's sister that the patient posed a risk to her

(*Rogers v. South Carolina Department of Mental Health*) (30). Following a hostile exchange between two sisters, the patient was admitted to the state hospital in July 1980. She was released 5 months later and was said to be doing well until August 1982, when her paranoid delusions reemerged, and she claimed that her sister was trying to poison her. Two weeks later she fatally shot her sister. The victim's representative filed a wrongful death action against the treating psychiatrist, alleging that he was negligent in failing to warn the decedent that the patient (her sister) might harm her. The appeals court rejected this claim, stating that the decedent had known about her sister's mental illness and potential for violence. Furthermore, there was no evidence that the patient had made specific threats against the sister while being treated by the defendant. It is interesting to note that this is the second "duty to warn" situation on which a South Carolina appellate court has ruled (31). In both cases, in addition to finding no duty owed, the court explicitly stated that "South Carolina law does not recognize a general duty to warn of the dangerous propensities of others" (32). Despite this holding, however, both of the South Carolina decisions imply that if a specific threat had been made toward a specific individual, South Carolina courts rule squarely in favor of a duty to warn.

Other recent duty to warn cases of note include a Sixth Circuit opinion, in *Sellers v. United States* (33), in which the court, interpreting Michigan law, found that a Veterans Administration hospital psychiatrist owed no duty to a third party injured by a patient with manic depression. In keeping with prevailing Michigan law (34), the court found that the psychiatrist had no duty to force a voluntary patient to remain confined and no duty to warn the general public. Instead, the duty to warn, as it applies in Michigan, is narrowly confined to readily identifiable potential victims. In *Sellers*, it was shown that the patient had never mentioned the victim to the psychiatrists and had not threatened the victim before the assault.

In Ohio, in *Littleton v. Good Samaritan Hospital & Health Center* (35), the state supreme court, in addressing the issue of when an *inpatient* psychiatrist might be held liable for releasing a patient who harms another person, concluded that such decisions must be evaluated in terms of the "professional judgment" applied in the case. In other words, a psychiatrist will not be held liable for releasing a patient who harms another person if, after carefully reviewing all of the relevant information, the psychiatrist made a good-faith professional medical judgment that the patient did not pose an immediate danger to others.

Two important distinctions underlie the *Littleton* opinion.

First, the court explicitly indicated that this opinion *did not* apply to outpatient treatment (36). Second, although the facts and underlying legal theory of this case are more appropriate to cases alleging "negligent release" or "failure to control," with no expressed allegation that an additional duty to warn someone was involved, the latter responsibility could become relevant if such a warning was, or should have been, part of a doctor's release plan but was not exercised. Under the professional judgment rule, however, liability for failing to warn could occur only in the absence of good faith or failure to exercise reasonable professional judgment.

When a new legal theory is adopted by a court or a court adds a different angle or twist to an existing theory or doctrine, claimants will often attempt to apply those "new theories" to their cases even when the facts are seemingly incompatible or significantly different. The *Tarasoff* decision and its progeny are good examples. Each year there are numerous cases in which *Tarasoff*-like "duty to warn" reasoning is applied to other, nonpsychotherapeutic situations, with varying success. For example, in *McCall v. Dept. of Health & Rehabilitative Services* (37), a Florida appellate court upheld a claim for failure to warn when one hospital inpatient was injured by another inpatient who was known to be dangerous, despite the lack of evidence of prior violence between the two patients. In *Eckhardt v. Kirts* (38), an Illinois court found that a psychiatrist had no duty to warn a husband about his wife's violent tendencies because the doctor was not made aware of any specific threats against the husband or any other foreseeable victims. Similarly, in *C.A.U. v. R.L.* (39), the court ruled that a man had no duty to warn his fiancée that he was infected with the AIDS virus, especially because confirmation of the disease was not made until after they had ceased having sexual intimacy. Last, the Massachusetts Supreme Judicial Court ruled in *A.L. v. Commonwealth* (40) that state and city officials were liable for their negligent failure to protect school children from a thrice-convicted child molester despite evidence that the defendants had no advance knowledge of the identity of specific victims.

Although cases involving the duty to warn appear to dominate much of the attention in psychiatric, mental health, and mental health law publications, cases involving the sexual exploitation of patients by health care providers continue to be filed at an increasing pace. Mental health professionals, principally psychiatrists and psychologists, continue to be the primary defendants in these cases, but these lawsuits extend beyond these professions and are not exclusively "psychotherapy" or "mental health" problems. For example, recent cases alleging some form of sexual exploitation of a fiduciary relationship have included the clergy (41), a chiropractor (42), a gynecologist (43), a general physician (44), a nurse (45), and a nun (46).

From the early strictures of Hippocrates (47) to the current code of medical ethics for psychiatrists (48), the medical and mental health professions have held that sexual contact between doctor or psychotherapist and patient is unethical. Despite the historic prohibition and the potential for lawsuits, criminal prosecution, and professional disciplinary action, some psychiatrists and other professionals continue to abuse and exploit their patients. There were far too many relevant cases in 1989 to summarize here, but a few are especially worth noting.

A New Jersey appellate court, in *Cosgrove v. Lawrence* (49) held that a mental health facility may not be held vicariously liable for the conduct of one of its therapists who engaged in sexual relations with a patient. In general, a hospital or facility is viewed as the sum of numerous individuals participating in a common enterprise (e.g., provision of mental health services). As a result, the primary source of hospital or institution liability is "vicarious," arising from the individual actions of the specific employees who injure a patient. For a vicarious liability to be upheld, however, three elements typically must be met. First, the alleged malfeasance must have been within the scope of an employee's professional duties; second, the malfeasance must have occurred within work-related limits of time and place; and third, the malfeasance must have represented some furtherance of the employer's wishes or directions. In *Cosgrove*, the defendant successfully argued that the therapist's sexually exploitive activity was not the kind of conduct for which he was employed, that much of the conduct took place away from the premises of the facility, and that the therapist could not be said to have been motivated by a desire to serve the facility. Citing consistent prohibitions against sex between therapist and patient by the employer and the therapist's own code of ethics (i.e., social work), the court held that a claim for vicarious liability was not met. There are relatively few decisions addressing the question of whether a mental health facility may be held vicariously liable for the sexual misconduct of an employee. Some courts have upheld claims (50), whereas others, as here, have not (51).

For the most part, defendants accused of sexually exploiting a client or patient have had little success in convincing a court that there was an acceptable reason for this conduct. Typically, if the defendant fails to deny the charge, or if there is credible evidence that the sexual activity did take place, there is little hope that liability will not be found (52). One "defense" theory that has generated a lot of commentary and opinion among professional groups such as the American Psychiatric Association is the propriety of sexual activity with a patient after therapy or treatment has terminated (e.g., "posttreatment sex"). The American Psychiatric Association's Ethics Committee recently published an addition to the *Principles of Medical Ethics* regarding this point that does provide some guidance. It notes, as an addition to Section 2, Annotation 1 of the Code of Ethics that "sexual involvement with one's former patients generally exploits emotions deriving from treatment and therefore almost always is unethical" (53).

At best, commentators would likely agree that this is a start, but its lack of definitiveness or at least clarification of situations that are clearly unethical and clearly ethical does create some problems. Only a few published cases have raised "posttreatment sex" as a defense. Raising such an argument relies on the fundamental rule that without a doctor-patient relationship, there can be no basis for a claim of malpractice because no duty of care is owed.

In a recent case in which lack of a doctor-patient relationship was part of a psychiatrist's defense, a New York trial court ruled that a cause of action for malpractice, among other things, was properly pleaded on the basis of a therapist's sexual relationships with a patient after the termination of treatment (54). Acknowledging that the court had not addressed this precise issue previously, the court, citing expert testimony that it was a departure from acceptable standards of care for a psychiatrist to engage in sexual relations with a patient or a *former* patient, concluded that the plaintiff's claim was analogous to a previous malpractice lawsuit that was founded on a physician's seduction of a patient. Unfortunately, other decisions that have addressed the defense of posttreatment sex have contained somewhat contrary reasoning in their conclusions (55).

An interesting artifact of malpractice cases involving alleged sexual exploitation is the surprising number of claims that are dismissed or rejected because the plaintiffs have pleaded an inappropriate theory for their cause of action. For example, in *Corgan v. Muehling* (56) an Illinois appellate court held that a suit against an unregistered psychologist was wrongly pleaded due to the absence of evidence that the defendant's conduct was calculated to cause the patient severe emotional distress. The plaintiff argued that the defendant's actions (sexual exploitation) placed her within a "zone of physical danger," but the court ruled that an action in *malpractice*, not negligent infliction of emotional distress, was the appropriate remedy. Cases involving allegations of sexual exploitation are definitely on the rise and are fast becoming a primary cause of action in mental health malpractice litigation. There are other areas of negligence involving psychiatrists that can result in a civil lawsuit, however.

For example, in *Hondroulis v. Schuhmacher* (57), the Louisiana Supreme Court held that a statutory presumption of the validity of a signed consent form may be rebutted by a showing that the patient was not adequately informed of a medical procedure's material risks. This decision is in accord with other recent opinions in Idaho (58) and Florida (59) and provides a strong *disincentive* for using generic or blanket consent forms.

In *Newton v. Louisiana Dept. of Health and Human Resources* (60), a psychiatrist was found not liable for the suicide death of a patient because of the psychiatrist's failure to have the patient committed. This case is similar to one reported in 1988, *Paddock v. Chacko* (61). In both cases, at the time of the patient's death there was no evidence of a doctor-patient relationship, the claimant was aware of the decedent's need for care but refused to pursue hospitalization, and the psychiatrist was not in a position to evaluate and possibly commit the patient. In each case, the court appeared to draw a line between the respective responsibilities of the doctor and patient and under what conditions responsibilities of the psychiatrist would arise.

Last, a growing number of cases, principally against local and state child protection agencies and workers, are being brought because of injuries arising from child abuse. All states have laws requiring professionals such as physicians, psychiatrists, and psychologists to report evidence of child abuse to proper authorities. A failure to comply with this law can result in a lawsuit. For example, in *Myles v. Osborn* (62), a mother took her 10-year-old daughter to a psychologist for treatment after the child had been repeatedly raped by her father. The psychologist did not report the rapes to the Department of Public Welfare, as required by state law. The young girl became pregnant, and the county welfare office assumed custody. The child's court-ordered guardian filed suit on her behalf, alleging that the psychologist had breached his duty to report child abuse and that this breach resulted in further rapes and pregnancy. The parties agreed to a structured settlement with monthly payments over approximately a 20-year period.

Cases such as this one are occurring with greater frequency, especially ones involving local protection agencies with which the responsibility for evaluating child abuse reports lies. Several state courts have held that child protection agencies and their employees (e.g., staff psychiatrists, psychologists, and social and case workers) have a duty to take reasonable precautions to protect a child who is at risk of abuse and that a violation of this duty is compensable under state law. Jurisdictions following this general rule include the District of Columbia (63), Arizona (64), Florida (65), and Michigan (66).

In a surprising opinion that appears to contradict the state opinions as well as several federal circuit opinions, the United States Supreme Court, in *DeShaney v. Winnebago County Department of Social Services* (67), held that state child protection agencies' employees have no constitutional duty to take measures to protect a child from a known danger of abuse. This tragic case involved a young child who was repeatedly beaten by his father and was initially referred to the local child protection agency. The agency conducted only a cursory interview of the father and declined further investigation. This same pattern was repeated the following year, when the child was examined in a hospital emergency room for suspicious bruises and abrasions. The examining physician suspected child abuse and notified the child protection agency. The child was placed in the temporary custody of the hospital while a team of medical, social work, and law enforcement officials considered the case. The team concluded that there was insufficient evidence of child abuse to retain custody and returned the child to his father with the agreement that the father would cooperate in implementing several voluntary measures. A month later, the child was again treated in the hospital emergency room, and suspected child abuse was again reported. The assigned caseworker concluded that there was no basis for action, but over the next 6 months the caseworker made periodic visits to the child's home, observed that the child had a number of suspicious head injuries, and noted that the child had not enrolled in school. No action was taken following the caseworker's observations nor was any taken when the child presented at the hospital emergency room for a third time. Four months after the last hospital report the father severely beat the child, causing him to fall into a coma.

A civil rights action, pursuant to 42 U.S.C. Section 1983 on behalf of the child and his mother was brought against the county, child protection agency, and several individual agencies alleging that their negligence had resulted in the child being deprived of his liberty without due process, in violation of the Fourteenth Amendment of the U.S. Constitution. The federal district court and the U.S. Court of Appeals for the Seventh Circuit granted summary judgment in favor of the defendants, and the U.S. Supreme Court affirmed. The

Supreme Court held that the due process clause of the federal constitution does not impose on the state an affirmative duty to protect its citizens against a private party's violent behavior. The court reasoned that the due process clause was designed to protect people from the *state* itself, rather than to have the state protect people from each other. The plaintiff argued that this situation should be afforded the same constitutional protection of adequate security and medical care that is provided to prisoners and involuntary mental patients. The court disagreed and distinguished the two situations on the basis that the latter cases involved persons whose freedom had been taken away by the state.

It is notable that the court did point out that states are free to impose tort liability on child protection agencies that fail to take reasonable measures to protect children who are at risk of abuse. In other words, the court argued that although children have no constitutional right to be protected by agencies responsible for their care and welfare, those same agencies can be held civilly liable for failing to reasonably protect abused and neglected children.

III. Criminal Law

The field of criminal law and criminal procedure was dominated in 1988–89 by several death penalty decisions handed down by the United States Supreme Court. The implications of these decisions with regard to psychiatrists and mental health professionals are likely to be of great interest and will be significant particularly for professionals who work with children, adolescents, and the mentally retarded, and in social and prison psychiatry. Three opinions in particular, *Stanford v. Kentucky/Wilkins v. Missouri* (68), *Penry v. Lynaugh* (69), and *Powell v. Texas* (70), have already generated a great deal of discussion, commentary, and uproar in the mental health community and the media.

Stanford v. Kentucky/Wilkins v. Missouri are two lower court opinions consolidated into one appeal to the high court because of their commonality of threshold issues. The central issue to be decided was, "May the death penalty be imposed on convicted murderers who were as young as 16 when committing their crime?" The court, in a bitterly split 5–4 decision, replied yes. Writing for the majority, Justice Scalia indicated that no national consensus currently consists that would make the practice (of executing someone who committed murder when 16) a violation of the Eighth Amendment (e.g., prohibition of cruel and unusual punishment). An important effect of this decision was that the Court declined to extend its decision in *Thompson v. Oklahoma* (71), which held unconstitutional the execution of any juvenile offender who was less than 16 years old at the time of the offense.

In concluding that there was "no national consensus" against executing persons 16 and older, the Court refused to consider the 14 states and the District of Columbia which oppose capital punishment altogether (72). The majority was further unpersuaded by the apparent fact that prosecutors and juries do not very frequently seek to impose the death penalty against 16- and 17-year-old offenders. This argument presumably was forwarded as evidence to support the conclusion that some consensus *did* exist with regard to a threshold age in which execution was offensive to the public. In the Court's view, however, it was "overwhelmingly probable that the very same considerations which induce the petitioners and their supporters to believe that death should *never* be imposed on an offender under 18 cause prosecutors and juries to believe that it should *rarely* be imposed" (emphasis added) (73).

Justice O'Connor once again was a key vote in capital cases; she cast the decisive fifth vote on *Stanford*. She argued that *Stanford* was distinguishable from *Thompson* because "whereas no state has expressly set a minimum age for capital punishment at below 16, three states have explicitly set 16 as the minimum, a fourth 'clearly contemplates' its imposition on 16-year-olds, and a majority of the States that permit capital punishment authorize it for crimes committed at age 16 or above" (74). Some commentators believe that it is conceivable that Justice O'Connor might eventually arrive at a different conclusion if several of the states that she specifically alluded to—Kentucky, Indiana, Nevada, and Florida—were to raise their minimum age standards.

As a result of *Stanford* and *Thompson*, at least for now, states will be free to execute 16- and 17-year-olds, *even if* certain due process procedures are waived by the defendant or not materially present (e.g., waiver of counsel, guilty plea, presentation of no mitigating evidence, request of the death penalty, or waiver of appeal) (75). Opponents of the death penalty and child advocates wonder whether, if enough states forbid these practices, a fifth justice might agree with the dissenting four that "juveniles so generally lack the degree of responsibility for their crimes that is a predicate for the constitutional imposition of the death penalty that the Eighth Amendment forbids that they receive that punishment" (76). In other words, juveniles are generally too vulnerable and immature to be considered sufficiently responsible for their actions and thus should be excluded from execution.

The second opinion, *Penry v. Lynaugh*, confronted the question of whether the death penalty may be imposed on convicted murderers who are mildly or moderately mentally retarded. Again, in an acrimonious 5–4 split, the U.S. Supreme Court said yes. This case actually produced two distinct 5–4 splits, with Justice O'Connor casting the controlling vote in each. Comprising Justice O'Connor, Chief Justice Rehnquist, and Justices Scalia, White, and Kennedy, the majority also relied on "national perception" in concluding that there was no public consensus regarding the execution of mentally retarded defendants. However, a second part of the *Penry* decision, in which Justice O'Connor joined Justices Brennan, Marshall, Blackmun, and Stevens, held that sentencing juries and judges must take into consideration a convicted murderer's mental retardation as a mitigating factor.

This second decision was aimed at providing greater balance of the relevant factors typically weighed during the sentencing phase in deciding whether the death penalty is appropriate. For example, in *Penry*, the defendant was not permitted to present evidence of his mental retardation and childhood abuse because of a Texas law that allowed juries to consider only whether a defendant had acted deliberately, whether the defendant probably would be dangerous in the future, and whether the defendant acted unreasonably in response to provocation (77). The Court deemed the Texas statute unconstitutional because it failed to permit juries to consider "mitigating" as well as "aggravating" factors and remanded Mr. Penry's case to the state for a new sentencing hearing. It is felt that the Court's decision to explicitly recognize mental retardation as a relative mitigating factor could lead to numerous reversals of many Texas death sentences because of their singular reliance on the three statutory sentencing criteria noted above.

Penry represents an interesting contrast to a 1986 Supreme Court case, *Ford v. Wainwright* (78), which addressed whether it was constitutionally permissible to execute a mentally ill prisoner. In deciding that such activity was generally not permissible, many commentators thought that *Penry* (i.e., the mentally retarded) would be afforded the same considerations noted in *Ford*. A primary argument for associating the mentally ill and mentally retarded in a criminal law context is that both presumably have a diminished capacity to understand and appreciate the gravity of their circumstances because of cognitive, intellectual, or psychiatric impairment. In the case of the mentally ill and execution, there is a historical and ethical presumption that a person must be capable of understanding and appreciating the reason for his or her punishment before he or she can be executed. In the case of the mentally retarded (e.g., *Penry*) this general rationale is applied to an analogous and even more basic principle. That is, for a person to be held criminally responsible he or she must have the *mens rea* (intent) to have committed the act charged. Theoretically, someone with mild mental retardation (IQ 55–70) or moderate mental retardation (IQ 40–55) is not intellectually capable of forming and appreciating this requisite intent. Moreover, and seen by some commentators as a principal flaw in Justice Scalia's majority opinion, is

> his failure to recognize that capital punishment is the most serious deprivation of liberty that the state can impose against a citizen and, a defendant's mental retardation, at the very least, creates doubt about whether he should be executed. At the minimum, the state, through the jurors, should be required to carefully consider a person's mental capacity, to ensure that he or she understands that the death penalty is to be meted out and why he or she is going to receive that punishment. (79)

For now, the Supreme Court does not fully agree with this presumption.

In an opinion that directly involves psychiatrists, the Supreme Court held that the Sixth Amendment (i.e., right to counsel) was violated when the prosecution presented future dangerousness testimony by a psychiatrist and a psychologist who were supposed to be conducting only a court-ordered examination of a defendant's sanity and his competency to stand trial. The unanimous opinion, *Powell v. Texas* (80), held that even if a defendant waived any Fifth Amendment (i.e., right against self-incrimination) violation by introducing psychiatric testimony in support of an insanity defense, "it certainly is not *unfair* to require the State to provide counsel with notice before examining the defendant concerning future dangerousness" (81).

Essentially, the *Powell* opinion represents a tenet of fundamental fairness and ethical consideration—that examinees should be apprised of the purposes of an examination so that they can voluntarily choose whether to participate. This position is really no different from the considerations a physician affords any patient in terms of informed consent before commencing a treatment or procedure. Essentially, what the Court is saying is that even a criminal defendant who is ordered by the court to appear for an examination has a minimal right, through counsel, to choose to participate and to what degree. To exercise that right, it stands to reason, the defendant must be provided with an adequate explanation of the possible purposes for which the information obtained might be used. Some psychiatric examiners associate this precaution with a sort of *Miranda* warning. Although the Court's judgment that a criminal defendant has a right to an adequate explanation of the purpose of psychiatric examinations does not require a formal or standardized "*Miranda*" warning, it does require some similar variation.

IV. Ethics and Professional Conduct

Articles in several prominent newspapers and publications have brought to the public's attention the seemingly inadequate and unresponsive job that physicians do in investigating and properly disciplining unethical, incompetent, and criminally culpable practitioners (82). For example, nationwide attention was focused on this problem when a series of articles, first appearing in the *Washington Post*, was published about a Navy surgeon who was charged with 4 counts of involuntary manslaughter and 24 counts of dereliction of duty for heart operations performed over a 2-year period (83). During the investigation it was discovered that the doctor had problems with his eyesight, was unfamiliar with some of the procedures he was performing because of his inactivity as a surgeon, and was given only minimal grades the few times the Navy evaluated his performance. Despite these problems and despite lingering questions about this doctor's surgical performance in medical posts he held before entering the military, the Navy failed to regularly evaluate the doctor or to have his work supervised until after several fatalities and alleged acts of negligence were reported.

This seemingly indifferent and lax response to addressing a serious lapse in medical care has often been cited as a difficult and long-standing problem in the medical profession. Data on the number of disciplinary complaints filed and acted on by state medical societies appear to provide some support for this contention (84).

Although no current figures could be found on complaints of unethical, illegal, or incompetent acts by psychiatrists made each year to state medical boards, it is reasonable to assume that they are on a par with the figures for other medical specialties. Case law makes it clear that a small percentage of psychiatrists are being disciplined each year for a variety of offenses. The most common offenses appear to involve allegations of sexual exploitation (85), insurance reimbursement improprieties (86), irregular prescription practices (87), and failing to provide adequate treatment or claims of irregular treatment (88). Disciplinary actions may be based on alleged violations of professional ethics, on deviations in customary professional practices and standards, or on evidence of criminal conduct. Physicians have been civilly sued and professionally disciplined for the same offense (89).

Perhaps because of the negative publicity that physicians and other professionals have been receiving, professional associations have taken greater responsibility to protect the public from doctors unfit to practice medicine (90). Moreover, some state licensing boards are becoming more active. For example, the consumer organization Public Citizen Health Research Group recently reported that there has been a 17% increase in disciplinary actions nationwide in 1987, compared with 1986 and 1985 (91). The Public Citizen Health Research Group report noted that the number of doctors disciplined (including psychiatrists) has increased in every state that has passed tougher laws regulating doctors or strengthening enforcement of existing laws. The report also concluded, however, that the regulation of doctors continues to vary widely from state to state and, as other studies have indicated (92), remains generally infrequent and of limited effectiveness.

V. HOSPITALS/INSTITUTIONAL CARE

Cases involving the liability of hospitals in general, as well as psychiatric facilities and institutions, rely on legal theories analogous to those pertaining to individual practitioners as well as to those peculiar to the institutional setting.

For example, in any case alleging malpractice, the person bringing the lawsuit bears the burden of establishing the standard of care that was owed and that the standard was breached. In actions involving individual doctors, as well as hospitals, evidence suggestive of the standard of care may include codes of ethics or professional standards, expert testimony detailing the prevailing norms within the profession or industry in question, and treatises or publications that are recognized in the field as authoritative.

Problems can arise, however, when a plaintiff attempts to establish the standard of care by which the defendant's conduct is to be judged. This most often arises in actions against hospitals when there is a "policy and procedures" manual that describes approved hospital practices for addressing a clinical situation that is analogous to the facts in the lawsuit. Contrary to what one might assume about such manuals, they are not necessarily definitive evidence of the standard of care to be applied against a hospital in a malpractice matter.

The problem of when a plaintiff uses rules and regulations promulgated by the defendant is illustrated in the case *Swarz v.*

Billington (93). One of the theories of liability against the hospital and the attending emergency room physician was that the physician improperly permitted the plaintiff to leave the hospital despite the possibility that the plaintiff was in danger of an imminent heart attack. The plaintiff introduced into evidence a hospital rule that required any patient who refused treatment or left the hospital against medical advice to sign a release form, a form the plaintiff never signed. The trial court refused the plaintiff's request for a jury instruction that a violation of the hospital's own policy would be evidence of negligence.

The jury returned a defense verdict, and the plaintiff appealed. The appeals court initially rejected the defendant's claim that the failure to obtain a release could not have caused any harm to the plaintiff because the sole purpose of the release was to protect the *hospital* by memorializing both its advice to the patient and the patient's refusal to follow that advice. The court reasoned, however, that the release form did serve another function—to impress on a patient the gravity of a decision to leave against medical advice. Implicit in that function, the court held, was the hope that the solemnity that accompanies the execution of such a document would lead the patient to reverse course and remain in the hospital. Nonetheless, the appeals court approved the trial court's refusal to give the plaintiff's requested jury instruction. The appeals court concluded that the proposed jury instruction overemphasized the value of the hospital's rule and that the hospital-defendant's violation of its own rules did not necessarily constitute conclusive evidence of negligence unless the jury concluded that the rule actually represented the appropriate standard of care. This finding is consistent with the rulings of several other courts that have held that a hospital's violation of an internal rule or regulation is admissible evidence on the standard of care but that it is not necessarily *conclusive* evidence (94).

Another area that is potentially problematic for hospitals and other institutions involves the establishment of the doctor-patient relationship. It is a well-established medical rule that without some express or implied contract, a private doctor has no duty to accept a patient who simply seeks medical or psychiatric treatment (95). There are situations, however, in which an "implied" contractual arrangement does exist, even among doctors and patients who have had no previous contact. For example, an emergency room doctor is generally acknowledged as available to provide services to all who seek them.

This arrangement also may be extended to include doctors and psychiatrists who are "on call" as backup or support to the emergency room staff. In such a case, *Dillon v. Silver* (96), a New York appellate court ruled that a question of fact (for the jury) existed regarding whether there was a doctor-patient relationship when an on-call surgeon refused to treat a patient referred by an emergency room doctor. The court reasoned that because the surgeon (the second doctor) was obligated under hospital bylaws to accept all referrals from the hospital's emergency room doctors, it could be argued that the patient in this case had become the surgeon's patient at the time the referral was made and acknowledged by the surgeon.

Many of the legal concepts governing the liability of individual physicians are applicable to hospitals as well, with some exceptions. As a general rule, a hospital, state institution, or facility is required to exercise reasonable care in accordance with sound hospital practices to protect the health and safety of its patients. Because a hospital is merely the sum of the input from its various employees (e.g., doctors, nurses, technicians), the primary source of hospital liability is "vicarious," arising from *individual* actions of specific hospital employees who may have injured a patient. Vicarious liability generally refers to the indirect legal responsibility that an employer has for the acts of an employee.

An exception arises for certain classes of physicians. Generally, a hospital will not be "vicariously" liable for the negligence of nonemployee physicians who merely exercise hospital "staff privileges." This is because most physicians with staff privileges are not employed by the hospital but rather are entitled to use hospital facilities for their patients. Thus, in most hospitals there are two classes of physician staff members—those holding staff privileges and those who are actually employees of the hospital. Interns and residents are among the most common of the latter group.

The threshold issue between the two classes, in terms of imposing vicarious liability on a hospital, is the amount of *control* the hospital exerts on the physician. For the doctor on staff or any employee, a hospital or facility has considerable control, whereas for a physician with staff privileges, the hospital's control generally is quite limited. An exception to this general rule may arise with regard to outside doctors with "staff privileges" when there is a direct economic relationship between the hospital and physician. For example, in some situations, a psychiatrist or other physician may share an economic relationship with a hospital but is not *technically* an employee. These cases typically involve physicians who have agreed to provide support services to the hospital through anesthesiology, pathology, psychiatry, emergency room, or other services. In some circumstances, the outside physician bills the patient directly. In others, the patient is billed by the hospital or facility, which in turn pays the physician.

The courts are divided on the question of whether physicians in such situations are "independent contractors" (implying that the hospital would not be vicariously liable) or "servants" (for whom the hospital would be considered the "master" and, therefore, vicariously liable). The determining fact to be decided is, "How much authority or control does the hospital have or is implied to have over the physician?" (97).

Some courts have found that as a matter of "public policy," it would be unduly burdensome to require patients to determine whether their treating physician was a hospital employee or an independent contractor (98). The reasoning given, at least by one court, is that because hospitals hold themselves out to the public as providers of quality health care, they should not be permitted to escape liability when inadequate care is provided at their facilities by independent contractors. This rationale may be the exception in that it enunciates a broad principle of public policy that could apply to any physician-hospital relationship and thus render immaterial any distinction between employee and independent contractor. Generally, courts have distinguished between the two classes in determining hospital liability and have treated these distinctions as issues of fact to be determined by a jury.

Two recent cases of interest involved facts common to psychiatric institutions and facilities. Because psychiatric hospitals, principally state mental institutions, provide care and treatment to patients who are often difficult to control, initially dangerous, and not rational, they are afforded a certain latitude in protecting patient and staff from possible harm from the patient's behavior. One method is to restrain and seclude patients until they no longer present a danger to themselves or others or until whatever emergency that precipitated their restraint and seclusion is no longer present. Of course, seclusion and restraint represent significant curtailments of a patient's freedom. Therefore, they must be used only in certain situations of demonstrated need and only in conjunction with a carefully considered and implemented plan. National guidelines for the appropriate use of seclusion and restraint have been developed by the American Psychiatric Association Task Force on the Psychiatric Uses of Seclusion and Restraint (99). When a facility violates one of these general conditions or fails to promulgate a clinically appropriate seclusion and restraint plan, it can be subjected to a court action.

In a 1988 case, *O'Sullivan v. Secretary of Human Services* (100), the Supreme Judicial Court of Massachusetts affirmed a preliminary injunction against state officials at the Bridgewater State Hospital for using seclusion and restraint procedures that were in violation of a state statute. The court particularly noted that the hospital had failed to properly monitor patients when they were in seclusion.

In this case, the issue in contention was whether the hospital was in compliance with a Massachusetts statute that required the monitoring of patients whenever they were placed in seclusion. The statute in question provided that patients could not be restrained without a person in attendance specially trained to understand, assist, and afford therapy to the person in restraint: "The person may be in attendance immediately outside the room in full view of the patient when an individual is being secluded without mechanical restraint." In an emergency, when a trained staff person was unavailable, the statute permitted restraint if the person was observed at least every 5 minutes, and a report was filed explaining the unavailability of a properly trained individual. After 8 hours of restraint of a patient in any 24-hour period, the superintendent, facility director, or designee was supposed to authorize any further restraint.

The major dispute in the *O'Sullivan* case was whether constant observation was necessary or whether clinical discretion could be applied in administering seclusion. The Massachusetts high court concluded that the statute's language on this point was clear. It indicated that because seclusion could be implemented only in emergency situations (e.g., when a patient harms or presents a serious threat of harm to self or others), constant observation was therefore necessary. On this basis, the court concluded that the granting of the preliminary injunction halting further seclusions (until this matter was clarified and settled) had been appropriate.

Another situation involving the responsibility of hospitals to carefully safeguard patients' rights occurs in cases of commitment. Again, as with seclusion and restraint procedures, civil commitment is well recognized as a deprivation of personal liberties that must be counterbalanced by certain protections against abuse. Every state has due process procedures that seek to ensure that a person's involuntary commitment is based on narrow grounds (e.g., that the person is mentally ill and represents a danger to himself or herself or others); that a patient, once committed, is treated in accord with certain minimum standards of conduct; and that the duration of the involuntary confinement will not be unduly burdensome or contrary to the original objectives of confinement. The failure of a hospital or facility to honor these requirements can subject it to a civil rights or tort claim.

In the 1988 case *Stock v. Forbes Health System* (101), a federal district court held that a psychiatric hospital was not immune from liability for its failure to afford a patient a series of reviews, examinations, and hearings regarding his commitment, as prescribed by law, because such failures resulted in deprivation of liberty without due process of law.

VI. Patient Rights

Cases involving various state and federal jurisdiction interpretations of committed individuals' right to refuse treatment or medication again dominate the 1988–89 case law decisions.

Two cases are most notable. In the first, the United States Court of Appeals for the Fourth Circuit has held that medical personnel at a mental institution may administer antipsychotic drugs over the objections of an involuntarily committed patient, subject to judicial review to ensure that the decision was not made arbitrarily. This case, *United States v. Charters* (102), has generated attention not only because of its conclusions but because of its interesting facts. The 1988 case involved a man who was involuntarily committed to a psychiatric facility at a federal correctional institution after he was indicted for threatening the life of President Reagan. The patient was subsequently found incompetent to stand trial. Periodic reviews of the patient's case resulted in continued confinement at the institution based on the conclusion that he was still incompetent and represented a danger to himself and others.

Approximately 2 years after the patient's initial confinement, the government sought to forcibly medicate the patient over his objections. The treating psychiatrist testified at a hearing that the patient was suffering from schizophrenia that could not be cured but that could be controlled symptomatically with medication. A lower court granted the government's request, concluding that although the patient had a constitutional interest in avoiding unwanted or unwarranted uses of antipsychotic medication, this interest had been adequately protected through the use of professional judgment of the psychiatric staff. A panel of the Fourth Circuit reversed this judgment, concluding that the professional judgment rationale was insufficient protection and that a patient could not be forcibly medicated without a more elaborate system of procedural protections. The circuit court held that the government was required to establish —in a two-stage adversarial judicial proceeding—that the patient was incompetent to make rational treatment decisions regarding whether medication would best serve his interests and that such treatments would in fact serve the patient's best interests.

A rehearing was subsequently heard by the entire Fourth Circuit, and it vacated the panel's ruling. Although the full court acknowledged that involuntarily committed patients retain certain constitutionally protected liberty interests in avoiding the forcible administration of medication, it explained that this interest sometimes must yield to legitimate government interests that are incidental to hospitalization. Due process, in these situations, requires only that the patient's rights be protected against arbitrary and capricious actions. In this regard, the court stressed that the government has an interest in treating the patient's mental illness and returning him to society, and that the laborious two-stage judicial procedure advocated by the panel was not likely to provide the patient with significantly greater or needed protection than the procedure originally provided by the hospital (e.g., judicial review of decision making in accordance with "professional judgment"). Such judicial review procedure, the Fourth Circuit noted, was consistent with other due process procedures, where the role of the court is to *review* medical decisions made by professionals (e.g., staff psychiatrists), rather than to *make* medical decisions. The court concluded that it was more appropriate for judges to review psychiatric decisions made by qualified professionals than to make primary psychiatric decisions on the basis of conflicting expert testimony. In response to the patient's concerns about the side effects of drugs as well as the lack of informed consent in these situations, the court reasoned that these risks are merely factors that must be taken into account in making a medical decision to forcibly medicate.

The significance of this decision, particularly for hospital psychiatrists who treat incompetent, involuntarily committed patients, is that it is the "medical judgment" of the professional that determines the decision to medicate or not. The court's role, according to the Fourth Circuit in this opinion, is simply to assess whether the medical decision reached was completely outside the bounds of professional judgment (i.e., arbitrary and capricious) (103).

The second opinion of note has the potential to resolve much of the controversy surrounding the circumstances and procedures applied in determining a patient's right to refuse treatment. This case, *Washington v. Harper* (104), has been granted *certiorari* (i.e., accepted for review) by the United States Supreme Court and will be argued sometime during the 1989–90 term.

Harper addresses whether a prison inmate is entitled to a court hearing and other constitutional safeguards before being forced to take antipsychotic medication. The Washington State Supreme Court concluded that inmates are entitled to these safeguards and reversed a lower court's dismissal of a civil rights action by a prisoner who alleged that the state had forcibly medicated him without a judicial hearing. The Washington high court specifically concluded that the prisoner's rights were not adequately protected by the administrative proceedings instituted by the hospital, especially because the patient-prisoner received no legal representation or had no real opportunity for an appeal. Moreover, it determined that *minimum due process* required that a judicial hearing be held.

At a judicial hearing, the state has to demonstrate that there was a "compelling state interest" in administering medication that was both necessary and effective in furthering the state's interest. A compelling interest, the court noted, could be demonstrated by one of the following criteria: *1*) preventing suicide, *2*) preserving life, *3*) protecting third-party interests, or *4*) maintaining the ethical integrity of the medical profession. In determining whether the medication was necessary and effective, the state must also show that it considered the patient-prisoner's prognosis with and without the treatment and that it considered alternative treatments and the patient's desires. In the judicial proceeding, after hearing the state's case, the court then would make a judgment on behalf of the patient as to whether forcible medication was necessary. This "substituted" judgment by the court is similar to or consistent with the medical treatment decision that is made for incompetent persons by health care professionals and other authorities (105). This decision-making process implicitly incorporates the notion that the judgment being made is ultimately in the "best interest of the patient."

The court noted that the state and its officials were immune from money damages as long as there was no evidence of malicious intent.

The importance of this case has not been overlooked by the American Psychiatric Association (APA). It has filed an amicus brief with the United States Supreme Court in support of overturning the Washington Supreme Court's decision (106). The brief puts forward three principal arguments (107). First, it argues that treatment involving psychotropic medication does not warrant a unique constitutional right. Second, it maintains that the due process clause of the Fourteenth Amendment secures a right to the exercise of professional judgment (by medical staff) in the administration of psychiatric care. Third, it contends that no judicial hearing is constitutionally compelled before a prisoner is administered psychotropic medication.

In essence, the APA, through this brief, is arguing that there is no constitutionally protected right to refuse treatment and that the state is not compelled to provide certain protections beyond those provided by the professional judgment of the treating doctors. In support of this position, the APA argues that the individual patient's primary interest is appropriate *care* and that it is in the interest of the government to *provide* that care. Moreover, assuming that psychotropic medication and other seemingly intrusive treatments (e.g., ECT) do involve certain risks to patients, the state, through its agents (hospital and treating doctors), and not the courts, is in the best position to provide the protections necessary to guard against any unreasonable risks. The involvement of the courts, the APA argues, is an unnecessary and burdensome procedure that interjects the opinions of a forum whose members are "less qualified than psychiatrists to render psychiatric judgments" (108).

The *Harper* case provides an opportune time for the United States Supreme Court to finally provide some clarity about the nature, if any, of constitutional protections owed to involuntary patients refusing psychiatric treatment. What procedures are necessary to ensure that those protections are provided? What is the standard by which compliance with those procedures will be judged? As noted in the APA's brief, although the *Harper* case involved a prisoner who refused antipsychotic medication, the Supreme Court's decision could potentially have far greater implications:

> If allowed to stand, the decision below will not only affect those prisoners in Harper's circumstances, but also the thousands of mentally ill persons involuntarily confined under state civil commitment statutes. At best, by interposing daunting, costly, and time-consuming procedural obstacles to the administration of necessary medical care, the decision threatens to delay and disrupt treatment of the refusing patient and others, while diverting scarce professional resources to costly and unproductive judicial proceedings. At worst, by enshrining the preferences of dangerous persons gravely in need of psychiatric treatment, the result threatens to consign those refusing antipsychotic medication to indefinite hospitalization, close confinement, and increased use of physical restraints. (109)

Aside from the major decisions in *Charters* and *Harper*, other decisions concerning various aspects of the right to refuse treatment question have emanated from states and federal districts and circuits in the past year. The following summarizes these latest actions, according to their jurisdiction.

Court of Appeals for the 10th Circuit (Federal)

Walters v. Western State Hospital, 864 F2d 695 (10th Cir 1988)
[physician at state hospital is not immune as a matter of law

from charges of involuntary administration of psychotropic medication and unlawful denial of visitation]

Colorado

Colorado ex rel M.K.M., 765 P2d 1075 (Colo Ct App 1988) [petition to compel patient to undergo ECT was properly denied given the state's failure to establish by clear and convincing evidence that treatment was needed]

Colorado v. Gilliland, 769 P2d 477 (Colo 1989) [denial of a motion to authorize the administration of antipsychotic medication to NGRI defendant was reversed and remanded]

District of Columbia

In re Bryant, 542 A2d 1216 (DC Ct App 1988) [application of substituted judgment for incompetent patient resulted in determination that patient would have wanted medication if competent]

Florida

Florida v. Moore, No. 88-8182CF10 *cited in* National Law Journal 9 (05/08/89) [antipsychotic drugs can be ordered against the wishes of a criminal defendant in an effort to make him competent to stand trial]

Iowa

In re Foster, 426 NW2d 374 (Iowa 1988) [involuntarily committed patient for psychiatric evaluation and treatment may not be forcibly medicated absent evidence that he was likely to injure himself or others if allowed to remain in general prisoner population]

Massachusetts

In re Guardianship of Linda, 519 NE2d 1296 (Mass 1988) [prior judicial approval of forcible administration of neuroleptic drugs to incompetent mental patient is required]

Minnesota

Matter of Jarvis, 433 NW2d 120 (Minn App 1988) [involuntary mental patient is entitled to second examiner for hearing with respect to involuntary administration of neuroleptic medication]

In re Steen, 437 NW2d 101 (Minn Ct App 1989) [failure to appoint independent mental health professional to examine patient before authorizing involuntary administration of neuroleptic medication deemed sufficient error to require a reversal of the original trial decision]

In re Lambert, 437 NW2d 106 (Minn Ct App 1989) [involuntary medication order was approved based on evidence that patient was incompetent to approve treatment and the order adequately outlined the course of treatment]

New York

Mental Health Legal Services v. Surles, No 88-12978 (Suffolk County Sup Ct, NY, Dec 1988) [antipsychotic medication may be administered over the objection of an involuntarily committed minor (17-year-old) if his parents consent to the treatment]

Matter of Jane Doe, NYLJ, Dec 19, 1988, at 29 at 6 (Westchester Cty Sup Ct, NY, Dec 1988) [failure to comport procedures and protections outlined in *Rivers* prevented forcible administration of medication to adult patient]

Sabatini v. Brown, NYLJ, Jan 21, 1988, at 15, col 5 (NY Cty Sup Ct, NY, Jan 1988) [failure to comport procedures and protections outlined in *Rivers* prevented forcible administration of medication to adult patient]

In re McConnell, 538 NYS2d 101 (NY App Div 1989) [order to forcibly medicate a psychiatric patient was sufficiently supported by evidence that it was "narrowly tailored to protect the patient's liberty interest (e.g., monitor for side effects) as well as serve his treatment interests" (e.g., "get better")]

Adele S. v. Kingsboro Psychiatric Center, 539 NYS2d 769 (App Div 1989) [order affirmed permitting administration of antipsychotic medication to involuntarily committed patient without her consent based on clear and convincing evidence that patient lacked capacity to make rational treatment decision, and the proposed medication was narrowly tailored to preserve patient's liberty interests]

In re Garrett, 538 NYS2d 919 (Sup Ct 1989) [lack of jurisdiction and violation of due process procedures outlined in *Rivers* prompted dismissal of petition to forcibly medicate patient where court papers had been given to the same physician who had initiated the petition instead of proper notice to the patient]

Middle District of North Carolina (Federal)

U.S. v. Waddell, 687 F Supp 208 (MD NC 1988) [forcible administration of antipsychotic medication to a defendant found incompetent to stand trial permissible only if decision is based on a modified substituted judgment test]

Wisconsin

K.S. v. Winnebago County, 433 NW2d 291 (Wis App 1988) [an involuntarily committed patient need not be informed of the advantages and disadvantages of medication, absent medically acceptable alternatives]

Suffice it to say, the law regarding the standards, procedures, and review of right to refuse psychiatric treatment decisions varies widely according to the individual circumstances of a case and the jurisdiction in which the case is brought. Unofficially, I have noted to date no fewer than 24 individual decisions in the federal courts and 46 decisions in state courts.

VII. Expert Testimony

Cases involving expert matters frequently arise when there are questions concerning what standard is to be applied in judging whether an expert's testimony is admissible, what is the scope of the subject matter on which an expert may offer testimony, and in what circumstances, if any, an expert may be held liable for his or her conduct in civil litigation.

For an expert's opinion to be considered relevant, and ultimately helpful to the trier of fact, it must be established that he or she is familiar with the standard of care that applies to the case being tried. This issue involves two distinct aspects. The first involves the standard of care applied in the "locale or jurisdiction" in which the case is being tried. The second deals with the nature and level of expertise, if any, that the person being sued might represent (e.g., general psychiatrist in a malpractice action).

The first consideration, in many jurisdictions, usually is not a problem in malpractice cases, because a "national" standard of care is applied. That is, it is presumed in these cases that the standard of care is uniform throughout the country. Some areas of the country, however, still apply a more narrow rule that requires experts to be familiar with the standard of care as it is practiced in that particular community. This is an example of the "locality rule."

In the second situation, an expert testifying about the standard of care as it applies to a malpractice defendant must also be familiar with any special circumstances or considerations that might characterize that defendant's practice or care in the case being tried. For example, if a case involves an allegation of negligence in the treatment of a minor by a board-certified child psychiatrist, then experts testifying in that case must demonstrate to the court their familiarity with the standard of care practiced by board-certified child psychiatrists.

A good example of both considerations—particularly what appears to be the latest way courts have limited the application of the traditional locality rule—is illustrated by an Indiana appeals case, *Wilson v. Sligar* (110). In *Wilson*, a trial court excluded the testimony of two board-certified orthopedic surgeons regarding the performance of a hip replacement, which the defendant is alleged to have done negligently, on the basis that the questions posed to the witnesses did not connect the standard of care to the community where the defendant practiced or to a similar community. The plaintiff had argued, unsuccessfully, that the standard of care applicable to board-certified orthopedic surgeons performing this procedure was the same regardless of where the procedure was performed.

An Indiana appeals court reversed the lower court on the basis that it had erred in excluding the proffered testimony. The court noted that though Indiana adheres to the locality rule, the rule should have been flexible enough to permit testimony from an expert who lacked familiarity with similar communities *if* the community standard and the national standard were the same. In essence, the court said that where there is a *minimum* standard of care that is uniform throughout the country in a particular practice, the locality rule will not bar the use of the minimum standard in trial.

The standard of care that a testifying expert would likely need to be familiar with involves one of four basic variations that courts across the country seem to apply. The "strict locality rule," which holds that a physician's duty to care is measured by the degree and care exercised by other practitioners in the specific community in which he or she practiced, has been virtually abandoned by states. In its place, many states have adopted the "same or similar locality rule," under which a physician's professional conduct must conform to the level of care and skill exercised by physicians practicing in communities similar to his or her own. This rule allows for testimony from experts who might be unfamiliar with the specific community where the defendant practices but who are familiar with prevailing standards in similar communities (111). Various courts that adhere to the locality rule have rendered rulings that limit or stretch the rule's effect under certain circumstances.

Some courts have indicated that a "national standard" may apply to certain types of procedures or treatments (112). Other courts have adopted a national standard of care for specialists, reasoning that specialists receive comparable training nationwide (113). Psychiatrists and psychiatric experts generally would fall in this category because of the fairly uniform education and training received by American psychiatrists today. Some cases reflect a recent movement by courts to hold that a national standard of care applies to *all* medical malpractice actions (114). Last, several states have attempted to codify the locality rule through legislation setting forth various qualifications for expert witnesses in medical malpractice actions. Some of the states that have done this are Tennessee (115), Delaware (116), Virginia (117), and North Carolina (118).

Questions also arise frequently in court about the nature, scope, and relevancy of an expert's proffered testimony. Cases involving psychiatric predictions of dangerousness are one such topic that frequently does engender controversy and objections. Often, testimony that is considered of questionable reliability is considered an issue for the jury to weigh and therefore is admissible to hear, within certain guidelines set by the judge. For example, in *Cross v. Lakeview Center, Inc.* (119), a lawsuit was brought against a psychiatrist and mental hospital arising from the release of a patient who shot and killed his father and a police officer 7 days after his discharge. It was held on appeal that the trial court did not abuse its discretion when it allowed expert testimony regarding the prediction of violent behavior, notwithstanding the defendant's contention that the field of violence prediction was not sufficiently developed to support expert testimony. The trial court concluded that when the defendants opened the door on this issue through testimony of their own experts, the plaintiff was allowed to present similar, but narrowly framed, testimony of its own.

Given today's litigious climate, it seems that any "bad or undesired result" is susceptible to allegations of negligence and civil liability. Psychiatrists and other professionals who provide expert testimony in malpractice actions or who serve as outside consultants in evaluating the mental status of employees at the request of an employer or other institutional third party no longer may be considered "suit proof." Several recent cases illustrate this point and important legal considerations associated with the role of expert witnesses and consultants.

In an Ohio case, *Willitzer v. McCloud* (120), several worker's compensation claimants brought an action against the Industrial Commission and an examining physician alleging intentional misrepresentations in medical examinations that resulted in denial or reduction of their benefits. The Ohio Supreme Court affirmed a finding by the Ohio Court of Appeals dismissing the claim against the Industrial Commission, but the supreme court allowed the suit to go forward against the examining physician.

It is generally accepted that in matters involving an adjudicatory process, judges, counsel, parties, and witnesses are absolutely immune from civil damages for defamatory remarks made during and relevant to the judicial proceedings. The adjudication of the workers' claims by the Industrial Commission, for example, is an analogous process in which the commission, too, is entitled to immunity. Immunity is not absolute in some circumstances, however. In this case, the defendant doctor claimed that his function of examining the claimants and filing medical reports was like that of a witness furnishing testimony at an adjudicatory proceeding and as a quasi-judicial officer. As such, the doctor argued, he deserved qualified immunity. The Ohio court disagreed. A distinction must be made, reasoned the court, between an activity that is "intimately associated with the adjudicatory process and that which is essentially investigative and administrative." Applying this functional analysis, the court maintained that the potential liability of the defendant was not predicated on the furnishing of testimony or submission of a report but rather on the manner in which he conducted his *earlier* medical examination of the claimants for the purpose of reporting their medical conditions to the Industrial Commission. The Ohio high court concluded that the defendant's out-of-court physical examination of the claimants was a medical-investigative fact-finding function—not a quasi-judicial function. As a result, these out-of-court physical examinations were not "intimately associated" with the quasi-judicial phase of the procedures for application of benefits under worker's compensation law. The court ruled that the defendant doctor was not immune from liability for any negligence or intentional conduct committed in examining the claimants.

Examinations on behalf of employers and insurance companies and other similar circumstances in which a benefit is being sought also occasionally result in lawsuits, but verdicts against the examining physician usually are not successful. In one suit, a Pennsylvania appellate court held that a physician who was employed by an insurance company to examine an applicant for an insurance policy may not be held liable to the applicant for failure to diagnose a heart condition (121). In affirming a lower court's dismissal of the action, the appeals court agreed that there was no doctor-patient relationship between the examining physician and the applicant and that therefore no duty of care was owed in terms of diagnosing and treating a medical condition. The examining physician's duty, the court held, was only to the insurer who employed him (i.e., the duty was to conduct a reasonable examination).

In another case with a similar finding, a Connecticut appeals court dismissed as inadequate a former postal employee's "breach of contract" action against a psychiatrist who had examined her on behalf of the postal service (122). The claimant was required to undergo a psychiatric evaluation to determine her fitness to remain on the job when she began experiencing difficulty coping with her employment. She was subsequently dismissed from work because of an "adjustment disorder" associated with her job. The employee filed suit against the psychiatrist, claiming that she was a third-party beneficiary of the psychiatrist's agreement with the postal service to evaluate her, and that by not conducting the service in a competent manner, the psychiatrist breached his contractual duty to her. The trial court dismissed the suit, and the appellate court affirmed. The appeals court concluded that the employee failed to demonstrate that the examining psychiatrist had any contractual relationship with the employee.

In addition to serving as examining doctors for various employment-related functions, some psychiatrists also provide expert testimony in civil lawsuits regarding questions of psychic injury, causation, and standard of care. A number of recent cases have raised the question of whether professionals may be held liable for their conduct as expert witnesses. Typical of the common response of courts thus far on this issue is the case *Kahn v. Burman* (123). The events leading to this case began when an attorney asked Burman, a physician, to evaluate whether Kahn, also a physician, had committed malpractice in treating a client of the attorney. Burman, the physician-consultant, prepared a report for the attorney in which he noted several errors made by the treating physician, Kahn. After reviewing this report, the attorney filed a malpractice action on behalf of his client, naming Kahn, several other physicians, and two hospitals as defendants. The consulting physician, Burman, was subsequently named as an expert witness in the malpractice action. He testified in a deposition that Kahn had been negligent in treating the attorney's client. Following the deposition, the expert prepared a second report for the attorney concerning the medical treatment provided by Kahn. Kahn then sued Burman, as an "expert," for negligence, fraudulent, intentional misrepresentation, defamation, and intentional infliction of emotional distress, based on Burman's deposition testimony and reports.

The court held that the *witness immunity doctrine* shielded the defendant, Burman, from civil liability for his deposition testimony in the malpractice litigation. The court further held that the immunity extended to witnesses for testifying also should apply equally to experts' reports prepared before or during litigation. The reasoning of this holding is based on the need of the judicial process to be unimpeded by fear of civil liability on the part of its participants—for example, witnesses. Also, if physicians as experts faced potential liability for preparing prelitigation reports in malpractice actions, fewer physicians would be willing to evaluate malpractice claims in advance of litigation. If physicians were intimidated from evaluating claims, fewer meritless suits would be weeded out before filing, and fewer plaintiffs with meritorious cases would be able to seek redress.

Other cases have resulted in similar findings of no liability. For example, in *Mercury Casualty Company v. Superior Court* (124), the court held that a physician who allegedly testified falsely in a personal injury trial may not be held liable to the claimant in that trial for causing the jury to return a low verdict (124). In a similar case, a court ruled that an expert retained by the claimant in a medical malpractice action may not be held liable for refusing to render an expert opinion at trial (125).

Questions regarding the potential liability of experts inevitably raise more questions—accurate or not—about the credibility of professionals who provide expert testimony in personal injury and other litigation. The issue of "hired guns"—professional witnesses who seemingly peddle their opinions to the side that pays their fee—has been the source of controversy for many years.

Recently, attacks on mental health experts have broadened in scope to criticize the fundamental courtroom roles of psychiatrists and psychologists. For example, a recent article in *Science* has questioned the effectiveness and viability of mental health professionals' opinions in litigation (126). In the article, two psychologists attacked the validity of expert testimony by psychologists and psychiatrists. They indicated that the clinical judgment of these two professional groups was neither reliable nor valid enough to be used in court as expert testimony. The authors argued that the courts should examine the possibility of excluding psychologists and psychiatrists as expert witnesses altogether. In response, both the American Psychiatric Association and the American Psychological Association have thoroughly disagreed with this position and have reaffirmed that mental health experts serve a valuable function in cases in which a psychological component is involved in the case (127).

At present, it appears doubtful that any significant part of the law will be amended to exclude psychological or psychiatric testimony. In part, this is because the Rules of Evidence, on which most states and all federal jurisdictions rely in determining the admissibility of expert testimony, are framed in quite broad terms. For example, Federal Rule of Evidence 702, Testimony of Experts, states: "If scientific, technical, or other specialized knowledge will assist the trier of fact to understand the evidence or to determine a fact in issue, a witness qualified as an expert by knowledge, skill, training or education, may testify thereto in the form of an opinion or otherwise." (128). A related basis for continuing to permit psychiatric testimony is that there is no reasonable alternative to the present psychological or psychiatric expert in presenting and interpreting this form of evidence.

The recent criticisms of the role of psychiatric experts, coupled with the courts' resistance to barring mental health professionals from providing expert testimony, create constant opportunities for opposing attorneys to attempt to impugn experts' credibility. Such attempts are common trial tactics, particularly when cases depend on the testimony of a particular witness, such as an expert. Criticism of a witness is generally an attempt to convince the jury that the witness or expert is in some way biased, incompetent, or unethical. In one case, for example, defense counsel literally called the plaintiff's experts "out-of-town hired guns" and mocked one of them as "absolutely the bottom of the barrel" (129). In another case, a court ruled that a defense counsel's remark during summation that the plaintiff's expert was like the television gunman Palladin—"Have Opinion, Will Travel"—although improper, did not require reversal as the trial court promptly gave a curative instruction (130).

Finally, opposing trial counsel frequently attempt to characterize expert witnesses as biased and subjective because they may receive a high fee for their time in a case or because they testify frequently as expert witnesses (131). The few court decisions that have been published dealing with this argument generally have permitted some examination of this topic (i.e., expert witness fees) but only when it is narrowly tailored to address the question of potential bias or untrustworthiness.

APPENDIX: VIII. LEGISLATION

This section is added as a resource on significant state and federal statutes that could affect psychiatrists. The lengthy and cumbersome language of many statutes makes it preferable here only to list citations or to summarize small, salient parts of the statutes. Readers thus are advised not to rely on these brief reviews themselves for professional purposes but to use them as guides to the full official federal or state statutes.

The following is a sample of the many mental health statutes, legislative actions, and administrative regulations promulgated each year on mental health issues.

CIVIL PRACTICE

HR 774, cosponsored by Congressman William Coyne (D-PA) and Senator Jay Rockefeller (D-WV), seeks to permit psychologists to obtain direct reimbursement under Medicare. The American Psychiatric Association argued at a committee hearing that the elderly and severely disabled need to have a medical differential diagnosis and that direct reimbursement also may be tied to a physical examination—both are services only a physician can provide.

CIVIL LIABILITY

Duty to Warn—Update

Alaska: Alaska Stat Ann § 08.86.200 (1988)

a) Immediate threat of serious physical harm to an identifiable victim made to a psychologist or psychological associate.
b) Disclosure to an appropriate authority.*

Maryland: MD Cts or Jud Proc Code Ann § 5-315 (1989)

a) Mental health care provider or administrator knew of the patient's propensity for violence, and the patient indicated to the

*The referenced statute does not specifically address what is to be done if the trigger element is met. The above stated "disclosure to appropriate authorities" is inferred by this writer based on the recognized Alaska exception to confidentiality for reporting child, elderly, or disabled person abuse.

mental health care provider or administrator of patient's intention to inflict imminent physical injury on a specified victim or group of victims.

b) Mental health care provider or administrator makes reasonable and timely efforts to 1) seek civil commitment of the patient; 2) formulate a diagnostic impression and establish and undertake a documented treatment plan calculated to eliminate the possibility that the patient will carry out the threat; or 3) inform the appropriate law enforcement agency and, if feasible, the specified victim or victims of the nature of the threat, the identity of the patient making the threat, and the identity of the specified victim.

Utah: Utah Code Ann § 78-14a-102 (Supp 1988)

a) "... communication of an actual threat of physical violence against a clearly identifiable or reasonably identifiable victim."

b) "... reasonable efforts to communicate the threat to the victim, and notifies a law enforcement officer or agency of the threat."

Sexual Exploitation—Update

Washington: Wash Rev Code Ann § 18.130.180 (24) (1988)

"The following conduct, acts, or conditions constitute unprofessional conduct for any license holder or applicant under the jurisdiction of this chapter. . . ."

Specifically, Subsection 24 states, "Abuse of a client or patient or sexual contact with a client or patient."

CRIMINAL LAW

On October 21, 1988, Congress passed the Omnibus Drug Initiative Act. This legislation was enacted to prevent the manufacture, distribution, and use of illegal drugs. Although the bill mandates the death penalty for persons who are convicted of drug-related capital offenses, an amendment prohibits imposing the death penalty on mentally retarded individuals who are convicted of such a crime. Congress has encouraged state legislatures and the courts to prohibit death sentences for persons with mental retardation found guilty of committing capital crimes (131). Readers interested in the law pertaining to capital punishment and the mentally retarded should read the recent United States Supreme Court opinion in *Penry v. Lynaugh*, 57 USLW 4958 (June 26, 1989).

DUTY TO WARN: CURRENT OVERVIEW AND TRENDS

Jurisdiction	Source of law	Status
Alaska	Statute	Accepts
Arizona	Case law	Acknowledges*
California	Statute	Accepts
Colorado	Statute	Accepts
Delaware	Case law	Accepts
District of Columbia	Case law	Accepts
Florida	Statute	Accepts
Georgia	Case law	Acknowledges*
Indiana	Statute	Accepts
Iowa	Case law	Accepts
Kansas	Statute	Accepts
Kentucky	Statute	Accepts
Louisiana	Statute	Accepts
Maryland	Statute	Accepts
Massachusetts	Case law	Accepts
Michigan	Case law	Accepts
Minnesota	Statute	Accepts
Montana	Statute	Accepts
Nebraska	Case law	Accepts
New Hampshire	Statute	Accepts
New Jersey	Case law	Accepts
New York	Case law	Accepts
North Carolina	Case law	Acknowledges†
Ohio	Case law	Accepts‡
Pennsylvania	Case law	Accepts/rejects§
South Carolina	Case law	Undecided
Texas	Case law	Accepts
Utah	Statute	Accepts
Vermont	Case law	Accepts
Washington	Statute	Accepts
Wisconsin	Case law	Accepts

*Acknowledged circumscribed duty, but none found in this case.
†No duty pursuant to case facts but a narrow one was acknowledged.
‡Opinion is expressly limited to inpatient situations.
§Two opposite trial opinions.

Tally (09/27/89)

Total jurisdictions	31
Statutes	14
Total cases	48 (involving mental health professionals)

Source. Researched and compiled by Steven B. Bisbing, Psy.D., J.D.

Common Terms and Abbreviations in Legal Citations

Symbols and Abbreviations

aff'd —lower court decision affirmed
aff'g —affirming
App —appellate (higher court)
App Div —appellate division (e.g., N.Y. Court of Appeals)
App Term —period in which appellate court hears cases
Cert —certiorari (discretionary device by a superior court to hear cases from a lower court). For example, when the U.S. Supreme Court grants *cert*, it means it has "voluntarily" decided to review a case.
Cert den —a petition for certiorari is denied/rejected
Cir —circuit/Circuit
Civ —civil/Civil
Crim —criminal/Criminal
Ct —court/Court
Ct Cl —Court of Claims
D —District (U.S. District Court) (federal jurisdiction)
Dist Ct —District Court (state jurisdiction or court)
id —cite to the immediate preceding authority
infra —citation found in upcoming passages
J/CJ —judge or justice/chief judge or chief justice
mod —opinion was modified
nd —no date available
reh'g —opinion was reheard
rev'd/rvsd —lower court opinion was reversed
slip op —slip opinion (advance publication of a recent opinion, typically in abbreviated form)
supra —previously cited authority that is not the immediate preceding citation
Sup Ct —Supreme Court (typically refers to state court)
S Ct or US —United States Supreme Court
Super Ct —Superior Court (trial-level court) (state)
vac —lower court opinion was vacated on appeal/rehearing

Terms

In re —in the matter of (e.g., all nonadversarial matters such as juvenile proceedings)

en banc —heard by the entire appellate court
ex rel —on behalf of
ex parte —by one, or for one, party (e.g., judges may choose to hear a matter, ex parte, or for the benefit of one party, without notice or response by an adverse party)
per curiam —opinion of the entire sitting court rather than the written opinion of one judge writing for the majority
sua sponte —of his own will (e.g., judge voluntarily hears a case on his own without prompting or a petition from a litigant party)
sub nom —a different name of a party in a subsequent history of a single case (For example, the defendant in the *Wyatt v. Stickney* case changed before the entire litigation process (appeals) had run; e.g., *Wyatt v. Stickney*, 344 F Supp 373 (MD Ala 1972) *aff'd sub nom Wyatt v. Aderholt*, 503 F2d 1305 (5th Cir 1974)

LIST OF CITED CASE LAW AND LEGISLATION BY CHAPTER OUTLINE

I. Civil Law—Professional Practice

Brune v Belinkoff, 354 Mass 102, 235 NE2d 793 (1968)
California Association of Psychology Providers (CAPP) v Rank, 247 Cal Rptr 641 (Cal App 1988) *on appeal*
Chizmadia v Smiley's Point Clinic, 428 NW2d 459 (Minn App 1988)
Creamer v Danks, 700 F Supp 1169 (D Me 1988)
In re A-85-04-38, 525 NYS2d 479 (Sup Ct 1988)
Justari v Nappi, 549 A2d 210 (Pa App 1988)
Lieb v Dept. of Health Services, 542 A2d 741 (Conn App Ct 1988)
Mazza v Huffaker, 61 NC App 170, 300 SE2d 833 (1983)
New York v Hawkrigg, 525 NYS2d 752 (Suffolk Cty 1988)
Shamburger v Behrens, 418 NW2d 299 (SD 1988)
Shilkret v Annapolis Emergency Hospital Association, 276 Md 187, 349 A2d 245 (1975)
Stepankoff v Kantor, 393 Mass 836, 473 NE2d 1131 (1985)
Wall v Stout, 310 NC 184, 311 SE2d 571 (1984)

II. Civil Law—Liability and Standard of Care

A.L. v Commonwealth, 521 NE2d 1017 (Mass 1988)
Block v Ambach, 528 NYS2d 204 (App Div 1988)

Bolton v Jones, 401 NW2d 894 (Mich App 1987) *vac on other grounds* 426 NW2d 183 (Mich 1988)
Buchanan v Lieberman, 526 So2d 969 (Fla App 1988)
C.A.U. v R.L., 438 NW2d 441 (Minn Ct App 1989)
Corgan v Muehling, 522 NE2d 153 (Ill App 1988)
Cosgrove v Lawrence, Nos A-350-86T5 & A-352-86T5 (NJ Super Ct, App Div, March 10, 1987)
Davis v Lihm, 335 NW2d 481 (Mich App 1983) *remanded on other grounds* 422 Mich 875, 366 NW2d 7 (1985) *on rem* 147 Mich App 8, 382 NW2d 195 (1985) *rvsd sub nom* Canon v Thumudo, 430 Mich 326, 422 NW2d 688 (1987)
DeShaney v Winnebago County Department of Social Services, No 87-154 (US S Ct, Feb 22, 1989)
Doe v United States, 618 F Supp 503 (D SC 1984) *aff'd* 769 F2d 175 (4th Cir 1985)
Eckhardt v Kirts, 534 NE2d 1339 (Ill App Ct 1989)
Florida First National Bank v City of Jacksonville, 310 So2d 19 (Fla App 1975)
Hamman v County of Maricopa, No CV-87-0070-PR (Ariz S Ct, Jan 19, 1989)
Hinkelman v Borgess Medical Center, 403 NW2d 547 (Mich Ct App 1987)
Honea v Prior, 369 SE2d 846 (SC App 1988)
Houndroulis v Schuhmacher, 531 So2d 450 (La 1988)
Jackson v New Center CMH Svcs., 404 NW2d 688 (Mich Ct App 1987)
Lipari v Sears, Roebuck & Co., 497 F Supp 185 (D Neb 1980)
Littleton v Good Samaritan Hospital & Health Center, 529 NE2d 449 (Ohio 1988)
Lyle v United States, No C-85-1824 (ND Cal 1986)
Mammo v State of Arizona, 675 P2d 1347 (Ariz App 1983)
Marston v Minneapolis Clinic of Psychiatry & Neurology Ltd., 329 NW2d 306 (Minn 1982)
McCall v Dept. of Health & Rehabilitative Services, 536 So2d 1098 (Fla Dist Ct App 1988)
Myles v Osborn, No 19,962-572, Hinds County Cir Ct (Miss, Dec 18, 1987)
Newton v Louisiana Dept. of Health and Human Resources, 536 So2d 560 (La Ct App 1988)
Noto v St. Vincents Hospital, NYLJ, Jan 10, 1989, at 22, col 4 (NY Cty Sup Ct, NY, Jan 1989)
Paddock v Chacko, 522 So2d 410 (Fla Ct App 1988)
Pass v Dorsey, Nos A8212-07040 & A8212-07041 (Multnomah Cty Cir Ct Ore, 5/14/84)

Perreira v Colorado, 768 P2d 1198 (Colo 1989)
Petersen v State, 100 Wn2d 421, 671 P2d 230 (1983)
Public Health Trust of Dade County v Valcin, 507 So2d 596 (Fla 1987)
Rogers v South Carolina Department of Mental Health, 377 SE2d 125 (SC Ct App 1989)
Rook v Trout, 747 P2d 61 (Idaho 1987)
Sellers v United States, 870 F2d 1098 (6th Cir 1989)
Sharpe v South Carolina Dept. of Mental Health, 292 SC 11, 354 SE2d 778 (Ct App 1987), *cert dsmd* 294 SC 469, 366 SE2d 12 (1988)
Strock v Pressnell, Nos 87-1550 & 87-1557 (Ohio Aug 24, 1988)
Tarasoff v Regents of the University of California, 17 Cal 3d 425, 131 Cal Rptr 14, 551 P2d 334 (1976)
Turner v District of Columbia, 532 A2d 662 (DC 1987)
Welty v State Board of Chiropractic Examiners, 759 SW2d 295 (Mo App 1988)
Woolverton v Kregar, No 11-86-4844-C, Cameron County, 197th, Judicial Dist (TX May 1988)

III. Criminal Law

Ford v Wainwright, 477 US 399 (1986)
Penry v Lynaugh, 57 USLW 4958 (June 26, 1989)
Powell v Texas, 57 USLW 3857 (July 3, 1989)
Stanford v Kentucky/Wilkins v Missouri, 57 USLW 4973 (1989)
Thompson v Oklahoma, 108 S Ct 2687 (1988)

IV. Ethics and Professional Conduct

Ackerman v Ambach, 530 NYS2d 893 (App Div 1988)
Danto v Michigan Board of Medicine, 425 NW2d 171 (Mich App 1988)
Lieb v Department of Health Services, 542 A2d 741 (Conn App 1988)
Reisner v Board of Regents, 535 NYS2d 197 (App Div 1988)

V. Hospitals/Institutional Care

Dillon v Silver, 520 NYS2d 751 (App Div 1987)
Kalssette v Mecklenberg County Area MHMR & SA Authority, 364 SE2d 179 (NC 1988)
O'Sullivan v Secretary of Human Services, 521 NE2d 997 (Mass Sup Jud Ct 1988)
Pampirin v Trinity Memorial Hospitals, 423 NW2d 848 (Wis 1988)

Salas v Gamboa, 760 SW2d 838 (Tex App 1988)
Smith v Baptist Memorial Hospital Systems, No 04-85-00558-CV Texas Court of Appeals *cited in* Medical Liability Reporter 5:31 (Jan 1989)
Stock v Forbes Health System, 697 F Supp 1399 (DC Pa 1988)
Swarz v Billington, 528 So2d 1371 (Fla App 1988)

VI. Patient Rights

Adele S. v Kingsboro Psychiatric Center, 539 NYS2d 769 (App Div 1989)
Colorado ex rel M.K.M., 765 P2d 1075 (Colo Ct App 1988)
Colorado v Gilliland, 769 P2d 477 (Colo 1989)
Florida v Moore, No 88-8182CF10 *cited in* National Law Journal 9 (05/08/89)
In re Bryant, 542 A2d 1216 (DC Ct App 1988)
In re Foster, 426 NW2d 374 (Iowa 1988)
In re Garrett, 538 NYS2d 919 (Sup Ct 1989)
In re Guardianship of Linda, 519 NE2d 1296 (Mass 1988)
In re Ingram, 689 P2d 1363 (Wash 1984)
In re Lambert, 437 NW2d 106 (Minn Ct App 1989)
In re McConnell, 538 NYS2d 101 (NY App Div 1989)
In re Steen, 437 NW2d 101 (Minn Ct App 1989)
K.S. v Winnebago County, 433 NW2d 291 (Wis App 1988)
Matter of Jane Doe, NYLJ, Dec 19, 1988, at 29 at 6 (Westchester Cty Sup Ct, NY, Dec 1988)
Matter of Jarvis, 433 NW2d 120 (Minn App 1988)
Mental Health Legal Services v Surles, No 88-12978 (Suffolk County Sup Ct, NY, Dec 1988)
Sabatini v Brown, NYLJ, Jan 21, 1988, at 15, col 5 (NY Cty Sup Ct, NY, Jan 1988)
United States v Charters, 863 F2d 302 (4th Cir 1988)
U.S. v Waddell, 687 F Supp 208 (MD NC 1988)
Walters v Western State Hospital, 864 F2d 695 (10th Cir 1988)
State of Washington v Harper, 759 P2d 358 (Wash 1988) *cert granted* No 88-599 (U.S. Supreme Court)

VII. Expert Testimony

Abbott v New Rochelle Medical Center, 529 NYS2d 352 (App Div 1988)
Capitol Hill Hospital v Jones, 532 A2d 89 (DC 1987)
Cross v Lakeview Center, Inc., 529 So2d 307 (Fla App 1988)

Curtis v Wolfe, 513 NE2d 1139 (Ill App 1987)
DiMaggio v Makeover, 536 A2d 595 (Conn App Ct 1988)
Ervin v American Guardian Life Assurance Co., 545 A2d 354 (Pa App 1988)
Footit v Monsee, 525 NE2d 423 (Mass App 1988)
Hastings v Baton Rouge Hospital, 498 So2d 713 (La 1986)
Haught v Maceluch, 681 F2d 291 (5th Cir 1982) (applying Texas law)
Jenkins v Parrish, 627 P2d 533 (Utah 1981)
Kahn v Burman, 673 F Supp 210 (ED Mich 1987)
McPherson v Ellis, 287 SE2d 892 (NC 1982)
Mercury Casualty Company v Superior Court, No C-483452 (Cal Ct App, 2d Dist, April 10, 1986)
Ogletree v Willis-Knighton Memorial Hospital Inc., 530 So2d 1175 (La App 1985)
Rhoades v Painter, 360 SE2d 174 (Va 1987)
Shuffer v Blue Ridge Radiology Associates, 326 SE2d 96 (NC App 1985)
Suarez v Wilmington Medical Center, Inc., 533 A2d 1249 (Del Super 1987)
Sutphin v Platt, 730 SW2d 455 (Tenn 1986)
Thomas v McPherson Community Health Center, 400 NW2d 629 (Mich App 1986)
Trower v Jones, 520 NE2d 297 (Ill 1988)
Willitzer v McCloud, 6 Ohio St 3d 447, 453 NE2d 693 (1983)
Wilson v Sligar, 516 NE2d 1099 (Ind App 1987)

VIII. Legislation

Alaska Stat Ann § 08.86.200 (1988)
Cal Health & Safety Code § 1316.5
MD Cts or Jud Proc Code Ann § 5-315 (1989)
Tenn Code Ann § 29-26-115 (1980)
Utah Code Ann § 78-14a-102 (Supp 1988)
Wash Rev Code Ann § 18.130.180 (24) (1988)

NOTES

1. Buie J: Right to diagnose is challenged in Florida. APA Monitor, Dec, 1988, p 23
2. Buie J: Physicians seek monopoly in legal case, brief states. APA Monitor, May, 1989, p 25
3. Buie J: Scope of practice debated in 12 states. APA Monitor, May, 1989, p 23

4. Cal Health & Safety Code § 1316.5
5. CAPP v Rank, 247 Cal Rptr 641 (Cal App 1988)
6. Hawaii rejects psychologist script privileges. Psychiatric News, April 7, 1989, p 1
7. Chizmadia v Smiley's Point Clinic, 428 NW2d 459 (Minn App 1988)
8. Brune v Belinkoff, 354 Mass 102, 235 NE2d 793 (1968)
9. Shilkret v Annapolis Emergency Hospital Association, 276 Md 187, 349 A2d 245 (1975)
10. Mazza v Huffaker, 61 NC App 170, 300 SE2d 833 (1983)
11. Stepankoff v Kantor, 393 Mass 836, 473 NE2d 1131 (1985)
12. Justari v Nappi, 549 A2d 210 (Pa App 1988)
13. Smith J: Medical Malpractice: Psychiatric Care—1989 Supplement 6–7. Colorado Springs, CO, Shephard's McGraw Hill, 1989
14. Tenn Code Ann § 29-26-115 (1980); Wall v Stout, 310 NC 184, 311 SE2d 571 (1984)
15. Shamburger v Behrens, 418 NW2d 299 (SD 1988)
16. Klein JI, Macbeth JE, Onek JN: Legal Issues in the Private Practice of Psychiatry. Washington, DC, American Psychiatric Press, 1984, p 38
17. American Psychiatric Association: The Principles of Medical Ethics With Annotations Especially Applicable to Psychiatry. Washington, DC, American Psychiatric Association, 1985, Section 4, No 2
18. Klein JI, MacBeth JE, Onek JN: Legal Issues in the Private Practice of Psychiatry. Washington, DC, American Psychiatric Press, 1984, p 38
19. Simon RI: Clinical Psychiatry and the Law. Washington, DC, American Psychiatric Press, 1987, pp 162–172
20. In re A-85-04-38, 525 NYS2d 479 (Sup Ct 1988)
21. Lieb v Dept. of Health Services, 542 A2d 741 (Conn App Ct 1988)
22. New York v Hawkrigg, 525 NYS2d 752 (Suffolk Cty 1988)
23. Creamer v Danks, 700 F Supp 1169 (D Me 1988)
24. Otten AL: More psychotherapists held liable for the actions of violent patients. Wall Street Journal, March 2, 1987, p 2
25. Bisbing S: Duty to warn: current overview and trends. Unpublished manuscript, Sept 27, 1989
26. Tarasoff v Regents of the University of California, 17 Cal 3d 425, 131 Cal Rptr 14, 551 P2d 334 (1976)
27. Hamman v County of Maricopa, No CV-87-0070-PR (Ariz S Ct, Jan 19, 1989)
28. Perreira v Colorado, 768 P2d 1198 (Colo 1989) [Note: This opinion supersedes the 10th Circuit's opinion in *Brady v. Hopper*, because in *Brady* a federal court was interpreting how it thought Colorado law might address the "duty to warn" issue. In *Perreira*, the Colorado Supreme Court, a much better authority for interpreting its own state law than a federal court, has clarified the issue.]
29. Lipari v Sears, Roebuck & Co., 497 F Supp 185 (D Neb 1980); Petersen v State, 100 Wn2d 421, 671 P2d 230 (1983)
30. Rogers v South Carolina Department of Mental Health, 377 SE2d 125 (SC Ct App 1989)

31. Sharpe v South Carolina Dept. of Mental Health, 292 SC 11, 354 SE2d 778 (Ct App 1987) cert dsmd 294 SC 469, 366 SE2d 12 (1988)
32. Rogers v South Carolina Department of Mental Health, 377 SE2d 125, 126 (SC Ct App 1989)
33. Sellers v United States, 870 F2d 1098 (6th Cir 1989)
34. Davis v Lihm, 335 NW2d 481 (Mich App 1983) remanded on other grounds 422 Mich 875, 366 NW2d 7 (1985) on rem 147 Mich App 8, 382 NW2d 195 (1985) rvsd sub nom Canon v Thumudo, 430 Mich 326, 422 NW2d 688 (1987); Hinkelman v Borgess Medical Center, 403 NW2d 547 (Mich Ct App 1987); Jackson v New Center CMH Svcs., 404 NW2d 688 (Mich Ct App 1987)
35. Littleton v Good Samaritan Hospital & Health Center, 529 NE2d 449 (Ohio 1988)
36. Littleton v Good Samaritan Hospital and Health Center, 529 NE2d 449, 455 n3
37. McCall v Dept. of Health & Rehabilitative Services, 536 So2d 1098 (Fla Dist Ct App 1988)
38. Eckhardt v Kirts, 534 NE2d 1339 (Ill App Ct 1989)
39. C.A.U. v R.L., 438 NW2d 441 (Minn Ct App 1989)
40. A.L. v Commonwealth, 521 NE2d 1017 (Mass 1988)
41. Strock v Pressnell, Nos 87-1550 & 87-1557 (Ohio Aug 24, 1988)
42. Welty v State Board of Chiropractic Examiners, 759 SW2d 295 (Mo App 1988)
43. Buchanan v Lieberman, 526 So2d 969 (Fla App 1988)
44. Honea v Prior, 369 SE2d 846 (SC App 1988)
45. Block v Ambach, 528 NYS2d 204 (App Div 1988)
46. Woolverton v Kregar, No 11-86-4844-C, Cameron County, 197th Judicial Dist (TX May 1988)
47. Stedman's Medical Dictionary, 22nd Edition. Baltimore, MD, Williams & Wilkins, 1979, p 579
48. American Psychiatric Association: Principles of Medical Ethics With Annotations Especially Applicable to Psychiatry. Washington, DC, American Psychiatric Association, 1985, Section 2, No 4
49. Cosgrove v Lawrence, Nos A-350-86T5 & A-352-86T5 (NJ Super Ct, App Div, March 10, 1987)
50. Marston v Minneapolis Clinic of Psychiatry & Neurology Ltd., 329 NW2d 306 (Minn 1982); Lyle v United States, No C-85-1824 (ND Cal 1986)
51. Doe v United States, 618 F Supp 503 (D SC 1984) aff'd 769 F2d 175 (4th Cir 1985)
52. Smith JT, Bisbing SB: Sexual Exploitation by Health Care Professionals, 2nd Edition. Potomac, MD, Legal Medicine Press, 1987
53. Patient-therapist sex in Mass. could lead to rape charges. Psychiatric News, May 5, 1989, p 1
54. Noto v St. Vincents Hospital, NYLJ, Jan 10, 1989, at 22, col 4 (NY Cty Sup Ct, NY, Jan 1989)
55. Pass v Dorsey, Nos A8212-07040 & A8212-07041 (Multnomah Cty Cir Ct Ore, 5/14/84)

56. Corgan v Muehling, 522 NE2d 153 (Ill App 1988)
57. Hondroulis v Schuhmacher, 531 So2d 450 (La 1988)
58. Rook v Trout, 747 P2d 61 (Idaho 1987)
59. Public Health Trust of Dade County v Valcin, 507 So2d 596 (Fla 1987)
60. Newton v Louisiana Dept. of Health and Human Resources, 536 So2d 560 (La Ct App 1988)
61. Paddock v Chacko, 522 So2d 410 (Fla Ct App 1988)
62. Myles v Osborn, No 19,962-572 Hinds County Cir Ct (Miss, Dec 18, 1987)
63. Turner v District of Columbia, 532 A2d 662 (DC 1987)
64. Mammo v State of Arizona, 675 P2d 1347 (Ariz App 1983)
65. Florida First National Bank v City of Jacksonville, 310 So2d 19 (Fla App 1975)
66. Bolton v Jones, 401 NW2d 894 (Mich App 1987) vac on other grounds 426 NW2d 183 (Mich 1988)
67. DeShaney v Winnebago County Department of Social Services, No 87-154 (US S Ct, Feb 22, 1989)
68. Stanford v Kentucky/Wilkins v Missouri, 57 USLW 4973 (1989)
69. Penry v Lynaugh, 57 USLW 4958 (1989)
70. Powell v Texas, 57 USLW 3857 (July 3, 1989)
71. Thompson v Oklahoma, 108 S Ct 2687 (1988)
72. Stanford, 57 USLW at 4976, n2
73. Stanford, 57 USLW at 4977
74. Stanford, 57 USLW at 4979 (O'Connor J, concurring)
75. Stanford, 57 USLW at 4984 (Brennan J, dissenting)
76. Stanford, 57 USLW at 4982 (Brennan J, dissenting)
77. Penry v Lynaugh, 57 USLW 4958, 4962 (June 26, 1989)
78. Ford v Wainwright, 477 US 399 (1986)
79. Parry J, The Rehnquist-Scalia court takes hold—part I: the death penalty and abortion. Mental and Physical Disability Law Reporter 13:319 (Aug 1989) citing Ford v Wainwright, 477 US 399 (1986)
80. Powell v Texas, 57 USLW 3857 (July 3, 1989) (per curiam)
81. Powell, 57 USLW at 3858
82. Schmidt S: Doctors rarely lose licenses. Washington Post, Jan 10, 1988, p Al; Disciplinary actions against physicians on rise, but still believed to be on low side. Psychiatric News, Jan 2, 1987, p 12
83. Spolar C: Billig Faces Charges in 5th Death. Washington Post, Sept 24, 1985, p C1
84. Disciplinary actions against physicians on rise, but still believed to be on low side. Psychiatric News, Jan 2, 1987, p 12; Schmidt S: Doctors rarely lose licenses—Maryland panel allowed rapist to keep practicing. Washington Post, Jan 10, 1988, pp A1, A16–17
85. Ackerman v Ambach, 530 NYS2d 893 (App Div 1988)
86. Danto v Michigan Board of Medicine, 425 NW2d 171 (Mich App 1988)
87. Lieb v Department of Health Services, 542 A2d 741 (Conn App 1988)
88. Reisner v Board of Regents, 535 NYS2d 197 (App Div 1988)
89. Padilla v d'Avis, 580 F Supp 403 (ND Ill 1984) action dsmssd sub nom Jones v City of Chicago, 608 F Supp 994 (ND Ill 1985); Padilla v

Minnesota State Board of Medical Examiners, 382 NW2d 876 (Mn Ct App 1986)
90. APA board sets up work group to assess sex problem between professionals, patients. Psychiatric News, Aug 3, 1984, p 4
91. Rensberger B: State watchdogs step up action against doctors. Washington Post, Sept 28, 1989, p A13
92. Disciplinary actions against physicians on rise, but still believed to be on low side. Psychiatric News, Jan 2, 1987, p 12
93. Swarz v Billington, 528 So2d 1371 (Fla App 1988)
94. Kalssette v Mecklenberg County Area MHMR & SA Authority, 364 SE2d 179 (NC 1988)
95. Salas v Gamboa, 760 SW2d 838 (Tex App 1988)
96. Dillon v Silver, 520 NYS2d 751 (App Div 1987)
97. Smith v Baptist Memorial Hospital Systems, No 04-85-00558-CV Texas Court of Appeals cited in Medical Liability Reporter 5:31 (Jan 1989)
98. Pampirin v Trinity Memorial Hospitals, 423 NW2d 848 (Wis 1988)
99. American Psychiatric Association: The Psychiatric Uses of Seclusion and Restraint (Task Force Report 22). Washington, DC, American Psychiatric Association, 1985
100. O'Sullivan v Secretary of Human Services, 521 NE2d 997 (Mass Sup Jud Ct 1988)
101. Stock v Forbes Health System, 697 F Supp 1399 (DC Pa 1988)
102. United States v Charters, 863 F2d 302 (4th Cir 1988)
103. Youngberg v Romeo, 457 US 307 (1982)
104. Washington v Harper, 759 P2d 358 (Wash 1988) cert granted No 88-599 (U.S. Supreme Court)
105. In re Ingram, 689 P2d 1363 (Wash 1984)
106. State of Washington v Harper, 759 P2d 358 (Wash 1988) cert granted—USLW—(U.S. Oct Term, 1989) (No 88-599) amicus for American Psychiatric Association et al
107. State of Washington v Harper, 759 P2d 358 (Wash 1988) cert granted—USLW—(U.S. Oct Term, 1989) (No 88-599) amicus for American Psychiatric Association et al at pp 9, 16, 22
108. State of Washington v Harper, 759 P2d 358 (Wash 1988) cert granted—USLW—(U.S. Oct Term, 1989) (No 88-599) amicus for American Psychiatric Association et al at p 25
109. State of Washington v Harper, 759 P2d 358 (Wash 1988) cert granted—USLW—(U.S. Oct Term, 1989) (No 88-599) amicus for American Psychiatric Association et al at p 7
110. Wilson v Sligar, 516 NE2d 1099 (Ind App 1987)
111. McPherson v Ellis, 287 SE2d 892 (NC 1982); Haught v Maceluch, 681 F2d 291 (5th Cir 1982) (applying Texas law)
112. Jenkins v Parrish, 627 P2d 533 (Utah 1981)
113. Hastings v Baton Rouge Hospital, 498 So2d 713 (La 1986); Thomas v McPherson Community Health Center, 400 NW2d 629 (Mich App 1986)

114. Capitol Hill Hospital v Jones, 532 A2d 89 (DC 1987)
115. Sutphin v Platt, 730 SW2d 455 (Tenn 1986)
116. Suarez v Wilmington Medical Center, Inc., 533 A2d 1249 (Del Super 1987)
117. Rhoades v Painter, 360 SE2d 174 (Va 1987)
118. Shuffer v Blue Ridge Radiology Associates, 326 SE2d 96 (NC App 1985)
119. Cross v Lakeview Center, Inc., 529 So2d 307 (Fla App 1988)
120. Willitzer v McCloud, 6 Ohio St 3d 447, 453 NE2d 693 (1983)
121. Ervin v American Guardian Life Assurance Co., 545 A2d 354 (Pa App 1988)
122. DiMaggio v Makeover, 536 A2d 595 (Conn App Ct 1988)
123. Kahn v Burman, 673 F Supp 210 (ED Mich 1987)
124. Mercury Casualty Company v Superior Court, No C-483452 (Cal Ct App, 2d Dist, April 10, 1986)
125. Curtis v Wolfe, 513 NE2d 1139 (Ill App 1987)
126. Faust F, Ziskin J: The expert witness in psychology and psychiatry. Science 241:31–35, 1988
127. Bales J: Expert witness controversy continues. APA Monitor, Jan 1989, p 21
128. Fed R Evid 702
129. Ogletree v Willis-Knighton Memorial Hospital Inc., 530 So2d 1175 (La App 1985)
130. Abbott v New Rochelle Medical Center, 529 NYS2d 352 (App Div 1988)
131. Footit v Monsee, 525 NE2d 423 (Mass App 1988); Trower v Jones, 520 NE2d 297 (Ill 1988)
132. HR 5210

Chapter 11

The Canadian Connection: A Canadian Perspective on Clinical Psychiatry and the Law

Selwyn M. Smith, M.D.

Marked differences exist between the Canadian and American experiences involving psychiatry and the law. In particular, the absence of a death penalty in Canada and the smaller number of landmark Canadian decisions involving psychiatry and the law are but two striking differences. Many recent Canadian decisions make reference to the Canadian Charter of Rights and Freedoms, specifically Sections 7, 9, and 15. These sections, concerned with unlawful arrest, confinement, and discrimination, are especially important in the area of patients' rights. They have impinged on procedures of involuntary commitment and shifted the dispositions of the courts somewhat toward patients' rights.

In general, many recent cases that focus on some specific principle of law reflect an aggregate of concerns that could be discussed under two or more headings. This is especially true in cases in which provincial health acts have been challenged by Charter or constitutional arguments; these cases are relevant to both patients' rights and legislative considerations. Expert testimony enters into cases discussed under the headings of criminal law and patients' rights.

It is difficult to assess changing trends in Canadian law based on such a small number of cases. However, shifts in emphasis and tensions between medical and legal aspects involving mentally disordered persons in Canada may be isolated.

This chapter reviews key legal developments relating to psychiatry and the law in Canada. I have addressed points of law or clinical practice specific to Canada and highlighted applications and exceptions in Canada. Dr. Bisbing's masterly chapter served as a useful guide.

I. CIVIL LAW—PROFESSIONAL PRACTICE

American legislation and consumer advocacy have seen salvation in adopting or at least learning from the Canadian health care system. Although Medicare has been very effective in guaranteeing Canadians reasonable access to quality medical care, it faces serious problems caused by an inability, or unwillingness, of provincial governments to pay the cost involved. Life expectancy is 2 years longer in Canada and infant mortality is lower than in the United States, and yet the Canadian government spends less than 9% of its gross national product on health care per year, in contrast to the United States, which spends 11.4%.

At present, serious conflicts exist with provincial governments over costs. Provincial governments are viewed as exerting inflexible budgetary controls on hospitals so that hospital boards have resorted to bed closures to balance budgets. Patients are discharged earlier, and more psychiatric treatment is performed on an outpatient basis. It is difficult to be certain what the future holds for the Canadian health care system. Most experts are cautiously optimistic that it will be maintained, even enhanced, if for no other reason than the public will demand it. Canadian physicians are currently locked into confrontation with their various provincial government paymasters. This battle is particularly heated in the provinces of British Columbia, Manitoba, Ontario, and Quebec. The right to binding arbitration, interestingly, has been won by Ontario psychiatrists who work in provincial psychiatric hospitals. This right is now also being demanded by the Ontario Medical Association as a precondition of any negotiated fee settlement.

Ontario is also forging ahead with health-profession legislation and hopes to introduce a bill during the 1990 spring session. This move comes despite serious concerns expressed by the College of Physicians and Surgeons of Ontario about how the legislation is to be enforced. The package proposed by the Ontario government includes legal and procedural, as well as scope of practice, provisions. This legislation is meant to develop a better regulatory framework for Ontario's health professions. At present, 17 health care professions are governed by eight different pieces of legislation, some dating as far back as 1925. Other professional groups have approached the Ministry of Health looking for ways to streamline regulation or become regulated.

The public has also lost confidence in the ability of certain professional groups to govern their members. A climate that will allow for a breakdown of the medical monopoly of the health care system appears to exist in Canada. Unlike the United States, Canada has not experienced the fever-pitch debate between psychiatrists and psychologists over hospital privileges, Medicare reimbursement, medication prescription rights, and the legal right to diagnose and treat organic disorders. Psychologists and other groups are lobbying for reimbursement under the various provincial health plans. Changes to the Medical Professions Act, which currently restricts doctors' ability to work with other health care professionals, are also being suggested. These efforts, if successful, may open up the controversy over the parameters of clinical practice between psychiatrists and psychologists that has occurred in the United States.

Because Canadians are less litigious than Americans, and because Canada is a much smaller country, there are far fewer Canadian court decisions involving patient records than such American court decisions. Many of the legal questions that arise in the United States have been considered by the U.S. courts. This is not so in Canada, where the answers remain speculative. In addition, American government agencies, both at the federal and state levels, promulgate regulation to a far greater extent than most of their Canadian counterparts. Answers to questions regarding records are often found in legislation in the United States, whereas Canadian lawmakers are silent on this issue. The result is that the practice of compiling health information is largely left in the hands of those who are gathering it, including government agencies operating the various health insurance programs.

The law governing health records in Canada is not found in one place (1). There are no health-record acts either at the provincial or federal level. Instead, there are provisions scattered throughout dozens of acts and regulations with references to numerous court decisions. Health-record legislation is found within broader legislation governing the institution or provider of service in which the record is found. Reference must be made to provincial hospital acts, hospital bylaws, nursing-home acts, public health acts, occupational health and safety acts, and so forth, and any regulations made under these acts.

A particular set of records will not be governed only by legislation directed solely at that particular provider of service. Legislation directed at particular circumstances, on which the records may from time to time be a part, will also govern. Information in a hospital record may be regulated by the hospital act of that province, the bylaws of the hospital, or the Public Health Act with respect to any information related to communicable disease. Records may also be affected by the Provincial Vital Statistics Act regarding the reporting of information. When the record is used in court, the evidence act will be applied.

To a certain extent, the law of health records is found in post-court decisions but to a lesser degree than in other medicolegal problems. Certain questions such as access to health records have been dealt with from time to time. By and large, however, most legal questions concerning health records have not been addressed by the courts. Judges occasionally comment in passing on certain matters involving health records, but these remarks cannot be taken as binding precedent.

Although the primary purpose of patient records is clinical, i.e., for the care or treatment of the patient, records are equally important as evidence in legal proceedings. Such proceedings may involve civil cases including divorce and personal-injury matters, criminal prosecutions, labor arbitration, and disciplinary actions.

Traditionally, the only evidence that has been permitted before the courts is that which a witness actually perceived through his or her own senses and not that gathered from other sources. Written or oral statements made by persons who are not before the court as witnesses are inadmissible as evidence that the information contained in these statements is true. Because of this, patient records were not admitted into court. They were in effect "hearsay" (2). The records contained statements of fact and opinion recorded by various individuals who were not before the court, and the credibility of these statements could not be tested by cross-examination. The statements written into the records may or may not have been true. Without the opportunity to test them, they were not admissible.

An exception to this hearsay rule occurred in a 1970 major Supreme Court of Canada decision. The Court in *Ares v. Venner* (3), examined the question of whether hospital records, including nurses' notes, could be admissible as an exception to the hearsay rule. The Court answered in the affirmative with the following rule:

> Hospital records, including nurses' notes, made contemporaneously by someone having a personal knowledge of the matters then being recorded and under a duty to make the entry of record should be received in evidence as prima facie proof of the facts

> stated therein. This should, in no way, preclude a party wishing to challenge the accuracy of the records or entries from doing so.

It should be noted that the decision in *Ares v. Venner* extends not only to hospital and nurses' notes but also includes records from extended-care facilities, clinics, and physicians' offices.

Canadian courts have not been faced with the problem of the patient taking action against the physician or the health care institution for the unwarranted disclosure of confidential information. Most experts have always assumed, however, that such disclosure, outside the context of a judicial procedure, would be grounds for legal action.

It should also be noted that an action for breach of confidence is still uncertain as far as Canadian common law is concerned. The Supreme Court of Canada has recognized the duty of confidentiality based on equitable principles (4). This was subsequently accepted by the Ontario High Court of Justice in a doctor-patient breach of confidence case (5). Breach of privacy actions, unlike in the United States, have not been developed in Canada.

II. Liability and Standard of Care —Actions Against Physicians

Canada has not experienced anything approaching the many lawsuits involving the "duty to warn" and the "duty to protect" that have arisen in the United States since the *Tarasoff* decisions. These decisions do not seem to have had much of an impact on the Canadian legal system. Recent actions do not flow in that direction, possibly due in part to the Canadian legal-fee structure and the consequent legal climate, which is less litigious than the American situation. Third-party issues have rarely reached the courts in Canada. Altogether, before 1980, there were few malpractice cases alleging improper treatment against Canadian psychiatrists. Canadian articles on issues such as the liability of hospitals for releasing patients in the context of an "open-door policy" tend to cite American cases (6).

The most important Canadian case concerning liability is *Mustafic v. Smith* (7), a 1988 decision. Ramiz Mustafic was a voluntary patient in the psychiatric unit of a hospital in Manitoba. The defendant, a psychiatrist, examined Mustafic and diagnosed him tentatively as being mildly depressed. Before reaching a final diagnosis, the doctor allowed Mustafic to leave the hospital on a day pass.

Mustafic left the hospital, wrote a suicide note, shot his two children, and killed himself. An action for negligence was brought against the psychiatrist on behalf of the patient's widow and one son, who survived the shooting. The defendant called two general psychiatrists to testify, and the plaintiff called two forensic psychiatrists. This is a rather unusual role for a forensic psychiatrist as far as Canadian legal cases are concerned.

Both forensic psychiatrists agreed that the initial referral to the Manitoba psychiatrist had been correct. The main issues at the trial were the initial diagnosis, responsibility to reach a final diagnosis quickly, and the accountability of the doctor for allowing the patient to leave the unit. The judge based his decision on his own interpretation of procedures outlined in DSM-III-R. The forensic psychiatrists called by the patient testified that in their opinion the defendant should have recognized the seriousness of the patient's illness, and they also testified that the medication prescribed was inadequate. The judge, however, found that at the time of the first interview, the patient "did not appear to have any of the major symptoms set forth in DSM-III-R as being determinative of a major depressive disorder." He further found the defendant reasonable in delaying a final diagnosis and ruled that the standard of health care had been sufficient. The facts, in his view, did not support a finding of negligence.

Important in the *Mustafic* judgment is the weight given to the testimony. The judge did not defer to the opinions of the two forensic psychiatrists, nor did he give them more weight than those of the general psychiatrists called by the defense. Both of the forensic psychiatrists felt that there should be a finding of negligence and substandard care, but the judge found for the defendant. He asserted that the plaintiff's witnesses were partial, and the psychiatrists called by the defendant were impartial, and therefore "where there is a conflict between the evidence of the experts called by Zumreta [the plaintiff] and those called by the defendant, I prefer and accept those called by the defendant." In the judge's ruling, it was stated that the "acts committed by the patient were not reasonably foreseeable." One thing that is clear in this decision is that Canadian courts have not yet had much experience with cases involving the liability of psychiatrists.

This case goes somewhat against the general tendency noted in Canadian decisions toward increasing specialization, uniform standards of health care, and the accountability of doctors (6). It has been observed that the so-called locality rule, a test of liability used earlier in Canada requiring only that a doctor demonstrate that the care given was of a standard equal to that in the community in which he or she practiced, has been weakened in recent years. In the *Mustafic* case, one wonders what the role of expert testimony is, if the judge himself, instead of relying on it, consults a textbook and makes up his own mind. This treatment of witnesses in an undifferentiated fashion is not likely to last long in Canada. In addition, the existence of malpractice insurance will probably contribute to an increased emphasis on the accountability of physicians for the care that they render.

The particular policy of exit privileges for patients involves specific provincial issues, of interest to professionals practicing in Manitoba. It has also been observed that in questions of liability, the courts take a stronger stance on the injury of a third party than on a patient's self-inflicted injury (6).

Litigation involving sex between a doctor and patient in Canada is rare. There have not been enough of these cases in Canada to establish a pattern; indeed, I was only able to discover one case recorded in 1989 (8). However, it appears likely that, similar to the American experience, it will be difficult for physicians to prevail in less clear circumstances.

In this case, a physician treating a 14-year-old girl for physiological and psychological problems had sex with her during a visit to her home (8). According to the Quebec Code (it is important to note that Quebec is the only province in Canada with civil law, as opposed to common law), the court had to determine whether most of the blame for the action should be placed on the patient or the doctor, and the court found against the physician. The physician, a general practitioner, had experienced serious psychotic episodes before the incident in question, and the lawyer for the Crown proposed that the judge find him not guilty by reason of insanity. This development—the Crown introducing the insanity defense when the defendant does not wish to use it for obvious reasons—will be subsequently considered. The judge considered the Crown's request, but found that the physician understood and appreciated the consequences of his actions at the time of the incident.

There is a dearth of Canadian litigation involving the incorporation of a duty to protect an adult or child. As emphasized in Dr. Bisbing's chapter, child protection agencies, staff psychiatrists and psychologists, social workers, and case workers must take reasonable precautions to protect children or adults who are at risk of emotional or physical abuse in the home. Although Canada has similar legislation to the United States involving the reporting of such cases, I have been unable to find a case involving successful litigation against a health care professional for failing to take reasonable precautions to protect a child or adult in the home setting. There may be cases pending. Also at the time of writing, there is a parallel flurry of cases having to do with the admissibility of children's testimony in abuse cases and the role of the psychiatrist in assisting the court in determining the credibility of the child's testimony. The outcomes of these cases are awaited with interest.

III. CRIMINAL LAW

Because there is no death penalty in Canada, that important issue is not covered here. Most of the recent cases dealing with criminal law involve the insanity defense. Insanity is defined under Section 16 of the Criminal Code of Canada and is based on a modified McNaughton rule. Recent decisions involve the categories of episodic dyscontrol syndrome, automatism, specific delusions, and intoxication.

Much of the activity in this area has been in the specific definition, for legal purposes, of a "disease of the mind." The Canadian definition of these legal terms most frequently referred to was formulated by Justice Brian Dickson in *R. v. Cooper* (1980) (9):

> Disease of the mind embraces any illness, disorder or abnormal condition which impairs the human mind and its functioning, excluding however, self-induced states caused by alcohol or drugs as well as transitory states such as hysteria or concussion.

In the same judgment, Justice Dickson defined the term *appreciate* as including more than knowledge of an action, and including an understanding of the nature and consequences of the action. Justice Dickson went on to become Chief Justice of the Supreme Court of Canada and has also made outstanding contributions in ruling on Charter issues. He retired in April 1990.

Recent cases involving judgments requiring the determination of "disease of the mind" still rely on Dickson's formulation. One wonders how far this formulation can be stretched to accommodate the cases that will arise in this decade and the next. Dickson's definitions were cited and relied on in *R. v. Stefan* (10), in which the defendant was found not guilty by reason of insanity of actions arising from arguments with his father. The defendant appealed, but the court held that at the time of his actions he was unable to "appreciate the nature and quality of his acts." The judge's statements are suggestive of the use of the definition given by Dickson.

The judge decided that it was not "necessary to put a label on the mental condition of the accused," and further that the only requirement was to determine that there was "present any illness, disorder, or abnormality which impairs the mind and its functioning." Being satisfied that this was the case, he upheld the verdict of not guilty by reason of insanity.

The definition of "appreciate" was the deciding factor in *R. v. Winters* (1985) (11), in which a woman was convicted of stabbing her son to death, and appealed on the basis that the trial judge made a mistake in instructing the jury on the insanity defense. The court of appeal in the Province of Newfoundland found the accused not guilty by reason of insanity under Section 16(1) of the Criminal Code, which includes that part of the definition of insanity relevant to this case, defining an insane person as one suffering from a disease of the mind to the extent that it renders him or her incapable of appreciating the nature or quality of an act. Also, Section 16(4) of the Criminal Code contends that each person is presumed to be sane until the contrary is proven. As outlined in the decision in this case, there are two parts to the test of insanity in Canadian courts, one being "the incapacity of the accused to appreciate the nature and quality of an act," and the second being the capacity "of the accused to know that an act is wrong." In this case, the first judge had equated appreciating with knowing. The trial judge failed to instruct the jury in how to apply the law of insanity to the evidence. The only psychiatric evidence positively established the patient's manic-depressive psychosis, which was evident during the period of the incident. The psychiatrist stated that when individuals are psychotically depressed, "they part company with reality," and such was the case here, to the extent that the appellant was unable to consider the consequences of her act, i.e., whether her actions were right or wrong. Here, the psychiatrist's expert opinion and testimony were based on examinations of the accused during remand and other usual procedures, including a review of her history. There was no outside evidence from various individuals to contradict the doctor's opinion, and the court held that if the jury in the first trial had accepted the evidence of the psychiatrist, it would have been obliged to return a verdict of not guilty by reason of insanity. It was noted that the trial judge did not instruct the jury as to the weight that they should give to the expert opinion of the psychiatrist and the supporting evidence of others.

Another case in which the definition of "appreciate" figured was *Kjeldsen v. R.* (12). The accused was detained at a psychiatric facility as a result of being found not guilty by reason of insanity of rape and attempted murder. He received a day pass from the facility, hired a taxi, and raped and killed the driver, striking her head repeatedly with a large rock. In his first trial for this offense, he was convicted of first-degree murder. In the first appeal, it was argued by the defense that the accused, who suffered from psychopathy, could not "appreciate" the consequences of his actions, in the sense that he could not "know that his acts were wrong." Psychiatrists for the defense and the Crown agreed that the accused was "a dangerous psychopath." Those testifying for the defense used a broad definition of "appreciating," including not only knowledge of the consequences of an action, but an understanding of the reactions of those affected by it. The psychiatrists called by the Crown used the term in a narrower sense, confining it to an understanding of the"physical consequences" of his actions. They stated that a psychopath "would be fully capable of appreciating the nature and quality of his acts though indifferent to such consequences." The court of appeal held that the broader interpretation should be used and found the accused guilty only of second-degree murder. Citing *R. v. Cooper* (1980) (9), in particular Dickson's formulation, the second appeal judge supported this verdict.

The definition of "appreciating" the consequences of the act was the deciding factor in *Landry v. R.* (13). The accused was charged with first-degree murder. He was diagnosed as suffering from paranoid schizophrenia at the time of the incident; he believed that he was God and that the victim he had killed was Satan. Following the correct procedure in cases in which the insanity defense is invoked, the judge instructed the jury on "disease of the mind" and its applicability to the verdict.

The jury interpreted the judge's explanation to mean that they should return a verdict of not guilty by reason of insanity only if "the accused was ill to the point of being incapable of knowing that he was committing a homicide at the time of the incident" [Section 16(1), Criminal Code C-34]—or if he was "ill to the point of being incapable of knowing that killing was illegal." Had these been the only instructions to the jury, they would not have allowed Landry to avail himself of the insanity defense, but the judge continued,

> On the other hand, if you are satisfied that it is more probable that it is not Pierre Landry, but Jesus Christ—or an internal force, following a cosmic influence or divine mission, who went to kill not Michel Fortin, but Satan or the demon, as the defense pleads, then you may correctly conclude that Pierre Landry did not have the material capacity necessary to appreciate the nature, quality, and consequences of his act or to know that it was illegal. He was

> then dissociated from reality, from our reality. He lived in his own reality, in a completely different reality, and his act was the result of his illness, of his chronic delirium, of his hallucinations. At that point he must be acquitted by reason of insanity.

These directives left the jury the task of deciding whether the defendant felt that he was God and the victim was Satan. The jury asked for further explanations of Sections 16(2) and (3), and details concerning hallucinations. After giving several examples, the judge stated that the test of Section 16(2) was whether the defendant knew that the act was "wrong" ("mauvais"), which the court interpreted as "illegal." This directive, as the Quebec Court of Appeal noted, left the jury with no choice but to find the defendant guilty. The court noted that

> If the Canadian Charter of Rights and Freedoms prevents Parliament from allowing a person to be stigmatized by a charge of murder except by a legal disposition in conformity with the principles of fundamental justice, Section 16 of the Criminal Code must be interpreted in a liberal manner. (13)

Further, another justice noted that "although the accused might have known that first-degree murder was legally wrong, there was no doubt that his mental illness led him to appreciate the quality of his action differently." The court of appeal overturned the verdict of the lower court and found the defendant not guilty by reason of insanity. In this judgment, we can see the influence of the Charter of Rights and Freedoms, intended to make the law accessible and understandable to Canadians. The Charter shifted the court toward a broader interpretation of the word "appreciate"—one favoring the accused.

In one unusual case, the defense was able to prove that the defendant was suffering from a disease of the mind, but the jury did not accept the insanity defense. In *R. v. Ratti* (14), the defendant, who had been found guilty of murdering his wife, appealed on the basis of the insanity defense. At the first trial, two psychiatrists, "well qualified in their field and well known to the justice system," gave convincing evidence of the accused's state of mind. In the appeal, the judge accepted this evidence and agreed that he was suffering from a disease of the mind, but held that the jury in the first trial was free to determine, from other evidence, that this disease of the mind did not fit the definition in Section 16 of the Criminal Code. Accordingly, the appeal was dismissed.

In *R. v. Mailloux* (15), concerning a defendant suffering from toxic psychosis, the insanity defense was not accepted by the jury, principally because of qualifications and reservations stated by the defense psychiatrists during cross-examination. The accused shot and killed a woman and her son while riding in a car with them. The defense pleaded insanity or, alternatively, intoxication, because the accused was paranoid and the problems in his personality were aggravated by the use of cocaine. The forensic psychiatrists called by the defense testified that the accused's use of cocaine resulted in the rare condition of toxic psychosis, and that he was, at the time, "incapable of forming the specific intent necessary to commit murder," or of "appreciating the nature and quality of his acts and of knowing that his acts were wrong." In cross-examination, they testified that he knew that the gun would go off when he pulled the trigger and therefore, was able "to appreciate the nature and quality of the act and to understand the immediate physical consequence which would flow from it." One of the psychiatrists agreed that the accused knew "that the act was wrong." This is another case in which it is clear that expert testimony alone is not decisive in the insanity defense. The courts reserve the right to interpret the medical evidence and determine whether the defendant could understand the consequences of his actions.

The decision in a case concerning episodic dyscontrol syndrome seems to have expanded the definition of "disease of the mind" (16). In *R. v. Butler,* the accused had a history of injuries to the head. He was charged with aggravated assault of his wife's infant son. The child had been badly beaten on the head, and the accused, while admitting that he was alone at home with the child, had no memory of beating the child on the head. The medical history of the accused was brought forward at the trial, and a neurologist ventured the opinion that he suffered from episodic dyscontrol syndrome, entailing an interruption of normal control mechanisms. His other violent acts were symptomatic. In the court decision, it was noted that disease of the mind had both a legal and medical component. Quoting from the judgment in a similar case, the judge observed that

> [t]he legal or policy component relates to the scope of the exemption from criminal responsibility . . . and the protection of the public by the control and treatment of persons who have caused serious harm while in a mentally disordered state . . . Since the medical component of the term reflects or should reflect the state of medical knowledge at a given time, the concept of "disease of the mind" is capable of evolving with increased medical knowledge with respect to mental disorder or disturbance. (17)

In line with other decisions, it was stated in the same case that "the opinions of medical witnesses as to whether an abnormal mental state does or does not constitute a disease of the mind are not, however, determinative, since what is a disease of the mind is a legal question." Here again we see that expert testimony is not always decisive in the insanity defense. The judge did emphasize that "the dissociative state must be considered as having its source primarily in the respondent's physiological or emotional make-up," rather than from an external source. The accused was acquitted by reason of insanity.

R. v. C. (R.M.) is another example of the difference between medical insanity and the legal definition of disease of the mind (18). The Manitoba Court of Appeal dismissed the appeals of two youths, young offenders, convicted of first-degree murder by a jury and sentenced to life imprisonment without eligibility for parole for 25 years, for "brutal, senseless" murder. In general, evidence showed that they were suffering from a type of megalomania, and "no doubt thought that they had extraordinary powers and, morally or amorally, were entitled to disregard the laws of the country at their own pleasure," thus showing that this delusion was not the type referred to in the Criminal Code. Consequently, they must be made responsible for their acts, even though the offenders might be deemed "medically insane."

> A person who has specific delusions but is in other respects sane shall not be acquitted on the ground of insanity unless the delusions caused him to believe in the existence of a state of things that, if it existed, would have justified or excused his act or omission. (13)

It is evident that the delusions of the defendant in *Landry v. R.* (13) would satisfy this test.

The landmark case in the area of self-induced intoxication is *R. v. Bernard* (19). The accused had been convicted in lower courts, and that conviction had been upheld, of sexual assault causing bodily harm. Witnesses testified that he had been drinking on the night of the assault, but he was walking straight and talking. The basis of the appeal was that the intoxicated state of the defendant removed the mens rea, the burden of which the Crown has to prove in such cases. The accused argued that intoxication should have been included in the finding of fact. The majority of judges held that only general intent need be demonstrated, in this case the intent to use force, which could be inferred from the accused's actions. They agreed that intoxication should have been part of a finding of fact, but stated that this omission did not create a miscarriage of justice. There was some discussion of the *Leary* rule (20), on which the judges relied to conclude that only a general or minimal intent need be demonstrated. Counsel for the accused argued that the application of the *Leary* rule effectively removed the burden of proof of intent from the Crown and therefore violated the accused's rights under the Charter. The majority of judges, however, held that the force of *Leary* was not absolute and the Crown was still required to prove intent; therefore, its application did not violate the Charter.

Chief Justice Dickson, who had dissented in *Leary*, dissented from the majority opinion in this case. He agreed that the *Leary* rule runs counter to the accused's right to a fair hearing and stated that the Crown must demonstrate specific intent in cases of sexual assault. In making his remarks, he explained that his judgment did not apply to intoxication in other offenses, such as impaired driving.

The definition of automatism was considered in *R. v. Oakley* (21). The accused had headaches, was dizzy, and heard voices while working with fiberglass. The voices in his head told him that people were threatening him, and he believed that his relatives were devils. He took his relatives' car forcibly and drove it at high speeds, colliding with several other vehicles and, when he was finally stopped by the police, struggling with the arresting officer. He was charged with theft, assault, and criminal negligence. At the trial, a psychiatrist described the incident as a "short-lived acute paranoid episode"; he was unable to give a medical opinion as to the cause of the episode, wherein the accused had no conscious ability to control his behavior.

When examined, the accused was able to describe all of his actions and activities within the context of his hallucination. At one point, he saw "devils in police uniforms." The psychiatrist testified as to a number of possible explanations for the psychotic episode, which included "a chemical blow to the integrity of the brain from exposure to toxic substances, an emotional blow, or a combination of both." It was established that there were emotional blows that may have been factors, i.e., that his parents had left home. It was further stated that a recurrence would be unlikely, but possible. The reason for this patient's epileptic seizures was undetermined, but perhaps was due to some toxic substance. The psychiatrist also stated that "although there was nothing psychiatrically wrong with the respondent at the time of the examination, there might be some underlying neurological condition that was the cause of the episode." He acknowledged the possibility that the psychotic episode was triggered by the exposure to toxic fumes while working with fiberglass.

In the trial, the judge followed the psychiatrist's analysis, and the accused was found not guilty on the grounds of noninsane automatism. The judge elected to establish the cause of the single episode, rather than consider that the accused had a disease of the mind. In the appeal, the Crown argued that the episode could not, in fact, be isolated in this way, and that the accused should be considered to suffer from a disease of the mind, because there was "evidence of serious mental illness of considerable duration." In the opinion of the judge, the actions of the accused were not unconscious or involuntary. The judge pointed out that

> they were the product of his delusions, but they were not involuntary within the definition of automatism. The fact that the respondent, as the result of his delusions, did not have the capacity to form a rational judgment, or that under the dominance of his delusions, which distorted his perceptions of reality, he considered that he had no choice other than to do what he did, does not constitute involuntary behavior. A person suffering from a severe, albeit brief, mental disorder, manifesting itself in a delusion that it is necessary to kill in self-defense, would not be entitled to a complete acquittal on the basis that his act of killing was so dominated by his delusion that he believed he had no other choice.

The court ordered a new trial on all charges except that of theft.

In the appeal of *R. v. Malcolm* (22), it was held that delirium tremens, which is brought about by the absence of alcohol after prolonged use, should be considered a disease of the mind (22). The defendant was charged with first-degree murder of his common-law wife and second-degree murder of her mother. The accused had drunk heavily for a day or two a week before the killings; he stated that he had suffered blackouts and hallucinations and could not remember the incidents or the hours before. Expert testimony was that he was probably suffering from delirium tremens at the time of the killings, and these experts explained that sufferers of delirium tremens really do not appreciate the nature and quality of their actions, and that "when compared to an intoxicated person, the chance was greater that a person suffering from the syndrome was totally out of touch with reality."

The trial judge did not make the defense of insanity available to the jury because he regarded the syndrome as a transitory state, resulting from the consumption of alcohol, and not as a disease of the mind. An important factor in his instructions to the jury was that the accused refused to undergo a psychiatric examination by the Crown's psychiatrist, and that the jury could draw "an adverse inference" from this refusal, in that "a sane and sober person intends the natural and probable consequences of his voluntary acts."

In the appeal, a new trial was ordered, because the judge held that "delirium tremens is not self-induced in the way drunkenness is self-induced, but rather is an abnormal state of mind which is the supervening result of the abuse of alcohol." In his judgment, it is a disease of the mind.

The court-ordered detention of a defendant considered to suffer from a disease of the mind was challenged by Charter arguments in *R. v. Swain* (23). Section 542(2) of the Criminal Code provides for the disposition of persons found to be not guilty by reason of insanity in a criminal case. In such cases, the accused is held "until the pleasure of the Lieutenant-Governor of the province is known." The Lieutenant-Governor is required to order that the accused be held in safe custody or released unconditionally, relying on a board to review cases and make recommendations. In the province of Ontario, there is a board of review charged with the review of every person in custody within 6 months of the original decision.

In *R. v. Swain,* the psychiatrist testifying for the Crown at the trial stated that if the accused continued to take his medication he would not be "a danger to the public." The verdict reached was not guilty by reason of insanity, and the accused was placed in a psychiatric facility. Two days later, the Lieutenant-Governor ordered him to undergo an examination. Based on the recommendations following this assessment, the Lieutenant-Governor ordered that he be confined to a hospital for treatment. In the appeal, counsel for the accused argued that the detention was unlawful under the Charter of Rights and Freedoms. The court, with one judge dissenting, held that the process is part of a larger scheme of treating mentally ill persons, and that as such it does not violate principles of fundamental justice. The appeal was dismissed. Justice Brooke, dissenting, stated that it should be possible to rebut the "presumption of continued mental illness or dangerousness" that follows a verdict of not guilty by reason of insanity.

The constitutionality of Lieutenant-Governor Warrants for those found unfit to plead or proceed with trial and for insanity acquittees is currently being considered by the Supreme Court of Canada. It will be interesting to see whether the Supreme Court of Canada follows the American court rulings on this important constitutional issue. In Canada, the public has difficulty in understanding the term *not guilty by reason of insanity.* The term *not responsible* is more meaningful to a confused public. At the time of writing, lawyers are arguing an appeal by Owen Swain of Toronto. Swain was found not guilty by reason of insanity in a 1983 assault on his wife and two children, and his lawyers argue that he is being held in arbitrary detention and that this is unconstitutional. In one highly publicized case, Emerson Bonner, a New Brunswick man, spent 16 years in a mental institution after being found unfit to stand trial. His crime? Trying to steal a woman's purse.

In addition to the constitutional challenge, amendments to the Criminal Code have been suggested that would change the words "not guilty" to read "not responsible by reason of mental illness." Several psychiatrists have argued for the adoption of a system similar to the one in Britain and other countries. A finding of diminished responsibility should be an option, and the court would decide what form of medical treatment or custody is required. Provisions could also be made to declare the dangerous mentally ill "dangerous offenders" and keep them in custody.

The current system involving review board hearings on the more than 400 Ontario residents detained under Lieutenant-Governor Warrants has been described as risk management by some and as a juggling act by others. It certainly is not scientific and errs on the side of public safety rather than the best interest of the individual. The typical Lieutenant-Governor Warrant patient, charged with manslaughter for example, serves between 7 and 8 years in the confines of the mental health system. That corresponds to the actual time served in most 12-year sentences as an extremely high sentence for the average manslaughter.

At present, as little as 1% of the mentally ill would qualify as criminally insane, and the public perception that an insanity plea is a means of "getting away with" something is unfounded. It is also clear that the current Lieutenant-Governor Warrant system leaves patients with fewer rights than people found legally guilty of crimes.

IV. Ethics and Professional Conduct

The regulation of psychiatrists in Canada is under the aegis of the provincial licensing bodies. The types of situations that will bring a psychiatrist before a disciplinary hearing are similar to those in the United States. Data are available from each provincial licensing body as to the number of complaints or incompetent acts made by psychiatrists. Such actions, if proved, are published on a regular basis. In addition, disciplinary actions against physicians, previously not open to the public, will shortly be open to the public in Ontario. Other provinces may well follow suit.

V. HOSPITALS AND INSTITUTIONAL CARE

With very few exceptions, patients in Canada who require inpatient hospital care are treated in publicly funded institutions. The psychiatric treatment of hospital patients and, in particular, the involuntary patient has been, unlike in the United States, virtually ignored in Canadian jurisprudence. Owing in part, perhaps, to the paucity of Canadian jurisprudence on the subject of the psychiatrist-patient relationship, few members of the legal profession or the public at large have a very clear idea of what actually goes on inside mental hospitals or the psychiatric wings of prisons. Fictional novels, plays, or television programs are adopted as fact by the Canadian public and lead to a distorted public image of psychiatric hospitals and routine psychiatric treatment. What is currently done to, for, and with mental patients and, in particular, mentally disordered legal offenders in Canada is done in relative secrecy. Such secrecy is sometimes the product of judicial, legislative, or administrative design.

VI. PATIENT RIGHTS—COMPETENCY

It is not surprising that the adoption of the Charter of Rights and Freedoms has prompted many challenges to laws and procedures of civil committal, treatment without consent, and competency. Indeed these are the issues of the legal impact of psychiatric care that average Canadians take to heart. The Charter was designed to appeal to the sense of justice of all citizens, and the rulings of the courts in these and other areas are beginning to alter the field of patient rights.

At the core of questions of involuntary committal is the question of whether the patient is "of danger to self or others." The definition of this consideration is brought to the fore and sharpened in *M. v. Alberta* (24). To understand this judgment and the progressive nature of the illness, it is necessary to review the patient's history.

In July 1979, after a urological operation, the patient experienced postoperative psychosis. The symptoms abated with medication in 2 weeks. During the year after hospitalization, the patient grew to believe that he had cancer. In October 1979, he went of his own accord to see the psychiatrist who had treated him for the postoperative psychosis. He was depressed and "85% of his day was preoccupied with delusions concerning cancer." The psychiatrist diagnosed him as being manic-depressive. The patient refused electroconvulsive therapy and was treated for 1 month in the hospital without effect. The patient denied suicidal intentions, but the psychiatrist was concerned about this possibility. He prescribed for the patient antidepressant and antipsychotic medications. This was of help to the patient, who went home to his parents. In November 1979, the psychiatrist thought that the patient's condition was worsening. Outpatient therapy was tried, but without success.

In January 1980, the patient, who by this time had lost weight, was apathetic, had trouble sleeping, and thought that he was being followed and eavesdropped on electronically by the police, was admitted to the hospital as a voluntary patient. The same psychiatrist treated him with antidepressant medication for 3 weeks, and the patient improved greatly.

In February 1980, the patient returned to the hospital for 6 weeks. His muscles twitched, and there were other signs of neurological degeneration. He still felt persecuted by the police and other institutions. He was diagnosed as suffering from manic depression or bipolar disorder. The psychiatrist felt that the patient did present a danger (although not an immediate danger) to himself and others, and if the patient had not been willing to be treated voluntarily, the psychiatrist would have moved to have him committed to the hospital involuntarily.

For 8 months, the patient seemed much less preoccupied with the police and cancer and worked in a clerical position. He returned to the hospital in July 1981, manic and preoccupied with the police, his family, and the psychiatrist, all of whom he thought were persecuting him. The patient's family reported that he had "grabbed a butcher knife" at home. The psychiatrist considered this an acting out of "suicidal feelings." Once again, the psychiatrist thought the patient dangerous, but did not apply for involuntary commitment because he could be treated voluntarily.

In September 1981, the patient returned to the hospital for 3 months as a voluntary patient. He spoke frequently of suicide and was depressed. The psychiatrist prescribed antipsychotic medication and sent him home. In July 1982, after threatening his mother, the patient returned to the hospital voluntarily. The family told the doctor that the patient was not sleeping well and had to be made to eat and take his medication. The results of a CAT scan showed "diffuse atrophy." The psychiatrist made a diagnosis of "paranoid psychosis with some organic, progressive basis. In his psychotic condition the patient suffered from paranoid delusions, his insight was impaired, he denied he was ill, and his judgment was grossly impaired." The psychiatrist also feared for his own safety with the patient.

The patient returned home, but by November 1983, his condition had become much worse. The psychiatrist found that the patient was "disinhibited" in his behavior toward the psychiatrist, and that he was a danger to himself and others and could no longer suitably be treated at that hospital. Accordingly, the psychiatrist signed a Certificate of Involuntary Admission. He wrote that the patient was "delusional," with his "insight and judgment grossly impaired," "unsuitable as a voluntary patient, very litigious, but harmless." He indicated on the form which facts he knew from his own examination and which were reported by the family. With the authority of this form, the patient was conveyed to the second hospital and admitted involuntarily. The psychiatrist testified later that by "very litigious, but harmless," he meant that the patient threatened to sue the hospital, but that the suit would not succeed. He said that he believed that the patient was dangerous in that "he might run into traffic in order to avoid a persecutor or might not eat, or might have gone out into the winter cold and not cared for himself." In the judgment, it was noted that the psychiatrist's conception of a person who is a "danger to himself or others" was one "unable to make sound decisions, which in turn might lead to dangerous behavior."

Psychiatrists at the second hospital interviewed the patient only briefly, and then at the times required for renewal Certificates of Involuntary Admission. One of these psychiatrists testified that the eventual diagnosis made by the first psychiatrist was correct, and that she considered the patient to be at risk of committing suicide because he had attempted it before and was a white male between the ages of 20 and 40 years with low overall stability. She estimated the risk of suicide to be 30 times greater, or 15%, because of the patient's "affective disorder." This psychiatrist treated the patient with the antipsychotic drug IMAP (fluspirilene), stating that without the drug he would relapse and become antisocial. She said that he had been violent toward his father, but the father did not testify to this effect. She explained her reasoning about the patient being dangerous—she thought that if he were released, he would have more time to think about his delusions, become isolated, deteriorate without the medication, and lose contact with reality. She admitted that she could not predict these results, but the combination of factors should be sufficient for detention.

At the time of one of the renewal certificates, an examining psychiatrist made a diagnosis of "paranoid psychosis." He told the court that his definition of dangerous included "emotional and psychological suffering." On more than one occasion, the patient refused electroconvulsive treatment. Eventually he was released, because the hospital staff felt that the next review board would not find him dangerous. After a brief period with his family, the patient was again committed to the hospital at his family's insistence. A review board granted a Certificate for Continued Detention, and the patient appealed that renewal certificate.

The evidence of all testifying psychiatrists was to the effect that the patient would not voluntarily keep appointments for injections of IMAP, and that without the injections his condition would deteriorate, he would not care for himself, and he would become dangerous. In the judge's opinion,

> I cannot say that the evidence satisfies me on a balance of probabilities that, if the patient stopped taking the present medication, there would be a serious risk of physical harm to himself or to others at present, even viewing the "present" in broad terms.
>
> I have already tried to make clear that if the patient stops taking the present medication, there will in a matter of weeks be a deterioration of serious proportions so that his condition will then properly be described as dangerous to himself, and even, perhaps, dangerous to others. If I am correct in my prognosis, then, when the deterioration has produced deterioration of such proportions, a physician could properly certify that the patient presents a danger to himself, and perhaps the physician could certify that he presents a danger to others.
>
> . . . I have been tempted to say that the patient is in a condition presenting a danger to himself and then use the power this court has under Section 32(8)(c) "to make any order it considers just" and order that the patient be subject to continuing detention only so far as is necessary to cause him to receive the injections he is now receiving. However, I have concluded against doing so. . . . First, I cannot in good conscience say that the evidence satisfies me that the patient is in a condition presenting a danger to himself or others. Second I regard the power given by Section 32(8)(c) as one which ought to be used only in special circumstances where otherwise injustice would occur. I do not think that there are here any such special circumstances.

The above case illustrates the problems in the assessment of whether the patient is dangerous to self and others, and therefore whether he or she should be detained. The courts insist on immediate, present danger, or some circumstances that can be predicted unerringly. The burden of proof is clearly on the review board. Here it is clear that they felt compelled to release the patient because they thought that a psychiatrist examining him would not grant a renewal certificate. The emphasis of the courts is no demonstrable immediate danger. Only this justifies detention.

In *Thwaites v. Health Sciences Centre Psychiatric Facility* (25), the sections of the Manitoba Mental Health Act pertaining to compulsory treatment and detention were subjected to a Charter challenge. Section 9 of the act allows authorities to convey to a psychiatric facility and detain any person suffering from "mental illness, mental retardation, psychoneurosis, psychopathic disorder, addiction, or any disability of mind caused by disease, senility or otherwise." The trial judge found the provisions of the act to be acceptable under the Charter, but the court of appeal struck down the act because of Section 9 of the Charter, which states that detention for "arbitrary" reasons is unlawful. In the case of the Manitoba Mental Health Act, the court of appeal found the language far too vague and the provisions too general, and therefore arbitrary.

On the same day as the above decision, the Manitoba Court of Queen's Bench ruled on the appeal of an order for probational treatment under Section 24(1) of the same act (26). The patient was diagnosed as having a "schizophrenia-affective disorder." Both sides in the dispute agreed that the patient had been properly admitted as an involuntary patient, but disagreed on the legality of the terms of her probation. The psychiatric facility released her on the condition that she "attend out-patient follow-up and receive and comply with medications (including intra-muscular injections)" as prescribed by the psychiatrists. The patient kept the appointments but refused to take the medication. The psychiatrist testified that the patient's condition would worsen without the medication, but the court noted that the act provided only for the requirement to attend appointments or report as conditions of release. It is unlawful to make the acceptance of medication a condition of probation.

The procedures of involuntary admission and detention in Ontario are highlighted by *Dayday v. MacEwan* (27). Dayday was admitted involuntarily because, in the opinion of examining psychiatrists, her mental disorder would result in violent actions against others. Two renewal certificates were issued. The patient challenged the second, on substantive and procedural bases, as well as Charter arguments.

The procedural issue is the most straightforward. The purpose of a review board, convened to issue a Certificate of Renewal for the involuntary detention of a patient, is to have a fresh evaluation of the patient by psychiatrists unfamiliar with the case. Accordingly, the same psychiatrist may not sit on two reviews of a patient's case. This happened in Dayday's case, and the judge was willing to quash the renewal certificate for that reason alone. He pointed out that although no objection was made at the time of the review board hearing, the prohibition in the Mental Health Act ensuring that members of a review board approach the issues free of any influence by reasons of prior involvement of any of its members in the same patient's case could not in law be waived.

Under Ontario law, a "mentally competent involuntary patient cannot be required to undergo treatment without his consent." Counsel for the patient argued that this means that involuntary detention is tantamount to imprisonment, and therefore renewal certificates should not be issued on the basis of hearsay evidence. The court held that hearsay evidence was admissible in a review board hearing, because of the strict time limits imposed on the board.

In the presentation of evidence that the patient was dangerous, the psychiatrists failed to convince the judge that the behavior they described and their prognosis justified involuntary commitment. Neighbors testified to "bizarre and hostile conduct." The judge stated:

> In my view, none of this evidence, whether direct or hearsay, revealed that the applicant had ever caused serious bodily harm to anyone. Rather, the evidence, if true, established that the applicant had been verbally abusive, an incredible nuisance and that she had inflicted what amounted to several relatively minor assaults on other persons. As a result of her behavior, some of her neighbors feared her and clearly did not want to have her in their midst. Of all of the allegations made against the applicant, the most serious was that she had sprayed a former neighbor in the face with some unknown aerosol substance. There was no evidence that the victim had been injured.

The judge cited excerpts from the transcript demonstrating that part of the psychiatrists' concern about releasing the patient was that they feared that her behavior would evoke responses from other people that might endanger her. This the judge did not find to be sufficient to meet the criterion of a mental disorder "of a nature or quality that likely will result in serious bodily harm to another person." For all of the above reasons, he canceled the renewal certificate.

Another important issue in patient rights is the determination of mental incompetency. A dispute between a father and son is a fascinating example of these issues (28). The patient was "cyanosed at birth" and "cerebral palsy, hydrocephalus and mental retardation were diagnosed at the Hospital for Sick Children in Toronto." He was taught to communicate using Bliss symbols and, by age 19, his intelligence test scores had changed from the midimbecile to the borderline retarded range. Doctors at the Rideau Regional Centre stated that he understood his gastric disorder, and what foods he could not eat.

In his Bliss conversations, the patient showed a great interest in his family, whom he had never seen, and in life outside the Rideau Regional Centre, in which he lived. Personnel at the center set up a trip allowing the patient to visit placement homes in Ontario and Quebec as a first step toward moving. The patient's father objected to this and the centre personnel canceled the trip. The father applied to have his son declared incompetent.

Teachers from the centre testified as to the patient's ability to learn quickly and his cheerful disposition. They felt that the cancellation of the trip would be a severe disappointment and cause introversion. The judge did not give much weight to the testimony of an outside psychologist who asserted that the patient should be declared incompetent because of mistakes he made in the Peabody Picture Vocabulary Test. This test requires a patient to distinguish between things such as waterfall and cascades, or faucet and tap, unrealistic distinctions for a boy confined to a center. In the opinion, the judge emphasized that physical infirmity does not imply mental infirmity, and ruled that the patient was competent and could make his own decisions and choose a home in which to live.

A similar decision concerning competency was reached in the case of an 89-year-old Manitoba resident (29) who suffered from short-term memory loss and disorientation. Her heating system was dangerous. Some of her children thought she should be institutionalized, but she was "stubborn and independent." The court ruled that she was competent and could decide to take risks if she wished. It ordered that her heating system be repaired and she be allowed to remain in her own home.

Provisions of the Ontario Mental Health Act were upheld in the face of Charter challenges in *Howlett v. Karunartne* (30). Counsel for the appellant, a 79-year-old voluntary psychiatric patient who had been determined to be mentally incompetent, argued that she could not be treated with medication against her will in the face of Section 7 of the Charter. The court ruled that mentally ill persons fall into a special category in society and they must be protected. Because the determination of incompetency was proper, she could be forced to undergo treatment.

The Charter was invoked in an unsuccessful attempt to challenge the Adult Protection Act of Nova Scotia (31). The Ministry of Community Services filed to institutionalize an elderly woman because they were unable to care for her in her own home. The court ruled that she was mentally incompetent and must be cared for, and that therefore institutionalization was not an infringement of her personal liberty. The obligation to care for incompetent individuals must outweigh Section 15 of the Charter.

The decision of whether to order the sterilization of a retarded woman provoked a great deal of commentary (32). The Mental Health Act does not provide for the sterilization of an incompetent person for nontherapeutic purposes. In this case, the family of an adult retarded woman wanted to have her sterilized to avoid the burden of bringing up children resulting from possible pregnancies. Permission was applied for under the *parens patriae* jurisdiction of the court. It was held on appeal that this consideration did not justify such extreme interference with a person's body.

VII. Expert Testimony

Although the Canada Evidence Act provides for the use of professional or other experts as witnesses at a trial, nowhere is it stated in the act exactly who such persons are. The general rule regarding qualifications of experts is that expert testimony will not be admissible unless the subject matter of the trial or inquiry involves issues beyond the competence of a lay jury to determine if unaided by such experts. Also, the witness's expertise must be gained through a course of study or habitual practical experience.

In the United States, a general practitioner is prima facie held to qualify as an expert on insanity regardless of the fact that he or she disclaims any such expertise and because his or her competence is a matter for the court's sole consideration. A number of older Canadian cases have invited the inference that a physician—or indeed, a non-M.D.—need not be stamped with the label "psychiatrist" to qualify as an expert on matters of the mind. Beyond that, it remains unclear exactly how qualified an "expert" must be before he or she will be permitted to testify on very specific psychiatric issues (33).

VIII. Legislation

All issues of legislation in Canada are now involved with sections of the Charter. Accordingly, some of the provincial acts have been discussed earlier in this chapter. Two cases have been retained for this section because their main interest is legislative.

In *Jenkins, Re* (34), an involuntary psychiatric patient challenged his detention under Section 7 of the Charter (34). He wanted to be able to present evidence that he should be released without going through the hearing of the review board. The court found that the provisions of the Mental Health Act did not violate principles of fundamental justice, and advised the applicant to apply for a review as dictated by the act.

In *R. v. Leblanc* (35), the accused made Charter challenges relating to the insanity defense based on Sections 7, 9, 12, and 15. The accused was convicted of second-degree murder by a jury in spite of his invocation of the insanity defense. He was sentenced to life imprisonment with no eligibility for parole for 10 years. He argued that he had been treated unfairly because of his mental disorder. The appeal court held that it was not the duty of the judge to interpret the verdict of the jury, and it was impossible to tell in what measure they had taken the insanity defense into account. The appeal court overturned the "guilty" verdict and registered a verdict of not guilty by reason of insanity.

NOTES

1. Rozovsky LS, Rozovsky FA: The Canadian Law of Patient Records. Toronto, Butterworth, 1984, p 3
2. Sopinka J, Lederman SN: The Law of Evidence in Civil Cases. Toronto, Butterworth, 1974, p 89
3. Ares v Venner (1970), SCR 608, 73 WWR 347, 14 DLR (3d) 4.12, CRNS 349
4. Slavutych v Baker (1976), 1 SCR 254, (1975) 4 WWR 620, 55 DLR (3d) 224, 38 CRNS 306, 75 CLLC 14
5. Damien v O'Mulvenny (1981), 34 OR (2d) 448, 128 DLR (3d) 258, 19 CCLT 48, at 50
6. Weisstub DN: Ethics and liability for malpractice: introductory note, in Law and Psychiatry in the Canadian Context. Edited by Weisstub DN. New York, Pergamon, 1980, p 753. See also the article reprinted on pp 765ff of this book from Fink VN: Medical malpractice: the liability of psychiatrists. 48 Notre Dame Lawyer 693, 1973
7. Mustafic v Smith (1988), 52 Man R (2d) 20, (1988) CCL 9934 (QB), affirmed (1988), 55 Man R (2d) 188 (CA)
8. R. v Theriault (1989), RJQ 1140 (CA)
9. R. v Cooper (1980), 1 SCF 1149, 31 NR 234, 51 CCC (2d) 129
10. R. v Stefan (1986), 51 Sask R 194 (Sask CA)
11. R. v Winters (1985), 51 Nfld & PEIR 271, 150 APR 271 (Nfld CA)
12. Kjeldsen v R. (1981), 2 SCR 617 (1982), 1 WWR 577, 17 Alta LR (2d) 97, 24 CR (3d) 289, 28 CR (3d) 81, 39 NR 376, 64 CCC (2d) 161, 131 DLR (3d) 121, 34 AR 574 (sub nom R. v Kjeldsen) (SCC), affirming (1980) 3 WWR 411, 20 AR 267, 53 CCC (2d) 55 (Alta CA)
13. Landry v R. (1988), 66 CR (3d) 158 (CA Que)

14. R. v Ratti (Nov 2, 1988) Doc No CA 355/87 (Ont CA), affirming Mar 2, 1987, Callaghan ACJ, Ont HC
15. R. v Mailloux (1986), 12 OAC 339, 25 CCC (3d) 171 (Ont CA). Leave to appeal to SCC granted (1986), 25 CCC (3d) 171n, 16 OAC 80n, 68 NR 160n (SCC)
16. R. v Butler (1988), 72 Nfld & PEIR 25, 233 APR 25 (PEI TD)
17. R. v Rabey (1978), 37 CCC (2d) 461, 79 DLR (3d) 414, 17 OR (2d) 1
18. R. v C. (R.M.) (1988), 53 Man R (2d) 29n (Man CA)
19. R. v Bernard (1988), 2 SCR 825, 67 CR (3d) 162, 90 NR 389, 44 CCC (3d) 570, affirming (1983), 36 CR (3d) 394, 9 CCC (3d) 94 (Ont CA)
20. Leary v R. (1978), 1 SCR 29
21. R. v Oakley (1986), 13 OAC 141, 24 CCC (3d) 351 (Ont CA)
22. R. v Malcolm (1989), 6 WWR 23 (Man CA)
23. R. v Swain (1986), 53 OR (2d) 609, 24 CCC (3d) 385, 13 OAC 161, 50 CR (3d) 97, 18 CRR 209 (Ont CA), reversing (Ont CA), Brooke, Houlden, Thorson JJ.A., Feb 11, 1986
24. M. v Alberta (1985), 63 AR 14 (Alta QB)
25. Thwaites v Health Sciences Centre Psychiatric Facility (1988), 3 WWR 217, 48 DLR (4th) 338, 51 Man R (2d) 196 (Man CA), reversing (1986), (1987) 1 WWR 468, 33 DLR (4th) 549, 45 Man R (2d) 187 (sub nom Thwaites v Health Sciences Centre), 27 CRR 325 (Man QB)
26. Demkiew v Health Sciences Centre Psychiatric Facility (Medical Officer) (1988), 53 Man R (2d) 301 (Man QB)
27. Dayday v MacEwan (1987), 62 OR (2d) 588 (Ont Dist Ct), additional reasons to Doc No DC 658/87, Ont Dist Ct, Nov 16, 1987
28. Clark v Clark (1982), 40 OR (2d) 383, 3 CRR 342, 4 CHRR D/1187 (Ont Co Ct)
29. Nova Scotia (Minister of Community Services) v R. (E.) (sub nom R. (E.), RE (1988), 88 NSR (2d) 301, 225 APR 301 (Fam Ct)
30. Howlett v Karunartne (1988), 640 OR (2d) 418 (Dist Ct)
31. Nova Scotia (Ministry of Community Services) v Carter (1988), 89 NSR (2d) 275, 227 APR 275 (Fam Ct)
32. Eve, RE (1986), 13 CPC (2d) 6, 31 DLR (4th) 1, 71 NR 1, 61 Nfld & PEIR 273, 185 APR 273 (1986), 2 SCR 388 (sub nom E. V. Eve), 8 CHRR D/3733 (sub nom E. V. Eve) (SCC), reversing (1980), 27 Nfld & PEIR 97, 74 APR 97, 115 DLR (3d) 283 (PEI CA), with additional reasons at (1981) 28 Nfld & PEIR 359, 79 APR 359, 115 DLR (3d) 283 at 320 (PEI CA)
33. Schiffer ME: Mental Disorders and the Criminal Trial Process. Toronto, Butterworth, 1978, p 198
34. Jenkins, RE (1986), 59 Nfld & PEIR 62, 178 APR 62 (PEI SC)
35. R. v Leblanc (1989), 68 CR (3d) 155 (CS Que)

Chapter 12

Expert Opinion: A Case of Tardive Dyskinesia

Thomas G. Gutheil, M.D.
Robert L. Sadoff, M.D.

Clinical Vignette

A 63-year-old floridly psychotic woman was brought to an emergency room of a general hospital by the police. Her landlord had called the police because of her continuous screaming. The attending psychiatrist on call to the emergency room saw the patient, diagnosed paranoid schizophrenia, and admitted her to the psychiatric unit. Because the patient was experiencing persecutory auditory hallucinations and delusions, haloperidol, 5 mg four times a day was started. The patient thought the psychiatrist was God. She viewed the taking of the medication as God's effort to purify her. The patient willingly took the haloperidol as prescribed.

Because the patient was so psychotic, the psychiatrist decided not to fully inform her about the risks and benefits of neuroleptic treatment. However, to ensure compliance, the psychiatrist did mention the possible side effects of dry mouth, blurring of vision, and constipation. The patient was taking her medication without coercion. The psychiatrist decided that neuroleptic treatment was the first priority. If he warned the patient that tardive dyskinesia (TD) was a possible side effect of neuroleptic treatment, he reasoned, the patient might incorporate this information into her delusional thinking and refuse treatment. The psychiatrist's reasoning was not entered into the medical records, however.

The psychiatrist learned that the patient had no family, lived by herself, and moved frequently. Social services contacted her landlord, who revealed that the patient was widowed many years ago, was quite wealthy, and had been hospitalized frequently for psychiatric reasons over the past 20 years. The patient was estranged from her only daughter. She saw a nephew infrequently.

The patient's clinical course was stormy. The auditory hallucinations remained initially refractory to haloperidol at 15 mg four times a day. At this level, she became overly sedated. After 2 months of neuroleptic treatment, the patient's psychotic symptoms went into remission. The patient began to question the need for continued medication. The psychiatrist was able to work out a compromise with the patient whereby she would continue to take half the dose of haloperidol. Shortly thereafter, the patient began to experience severe dystonic movements of the face, trunk, and lower limbs. The patient became physically incapacitated by these symptoms, requiring assistance in eating, toileting, and walking.

The old medical records from her 11 previous psychiatric hospitalizations eventually were obtained by the psychiatrist. He discovered that she had received high doses of neuroleptics intermittently for 20 years for a diagnosis of chronic paranoid schizophrenia. She frequently would stop taking antipsychotic medications because of difficult-to-control extrapyramidal side effects requiring rehospitalization. The patient was discharged after 3 months to a nursing home for further care.

The patient brought suit against the psychiatrist for TD and lack of informed consent. Had she known that she was taking neuroleptic medication, the patient stated, she would have refused. It was her belief that medications in the past had produced more harm than benefit. The patient contended that she was not so psychotic as not to be able to make an informed decision.

In the psychiatrist's jurisdiction, two recent state supreme court decisions ruled on the matter of informed consent and the right to refuse treatment. In the first decision, the court ruled that physicians were required to inform patients according to the "reasonable man" standard. The medical custom standard was struck down. In the second ruling, the court held that incompetent mental patients who were refusing treatment required the substituted consent of the court, absent a defined emergency, before treatment could be started.

ARGUMENT FOR THE PLAINTIFF

THOMAS G. GUTHEIL, M.D.

Litigation for tardive dyskinesia (TD), regrettably, is only in its early stages nationally. All too many cases, moreover, represent at heart litigation for generally bad and even negligent care. Thus, some early cases involved retarded patients for whom even indications for neuroleptics were at least controversial. Almost no cases provide the rigorous legal analysis desirable to probe the core question in this matter: the risk-benefit analysis of antipsychotic treatment (1).

To discuss the plaintiff's side of the case based on the hypothetical vignette, I examine four aspects of the issue and conclude with some discussion. The aspects are the patient's membership in a high-risk population, the questions related to informed consent, problems inherent in TD as an entity, and analysis of the liability process.

Patient as High Risk

Demographic factors. This patient fits the category for high risk of TD on several dimensions. First, her advanced age and gender conspire against her as synergistic risk factors, because both are associated with a higher risk of TD.

Situational factors. More significantly, this patient was known at the time of initial presentation only to have been previously hospitalized repeatedly for a known chronic illness. Although, as is typical, the old records arrived extremely late, the physician had two ways to bypass this lack of information.

The first approach would be to call one of the previous hospitals and attempt to obtain information if the latter was willing to give it either under the patient's verbal consent over the phone or under color of the emergency situation. This might or might not have been successful.

More useful is the approach whereby the physician simply operates according to a few statistically likely and hence conservative assumptions. First, the psychiatrist might assume that the patient probably has been medicated with neuroleptics in the past and perhaps even overmedicated or exposed to polypharmacy in at least some previous care systems. Second, the psychiatrist should not assume that careful, respectful, and complete informed consent has *ever* been obtained by any previous caretaker. This position is not only likely to be true but also ensures that the current treating clinician assumes personal responsibility for undertaking the entire informed consent process anew. Taking this approach provides direct contemporary evidence of informed consent and permits the treating physician to adapt informed consent to the specific relationship with the patient that is being formed. I will say more on this point below.

Informed Consent Issues

Informed consent as dialogue. For all too many clinicians—not only psychiatrists—obtaining informed consent means getting the patient's signature on a form. As colleagues and I have suggested, this conceptualization is no more than "formed consent" or "pro forma consent," because it honors the letter but not the spirit of true informed consent (2). We have argued that informed consent in its true spirit is a dialogue conducted in an atmosphere of openness and honesty that permits doctor and patient to share medical uncertainty (2,3). Thus, there is no such thing as an informed consent "session" or "discussion" as a single event. The process is coextensive with the entire therapeutic relationship.

The information representing the "informed" in informed consent is usually characterized as the risks and benefits of the proposed treatment, of alternative treatments, and of no treatment. The consent refers to a competent agreement with the proposed plan; hence, the third element of informed consent is competence. Note that simple agreement with treatment by an incompetent patient is *assent, not consent*. Note further that the fact that the woman was psychotic does not in itself imply she was incompetent. Many chronically ill patients are incompetent in some areas but not in others.

Timing of information. Clinicians are justifiably concerned with informed consent in relation to use of neuroleptics with acutely psychotic patients such as the woman in the vignette who, in addition to being difficult to reach, may be actively paranoid and suspicious of caretakers. In this context a classic catch-22 presents itself. The clinician seeks trust from the patient by being frank and candid, but candid recitation of a "bad news" list of side effects and dire consequences of medication may heighten the patient's distrust. Yet the main route to decreased paranoia is this very medication.

Clinicians may adopt a compromise in the informing process described elsewhere (4). In brief, the patient is told during the acute phase about the immediate likely effects—hypotension, extrapyramidal symptoms, urinary retention, and so on.

Later—often at the point of discharge to outpatient status, when the patient might be expected to be competent—the long-term view may be explored. At this point TD should enter into the discussion in the context of a risk-benefit analysis for the long term. This delay may be justified, despite the law's vision of "informed consent from day one," because if the disease turns out to be a short psychotic episode (unlike the vignette), the neuroleptic may be stopped, and the issue of TD becomes academic. The physician and patient, in joint consideration, may wish to stop medication on a trial basis and see if relapse occurs. Where the illness is chronic or recurrent, and medication has been proved essential to prevent relapse, doctor and patient still may wish to review the TD risk afresh.

Therapeutic privilege. Of the several exceptions to the requirement for informed consent, emergencies are the most common and familiar. A less familiar one is the concept of therapeutic privilege (4). Simply put, this means that the physician can elect to withhold information about an illness or treatment from the patient if that information will directly harm the patient. A classic example is not telling a patient that he has just had a heart attack because hearing this pronouncement will further stress the patient and may itself produce noxious cardiac effects. In psychiatry, a similar question may arise about, say, telling this patient she has schizophrenia (5) and needs medication for it.

The most common misperception of the notion of therapeutic privilege is that it can be invoked because the doctor fears that the patient, once told of side effects, will refuse the treatment. This last example of paternalistic withholding is precisely what the doctrine of informed consent attempts to avoid. Competent refusal of treatment based on wishes not to have side effects is a fully valid exercise of informed consent. Thus, the competent decision to stop medications because of a fear of TD must be respected.

The reasonable man standard. The case vignette hypothetically takes place in a jurisdiction where the standard for informed consent is the so-called reasonable man standard. The physician is expected to reveal to the patient the risks and benefits that a reasonable person would want to know to make an informed decision. This means, among other things, that every last reaction in the *PDR* need not be listed nor every eventuality foreseen. The potential of neuroleptics to induce TD is clearly comprehended by this standard, however, because of the seriousness and general irreversibility of TD.

Substituted consent. A further legal doctrine in the vignette is one seen in several jurisdictions nationally: court-mandated substituted consent for antipsychotic medications (4,6), problematic though this model may be (7). Although the vignette describes this rule as applying to incompetently refusing patients, it is common for courts, in footnotes or dicta in such cases, to extend the legal procedures to the "incompetent assenter," the patient whose agreement is not valid because of incompetence. The case example would likely be subsumed under this procedure.

The TD Dilemma

Tragic choices. TD represents a classic instance of what is called in decision analysis a tragic choice: one in which both forks of the decision tree lead to undesirable or harmful outcomes. The tragic choice here poses TD against untreated major mental illness, each with its own severe negative consequences. Physicians, who played no role in giving the patient the underlying schizophrenia, confront the problem of inducing iatrogenic illness or leaving a severe pathology essentially untreated.

Reversibility of TD. TD, once thought irreversible, is now known to demonstrate at least partial reversibility under some circumstances when antipsychotics are stopped. This finding suggests that patients with early TD should be given at least a trial off medication to test this possibility.

Treatment of TD. In general, active pharmacologic treatment of TD has been disappointing. But many of the attempted regimens have shown at least limited or partial success. Hence, this avenue might have been tried, in consultation with specialists, with the patient in the case example. In addition, facts about treatment and reversibility of TD, no matter how limited, belong appropriately in the informed consent dialogue between physician and competent patient.

The Litigation Dimension

Hindsight factors. In almost all litigation the case unfolds under the retrospective view—that is, by hindsight. Despite our knowledge of actuarial risk factors, we cannot always predict who will and will not suffer TD. All we know is that if a suit for TD is brought, the person did suffer it and was sufficiently bothered by it to litigate. This last point alludes to the fact that a number of patients are not markedly impaired by their TD, accept it as the cost of remaining free of psychosis, or both. Note in the case vignette the plaintiff's claim that had she known of the TD risk, she would have refused medication. This is estimation by hindsight. From her current nonpsychotic state, the woman was performing a retrospective risk-benefit analysis that, however sound at present, cannot bring us back to the prospective decision-making situation in which real life is lived.

TD litigation. As noted earlier, TD litigation requires not only the presence of TD symptomatology but the patient's sense of being aggrieved by it—what I have called the malignant synergy of a bad outcome and bad feelings. Although this view may represent the patient-plaintiff's own position, legal advocates for the mentally ill also may bring TD litigation against a health care system as part of a broader critique of quality-of-care issues that often underlie ostensibly narrow medicolegal questions (8).

Finally, TD litigation is conceptually no different from any other litigation concerning adverse medication reactions—side effects, contraindications, allergic reactions, toxicities, and the like. For reasons to be addressed in the next section, however, TD issues set themselves apart (1).

Problems in the courtroom. The core issue in TD litigation, as noted at the outset, is the risk-benefit analysis of treatment with antipsychotic medications. Yet this picture is too simplistic once we arrive in court. Here is why: The patient in question already has TD. The woman in this case can be shown to the jury right in court, with a dramatic effect that is proportional to the severity of the condition. In other words, the "risk" side of the equation can be displayed palpably to the lay jury. The injury is clear.

The other side of the equation, in contrast, is an abstraction: How can one reveal anywhere nearly as dramatically the concept of "years of hospitalization avoided" or "months of freedom from symptoms" or "years of uninterrupted employment," or even "hundreds of patients who never get TD with the same treatment"? Here the ultimately misleading hindsight perspective can powerfully distort the picture.

Case Analysis and Conclusion

With the foregoing analysis as background we now can turn to the plaintiff's side of the hypothetical case and its rationale.

First, the case reveals that the patient was an "incompetent assenter" because her compliance, although clearly incompetent because of her psychosis, was based on a perception of the doctor as God rather than on the basis of a genuine or rational informed consent. According to the standard of care, her incapability of forming competent consent should have triggered simultaneously 1) treatment that the emergency aspects of her condition required (which do not emerge convincingly from the protocol, i.e., imminent risks to self and others) and 2) submission of the case to the court of competent jurisdiction for a reading on the case. Had the patient been formally ruled as competent, treatment could have proceeded in the appropriate manner.

Second, the doctor violated principles of informed consent by misusing the concept of therapeutic privilege. That is, the doctor's withholding information for fear that the patient might use side effect data—no matter how psychotically—as a reason not to take medication may be viewed as an attempt to bypass informed consent. If the patient competently refused for fear of TD, that must be respected; if the patient is incompetent, why isn't she in court? Note that the doctor's failure to document his original reasoning, as often emerges in subsequent litigation, even further weakens any arguments of therapeutic privilege.

Next, the patient was treated with markedly high doses of haloperidol even though she was a member of a group at risk for TD—elderly females. Moreover, there is no record of attempts (or even of consideration of attempts) to use other antipsychotics that might have been effective at lower doses or combinations of lower-dose haloperidol with benzodiazepines, an effective regimen that may decrease the need for antipsychotics. Instead, haloperidol was continued despite little positive response. Nor is there evidence that the doctor weighed the long past history as a cautionary factor, as described earlier.

Next, when the patient finally became nonpsychotic and questioned the use of medications, the time would have been ripe for a "phase two" discussion of TD in the context of the long-term effects of neuroleptics. Even though the patient accepted a lower dose, there is evidence neither of a risk-benefit analysis specifically incorporating discussion of TD, nor of consideration of other antipsychotic dosages that might have a lower risk of TD. Similarly, the record contains no evidence that the psychiatrist considered stopping medications when the first signs of (at least potentially reversible) TD appeared, nor does it show attempts, no matter how uncertain, at pharmacologic treatment of the TD symptoms.

On the basis of these deviations from the standard of care, the plaintiff might advance her claim.

ARGUMENT FOR THE DEFENDANT
ROBERT L. SADOFF, M.D.

There are two major ways of approaching this particular case—the legal method and the medical method. If one considers only the legal issues involved in treating this 63-year-old floridly psychotic woman in an emergency, then one adheres to the two recent state supreme court decisions regarding a patient, as noted in the clinical vignette. The first is the matter of informed consent in that physicians are required to inform patients according to the "reasonable man" standard. My interpretation of that standard is that the psychiatrist in any treatment situation, according to the supreme court ruling, must assume the role of a reasonable psychiatrist and assume that the patient is a reasonable person who can understand information about the illness and its treatment. This concept is close to what has been known as the reasonable person's standard in the law. Ideally, the psychiatrist should explain to this "floridly psychotic" woman in an emergency that she has paranoid schizophrenia and that she requires antipsychotic medication. The psychiatrist must explain to her the side effects, including tardive dyskinesia (TD) and hope that in a reasonable way she will accept his recommendation for treatment. Of course, he should also tell her about alternative forms of treatment and no treatment, and what the consequences of such alternative methods would be for her under these conditions.

The patient contends that had all of this been explained to her in her psychotic condition, she would have been sufficiently competent to understand and would have rejected the neuroleptic medication because she had taken it so many times before and had had side effects from it. (There is nothing in the history to indicate that she had ever had TD or symptoms similar to TD in the past.)

The second legal ruling by the court, as noted in the clinical vignette, held that incompetent patients who refuse treatment would require the substitute consent of the court, "absent a defined emergency," before treatment could be started. It appears that in this scenario, there is a "floridly psychotic" woman in an emergency, so that the legal standard would not apply. But, assuming that the doctor considered the patient incompetent and withheld treatment until he could find a judge who was willing to give "substituted consent," the patient would have continued in a "floridly psychotic" state.

This becomes one of those cases in which the law does not always apply to the practicalities of emergency room medicine and psychiatry. If the treating psychiatrist had waited to obtain substituted consent from a court, his floridly psychotic patient would have continued in a seriously mentally ill state. He would then have been criticized for withholding the very treatment for which she was brought to the emergency room. Comparable situations do not occur in medicine outside of psychiatry. If a floridly ill person is brought as an emergency to the emergency room for treatment of a medical or surgical condition, if the physician holds back in applying or administering emergency medical care, serious consequences can occur to the patient, which would result in a malpractice action against the doctor for negligently withholding emergency treatment. Therefore, emergency room physicians are trained to treat emergencies that are brought before them and to consider legal issues after the medical emergency has been taken care of.

In this particular case, we have a genuine medical psychiatric emergency in a "floridly psychotic woman" who was brought to the emergency room for treatment. It should be noted that the definition of *emergency* may vary in different jurisdictions. It is not proper to withhold treatment that will help this paranoid schizophrenic woman to obtain substituted consent for treatment. Doctors can certainly cover themselves by deferring to judges to make decisions about treatment. The doctor can cite state supreme court decisions that his interpretation mandates referring the case to the court rather than acting as a physician in an emergency situation. Then, if the court refused to allow the use of neuroleptic medications in this "floridly psychotic woman," the physician could blame the legal system when the patient continues to suffer in her psychosis.

But self-serving medicine is not necessarily good medicine, and it should not be encouraged in emergency situations. The proper interpretation of the supreme court cases in this clinical vignette makes an exception for emergencies, as this case appears to be. There are other exceptions to the informed consent rule in the practice of medicine. The concept of implied consent occurs when a patient is unable to give consent at a time when treatment is necessary. The consent is implied or presumed to be given, such that if the patient were competent, he or she would give consent to the treatment that is necessary. In a balance of life-or-death situations, courts often have allowed emergency treatment without informed consent, noting that the patient in an emergency waives his or her right to consent when life is on the line.The psychiatrist does not have the luxury of time to withhold treatment and wait for a judicial opinion. He has to make an immediate assessment of the patient's competency to understand her condition and necessary treatment. Absent an emergency, it is proper for the psychiatrist to withhold treatment of the incompetent patient to have substituted consent by family members (sometimes known as proxy consent) or professional consent by treatment review panels or through proper legal channels. But in this type of emergency, it is improper for the psychiatrist to withhold treatment in a suffering, medically ill psychotic woman. In this case, the patient did not refuse the medication that was offered, although she did accept the medication as part of her psychotic delusional system. There is really no way to be certain that the patient would have refused this medication if she had been told about TD as a potential side effect or if she had been told that she was going to take neuroleptic medication. Two months later, after the fact, when she is competent, she argues that she would have refused, even when she was in an emergency and incompetent state.

Certainly, this particular patient has had sufficient experience with neuroleptic medication over the past several years and her past several hospitalizations to know that the medication would be similar to what she had taken before, if she were competent to understand that. When she became more able to understand the nature of her medication and was told by the doctor what she was taking, she became upset about it, but did agree to a compromise with the doctor to take half the medication she had taken before.

In the course of treatment, the physician learned about the patient's past treatment and her frequent psychiatric hospitalizations during the previous 20 years. He did obtain medical records from her 11 previous psychiatric hospitalizations and discovered that she had received high doses of neuroleptics over the period of 20 years. He also learned from the records that she had never developed any symptoms of TD in the past, even from the high doses of neuroleptic medications she had taken intermittently for 20 years. It can be assumed that during the course of her treatment over the past 20 years, she had been told of the side effects of neuroleptics by doctors who had treated her during her previous hospitalizations. She had to be aware of the side effects that were discussed with her by her current psychiatrist, and even of the side effect of TD which this psychiatrist chose not to discuss with her for fear she would refuse necessary treatment.

Her current treating psychiatrist chose to use therapeutic privilege to effect a medical goal of helping his patient. Therapeutic privilege applies if informing the patient would tend to worsen the patient's condition or to confuse the patient to such a point that she could not give informed consent. As always, when treating patients, the psychiatrist must consider the best interest of the patient paramount in all phases of the treatment process. This, again, is a medical rather than a legal goal that physicians find important in the total treatment of their patients.

Lawyers would argue to the contrary that patients should be told every side effect that might affect their clients. Lawyers are not as concerned about medical improvement as they are about upholding the rights of their clients. It is in this particular area of medical-legal confrontation that physicians and lawyers may disagree. Lawyers argue for autonomy and independence of the patient who should make considered judgments and decisions for himself or herself. Physicians argue that patients who are functionally incompetent cannot make proper or reasonable decisions in the face of emergency conditions and require, at times, the substituted judgment of the physician who has experience in treating similar cases. The determination by the physician that the patient is incompetent is a total evaluation and is not based on diagnosis alone. Psychotic patients may still be competent to make treatment decisions.

In looking at this particular case, it is my opinion that this 63-year-old floridly psychotic woman, who was experiencing persecutory auditory hallucinations and delusions, was incompetent at the time of treatment to make a reasonable judgment about her condition and about her treatment needs. She required treatment at once—not a delay that may have aggravated her psychotic condition. The treating psychiatrist acted properly when he administered the neuroleptic medication with implied consent from the patient, without telling her of all the side effects that might occur. She did not refuse the medication and did not require the substituted consent of the court at that time, because she was in an emergency. Because she did not refuse the medication, the psychiatrist may presume that she was willing to accept it. Courts have occasionally accepted behavioral assent in lieu of formal verbal informed consent. When she improved and began to resist the neuroleptic medication, she agreed to a compromise with the physician to accept a half-dose of the medicine.

The decision of the state supreme court in the clinical vignette that physicians are required to inform patients according to the "reasonable man" standard does not mean that the physician must regard all incompetent patients in emergency situations as "reasonable" people who can make "reasonable informed decisions."

The patient is suing the physician because she developed TD and because of lack of informed consent. One cannot predict that a patient will develop TD, and the fact that the patient had had high doses of neuroleptic medication over the past 20 years without ever developing symptoms of TD indicates that there was no predilection for it in her case. The physician, of course, must be aware of the possibility of the development of TD and must observe the patient for early signs or symptoms. However, he cannot withhold the medication in such an emergency because he is afraid that the patient may, in the future, develop TD. He must treat according to the proper medical guidelines, and, in my opinion, he did so in this particular case.

The other part of the suit is lack of informed consent. The patient may reasonably argue that she was not told about the possibility of TD and that if she had been told, she would not have taken the medication. She also argues that she was not told she was getting neuroleptic medication at the time of her admission to the hospital. It is very likely that had the psychiatrist told her in her emergency condition that she was to receive neuroleptic medication and that TD was one of the side effects, she still would have accepted the medication because of her incompetent condition in that emergency situation. Her argument that she was sufficiently competent to make such a discrimination and distinction is overcome by the facts of the case, that she "thought the psychiatrist was God" and "viewed the taking of the medication as God's effort to purify her." In my opinion, under those conditions, giving her all the specifics of the side effects of the medication may have confused her even more and aggravated her condition. It was proper not to have burdened the psychotic patient with the information that she could not have handled or assessed and not to delay treatment any longer when this would have worsened her condition.

Telling the patient at that time is not the essential issue. What is important is the proper use of such medication, the proper caution by the physician for its use, and continued monitoring and observation of the patient's condition. The standards of medical care are not always equivalent to standards of legal care.

Summary and Conclusions

This complicated case exemplifies a common conundrum in the practice of psychiatry—whether to adhere to legal guidelines or to follow sound medical practices. Often, the two can be reconciled and are not antagonistic. But cases do arise in which medical needs in the emergency situation do not lend themselves to proper legal guidelines that are considered sound in nonemergency situations. Ideally, it would have been legally proper for the psychiatrist to tell the patient the nature of the medication and all side effects, including the possibility of TD. If the patient then refused the medication, the psychiatrist would have petitioned the court for substituted consent for treatment. That takes time and is not practical in emergency situations such as this one. Thus, it is my opinion that the psychiatrist did not deviate from the standard of care when he treated this "63-year-old floridly psychotic woman" in an emergency situation. Despite the supreme court decisions, this case did not apply because of its emergency nature. The mere development of TD does not mean the doctor was negligent in his care of this patient. Some patients develop TD, and others do not. The standard of care is what determines whether negligence and malpractice have occurred. In this case, the physician followed the medical standards of care and did not deviate. Thus, there was no malpractice. The result is unfortunate for the patient, but it was not proximately caused by any deviation from the standard of care by the treating psychiatrist.

NOTES

1. Gutheil TG: Forensic aspects of tardive dyskinesia, in Disorders of Movement in Psychiatry and Neurology. Edited by Joseph A, Young R. Cambridge, Blackwell Scientific (in press)
2. Gutheil TG, Bursztajn H, Brodsky A: Liability prevention through informed consent: some new approaches for the clinician. Risk Management Foundation Forum 7:8–9, 1986
3. Gutheil TG, Bursztajn H, Brodsky A: Malpractice prevention through the sharing of uncertainty: informed consent and the therapeutic alliance. N Engl J Med 311:49–51, 1984
4. Gutheil TG, Appelbaum PS: Clinical Handbook of Psychiatry and the Law. New York, McGraw-Hill, 1982
5. Masnik R: Telling a schizophrenic patient his diagnosis. Am J Psychother 28:452–457, 1974
6. Appelbaum PS: The right to refuse treatment with antipsychotic medications: retrospect and prospect. Am J Psychiatry 145:413–419, 1988
7. Gutheil TG, Appelbaum PS: The substituted judgment approach: its difficulties and paradoxes in mental health settings. Law, Medicine and Health Care 13:61–64, 1985
8. Appelbaum PS, Gutheil TG: The right to refuse treatment: the real issue is quality of care. Bull Am Acad Psychiatry Law 9:199–202, 1981

SUGGESTED READING

Cole JO, Gardos G: Tardive dyskinesia and malpractice suits. McLean Hospital Journal 4:35–48, 1989

Simon RI: Clinical Psychiatry and the Law. Washington, DC, American Psychiatric Press, 1987

Wettstein RM: Legal aspects of neuroleptic-induced movement disorders, in Legal Medicine. Edited by Wecht CH. New York, Praeger, 1985

Chapter 13

The Psychiatrist in the Courtroom: Suicide Litigation

Jeffrey D. Robertson, J.D.
Robert I. Simon, M.D.

THE TRIAL OF A SUICIDE CASE

JEFFREY D. ROBERTSON, J.D.

Suicides account for the greatest number of malpractice suits against psychiatrists and the largest percentage of settlements and verdicts paid by malpractice insurance companies (1). Yet most psychiatrists do not understand the law that governs the suicide case, and, as a result, they practice poor risk management.

Obviously patients should be admitted if there is clear evidence that they may harm themselves. But this is often a judgment made by the psychiatrist rather than a strict question of law. An error of judgment is a valid defense, provided the physician was cognizant of all the pertinent records and facts. The court will not insulate the psychiatrist if his judgment was made without proper medical foundation and not predicated on a careful examination and assessment of the patient. Of course, psychiatrists cannot predict the future. But psychiatrists rarely document reasons for not involuntarily admitting patients and fail to record the basis of their suicide assessment. Without seeing clear suicidal signals and symptoms the psychiatrist cannot commit a patient against the patient's will. Although all seriously depressed patients are at risk for suicide, the criterion is usually one of imminent and immediate danger. It is this dichotomy between the psychiatrist's duty to protect the patient's life and at the same time to respect the patient's civil rights that is at the heart of every suicide case. The law, in theory, protects the psychiatrist from the mere error in judgment, provided that the judgment was based upon full knowledge of all pertinent facts. It is well settled that physicians who exercise such judgment cannot be held liable for malpractice even if in hindsight the decision was erroneous (*Centano v. City of New York*) (2). Yet, as the following case dramatically illustrates, this defense is not often successful when a jury is confronting a fait accompli and conflicting expert opinions (3).

In *Bell v. New York City Health and Hospital* (4) the court imposed liability for the premature release of a patient who attempted suicide a week after discharge by dousing himself with gasoline and setting himself on fire. He heard voices that told him to do it. The defendant psychiatrist acknowledged that the decision to release the patient turned on whether the patient presented a risk to himself. The psychiatrist defended himself on the basis of the "best judgment" doctrine. But he admitted that he did not inquire into the nature of the patient's auditory hallucinations, even though the nurse had recorded her own observations of the patient's hallucinations for 3 days before the discharge. The doctor also acknowledged that a history of auditory hallucinations could lead a patient to kill himself, depending on what was said and believed by the patient and the identity of the voices.

Liability was also predicated on the psychiatrist's failure to request prior records concerning the patient's psychiatric history, even though the patient refused to cooperate. The records would have revealed an earlier suicide attempt. The doctor admitted that the prior records would have been helpful in stabilizing the patient and for future treatment purposes.

The day before the patient's release, the hospital record revealed, the nurse had had to place the patient in restraints because of his physical behavior. The need for restraints indicated the patient's assaultive tendencies, but the psychiatrist made no inquiry into this extraordinary event. The court also found an extraordinary failure of communication between the doctor and the nursing staff concerning the patient liability. As a result of all of these factors, the court found that "the decision to release the patient cannot be deemed to have been a professional judgment founded upon careful examination" (5). To fully appreciate the way the jury saw this case and viewed this psychiatrist in court we may examine the actual cross-examination of the defendant who authorized the discharge.

Questions by the Plaintiff's Counsel

Q.—Doctor, can you answer my question and relate it to this specific case. Was John Bell stabilized on the 9th?

A.—According to my note, yes, he was.

Q.—And according to the nurses' note he wasn't; is that true?

Comment. Plaintiff's counsel is trying to drive a wedge between the hospital staff and the psychiatrist and suggest a total lack of communication and failure on the part of the doctor to even review the nurses' notes.

A.—The note that the nurse wrote was on the 7th, not on the 9th. He was receiving 600 milligrams of Thorazine a day.
Q.—Doctor, let me ask you this: Do you consider a delusional patient stabilized?
A.—Stabilized enough so that he did not have to remain in the hospital. It depends on the delusion. There are delusional patients who are stabilized enough to go for outpatient treatment. I do not think that a delusional patient should not get treatment. I'm just saying a delusional patient does not have to necessarily remain in a hospital.
Q.—Depending on the delusions.
A.—Depending on the delusions.
Q.—Doctor, the record says 9/8/76: "Awake since change of tour. Delusional and restless." Is there any indication, Doctor, that the important element that you just mentioned, namely inquiry into the type and circumstances of the delusions, was made?
A.—No.
Q.—And that's a departure from accepted medical practice, isn't that true, Doctor?
A.—Yes.
Q.—And, Doctor, you didn't make any inquiry into the nature and circumstances of the delusions? That's certainly something that would find its way onto the chart in accord with accepted medical practice, isn't that true?
A.—Yes.
Q.—Is there anywhere in the chart that it says anything about that inquiry?

Comment. Of course if the doctor did make such an inquiry but failed to note it he still should have insisted on volunteering this fact in his answer, rather than allowing himself to be intimidated by the cross-examiner. He has given the impression that he failed to review the patient's record or status in any way whatsoever.

A.—The only thing that the chart says was the dictated note that there was no clear delusional thinking, but there is considerable amount of suspiciousness on the part of—on his part—and the preoccupation of Jesus Christ loving him.
Q.—That's the note written on the 7th, isn't that correct?
A.—Yes.

Q.—And yet the nurse's notes on the 8th and 9th state delusional and no inquiry was made, isn't that correct?
A.—According to the chart, that's correct.

Comment. If the doctor knew that he or the nurses did make inquiries even if not noted in the record, now was the time to state it. Of course, if no inquiry was ever made, liability appears obvious.

Q.—Doctor, the voices described by Nurse Brown might well have been voices indicating harm, isn't that correct? She never made her follow-up inquiry.
A.—It's always possible.
Q.—And, Doctor, the delusions that Mr. Bell was having on the 8th and 9th into which no inquiry was made might well have been delusions that would endanger him or others, isn't that true?
A.—Yes.
Q.—Doctor, wasn't it a departure from basic accepted medical practice for you to write that in the record without inquiring into those voices and into those delusions further?
A.—Yes. (6)

Comment. The patient testified that he did later hear voices telling him to set himself on fire. Once the defendant admits a "departure from accepted practice," liability is basically a foregone conclusion. It may not even be necessary to call an expert on the plaintiff's case. Of course, the departure must be established as the proximate cause of the injury, or there is no legal malpractice. This case appears to illustrate poor patient management and staff communication problems and obviously led to a plaintiff's verdict.

Best Judgment Defense

It has been said that to err is human but to blame it on someone else is genius. In this case the defendants tried just such a tactic, perhaps out of desperation. They claimed that even if they were negligent, they were not responsible, because the proximate cause of the suicide attempt was the patient's wife's argument with and abandonment of her husband after his discharge. The court soundly rejected this argument, however. The wife's leaving was not a supervening independent cause. In fact, the court held that her conduct was set in motion by the negligence of the defendants in prematurely releasing her husband. Mr. Bell threatened his wife at home, calling her "the devil" and threatening to kill himself and their oldest son. She therefore was quite justified in leaving him. As the court poignantly and prophetically put it:

> Who is to say that the act of leaving may not have saved yet another tragedy. In any event the peril which Mrs. Bell responded to was activated by the defendant's wrongful discharge of her husband. For just as danger invites rescue, it also provides for a retreat to safety. Mrs. Bell's conduct was not an intervening act, but part of a continuum of events initiated by the defendant's original misconduct. Her leaving was, at the very least, a concurrent cause of the attempted suicide for which defendants would not be released from their responsibility. (7)

Despite the ruling in *Bell,* the courts generally will uphold a psychiatrist's best judgment defense where it is based on proof of a careful examination of all the salient factors and records. In *Topel v. Long Island Jewish (8),* New York's highest court proclaimed that if the best judgment was exercised properly it would not subject the psychiatrist's judgment to the "second guess of a jury." *Topel* involved a police officer who was brought to the emergency room after making two suicide attempts in one day. The defendant psychiatrist was advised of the prior suicide attempts. He examined Mr. Topel, and in his best judgment, observation every 15 minutes was appropriate. Twenty-four-hour surveillance was contraindicated and counterproductive, in his opinion.

However, on the third day of hospitalization, a staff nurse ordered constant observation when she noted Mr. Topel prying the windows open. The following day the psychiatrist reduced the observation back to 15 minutes in an effort to calm the patient. However, unlike the situation in the *Bell* case, the psychiatrist had reviewed and considered the nurse's note. He was thereby establishing a firm foundation for the best medical judgment defense. The psychiatrist based his decision to order only 15-minute observation instead of constant observation on Mr. Topel's poor reaction to constant observation, on the rehabilitative aspects of an open ward, and on the enhanced possibility that the patient would consent to electroconvulsive therapy (ECT) in a more relaxed atmosphere.

The plaintiff's counsel claimed that the failure of the defendant to keep the patient under constant observation during the acute stages of his illness constituted negligence and led to his death. The plaintiff's case was supported by an expert who testified on the basis of recorded facts that the treatment rendered by the defendant deviated from accepted medical practice, and that lack of reasonable care inherent in this departure proximately caused the suicidal death.

Although the jury returned a verdict in favor of the plaintiff, the trial court set it aside. The court of appeals affirmed, holding that "the decision whether to keep Mr. Topel on constant observation at 15 minute intervals was a matter of professional judgment for which defendant doctor *cannot* be held liable." The court found that the defendant weighed various factors before determining "on balance" that the prescribed program was worth the risk involved.

> [W]hile the line between medical judgment and deviation from good medical practice is not easy to draw, we conclude that more is required to make out a prima facie case against a doctor than was presented by plaintiff's expert testimony [citations omitted]. To hold otherwise on the basis of an expert's opinion which does not negate the factors, listed above, on which the attending physician based his judgment is to subject every judgment made by a doctor, no matter what its basis, to the second guess of a jury.

The Second Guess of a Jury

A recent case where the jury did "second guess" the judgment of the psychiatrist involved weighing various factors in determining whether to admit a patient involuntarily and resulted in a plaintiff's verdict. The case was settled on appeal, however, and therefore no admission of liability can be inferred.

The major issue was whether the defendant departed from accepted psychiatric standards by not committing his patient involuntarily to the hospital on September 20, 1983. The doctor's defense was that in his best judgment, the patient was never imminently suicidal. He also testified that the patient's wife failed to stay home with the patient, as she had been instructed the night before the suicide.

The case is a perfect example of how difficult it is to educate a jury on the dilemma facing the psychiatrist. The major issue was whether the defendant departed from accepted psychiatric standards by not committing his patient involuntarily to the hospital on September 20, 1983. The doctor's defense was that in his best judgment, the patient was never imminently suicidal during 3 months of treatment.

Although the doctor recognized that this patient, like all with major depression, was always potentially at risk, it was his judgment that the patient never was suicidal and could not be involuntarily committed under the state's mental hygiene law. During the 10 weeks of treatment, the patient never made any suicidal attempts, gestures, or threats and never expressed any suicidal ideation. He was never psychotic, paranoid, or delusional. After weighing and balancing all the positive and negative factors, the defendant's opinion was that the plaintiff was not suicidal on the date of the last visit. A summary of the patient's treatment record, which was the basis of the doctor's opinion, follows.

Psychiatric Summary of Treatment

June 1983. The patient had no prior psychiatric history until June 1983, when his employer suddenly passed away. He then became psychotic and went to Holland to visit his father on June 6. While embracing his father, he cut his wrists and cut his father. He later told the defendant that he thought they would go to Heaven and didn't really intend to harm either one of them. In the doctor's opinion, it was actually part of his delusion. After a brief hospitalization for psychotic paranoia, he was discharged and advised to see a psychiatrist upon his return to New York.

July 6. The plaintiff was referred to the defendant, a board-certified psychiatrist who was formerly regional director of the state mental health department. The doctor reviewed all of the psychiatric records from Holland, conducted a thorough examination, and elicited history from both the patient and his wife. He concluded that the patient was no longer "psychotic" and not "currently suicidal" based upon an evaluation of the following positive and negative factors:

1. The absence of any suicidal ideation.
2. The absence of depressed agitation.
3. The absence of delusions or paranoia.
4. The absence of feelings of worthlessness and hopelessness.
5. Consideration of the prior suicide attempt.
6. The prognostic statistics such as age, sex, and race.
7. The patient's judgment and insight.
8. The patient's family history of depression and his mother's suicide when he was young.
9. The history of the patient.
10. Behavioral characteristics such as impulsiveness and compulsiveness.

The defendant diagnosed the patient as suffering from major depression and recommended as the "primary and foremost" treatment hospitalization with ECT. This would have provided the best structure and the fastest opportunity for recovery. The patient was terrified of hospitalization, however, and refused. He wanted to stay at home with his family. Because the doctor could not admit him involuntarily, the only other alternative was to rely on medications and supportive therapy on an outpatient basis. As time went on, the patient made steady progress, as summarized in the following excerpts from the medical records.

July 9. No psychotic symptoms.

July 12. Feeling much better.

July 21. Not suicidal . . . not delusional . . . afraid of hospitalization.

August 12. No psychotic symptoms.

August 19. Wife says he is 60–70% of normal self, no paranoid or delusional ideas . . . no self-destructive thoughts . . . feeling good . . . sleeping well, keeping on weight . . . appetite good . . . enjoys company of son . . . is improving.

September 2. Not delusional . . . ("I think clearly") . . . generally doing better around the house . . . cooking . . . taking care of maintenance . . . feels better in p.m. . . . appetite fair, sleep—good.

Even the patient's wife testified that as time went by, her husband was more relaxed, less nervous, and showed a general improvement. In September he was playing with his young son, was thinking more clearly, and went on a camping trip with the family.

September 20. Despite this improvement, the patient began to show some signs of regression on the last visit. He was "preoccupied with his inability to function" in the last 2 weeks, according to the doctor's notes. The doctor was concerned about the tone of his reporting but testified that this did not mean that the patient was more severely depressed than before, or suicidal. In assessing the suicide risk on this last visit before the suicide, the doctor testified that he weighed the following positive and negative factors:

1. The patient did not express suicidal ideation.
2. He did not express any hopelessness.
3. He was competent, lucid, and able to understand the discussion.

4. He was not agitated.
5. His judgment was appropriate.
6. He was free of psychotic preoccupation and symptoms.
7. He had made a prior suicide attempt in Holland in June.
8. The plaintiff's psychiatric anxiety might increase because of the recommendation for hospitalization and ECT.

The psychiatrist also was mindful of other factors such as the patient's family history, statistical factors, and the patient's behavioral characteristics. Because the doctor could not hospitalize the patient against his will, the defendant urged the patient to reconsider ECT and hospitalization. The patient again refused. The psychiatrist asked the patient and his wife to think it over carefully that night and call him in the morning with their decision.

He recognized that the patient might experience increased anxiety over this decision and therefore prescribed Sinequan, for antianxiety and sedative purposes. He asked the wife to stay with her husband at all times to "reassure and comfort him, report any significant changes and to discourage any acting out, even suicidally." The wife had been a very responsible and reliable spouse who stayed at home with her husband in the past. Unfortunately, she denied ever being told to stay home. Her attorney argued, however, that if she was told to stay it actually constituted proof that the defendant considered the patient suicidal. If the patient might "act out, even suicidally, then why take any chances?" he argued to the jury in his summation. The doctor, however, denied that he thought the patient would act out suicidally. "It was only a precaution," the psychiatrist explained, "there was no real evidence it might happen." Nevertheless, this testimony influenced the jury in favor of the plaintiff.

The patient's wife left her husband alone the next day to go to her part-time job because "she did not believe he was in any danger" and because "it was not his worst day." She spoke to him in the morning and believed that he was rational. Actually, this testimony was helpful to the defense, because it contained the doctor's evaluation:

Q.—What did you say to your husband?
A.—I asked him if he thought it would be necessary for him . . . I would be with him today.
Q.—And he said "No, it's okay, you can go to work?"
A.—Yes, he said "No, you can go to work."
Q.—You didn't think he would do anything like take his life or you

would not have left?
A.—I would not have left, no.

Sometime later that morning she called a neighbor to check on her husband. He was found hanging in the basement.

Plaintiff's Case

The plaintiff's case was based on the testimony of an expert psychiatrist who was retained just before the trial. He came to the attention of the lawyer as a result of a mass advertising campaign. The psychiatrist prepared a mailing list of attorneys from the local Jury Verdict Reporters and sent a series of form letters to 100 attorneys advising them of his "availability to perform consultations . . . and . . . do whatever I could to inform these attorneys of my findings and . . . willingness . . . to appear in court." Although this psychiatrist had experience as chief of a metropolitan hospital years before, he no longer treated patients in hospitals or had any psychiatric hospital affiliations. He admitted that he was "not current on what exactly has to be done once a patient reaches a ward." He had never performed ECT. When cross-examined about the procedure for admitting a patient to a hospital against his or her will he testified, incredibly, as follows:

Q.—Doctor could you put a patient in a hospital against his will and sign a certificate that he was in danger of hurting himself without examining the patient under the laws of psychiatry?
A.—I most certainly could.
Q.—Without ever having examined the patient?
A.—I most certainly could.

He later amended this answer to admit that he has seen patients for about a few moments before certifying them for involuntary admission.

Nevertheless, the jury was persuaded by his testimony. Calling the patient "about the highest risk patient you could ever have in the way of suicide potential," the witness testified that the defendant departed from good and accepted psychiatric practice by not involuntarily admitting the plaintiff to a hospital and that this was the proximate cause of his death. His opinion was based on his consideration of the following factors:

1. The patient began to backslide from his initial improvement and was preoccupied with thoughts of hospitalization and ECT.

2. The patient's wife was not competent to stay with her husband to discourage acting out, even suicidally.
3. The defendant underestimated the importance of the prior suicide attempt.
4. The patient had a family history of depression, and his mother had committed suicide while he was young.
5. The defendant admitted that he didn't like the tone of the patient's reporting the visit before the suicide risk.

The expert also testified that the following important factors were not adequately considered by the defendant:

1. Statistical studies show a greater incidence of suicide among white male patients over the age of 40.
2. The patient had an impulsive nature.
3. The patient was not working and was living in an unstructured environment at home.
4. The patient's judgment was impaired.
5. The thought of hospitalization and ECT would have increased the patient's anxiety.

Defense's Case

The defendant argued the best judgment rule. The doctor considered all of these factors, but simply accorded a different weight and significance to them. The patient was not suicidal at the time of the last visit. In explaining how a psychiatrist assesses suicide potential, he testified that although there is always a potential risk, one weighs and balances positive and negative factors:

> When we make a diagnosis of a patient it is very important that we keep in mind several things. We don't only look at what is bad. What is negative. We also look at what is positive.
>
> In the case of the patient, a depressed individual, it becomes extremely important from day one that one rules out the possibility of suicide because there are a number of considerations in any patient who is suffering from depression regardless of whether he is psychotic or nonpsychotic or neurotic. Depression always brings to our mind whether there are suicidal possibilities. So you asked about it, have you ever thought about killing yourself? If the patient says no, that is not the end of it. You also want to look at other ways that you can get to the situation. We have learned in the practice of psychiatry it is very important that one look at other signs of suicidal behavior. . . .
>
> Every time a psychiatrist sees that patient, every single session he has got to review that in his own mind. Is he suicidal? Is his judgment impaired? Is he not responding to treatment? What is his

> response to medications? How is he relating to you?
>
> All of these things are essential components that one practicing in psychiatry will have to take into account. . . . A continuous evaluation of the patient at every visit and continuous evaluation along all the parameters, medication, symptoms, his progress, lack of progress, new developments . . . with this patient, at all times I am concerned and considering the possibility of suicide. I cannot overemphasize that. . . .

Perhaps the psychiatrist summed it up best when he testified that "[w]hen I will make a judgment based upon my clinical assessment of the patient I cannot as a psychiatrist, regardless of how well trained or how good I am, predict the future with any certainty. . . . I cannot read minds."

Suggestion for Trial

In preparing for the deposition or trial of a suicide case, the psychiatrist should be prepared to be cross-examined on the following questions:

1. Had the patient any history of prior suicide attempts? If so, what methods were used? Isn't it true that the more lethal and serious the attempt, the more serious the risk?
2. Had there been any recent suicidal ideation? How often? Was there a specific plan, or was it just manipulative talk?
3. Were there any recent suicide gestures involving deadly objects such as knives, windows, roofs, stoves, or medication?
4. Was there a recent divorce or separation or loss of a loved one?
5. Was there trouble at work? Did the patient suffer a loss of self-esteem, face, or self-confidence? Has he lost a job and been humiliated by attempts to find new employment?
6. Is the patient alcoholic, a drug addict, or an addictive personality?
7. Was there a spouse, friend, or strong family to support the patient emotionally or monitor his safety physically?
8. Were the suicidal thoughts persistent in nature, in contrast to transitory ideas?
9. Had the patient finalized his business affairs or recently written or revised a will?
10. Did the patient live alone and have few or no human contacts?
11. Had there been any suicides in the family? Who were they, and what relationship did they have to the patient?
12. Was there a history of previous psychiatric treatment or hospi-

talization? Did the patient suffer from episodic moods of elation and depression of a manic-depressive type?

13. Did the plaintiff experience feelings of depersonalization? or of feeling that he or the world around him is "unreal," such as in a schizophrenic divide?
14. Did the patient suffer from a severe medical illness with intractable pain accompanied by intense feelings of depression? Was he feeling hopeless?
15. Did you record the fact that you made these inquiries and discussed the answers with the patient?
16. Had there been any change in the patient's condition during hospitalization?
17. Were restraints indicated? Why? Is there a suicide assessment in the record? Did you consider a consultation or second opinion in a difficult case?
18. Was the patient having any delusions or hallucinations?
19. Did you inquire into the nature of these delusions, hallucinations, or voices?
20. Had any change been made to the medication regimen that may have affected the patient's progress?
21. Was the patient dwelling on suicidal thoughts?
22. Was the nursing staff following through with the supervision orders?
23. Were there reasons that constant observation would have been detrimental for this patient?
24. Was the patient interacting with staff and patients, or was he remaining isolated?
25. Was the patient kept in a room close to the nursing station, and was he closely monitored by the staff?

If a patient refuses to be admitted and the psychiatrist determines, after a competent examination, that the patient is a danger to himself or herself, there may arise a duty to involuntarily admit the patient pursuant to the specific requirements of the applicable state mental health law (9). In some states, affidavits from two physicians are necessary. Ironically, if there is not valid reason to admit, a psychiatrist could be liable for false imprisonment or negligent admission, absent an immunity statute. But, if the psychiatrist was acting in good faith, liability is unlikely.

Even after admission, the psychiatrist is at risk for failing to take adequate precautions to protect the patient. One expert warns that merely writing "suicide precautions" on the order sheet is not enough, because hospital rules are ambiguous or subject to change or interpretation by the nursing staff (10). The psychiatrist must specify either constant observation, hourly observation, or observation every 15 minutes. The psychiatrist should confirm whether these precautions are being carried out. The nursing staff also must advise the doctor if the patient's condition deteriorates, because stricter precautions may be necessary. If the staffs fail to advise the doctor, the hospital may face primary responsibility for the suicide. Flagging the beds and charts of such patients might be helpful in alerting all ward personnel to the potential danger, even if the physician fails to order constant observation or if the order is canceled or expires.

Allegations in the Complaint and Defenses

To better understand the practical aspect of the suicide case we may look at a typical complaint. The most common allegations found in the plaintiff's complaint are the following:

1. Failure to predict or diagnose the suicide.
2. Failure to control, supervise, and restrain.
3. Failure to take proper tests and evaluations of the patient to establish suicidal intent.
4. Failure to medicate properly or restrain the patient.
5. Failure to observe the patient continuously (24 hours) or on a frequent basis (every 15 minutes).
6. Failure to take an adequate history.
7. Inadequate supervision and failure to remove belt or other dangerous objects.
8. Failure to place a patient in secure room.

Defenses

Psychiatrists can employ many legal and strategical defenses, as outlined below (3).

Best judgment defense. This defense excuses the defendant if he or she honestly used his best judgment after careful evaluation, testing, and consultation. Such defenses are often more effective on appeal than at the jury level. If the defendant failed to review the proper records or to conduct an adequate examination, there is no basis for this defense.

Impossible to predict. This defense is often based on the statistical impossibility of predicting suicide and often can be documented by lack of any suicidal ideation, attempts, or gestures. The defendant should be able to argue that the patient, family, or both denied any suicidal gestures, threats, or ideation and that there was no clinical reason to anticipate the suicide.

Family's responsibility. Sometimes a spouse or other family member refuses to reveal a prior suicide history or neglects to follow the doctor's orders or to monitor medication as requested. It is often effective psychologically, as well as legally, to challenge the responsibility of the surviving family. Often the surviving spouse was given the responsibility for monitoring a patient or for administering medications. In some cases, failure of the family to observe the patient at home or to report a change in condition can be a contributing factor. Sometimes families even can be shown to have provoked a confrontation. A common theme in defense cases is that the surviving spouse "drove the patient to it." This approach can have a certain practical appeal to a jury, particularly if it comes to see the surviving spouse not only as someone who was negligent but who is now seeking substantial monetary gain. Such defenses are dangerous without specific evidence, however, and this can easily backfire on the defense. But if the marriage was a rocky one, and there is evidence of infidelity, separation, or strife, the jury may be more likely to punish than to reward the spouse.

Family- or widow-guilt complex. One subtle defense theme is that the surviving spouse feels so guilty over his or her role in the suicide that the lawsuit is only based on guilt projected on the defendant. This is a sensitive argument and should not be used to "bury" the widow but to excuse her and the defendant at the same time from any culpability.

Intervening and supervening causes. Some suicides occur after the patient is discharged or when he or she is not under active treatment. A change of circumstances or long delay between discharge and the suicide is essential to sustain such a defense.

Contributory or comparative negligence. In some jurisdictions the patient can be held partially or wholly responsible for his or her own negligence. Most jurors are reluctant to make this judgment, however, because jurors usually consider patients inherently impaired in judgment if they attempt to take their own lives. But if a patient is proven incompetent by medical testimony, the plaintiff is responsible for his or her actions under the comparative negligence doctrine.

If a patient conceals a history of prior attempts, refuses to be hospitalized, or fails to follow orders and take medication, the jury could reduce any award by the percentage of comparative negligence they assess against the patient.

Can the Family Be at Fault?

Can a patient or a patient's family be held liable for not advising the psychiatrist of the patient's full psychiatric history? The answer is yes. Just as a patient can be responsible for not taking medication that patient or the patient's spouse can be liable for not revealing an accurate history. In *Krapvika v. Maimonides* (11), the court reversed a lower court's decision in favor of the plaintiff and dismissed the complaint. The decedent and his wife were recent Soviet émigrés. The decedent's psychiatric history was taken at the time of admission. He denied any prior suicide attempts. His wife was not directly asked about suicide attempts but testified that she intentionally withheld information about prior attempts because of her concern over their immigration status and harm to their family back in the Soviet Union. The decedent's wife also denied a history of prior suicide attempts by her husband during her deposition.

The court, in dismissing the complaint, held that

> [t]he record does not support the jury's finding that the defendant's staff failed to take proper medical history . . . and that failure to do so was a departure from good and accepted medical practice which caused or contributed to his death. The absence of a notation in the decedent's hospital records indicating that the decedent was questioned about prior suicide attempts and that there was a family history of suicide is not proof that the decedent was not so questioned [citation omitted]. Furthermore, three members of the defendant's psychiatric staff testified that the decedent's psychiatric history was taken as part of a routine procedure and that the decedent denied having made any prior suicide attempts. A positive response would have been recorded.
>
> The failure of the defendant's staff to question the decedent's wife, his rabbi, the doctor who drove him to the hospital and the psychiatrist who previously met him for one treatment session regarding the decedent's psychiatric history was also not a deviation from accepted medical practice which proximately caused or contributed to his death, since the plaintiff's wife admitted that she purposely withheld information about the decedent's prior suicide attempts, and the other persons had little or no relevant information to offer. In any event, there is no indication that more stringent supervision and restrictions would have been mandated had the hospital known of the decedent's prior suicide attempts.

Therefore, the court held that the decision of the defendant's staff not to place the decedent in the intensive care unit of its psychiatric ward but to allow him some measure of freedom within the ward for therapeutic purposes was an exercise of medical judgment. It was not made without proper medical foundation. The court concluded that "the prediction of the future course of a mental illness is a professional judgment of high responsibility and in some instances it involves a measure of calculated risk" (*Centano v. City of New York*, 40 NY 2d 932, 48 AD 2d 812, 813; *aff'd*, 40 NY 2d 932). Liability cannot be based merely upon the disagreement of another physician with the manner in which treatment is provided (12).

Subsequent Treating Doctor

If the suicide actually occurs months after the defendant treated the patient, a subsequent treating doctor is a key witness. If this doctor also did not hospitalize the patient, the doctor's testimony will be very helpful. It is often better to enlist the aid of prior or subsequent treating physicians than to alienate them by threatening to bring them into the lawsuit. In fact, often the records of a prior doctor help to establish that there was no diagnosis of suicidal ideation or gestures or need for involuntary hospitalization. The prior or subsequent treating doctor therefore can help substantiate the defense that one could not predict the tragedy.

Least Restrictive Alternative

Psychiatry recognizes that sometimes the least restrictive alternative is the most appropriate. Hospitalization with constant 24-hour observation actually might be harmful to some patients. The doctor may consider the least restrictive alternative treatment as an appropriate alternative treatment. As one court put it, "If liability were imposed each time the prediction of the future course of mental disease was wrong, few releases would ever be made in the hope of recovery, and rehabilitation would be impeded and frustrated" (13).

The trial of a suicide case is one of the most agonizing experiences for psychiatrists on both the personal and professional levels. But if psychiatrists give forethought to the medical decisions they reach during treatment, and if they document these decisions carefully in the medical record, they may be able to minimize at least the legal trauma of a suicide and maximize their own basis for a successful defense.

NOTES

1. Twenty-one percent of all cases filed are suicide related. Forty-three percent of all claims are for negligence claims arising out of successful suicides, according to the Medical Protection Company, as cited in Psychiatric News, April 6, 1987, p 12.
2. Centano v City of New York, NE 40 NY 2d 932 (1976)
3. See Robertson J: Psychiatric Malpractice. New York, Wiley Law Publications, 1988, for a general discussion on the law and practical aspects of depositions and trials in the suicide case.
4. Bell v New York City Health and Hospital, 90 AD 2d 270, 276, 456 NYS 2d 787 (1982)
5. Bell v New York City Health and Hospital, 456 NYS 2d at 796
6. Id at 790
7. Id at 797
8. Topel v Long Island Jewish, 55 NY 2d 682, 446 NYS 2d 932 (1981)
9. Every state statute authorizing confinement for a suicidal individual requires also the individual evidence indicia of mental illness. See, e.g., Ala Code § 22-52-10 (1984); Alaska Stat § 47.30.700 (1984); Ariz Rev Stat Ann § 36-523 (1986); Ark Stat Ann § 59-1406 (Supp 1984); Cal Welf & Inst Code § 5150 (West 1984); Colo Rev Stat § 27-10-105 (Supp 1984); Conn Gen Stat Ann § 17-183 (West Supp 1985); De Code Ann tit 16, § 5122 (1983); DC Code Ann § 37-3-41 (1982); Fla Stat Ann § 394.463 (West Supp 1984); Ga Code Ann § 37-3-41 (1982); Haw Rev Stat § 334-59 (Supp 1984); Idaho Code § 66-326 (Supp 1985); Ill Ann Stat ch 91, para 3-600 (Smith-Hurd Supp 1986); Ind Code Ann § 16-14.917 (West Supp 1985); Iowa Code Ann § 229.22 (West 1985); Kan Stat Ann § 59-2908 (1983); Ky Rev Stat Ann § 202A.026 (Baldwin 1985); La Rev Stat Ann § 28:53 (West Supp 1985); Me Rev Stat Ann tit 34B, § 3863 (Supp 1984); Md Health-Gen Code Ann § 10-622 (1982); Mass Ann Laws ch 123, § 12 (Law Co-op Supp 1985); Mich Stat Ann § 14.800 (438) (Callaghan Supp 1985); Minn Stat Ann § 253A.04 (West 1982); Miss Code Ann § 41-21-69 (Supp 1985); Mo Ann Stat § 632.305 (Vernon Supp 1986); Neb Rev Stat § 83-1020 (Supp 1981); Nev Rev Stat § 433A.160 (1983); NH Rev Stat Ann § 135-B:19 (Supp 1985); NJ Stat Ann § 30:4-26.3 (West 1981); NM Stat Ann § 43-1-10 (1984); NY Mental Hyg Law § 9.39 (McKinney 1983); NC Gen Stat § 122-58.18 (1981); ND Cent Code § 25-03.1-25 (Supp 1983); Ohio Rev Code Ann § 5122.10 (Anderson 1981); Or Rev Stat § 426.175 (1981); Pa Stat Ann tit 50, § 7301 (Purdon Supp 1985); RI Gen Laws § 40.1-5-7 (Supp 1983); SC Code Ann § 44-17-410 (Law Co-op 1985); SD Codified Laws Ann § 27A-10-1 (1984); Tenn Code Ann § 33-6-103 (1984); Tex Rev Civ Stat Ann art 5547-27 (Vernon Supp 1985); Utah Code Ann § 64-7-32 (Supp 1985); Vt Stat Ann tit 18, § 7505 (Supp 1985); Va Code Ann § 37.1-67.1 (1984); Wash Rev Code Ann § 71.05.050 (Supp 1985); Wyo Stat § 25-10-109 (1982)

10. Perr H: Liability of hospital and psychiatrist in suicide. Am J Psychiatry 122:631, 1965
11. Krapvika v Maimonides, 60 AD 2d 871, 501 NYS 2d 429 (1986)
12. Krapvika v Maimonides, 501 NYS 2d at 431
13. Taiq v State, 19 AD 2d 182, 241 NYS 2d 495 (1963)

The Suicide Prevention Pact: Clinical and Legal Considerations

Robert I. Simon, M.D.

It is well established that once a psychiatrist enters into a treatment relationship with a patient, he or she owes that patient a duty of at least ordinary care (1). Probably in no clinical situation is this duty of care more critical than when a psychiatrist is treating someone who is potentially dangerous or violent, such as a suicidal patient.

Volumes have been written regarding the strategies, prevention plans, and risk management procedures that psychiatrists employ to defuse a patient's suicidal impulses and reduce the chance of self-destruction (2). Yet, with a few exceptions, very little has been written concerning the suicide prevention pact itself (3,4). One practice that is sometimes used is the "suicide prevention contract." Generally described, this is an expressed understanding between the psychiatrist and patient that if the latter begins to feel "suicidal" he or she will engage in some preventive act, such as calling the psychiatrist, rather than give in to the suicide impulse. Through such an agreement, psychiatrists attempt to therapeutically engage suicidal patients and prevent them from committing suicide.

All kinds of contracts are being used in psychotherapy. In residential placements, patients who have been violent are asked to promise that they will not be violent. If the patient becomes violent, privileges are canceled in accordance with the agreement. In group therapy, a promise to pay a certain sum is part of a "contract" against breaches of confidentiality (5).

Suicide prevention "contracts" appear to be used more often in outpatient settings, because the outpatient therapist has less control and fewer security options than does a staff psychiatrist in a hospital. Still, these agreements or contracts against suicide also are used in psychiatric hospitals, particularly when patients are issued passes or discharged. The agreement may be oral or written, but is always

I thank Ralph Slovenko, LL.B., Ph.D., and Steven B. Bisbing, Psy.D., J.D., for their critical review.

expressed rather than implied. That is, the agreement's terms are specifically declared and agreed on, usually at the time the pact is made, either orally or in writing. Sometimes the suicide prevention contract is motivated by the therapist's fear of being sued, should the patient commit suicide. The appropriate and inappropriate uses of such a suicide prevention pact, as a clinical tool and a risk management approach, are discussed, as are its legal implications.

Suicide Risk and the Therapeutic Alliance

The therapeutic alliance as an element of adaptive change in patients is crucial, as is the responsibility of the clinician to maintain this alliance under "optimal conditions" (6). The alliance can be defined as a primarily conscious and active relationship between therapist and patient in which they implicitly agree to work together to help the patient with his or her problems. The presence of a therapeutic alliance is a bedrock indicator of the patient's willingness to seek help and sustenance through personal relationships during times of serious emotional crises (7).

The importance of a therapeutic alliance with suicidal patients is that the healthy part of a patient's personality is willing to work with the therapist based on a life-affirming statement such as, "I believe you can help me learn to cope better and be happier." This is the antithesis of the life-denying feelings that impair the therapeutic alliance, such as, "There is no hope for the relief of my pain. I am going away."

The therapeutic alliance also can be used by clinicians as a here-and-now indicator of a patient's suicidal state. If the alliance does not develop because of problems in the therapist or because of some nontherapeutic therapist-patient interaction, then the presence or absence of other sustaining personal relationships must be assessed. Therapist-patient impasses need to be addressed directly. If a stalemate persists, resolution of suicidal ideation or impulses will be unlikely. If a stalemate cannot be constructively resolved, the patient should be seen in consultation or referred elsewhere, if possible.

There are patients who, because of their illness, may not be able to form or sustain a working alliance. Borderline patients can fluctuate rapidly in and out of a working alliance. Schizoid patients may have great difficulty in reaching out to anyone. Paranoid patients tend to treat any close relationship with extreme fear. Nonetheless, unless they are bent on committing suicide, even these patients usually maintain at least a modicum of a relationship with someone. In the hospital, the staff can be extremely important in providing sustaining relationships for a person in a suicidal crisis. For some patients, the staff is the *only* "significant other" in their lives.

There are some notable exceptions to the general rule that the presence of a strong relationship with someone is relatively antithetical to suicide. Some patients may develop intense relationships based on feelings of anger. In patients with borderline personality disorder, splitting defenses may turn the rage meant for others toward oneself, where the object is valued but the self is suicidally devalued (8). Individuals who maintain very close relationships may make an actual pact to commit suicide with their partner and may induce the partner to join in a double suicide. Social isolation, dominance, and aggression seem to characterize persons who form such suicide pacts (9).

The Suicide Prevention Contract and the Therapeutic Alliance

Some therapists attempt to formalize a therapeutic alliance with suicidal patients by a verbal or even a written agreement stating that the latter will call on the therapist if serious doubts about control of suicidal thoughts or impulses arise. Other conditions sometimes enunciated in these suicide prevention contracts include contacting a local mental health center or suicide hotline, calling the police, or having a trusted friend stay with the patient.

A simple agreement intended to address the patient's clinical needs and circumstances may read as follows:

> We (doctor and patient) agree that you (patient) will call me if you find that you are worrying about harming yourself. I will get back to you as soon as I am able. If you feel you need immediate help and cannot reach me at that moment, you will go directly to the emergency room (specifically designated). I will then be in touch with the emergency room. If you need to be seen between appointments, I will be available to see you.

Some therapists require the patient to sign such a statement, but the patient's signature is not critical. Although some patients may indicate acceptance of these conditions, others will honestly state that they cannot be sure that if self-destructive impulses strike, they can or will want to call. A problem with patient agreements against suicide is that they may falsely ease the therapist's concern and lower the clinician's vigilance without having any appreciable effect on the patient's suicidal intent. Forensic psychiatrists who have reviewed numerous suicide cases can attest that the road to suicide by patients is strewn with broken antisuicide "contracts." Not infrequently, such "agreements" reflect the therapist's attempt to control his or her inevitable anxiety in treating suicidal patients.

In *Stepankoff v. Kantor* (10), a psychiatrist was sued for the wrongful death of his patient. The psychiatrist indicated at trial that he felt that he had a "solid pact" with his patient, who suffered from manic-depressive illness, to contact him if the patient felt suicidal (11). In fact, on several occasions just before his suicide, the patient did contact the psychiatrist or his designated replacement. The combination of the patient's defense mechanisms and a favorable telephone assessment of the patient's psychological stability led the psychiatrist to feel that the patient was unlikely to commit suicide. But the patient did commit suicide. The plaintiff's appeal of this case was based on a number of questions about the standard of care provided by the defendant psychiatrist. Despite conflicting expert testimony, the Massachusetts Supreme Judicial Court upheld a lower court's finding that the defendant's care and treatment were consistent with the standard of care and that the psychiatrist had not acted negligently. Although there was no expressed commentary addressing suicide prevention pacts, it could be presumed that the "pact" with the patient against suicide fell within such a standard. More than likely, however, the suicide prevention pact was a minor issue, given the many clinically appropriate or reasonable procedures in which the psychiatrist engaged (e.g., contact assessment, frequent contacts, documented consideration of involuntary hospitalization, and use of an "active" substitute therapist while the principal therapist was away on vacation).

Some therapists may gauge a patient's suicidal intent by a willingness or unwillingness to formalize the alliance into a written agreement. Contracts against suicide can have some narrow but important clinical utility. In certain instances such agreements may reaffirm the therapeutic alliance and the therapist's desire to help the patient, but their limitations should be clearly understood. Therapists must understand that the only sure way to avoid personal agony when a patient commits suicide is not to take patients.

Suicidal patients who outright refuse to accept suicide contracts at least disabuse the psychiatrist of any false security associated with creating such contracts. Although the refusal to sign may not necessarily mean that the patient is suicidal, the clinician should immediately reassess the state of the therapeutic alliance.

The Suicide Prevention Contract: Is It a Legal Contract?

A common question raised by therapists who use suicide prevention contracts is what, if any, legal authority these agreements have. Put another way, will a written or oral agreement with a patient to not kill or harm himself or herself immunize a therapist from a lawsuit if the patient subsequently commits suicide?

In this scenario, a defendant's presumed defense of "breach of contract" is *not* likely to be sustained for several reasons, each of which, on its own, serves as a basis for rejecting the clinician's pseudo-contract as legally enforceable.

A contract can be defined as "an agreement between two or more persons which creates an obligation to do or not do a particular thing" (12). Some of the general requirements that are essential to making a contract or agreement legally enforceable include the following.

1. *The parties of the contract must be legally competent parties.* A person must have sufficient cognitive capacity—or the ability to understand the nature and consequences of a proposed transaction—to be considered *competent to contract* (13). A contract is *voidable* if the party "by reason of mental illness or defect . . . is unable to act in a reasonable manner in relation to the transaction and the other party has reason to know of this condition" (14).

   There is a *presumption* that all adults are competent. However, in the case of a psychiatric patient, especially one who is suicidal, serious questions would be raised regarding the *legal competency* of the patient to enter into any agreement (e.g., suicide prevention contract) with his or her psychiatrist. Other factors such as medication effects and transference phenomena in an already emotionally weakened individual also will undermine any conclusion that a patient was sufficiently competent to contract (15,16).
2. *The agreement or contract must include a valuable consideration—an inducement for each party to carry out his or her part of the bargain.* Consideration is something of value requested by the offerer (i.e., psychiatrist) in exchange for the psychiatrist's promise to the offeree (i.e., patient). In the case of any agreement between a therapist and a patient basically "not to commit suicide," no consideration is given by either the psychiatrist or the patient.
3. *A mutual obligation must be imposed on each party.* As noted earlier, in a suicide prevention pact, the only party actually agree-

ing to forbear or not do something that he or she is under no legal obligation to give up is the patient (e.g., not to harm himself or herself, to call the psychiatrist if he or she feels suicidal). The therapist's promise to be available for the patient is nothing more than an extension of the duty of care that he or she already owes the patient. Therefore, the therapist's obligation in a suicide prevention agreement is illusory and defeats the requirement of a "mutual obligation."

4. *The contract must not contravene public policy* (17). From a legal defense perspective, a suicide prevention "contract" is a classic illustration of an "exculpatory clause" (18). There is general agreement that a person may *not* enforce a contract term that would relieve him or her from liability for any harm caused by his or her negligence. Therefore, a suicide prevention agreement with a patient would not immunize a therapist from liability if his or her conduct was negligent and it was this negligence that proximately caused the patient's suicide death or injury. Doctors cannot contract to provide less care than what is normally owed, regardless of whether a patient implicitly or explicitly agrees to the arrangement. To do so is a violation of public policy. Negligence cannot be "contracted" away.

The Suicide Prevention Pact as Pseudo-contract

The mere use of the term *contract* or *agreement* fails to meet the essential requirements of a legally enforceable contract. Moreover, its very intent—however noble or clinically based—is likely to be construed as morally suspect and contrary to the public's welfare. Therapist-patient agreements "not to commit suicide" may have some intrinsic, psychological value in that they communicate to a patient a sense of caring and hopefulness. But clinicians should not rely on such "contracts" to provide any legal protection in themselves. In the *Stepankoff* case, the defendant did have a suicide prevention pact with the patient. Nevertheless, it was not the "pact" as such that protected the defendant from liability; instead, it was the many clinical procedures that the psychiatrist used that persuaded the court that his actions were consistent with the standard of care.

Risk Management

Psychiatrists who look on suicide prevention contracts as valid legal instruments commit a twofold error. First, the idea that a legal document could prevent a patient from committing suicide is naive and self-delusive. Still, clinicians who are under considerable pressure in managing difficult suicidal patients may regressively grasp at any straw for reassurance. Second, waving around a suicide prevention contract signed by a deceased patient will not immunize the psychiatrist against legal liability. On the contrary, unless the clinician has performed an adequate assessment of suicide risk and has made adequate risk-benefit assessments before clinical decisions, the suicide contract could *indict* the clinician who relies solely on it to prevent a patient's suicide. In the treatment of any patient, but especially the vulnerable patient, liability will be evaluated based on the *reasonableness* of all the therapist's actions—assessment, treatment, and management (19).

Suicide prevention contracts are useful risk management strategies only when they facilitate good clinical care. Some patients are reassured by the psychiatrist's interest and availability. The therapeutic alliance can be greatly strengthened and the suicide threat likely averted. Behavioral contracts also may offer patients and therapists an obsessive defense to hang onto during a suicidal crisis. Good risk management is always derivative of good clinical care.

Suicide prevention contracts also may be used to assess the competence of patients to collaborate with treatment and management decisions. The ability to reach out to another person in a time of crisis indicates the presence of a basic level of adaptive competence. Patients with Axis I disorders, particularly acute schizophrenic and affective disorders, may not possess the mental capacity to enter into a behavioral contract. Patients with Axis II personality disorders usually have the mental capacity to collaborate with psychiatric treatment, but because of their maladaptive character structures and defenses, their ability to cooperate with a behavior contract may be impaired. Gutheil recommends that clinicians should specifically evaluate the patient's competence to participate in clinical decisions (20). Patients who are not competent to collaborate with a psychiatrist require more conservative management.

Clinical Vignette

A 38-year-old divorced woman with the diagnosis of borderline personality disorder has been treated in twice-per-week psychotherapy for 2 years. Her main difficulties include chaotic relationships, poor work performance, lack of clarity in personal identity and life goals, recurrent depression, and frequent suicidal ideation.

Currently, the patient is experiencing increasingly frequent thoughts of suicide following the breakup of yet another relationship. No previous suicide attempts have been made. Vegetative signs of depression such as terminal insomnia, loss of appetite, and psychomotor retardation are present. The patient is still able to work, however. After careful assessment of suicide risks and the evaluation of both the risks and benefits of psychiatric hospitalization versus outpatient treatment, the psychiatrist concludes that continuing outpatient care is the best option.

The psychiatrist asks the patient to enter into a suicide prevention pact in lieu of hospitalization. In addition, the psychiatrist hopes to enhance, as well as test, the faltering therapeutic alliance. She directly engages the patient through an expressly stated mutual agreement of cooperation should a suicide crisis develop. The psychiatrist records the diagnosis of borderline personality disorder and major depressive episode.

The patient signs a written document that clearly spells out the psychiatrist's availability to help the patient at any time. The contract also states the patient will call the psychiatrist at any time if suicide thoughts or impulses threaten. Although the patient signs the agreement, she is not sure if she can comply because, she says, "I may want to kill myself." The thought of suicide has been comforting to the patient as a possible means of controlling or escaping extremely painful feelings.

One month after signing the contract, and without contacting the psychiatrist, the patient takes an overdose of tricyclic antidepressant prescribed by the psychiatrist. It is discovered later that the patient had been hoarding antidepressants for some time. The patient recovers from the overdose but is left with mild to moderate brain damage. A malpractice suit is brought against the psychiatrist. At the time of trial, the suicide prevention contract is used in the psychiatrist's defense. The psychiatrist's expert asserts that the suicide prevention contract was part of the assessment of suicide risk and represented additional evidence that the psychiatrist met the standard of care in assessing and treating this suicidal patient. The plaintiff's psychiatric expert states that the suicide contract was worthless and could not be relied on in managing a suicidal patient. Furthermore, the expert testifies that the defendant had unreasonably relied on a behavioral contract instead of hospitalizing the patient. The patient's diagnoses and clinical condition, the expert opined, required psychiatric hospitalization.

Discussion of Vignette

The psychiatrist in the clinical vignette did not rely on the suicide prevention contract to replace adequate suicide risk assessment. This is a most important point. The plaintiff's expert is in error in asserting that the suicide prevention contract was worthless in this case. The most important clinical use of the contract in this case was to assess the state of the therapeutic alliance. Although a patient intent on committing suicide may sign such a contract to deceive the clinician, other aspects of the therapeutic alliance usually will be absent. For example, therapy may be stalemated, or a feeling of "unrelatedness" is sensed by the therapist in working with the patient. In the clinical vignette, the psychiatrist used the contract to assess the therapeutic alliance and the degree of "connectedness" the patient had with the treatment process. The patient appeared to openly state that she did not know if she could comply with the contract rather than attempting to deceive the psychiatrist. The patient's candor, in the clinical judgment of the psychiatrist, was a positive collaborative development.

The psychiatrist did indicate that she would be available to the patient at all times. Although the patient did not call before her suicide attempt, she could have called when the psychiatrist was unavailable. Some patients do find suicide prevention contracts very helpful and reassuring during a time of emotional crisis. They will call as promised. In establishing the suicide prevention contract, the psychiatrist must indicate that he or she may be unable to respond for brief periods. But the patient should be reassured that every attempt will be made to get back to the patient as soon as possible. Obviously, if the psychiatrist cannot be available for most of the time, promising to be *always* available to the patient would be an extremely destructive sham, should the patient call. If the patient needs immediate help, and the psychiatrist is not available, the patient should have the number of the nearest emergency room or access to other suitable assistance. This option should be clearly stated in the contract. If the patient cannot tolerate brief absences of the psychiatrist, then psychiatric hospitalization should be seriously considered.

The psychiatric defense expert asserted that the defendant psychiatrist's use of an antisuicide contract met the standard of care. To support this conclusion, he highlighted the defendant's use of the contract in conjunction with a full assessment of suicide risk and a risk-benefit analysis. The contract was also a means of affirming the psychiatrist's availability to the patient. It was not used as a defensive procedure (e.g., as a tool to expressly thwart any future malpractice suit). The contract was not used as a convenient substitute for hospitalization.

The court found in favor of the defendant psychiatrist. It reasoned that the presence or absence of the suicide contract was not, by itself, material to the determination of the standard of care provided by the psychiatrist. Finding that the psychiatrist's assessment of suicide risk and subsequent risk-benefit analysis met the standard of care, the decision that the patient could be treated as an outpatient was found a valid exercise of professional judgment. It should be noted that courts, as in this case vignette, generally will not hold a psychiatrist liable for mere honest mistakes (21). The threshold issue in assessing liability will be whether the totality of the defendant's actions were *reasonable* under the circumstances (22).

Summary

Psychiatrists who make clinical decisions and interventions based on the treatment needs of the patient should try to avoid being overly concerned about defensive practices. A suicide prevention pact established with a patient who is struggling against suicidal impulses can be an important part of the clinical care provided. But if such a behavioral contract is used in the place of adequate assessment of suicide risk, the patient may be harmed. The suicide prevention pact can be used as an important aspect of good clinical care—*never* as a substitute for it. The clinical care provided after an understanding is reached is much more important than the mere presence of a "contract" in hand. An additional danger attendant to suicide prevention pacts is their delusive use by therapists to allay anxieties in treating difficult suicidal patients. Furthermore, it is a serious error to view such "contracts" as a sure legal defense to a subsequent malpractice suit if the patient fails to comply with the terms of the agreement.

Can the suicide prevention pact immunize a negligent psychiatrist from a malpractice action? When such a pact is used by itself, the answer is no. But when a suicide prevention pact is used as part of the provision of reasonable clinical care, the *reasonableness of the care itself* is the best defense against an allegation of malpractice.

NOTES

1. 70 Corpus Jurus Secundum. Physicians & Surgeons § 41 (1951)
2. See e.g., Busteed EL, Johnstone C: The development of suicide precautions for an inpatient psychiatric unit. J Psychosoc Nurs Ment Health Serv 21:15, 1983; Farberow N: Suicide prevention in the hospital. Hosp Community Psychiatry 32:99, 1981
3. O'Farrell TJ, et al: Behavior contracting for repeated suicide attempts. Behav Modif 5:225–272, 1981
4. Brown RS (chairman): Forensic issues in suicide. Presented at the 20th annual meeting of the American Academy of Psychiatry and the Law, Washington, DC, Oct 20, 1989

5. Ralph Slovenko: Personal communication, Feb 22, 1990
6. American Psychiatric Association: Principles of Medical Ethics With Annotations Especially Applicable to Psychiatry. Washington, DC, American Psychiatric Association, 1983, Section 6(1)
7. Simon RI: Concise Guide to Clinical Psychiatry and the Law. Washington, DC, American Psychiatric Press, 1988, p 89
8. Gutheil TG: Medicolegal pitfalls in the treatment of borderline patients. Am J Psychiatry 142:9–14, 1985
9. Simon RI: Clinical Psychiatry and the Law. Washington, DC, American Psychiatric Press, 1987, p 261
10. Stepankoff v Kantor, 473 NE 2d 1131 (Mass 1985)
11. Id at 1133
12. Black's Law Dictionary, 5th Edition. St. Paul, MN, West, 1981, pp 291–292
13. Cundick v Broadbent, 383 F2d 157 (10 Cir 1967) cert den 390 US 948 (1968)
14. Restatement Second, Contracts § 15; Ortelere v Teachers' Retirement Board of the City of New York, 25 NY 2d 196, 303 NY 2d 362, 250 NE 2d 460 (1969)
15. See e.g., Sharpe: Medication as a threat to testamentary capacity, 1957. North Carolina Law Review 35:380, 1957
16. See generally, Williamson v Matthews, 379 So2d 1245 (Ala 1980); McPheters v Hapke, 94 Idaho 744, 497 P2d 1045 (1972)
17. See e.g., Roy v Hartogs, 366 NYS 2d 297, 301 (Civ Ct 1975)
18. See e.g., Porubiansky v Emory University, 156 Ga App 602, 275 SE 2d 163 (1981); Meiman v Rehabilitation Center, 444 SW 2d 78 (Ky App 1969); Olson v Molzen, 558 SW 2d 429 (Tenn 1977)
19. See e.g., Meier v Ross General Hospital, 69 Cal App 2d 420, 526, 445 P2d 519, 525, 71 Cal Rptr 903, 909 (1968)
20. Gutheil TG: Malpractice liability in suicide. Legal Aspects of Psychiatric Care 1:1–4, 1984
21. See e.g., Fiederlein v New York Health and Hospital Corporation, 437 NYS 2d 321 (App Div 1982)
22. See e.g., Weatherly v State, 109 Misc 2d 1024, 441 NYS 2d 319 (1981); Abile v United States, 482 F Supp 703 (ND Cal 1980)

Afterword

Volume 3 of the *American Psychiatric Press Review of Clinical Psychiatry and the Law* will present the following important psychiatric topics: "Patients at Suicide Risk: Assessing the Unpredictable" by Robert I. Simon, M.D., "The Psychiatrist as Double Agent" by Henry C. Weinstein, M.D., J.D., "Informed Consent in Psychiatric Practice" by John Malcolm, J.D., and "Psychiatric-Legal Issues in Hospital Psychiatry" by John R. Lion, M.D.

The Features section will continue to bring "Recent Legal Developments and Psychiatry" by Steven B. Bisbing, Psy.D., J.D., covering legal cases of clinical importance to psychiatrists decided since the publication of Volume 2; "The Canadian Connection: A Canadian Perspective on Clinical Psychiatry and the Law" by Selwyn M. Smith, M.D.;"Expert Opinion"—a discussion by Robert L. Sadoff, M.D., and Thomas G. Gutheil, M.D., of a sexual misconduct case from both plaintiff and defense perspectives; and "The Psychiatrist in the Courtroom" with advice for psychiatrists on managing courtroom testimony by Jeffrey D. Robertson, J.D.

Volume 3 of the *American Psychiatric Press Review of Clinical Psychiatry and the Law* will continue the important task of informing psychiatrists about the latest developments in the critical area of psychiatry and the law.

Robert I. Simon, M.D.

Index of Cases

Subject Index